Routledge Revivals

Political Trials in Poland 1981-1986

First published in 1988, *Political Trials in Poland 1981-1986* describes the major political trials which took place in Poland between 1981 and 1986. Based on extensive original research using both official and unofficial information from Poland and interviews with Solidarity activists, it shows how the trials constituted an attempt by the Jaruzelski regime to break the back of the independent Solidarity movement by judicial and penal measures. It discusses how the authorities abused the law and how the law itself leaves much to be desired and it charts the different human rights that were violated in each case. It considers the implications of the abuse of law in this way for the rule of law and the image of the state in communist countries. This book will be of interest to students of history and political science.

Political Trials in Poland 1981-1986

Andrzej Swidlicki

First published in 1988
By Croom Helm Ltd.

This edition first published in 2024 by Routledge
4 Park Square, Milton Park, Abingdon, Oxon, OX14 4RN
and by Routledge
605 Third Avenue, New York, NY 10017

Routledge is an imprint of the Taylor & Francis Group, an informa business

© 1988 Andrzej Swidlicki

All rights reserved. No part of this book may be reprinted or reproduced or utilised in any form or by any electronic, mechanical, or other means, now known or hereafter invented, including photocopying and recording, or in any information storage or retrieval system, without permission in writing from the publishers.

Publisher's Note
The publisher has gone to great lengths to ensure the quality of this reprint but points out that some imperfections in the original copies may be apparent.

Disclaimer
The publisher has made every effort to trace copyright holders and welcomes correspondence from those they have been unable to contact.

ISBN: 978-1-032-74151-2 (hbk)
ISBN: 978-1-003-46787-8 (ebk)
ISBN: 978-1-032-74152-9 (pbk)

Book DOI 10.4324/9781003467878

Political Trials in Poland 1981-1986

ANDRZEJ SWIDLICKI

CROOM HELM
London • New York • Sydney

© 1988 Andrzej Swidlicki
Croom Helm Ltd, Provident House, Burrell Row,
Beckenham, Kent, BR3 1AT

Croom Helm Australia, 44-50 Waterloo Road,
North Ryde, 2113, New South Wales

Published in the USA by
Croom Helm
in association with Methuen, Inc.
29 West 35th Street
New York, NY 10001

British Library Cataloguing in Publication Data

Swidlicki, Andrzej
    Political trials in Poland 1981-1986.
    1. Trials (Political crimes and offenses)
    — Poland
    I. Title
    344.3805′231 [LAW]
    ISBN 0-7099-4444-6

Library of Congress Cataloging-in-Publication Data

ISBN 0-7099-4444-6

Printed and bound in Great Britain by Mackays of Chatham Ltd, Kent

Table of contents

Acknowledgement	
Introduction: NORMALIZATION	1
I THE RIGOURS OF MARTIAL LAW	16
1. Extraordinary legislation	16
2. Internment	25
3. Military courts	33
4. Militarized enterprises	38
5. Compulsory labour	46
6. Special procedures	51
7. The use of force	61
II THE TRIALS OF DECEMBER 1981 STRIKERS	67
III THE TRIALS OF THE INTERNEES	112
IV THE SEDITION TRIALS	126
V THE TRIALS OF THE UNDERGROUND SOLIDARITY ACTIVISTS	156
VI THE BASIC FREEDOMS AND THE COURTROOM	192
1. The right to a defence	192
2. The right to freedom of association	213
3. The right to freedom of expression	234
4. The right to peaceful assembly	253
5. The right to protest	272
6. The right to work	284
7. Freedom of conscience and religion	298
VII THE POLICE AND THE PROSECUTION	323
VIII THE PRISON SYSTEM	364
IX FREEDOM UNDER THE PPR LAW	386
Glossary of Terms Used in this Book	410
Index	415

Acknowledgement

The production of this book, dedicated to all who have been persecuted in the cause of freedom, has been made possible by the generous support of The Airey Neave Memorial Trust.

Airey Neave, MP, who devoted so much of his life to helping the oppressed, was murdered by terrorists in the precincts of the House of Commons in 1979. The Trust founded in his memory exists to provide scholarships for research into subjects directly concerned with individual freedom under the law.

Airey Neave was a good friend of Poland. It is therefore fitting that the administrators of the Trust should take an interest in the fight for freedom and justice in Poland. Individual freedom under the law is the philosophy on which Solidarity is founded and it is this ideal which brings hope to millions of Poles now existing in a totalitarian state without national sovereignty.

Introduction: NORMALIZATION

Lawlessness, far from being a sickness of Communism, is its health.

(Leszek Kołakowski)

The Independent Self-Governing Trade Union Solidarity was a national and social movement in a trade union formula. Although it tried to avoid political tasks, its very existence in a totalitarian Soviet–style environment was of major political significance. Its very independence of the authorities forced the union to take up tasks not normally associated with trade union activities. It could not limit itself to defending the strictly material interests of its members because these were inextricably linked with the functioning of the system as a whole, a system that had long ceased to be workable and made a mockery of popular aspirations, a system that was economically, spiritually, culturally and politically bankrupt. The people wanted freedom and rule of law at least as much as they wanted improved social benefits. The union, with its adherence to Christian and democratic values, considered that it had a responsibility to represent not only its members but also the nation at large, reduced as it was to poverty, deprived of its rights, fed with mendacious propaganda, and ruled by an unrepresentative nomenklatura. As a result, the issues of truth in public life and in the media, social justice, and reform of the law which would not normally be the province of trade union activity were important elements of the Solidarity programme.

Solidarity was a movement for the reconstruction of civil society. This was to be achieved through the democratization of public life, economic reform, truthfulness in the media and the rule of law. Instead of remaining the silent monolith it had been in recent years, with the exception of a few outspoken dissident groups, society began to be transformed during the Solidarity period into a plurality of independent associations. The changes also affected the Communist party itself which was openly split

Introduction: Normalization

by factionalism and began to drift apart. The ruling apparatus, however, held on to power and prepared itself in secrecy to reclaim the initiative from Solidarity by whatever means proved necessary. The ensuing impasse was aptly characterized by Jacek Kuroń: 'the Communist party's former power monopoly is already broken and the democratic reforms sought by society have not yet been realized'.[1] The party's unwillingness and inability to reform itself, coupled with the authorities' procrastinating tactics, were the main reasons for the deepening crisis.

The basic issue confronting Solidarity was how to bring about a change in the way power was exercised in the country without being forced into a struggle for power. According to Paul Thibaud, Solidarity was caught in a dilemma: it had neither the means for effectively influencing power, nor was it a candidate for taking over power.[2] Poland's 'self–limiting revolution' which originated in the 'social contract' of August 1980 was based on a concept of dialogue and negotiations between society represented by Solidarity and the authorities. The negotiations were difficult if not impossible. The authorities, although they would not for tactical reasons have admitted it, resented the very existence of Solidarity, while the union's representatives — not without reason — were mistrustful of the authorities. The negotiations also served as an element of the 'status–orientated politics' that Solidarity pursued vis-à-vis the authorities. Real issues were often inextricably linked with symbolic politics.[3]

On the one hand a sense of realism prompted Solidarity leaders to seek negotiations since the means to enact a change in the system were objectively in the hands of the authorities. On the other hand, looking upon the authorities with contempt and preoccupied with its internal affairs, the union as a whole tended to disregard the actual power structure and underestimate the resolve of those in power. This ambiguity resulted in the growing frustration, politicization and verbal radicalism of the Solidarity rank–and–file. In practice it was impossible either to put up with the inaction on the part of the authorities or to ignore them completely and act independently. The union found itself in the unenviable position of deciding how to arrive at a compromise with a partner one did not trust or how to ensure that the negotiated compromise was indeed observed. Solidarity leaders soon realized that pressure put on the authorities in the form of strikes or strike threats had its limits.

As Paul Thibaud put it, Solidarity was 'locked in an illusory

Introduction: Normalization

logic' based on misconceptions about the PUWP apparatus:

> 'Not to want to change power but to control and reform it was a gamble on the rationality, the political capacity of the apparatus of the Polish United Workers' Party, which was expected out of reasonableness, humaneness and patriotism, to play the game without being physically forced to do so, since there was no means to remove it and this was publicly acknowledged...'[4]

According to Adam Michnik, Solidarity lacked a clearly defined concept of co-existence with the Communist regime.[5] It was therefore easily provoked into a conflict. Its basic weapon — the strike — lost its effectiveness after the first few months. Instead of a practical programme expressed as partial aims and divided into stages, Solidarity had only a vision of the liberation of society through the reaffirmation of the Christian values of human dignity and labour, democratization and self-management. The union leadership did not believe in the imminence of a decisive clash with the regime. Although they did not rule out the possibility of such a clash, the union's silent majority thought that the will of the people would eventually prevail. After all, it was thought, Solidarity had 10 million members, the party was disintegrating and its apparatus, which bore the blame for the crisis, was morally and politically bankrupt. The laws on state enterprises and self-management would break the grip of the *nomenklatura* — the privileged hangers-on of the party apparatus — over the economy and thus release social initiative and tap the human potential required for the success of the economic reform. The union, however, mistook the weakness of the apparatus for a power vacuum. The privileged position of the ruling apparatus was eventually rescued by the party's military arm or, to use George Malcher's expression, the 'military party'.[6]

The conflict between Solidarity and the regime was enacted within the legal framework of the PPR Constitution. Under the Gdańsk Agreement the independent union agreed to operate within the limits of the country's constitution, together with its provision concerning 'the leading role of the party in the construction of socialism'. It did so in the belief that 'the leading role' would not be exercised with regard to the trade union movement and in the hope that this general provision could be

Introduction: Normalization

precisely defined by the law. Acknowledging the de facto rule of the PUWP (not to be confused with the right to rule) the workers' representatives wanted to fight for freedom under the law. Government was to be based on rule of law and the existing provisions were to be amended to guarantee the people their basic civil freedoms including trade union rights. The democratization which began with the signing of the Gdańsk Agreement was to be institutionalized in order to guarantee its permanence. Again, these guarantees were to be found in law, in particular the law on trade unions and on censorship. The struggle for democratic reform of the law involved not only specialists but a broad cross-section of the community. Bills were drafted as a result of comprehensive consultations between lawyers, representatives of other professions and the trade unions. Solidarity and the government both had their legal experts and advisers and more often than not two separate drafts were submitted for discussion — a government one and an independent one. The two drafts were compared and differences discussed during negotiations between Solidarity and the government. The Sejm, Poland's rubber-stamp parliament, was also involved in mediation efforts, helping to hammer out the final shape of the legislative acts which, in contrast to normal Communist practice, was quite often unknown until the last moment.

The existing body of legal provisions was widely considered unsatisfactory with regard to civil rights which were granted to the PPR citizens only on paper and all too often turned out to be a dead letter since the principle of equality of all citizens before the law was not observed. The respect for law and order in particular by the local authorities, which in several instances provoked local conflicts that threatened to escalate into confrontations on a national scale, was a demand repeatedly voiced, albeit Solidarity considered law and order too sensitive and potentially explosive a matter to make it a front-line issue and avoided putting too much pressure on the authorities in this connection. It is possible that the union might have won some concessions from the authorities with respect to greater observance of law and order by police and other officials had it not been for the so-called Bydgoszcz affair in March 1981, when three Solidarity activists were beaten up by the police. In what proved with hindsight to have been a decisive war of nerves, the union finally backed down from its decision to call a general strike, demobilizing the masses and letting the authorities regain the

Introduction: Normalization

initiative. With the pressure removed, the authorities were no longer prepared to compromise on the issue. The police, prosecution and courts remained staffed with people who would carry out any instructions, regardless of legal norms and the principles of justice. Solidarity did not offer its unequivocal support to the independent trade union of policemen that was set up in the Spring of 1981 and did not react when prosecutors and policemen known for their pro-Solidarity sympathies or activities were sacked long before martial law was introduced. Its position was that it was up to the legal profession itself to fight for its rights. Certainly, a number of judges tried, albeit unsuccessfully, to demand that their statutory independence be respected and expressed in new guarantees such as the principle of self-government with judges having the right to nominate the court chairman.

Martial law was also in many ways a result of the collision of two differing concepts of law. Solidarity represented the traditional concept of law as a system of rules and restrictions that applied to both the authorities and the citizens. The ruling apparatus, on the other hand, did not feel itself bound by the existing legal provisions and reached for non-constitutional, emergency powers to restore its position as the uncontested authority in making, interpreting and applying the law. Martial law was devised in such a way as to leave the authorities (headed by the party's military arm) free to apply forms of repression of whatever scale and duration they considered necessary. Law was to become an instrument of pacification and of normalization, a means of crushing all independent social initiatives, restoring the monopoly of the Communist party and strengthening its position. The writer and satirist Sławomir Mrożek wrote that since this monopoly had never been legitimized by the people through democratic elections, it could hardly be defended by democratic means and the open use of force at this stage was only proof of the illegitimacy of the ruling apparatus. Martial law — wrote Mrożek — revealed starkly the 'original sin' of the Communist authorities in Poland — their illegality and illegitimacy.[7]

The coup of 13 December was, in fact, a return to the practices of war Communism which had, in the USSR and other Soviet-style people's democracies, provided a model for disciplining the workers and the peasants by incorporating their labour into the party-controlled military effort and subjecting them to the commands of the party apparatus. The apologists of

Introduction: Normalization

martial law have recalled, with some nostalgia, the period of 1944–8 when the Polish Communists, having with Soviet aid crushed the opposition, installed themselves as the supreme authority in Poland. The post–Solidarity reaction, spearheaded by the military arm of the party, was in many respects comparable to the imposition of 'people's rule' which the Communists call 'revolution'. The notions of revolution and war on the enemy are inseparable in Communist language. Although the name of the great heretic of Communism Leon Trotsky was not mentioned by the apologists of normalization in Poland, they would most probably have agreed with him that the enemy must be rendered harmless and that meant that he had to be destroyed in time of war. The 'strategic objectives' of the Polish military were the trade union freedoms won by the Polish workers in August 1980. All of them were to be retracted.

One of the strategic features of Jaruzelski's normalization was an obsession with legislation. As revealed by Col. Ryszard Kukliński from the General Staff, who defected to the US in early November 1981, the actual coup had been preceded by months of intensive legislative preparation. The law was exploited for a dual purpose: to disarm society with immediate effect and protect the power elite from any Solidarity-style upheaval in the future. The new self-appointed supreme authority in the country — the Military Council of National Salvation (WRON) — was already in full control when the Council of State was formally requested to approve the four decrees which formed the basis of martial law. These decrees were eventually rubber-stamped by the very Sejm whose prerogative had been usurped on the night of December 12. Subsequent emergency legislation supplemented statutory law, institutionalizing martial law. Lacking popular approval for their policies, Jaruzelski and his group strove for the appearance of legality. Their precept was *dura lex sed lex* i.e. the law must be observed however unpleasant its content. The aim of Jaruzelski's legislative efforts was to transform criminal law into a still more efficient instrument of political repression, redefine the institutional framework of the one-party state to reflect the new balance of forces within the ruling elite, create an appearance of mass support for the regime and facilitate economic reform on its own terms.

Implementation of these aims was achieved through a specific type of repression which differed from the earlier Hungarian and Czech models. It was neither the mass terror applied in Hungary

Introduction: Normalization

nor the ideologically motivated purges of the intelligentsia and the liberal wing of the Czech and Slovak Communist Parties, but 'the Jaruzelski group', to quote Jadwiga Staniszkis, 'recalls rather bureaucratic Stalinism, non-ideological and based on the state not the party'.[8] Demobilization of the masses through penal and economic repressions was, indeed, accompanied by attempts to build an authoritarian and bureaucratic rather than ideological state which the philosopher Leszek Kołakowski has called 'a new curiosity — a Communism without ideology'.[9]

These attempts went hand in hand with a new rationalization for the changes which had been imposed from above. The real legitimacy of the ruling elite was force. To make the people accept this new legitimacy, the threat of a direct Soviet intervention was evoked. Jaruzelski credited himself with having prevented such an outcome and presented his coup as 'a lesser evil'. Jaruzelski's message to the people was that his efficient, untainted and patriotic army was serving the interests of nation and state. These arguments were meant to obscure the fact that Jaruzelski, while engineering his coup, was not acting on his own and could not have staged a military operation on such a scale without Soviet approval and backing. It was, in fact, not the sovereignty of the nation and the state which he wished to safeguard but, on the contrary, Poland's continued dependence on her powerful neighbour.

Martial law changed Poland's institutional framework. At the outset of martial law Jaruzelski occupied the highest posts in the party (First Secretary), the army (the head of WRON) and the government (Prime Minister and Minister of Defence). While consolidating his power he gave up both the government posts, becoming the head of the National Defence Committee (KOK), the Supreme Commander of the armed forces and the Chairman of the Council of State. The prerogatives of both the KOK and the Council of State were substantially increased as a result of legislation. The law of 21 November 1983 which amended the Law on Universal Military Service furnished the KOK with wide prerogatives concerning the formulation of the broad lines of the PPR's defence policy, as well as the introduction of a state of emergency, martial law, general mobilization and declaration of war. The Chairman of KOK not only supervises the Minister of Defence and vets candidates for this post, but also appoints and recalls, albeit at the latter's recommendation, the general chief of staff and the commanders of military districts. The KOK, which

Introduction: Normalization

is not even formally accountable to the Sejm, is, however, an integral part of the system of command of the Warsaw Pact.

The Law on the State of Emergency of 5 December 1983 increased the powers of the Chairman of the Council of State who has been empowered, in extraordinary circumstances, to proclaim a state of emergency on his own initiative. Thanks to this provision the post of the Chairman of the Council of State has ceased to be ceremonial and its actual incumbent has been empowered to 'suspend', without notice, the civil rights of the citizens. The post was entrusted to Jaruzelski in December 1985. The same law made KOK 'the administrator of state defence and security'. In this way, Jaruzelski is now able to announce a state of emergency as the Chairman of the Council of State, and administer it, as the Chairman of KOK.

The role of the army as a whole has also been enhanced with new far-reaching powers. Through the Voivodship Defence Committees the military have been granted direct control over the regional and local administrative authorities and charged with co-ordinating civil organizations and economic enterprises in the region. Control can also be exercised through inspection commissions. The military also play a major role in the Council of Ministers' Committee on the Observance of Law, Order and Social Discipline. The Committee, which was set up in December 1983 under the chairmanship of the Minister of Internal Affairs, General Czesław Kiszczak, has the prerogatives of initiating new laws and influencing the work not only of the Ministry of Justice but also of the Supreme Court. By virtue of its composition the Committee cuts through the government, the judiciary, the prosecution, the military and the police. It is a new, practical way of expressing the Communist dogma of unity of all powers as opposed to the separation of powers. The supreme position of General Kiszczak's Committee proves clearly that the judiciary is subordinated to the government and the party. The police and prosecution authorities whose representatives sit on the Committee have been treated on a par with the courts, thus blurring the difference between law enforcement, crime investigation and adjudication. Kiszczak's Committee is another example of the militarization of the system, a process which began even before the imposition of martial law, encompassing first the government, the administration and the party and later also the judiciary and the prosecution. Militarization of the system helped to fill the power vacuum caused by the weakness of the party after August

Introduction: Normalization

1980 and consolidated a new military–political order.

The process of overhauling the system's basic institutions affected both the civilian and military wings of the party first of all. The architects of martial law had to break substantial opposition among the 'Communists in uniform' and later also among the civilian party membership. According to Malcher, some 13,000 military officers were expelled from the party after 13 December 1981.[10] Army activists in uniform were given the task of rebuilding the civilian party organizations which were affected by low morale and loss of membership. During the first few weeks of martial law the civilian party was run by the military wing of the PUWP by orders.[11] The combination of party and military discipline was a miracle cure designed to resuscitate the party.

The uniformed Communists, having achieved a supreme position within the power elite, proceeded to consolidate their hold on the government and the party. This task was approached through the verification of personnel by party control commissions as well as through legislative changes. The sheer number of laws passed by the Sejm after 13 December might seem to suggest that the role of the Sejm had been enhanced, but the opposite was, in fact, the case. The general trend of Jaruzelski's programme of legislation was to strengthen the militarization of the civilian sector. The most important acts were clearly disciplinary in character. All the emergency powers with which the authorities had armed themselves during martial law were transferred one by one to statutory law. The drafts of most of the laws were prepared in secret and the proper procedure of voting on them was not always observed in Sejm. The most glaring example of this tendency was the trade union bill which was submitted to the Sejm deputies marked strictly confidential only three days before it was due to be voted. The trend towards increased repression and penalization was maintained despite the gradual dismantling of martial law and an easing of the situation from the authorities' point of view.

In a narrower sense Jaruzelski's normalization was directed against the active centres of the opposition: Solidarity's national and regional structures, factory commissions, professional associations, student unions, nascent political parties, individuals known for their past record of 'anti-state activity'. In a larger sense normalization was an opportunity to re-impose Communist-style regimentation on society as a whole. Although

Introduction: Normalization

non-doctrinaire in character and lacking the elements of an ideological crusade, Jaruzelski's normalization proves that the Polish Communists, in the same way as their Hungarian and post-Dubcek Czechoslovak counterparts, were determined to hold on to power in the same way as they had seized it, i.e. by violence. The actual degree of violence may differ (Jaruzelski's normalization was based on controlled repression), but the basic ingredient in all three cases was state terrorism. The distinction between the active and passive phases of state terrorism made by Istvan Lovas and Ken Anderson with regard to Hungary after 1956 is also relevant to the current Polish situation.[12] While active terrorism aims at the transformation of society, passive terrorism is directed towards efficient social control. Overt coercion ceases and is diluted throughout the system. If the period of martial law can be described as active state terrorism and, in many ways, a repetition of the early period of Stalinization of Poland, then the post-martial law reality with its institutionalization of martial law corresponds to the passive phase of state terrorism. 'It is the rational desire for efficiency which prompts the state to end the active phase of terrorism and engage in what is called a passive stage ... terror adapts itself to the needs of production ... potential organs of state terror are incorporated into the infrastructure of society'.[13] In post-martial law Poland there is little overt violence but quiet forms of repression such as the employment policy, financial penalties, forced emigration, denial of exit visas for foreign travel, increased surveillance at the workplace or the presentation of criminal charges in order to obscure the political character of criminal proceedings linger on. The potential for terror exists, however, and should the ruling elite feel threatened at any time, all the rigours of martial law can be activated — this time in accordance with the law.

One of the forms of state terrorism in Soviet-style societies is the political trial which fits neatly into the mechanisms of domination and social control used by the ruling elites. The major political trials are programmed, co-ordinated and supervised at the highest level of power. The Investigations Bureau of the Ministry of Internal Affairs plays a key role in co-ordinating the preparations for such a trial. It takes an active interest in the investigations carried out by the prosecutor's office and passes its recommendations higher up. The Bureau is not a monopolist since the Prosecutor General's Office and Kiszczak's Committee also play an active role in the preparation of a political trial.

Introduction: Normalization

The political trials held in Poland during martial law and after cannot be described as Stalinist show trials although they testified to the terrorist nature of the Communist state. Although they were part of an overall pattern of repression, they were designed to serve not as an instrument of political education of the masses, but as the instrument of their demobilization. The defendants in Soviet Stalinist show trials were frequently themselves party members who rendered their last service to the party by admitting to the most incredible charges. These trials were a sign of purges within the party. In martial law Poland, however, it was the elected officers of Solidarity who were the first to be put on trial for defending the union. It is true that the question of guilt and punishment in the courts of martial law Poland was governed by political expediency just as in Stalinist times, but the trials were not simply a masquerade, the defendants did not strive to act the parts assigned to them, defence lawyers did not sit passively throughout the hearings, and it was not the prosecutor but the judge who dominated the hearing. Whereas Stalinist trials were a farce played out in the courtroom for the edification of the masses but having nothing to do with the law, the martial law trials were rather an example of the abuse of law, an expression of its undemocratic content, and an act of vengeance on the part of the authorities against those who thought or acted in a manner independent of the officially approved canons. These trials took place because the PPR citizens were, and still are, deprived of political rights, in particular the right to participate in public life, as well as of the fundamental individual freedoms. The very fact of staging political trials attests to the authorities' intention to extend and maintain control over all aspects of social life in the country.

The political trials discussed here may be divided into three stages, each having its own specific dynamics. The first stage — from the introduction of martial law until the delegalization of Solidarity — was marked by the trials of Solidarity activists who defended their union's right to exist. The indictment was based in most cases on the Martial Law Decree. This stage of normalization is more appropriately described as pacification proper. The military authorities broke up Solidarity's organizational structure but failed to prevent the forming of skeleton union structures underground. Independent demonstrations in May and August 1982 complicated the authorities' task. None the less, the underground leadership,

Introduction: Normalization

trapped within overground Solidarity's formula of mobilizing anti-regime sentiments while still seeking a negotiated accommodation with it, refused to see that the cornerstone of Jaruzelski's normalization programme was the negation of August 1980 and to accept that the blow thus dealt to Solidarity was irreversible. They were, therefore, unable to put forward any objectives that would relate to Jaruzelski's long-term strategic thinking. The dissolution in October 1982 of Solidarity and other post-August 1980 trade unions and the failure of the general strike of 10 November made the August 1980-oriented tactics still more a thing of the past. This first stage also dispersed any illusions as to the real prospects for economic reform. A packet of economic reforms adopted by the Sejm on 25 February 1982 did not yield the desired results and it became evident that it was little more than a cover for the introduction of martial law.

The second stage of normalization in Poland began with the suspension of martial law and ended with the amnesty of July 1984. Martial law was formally lifted on 21 July 1983 and a partial amnesty declared but the problem of political prisoners continued to remind public opinion about the legacy of the military crackdown. Jaruzelski and his group proceeded to build up support for the new order through the Patriotic Movement for National Rebirth (PRON) and to re-impose a Soviet-style regime. A party-sponsored trade union movement was gradually rebuilt, though not without widespread opposition and deep-rooted resentment. The second stage of normalization was marked by preparations for the trials of the four members of KOR and the seven members of Solidarity's National Commission, as well as by the trials of underground Solidarity activists. It was during this stage also that major legislative acts were passed by the docile Sejm deputies. Among the most important were the Law on State and Official Secrets of 14 December 1982, the Law on the Minister of Internal Affairs and the Police Force of 14 July 1983, the Law on the State of Emergency of 5 December 1983, the Press Law of 26 January 1984 and the amendments passed to the Law on Universal Military Service of 21 November 1983, the Law on Censorship of 28 July 1983 and the Penal Code of 18 December 1982 and of 28 July 1983. On two occasions the Sejm passed 'Special Regulations' (for the Period of Suspended Martial Law and for the Period of Overcoming the Socio-Economic Crisis). The latter regulation was in force until 31 December 1985. One of the effects of these special regulations was to extend

Introduction: Normalization

administrative control over the workforce, social and cultural associations, universities, the teaching profession and students. Under the terms of the July 1984 amnesty which brought this stage of normalization to a close, the overwhelming majority of political prisoners were released, leaving 22 still incarcerated.

The third stage of normalization which began in July 1984 was marked by the regime's attempts to find recognition in the West, its preoccupation with minimizing workers' unrest caused by the deteriorating standard of living, and its increasing impatience with continuing dissent. Underground activists were charged with treason and sedition. The Gdańsk trial of Frasyniuk, Lis and Michnik was intended to shake the opposition into submission. Criminal charges were increasingly presented to the activists of the opposition. The authorities also gave what seems to have been a final warning to Lech Wałęsa by bringing him to trial on a formal charge of slandering election officials and abandoning proceedings after a compromise was reached. The Law on Special Criminal Liability of 10 May 1985 made criminal law still more repressive in order to discipline the population still further. The regime's front organizations: the people's councils, the Sejm, PRON and the youth organizations finally reasserted themselves. The remnants of independence were purged from the universities, the Chief Barrister's Council, the official scout organization. The already narrow margin of independence of the judiciary was restricted still further by the passage of the Laws on Courts, the Supreme Court and the Prosecutor's Office. The passage of these laws amounted to the most extensive changes to the judiciary and the prosecution since the early 1950s. The Minister of Justice and the courts' chairmen were granted prerogatives enabling them to influence the course of adjudication. The systematic growth in the number of political prisoners was visible proof of the resilience of the opposition. The course of the Tenth PUWP Congress, on the other hand, reflected the regime's growing self-confidence. From the authorities' point of view, the basic purpose of martial law — rebuilding the party — has been achieved.

The third phase of normalization ended in September 1986 with the release of almost all of the political prisoners on the basis of the Law on Special Procedure for Perpetrators of Certain Offences of 17 July 1986. The authorities took stock of their policies. General Kiszczak indirectly acknowledged the resilience of social resistance admitting that from 1981–6 the police

Introduction: Normalization

had broken up about 1,600 illegal groups, uncovered about 1,200 underground printing and distribution facilities and seized almost 700 pieces of printing equipment. He said that the police action had prevented about five million leaflets and hostile publication from being disseminated.[14] The official self-confidence was reflected in Jaruzelski's speech of 16 September 1986 at a party conference in Zielona Góra where he said 'today the strength of the authorities is not measured by the number of overpowered opponents but in the number of supporters won over'.[15] The amnestied political prisoners pledged, for their part, to continue fighting for political freedoms as long as the authorities prevented the formation of a legal opposition. The political impasse resulting from the authorities' reluctance to risk any meaningful political or trade union pluralism, combined with the continuing economic crisis will, to judge by previous experience, eventually lead to stagnation and a new crisis.

The most important consequences of normalization in Poland were first, the creation of a new power elite by the integration of the military into the civilian party apparatus and ultimately into the traditional elite of government, local administration, economic bureaucracy and the police; secondly, the creation of a new institutional basis for the power elite to transmit orders and ensure conformity (KOK, Voivodship Defence Committees, the Council of Ministers' Committee for the Observance of Law, Order and Social Discipline, new powers for the Council of State to declare a state of emergency, and a further decline of the supposedly representative Sejm); thirdly, the ex-post 'legalization' of martial law and its permanent institutionalization; and finally, the drastic limitation of the freedoms enjoyed by the citizens under the law.

In the course of normalization repression was disguised as law and the system of police surveillance revamped. Both can be activated at any time. Although normalization ultimately rests on the threat of force, in its mature stage the authorities prefer to rely on various forms of invisible repression, such as administrative surveillance, a coercive employment policy, fiscal penalties and arbitrary passport policy. Social control is exercised rather less through the courts and rather more through the police who enjoy almost unrestricted discretionary powers and through petty offences tribunals.

Despite the authorities' efforts, there is no feeling of irreversible defeat among the Poles. Dissatisfaction with the

Introduction: Normalization

regime, due to growing pauperization and the deprivation of political and trade union rights, is as strong as ever. The independent trade union movement is still widely believed to be a vehicle of change and a symbol of freedom to come.

Notes

1. *TELOS* no. 47 Spring, 1981 reprinted from *Der Spiegel*, 15 December 1980.
2. Paul Thibaud, 'The Extent of the Defeat', *TELOS* no. 53, Fall 1982 reprinted from *Esprit*, March 1982.
3. Jadwiga Staniszkis, *Poland's Self-Limiting Revolution*, Princeton University Press, 1982. For an excellent and lucid historical narrative of the events and atmosphere of the Solidarity 'revolution' see Timothy Garton Ash, *The Polish Revolution: 1980–1982.* Jonathan Cape. London 1983.
4. Thibaud, 'The Extent of the Defeat'.
5. *Krytyka* no. 12, 1982.
6. George C. Malcher, *Poland's Politicized Army: Communists in Uniform*, Praeger Special Studies, 1984.
7. *Kultura* no. 1 / 2, 1982.
8. J. Staniszkis, *Poland's Self-Limiting Revolution.*
9. *Kultura* no. 3, 1984.
10. Malcher, *Poland's Politicized Army.*
11. Ibid.
12. *TELOS* no. 54, winter 1982 / 83.
13. Ibid.
14. Quoted in *Trybuna Ludu*, 6 May 1986.
15. PAP, 17 September 1986.

I
THE RIGOURS OF MARTIAL LAW

1. Extraordinary legislation

The destruction of independent social organizations

In their determination to demobilize the masses and regain the initiative, Poland's martial law authorities devised a comprehensive system of repressive measures. Their essence was defined in the Martial Law Decree itself and the three other decrees: on Special Procedures, on Military Courts and on the Abolition Decree which were all issued by the Council of State on 12 December 1981. A barrage of ordinances providing detailed regulations on the application of the principles of martial law in various spheres was issued within a very short time by the Council of Ministers or the ministers concerned.

The extraordinary legislation of martial law was given priority over the existing body of laws passed before the imposition of martial law (Art. 57.1 of the Martial Law Decree). In particular the Council of Ministers was empowered to '... issue provisions stipulating conditions of work, social insurance benefits and social welfare activity in enterprises differing from the provisions of the labour law' (Art. 29.8 of the Martial Law Decree).

The public was surprised not only by the stringent nature of the new regulations but also by their scope for interference with the individual's everyday life. Not only were the people deprived of such fundamental rights as inviolability of the person, inviolability of the home, secrecy of correspondence, freedom of movement within one's own country or freedom of expression but also new obligations were imposed upon them. For instance, they had to seek permission in order to change their place of residence for more than 48 hours.

The obligations and restrictions imposed upon the public corresponded to the new prerogatives granted to the police, the army and the administration. These new powers were intended to restore the barrier of fear between the rulers and society at large. They provided for censorship of mail and telephone conversations (Art. 18 of the Martial Law Decree), the use of force including firearms (Art. 26 and 27), the imposition of a curfew, special contributions for the needs of the food economy which involved 'restrictions on trade in, and the processing of, specified agricultural produce for the needs of the state' (Art. 30.1) or 'partial rationing of the supply of staple foods and certain articles other than food' (Art. 31.1).

All premises and buildings became liable for administrative appropriation by the authorities (Art. 32.1) and those 'deprived of their homes as a result of military operations' could be billeted wherever the authorities saw fit. Real estate could be expropriated (Art. 32.2) 'for the needs of the defence of the state or the performance of important socio-economic tasks' (Art. 32.3). Administrative decisions concerning matters stipulated in the Martial Law Decree were final and not subject to appeal in the administrative court (Art. 53.2).[1]

Among the political rights proscribed under the Martial Law decree the most important was the freedom of association, including the right to belong to the trade union of one's choice (Art. 15). The Prime Minister was empowered to suspend social organizations ranked as being 'of greater public benefit', trade unions, associations as well as socio-professional organizations if their activity 'struck at the political and social system or the legal order of the PPR or otherwise endangered the interests of the security or defence of the state, as well as for other valid reasons'. The 49 voivods had similar powers with regard to registered or ordinary societies, associations and socio-professional organizations whose field of activity remained within the boundaries of their voivodships.

It was on the strength of this provision that the Prime Minister issued order no. 51 of 13 December 1981 proscribing all trade union activity. Trade union assets were entrusted to the custody of factory managements and local administration officials.

Other political rights won by Solidarity and taken away by

the martial law authorities included the freedom of speech, of the press, of assembly, and of meetings, marches and demonstrations stipulated in Art. 83.1 of the Constitution of the PPR. The Martial Law Decree, in contrast to the Law on Censorship of 31 July 1981, extended censorship to internal circulation trade union bulletins and printed matter and the internal publications of social and political organizations, as well as to academic publications by educational and scientific institutions such as diploma and doctoral theses, second editions of publications already censored in the PPR, literary works published before 1918, visual arts and photographic exhibitions, manuscripts published in fewer than 1,000 copies and performances for selected audiences.

The spoken word was no less subject to control. Local radio and television programmes were discontinued, and only one national radio and one television programme were broadcast. Editorial and technical duties were assigned to a special emergency team set up in secret a few months earlier, one more indication that martial law had been planned well in advance. On 28 April 1981 the Council of Ministers issued resolution no. 185 which was not made public because of the sensitive nature of its contents. It was, however, later quoted as the legal basis on which the Chairman of the Radio and Television Committee issued an order introducing sweeping changes in the functioning of radio and television. All forms of public meetings, with the exception of religious services, were banned (Art. 13).

The Martial Law Decree also suspended fundamental social and economic rights such as workers' self-management in state enterprises (Art. 16). The tasks of the self-management bodies were taken over by the enterprise directors. In its order of 30 December 1981 the Council of Ministers stipulated that it was up to the individual ministers within whose sphere of interests the relevant enterprises lay to decide when self-management bodies could resume their activities. The important right to select and recall the enterprise director which had become one of the key issues of self-management before martial law was, however, withdrawn.

The workers were also deprived of their basic weapon — the strike (Art. 14.2). Participation in a strike was punishable by up to three months' imprisonment or a fine of up to 5,000 zloty (Art. 50.1), and it provided sufficient grounds for the immediate termination of the labour contract, with the worker being declared the guilty party.

The Rigours of Martial Law

Denial of the right to strike was accompanied by a tightening of discipline. The worker was made more dependent on his employer, who could stop him from leaving the job, extend his working hours, re-allocate duties or change his conditions of work without consulting the unions.

The martial law authorities did not stop there. They tried to bring their citizens even more under official control. Private currency accounts were frozen. Restrictions were placed on the maximum amount of cash that could be withdrawn from private savings accounts. No more credit loans were issued either to the public or to state enterprises. All internal and external air traffic was suspended and the borders were sealed off. There was a ban on petrol sales to the general public. The daily and weekly press was suspended but for a few officially sponsored titles.

The Martial Law Decree also introduced new offences and stringent penal regulations. For instance, offences under Art. 271.1 of the Penal Code (dissemination of 'false information' liable seriously to harm the interests of the PPR), Art. 282 (publicly inciting to disobey the law), and Art. 287 (possession or manufacture of a radio transmitter without permission) were henceforth to be punished by the single penalty of up to five years' imprisonment.

The broad scope of repressions provided by the Martial Law Decree can be explained by the fact that the authorities could not have known at the time these measures were being prepared how Solidarity and society at large would react to the proclamation of martial law. The key element for the success of the operation was breaking the popular will to resist. To this end the authorities equipped themselves with very far-reaching powers. Since they managed, however, to contain the wave of strikes and protests following the introduction of martial law, they found that they could dispense with some of the most repressive measures stipulated in the Martial Law Decree. In particular, the provisions on special contributions to the national defence effort and for the needs of the food economy remained unused. Likewise, the Council of Ministers' resolution no. 262 of 12 December 1981 on 'units and organizations formed for the protection of public order and property and the procedure for issuing them with firearms'. was not enacted.[2] Martial law was, in fact, a system of controlled repression coupled with a potential for still greater violence. The martial law authorities adopted a strategy of combining toughness with flexibility. The latter required a readiness to discontinue or not resort to those repressive measures which were no longer necessary, while the former meant a determination to apply some of the more repressive measures held in reserve should popular resistance prove to be stronger or more prolonged. The Martial Law Decree was construed in such a way as to leave the authorities freedom of manoeuvre. The phraseology of the decree is most characteristic in this respect with its recurrent use of the conditional mood, e.g. 'The Council of Ministers may by decree impose...' or "The Council of Ministers is hereby empowered...'

If the demobilization of the masses was the immediate aim of martial law, the long-range aim was to bring about a shift from the traditional type of Communist party-state to a bureaucratic, authoritarian army-state. An important step in this direction was the setting up of a non-constitutional body known as the Military Council of National Salvation (WRON).

WRON – The major focus of power

The WRON was constituted in an illegitimate manner even in the light of the PPR law. The PPR Constitution does not envisage such a body. General Jaruzelski seemed to have been aware of this when in his speech of 13 December 1981 he declared that the WRON was not replacing constitutional agencies of power. Its sole task was to be 'the protection of the legal order in the country and the creation of executive guarantees that would make it possible to restore order and discipline'. In its proclamation of 13 December 1981 the WRON described itself as a temporary body which would function until the situation returned to normal. Its prerogatives were not clear. The proclamation stated that it did not violate the jurisdiction of and did not 'remove responsibility from any cell of the people's authorities'. None the less, the WRON was set up with no legal base at all but it wielded the real power in the country since it emanated from the armed forces. Although, under the PPR Constitution, it is the Sejm and the people's councils which, by virtue of their representative character, take precedence over all other state authorities, the WRON and its commissars were not subject to any control by either the Sejm or the people's councils. The commissars through which the WRON exercised authority were appointed, in accordance with the provisions of the Law on Universal Military Service, by the National Defence Committee (KOK), a body attached to the Council of Ministers and responsible for the country's defence. They were detailed to supervise the implementation of martial law

The Rigours of Martial Law

regulations at all levels of state administration and in certain economic units. In the countryside they were aided by special military task forces set up by the commanders of military districts. On the voivodship level regional subdivisions of the National Defence Committee were set up. The role of the Voivodship Defence Committees was to co-ordinate the activities of the local administration, state enterprises, co-operatives, state institutions and social organizations.

As the supreme authority during martial law, the WRON undertook the task of overhauling the state administration and the economy. The very existence of the WRON clashed with the dogma of 'the leading role of the party'. But in fact there was no real conflict of interests. The party continued to act through those of its members who were also members of the WRON. Both the WRON and the party were headed by General Jaruzelski. The WRON did not stand above the party but was, in fact, constituted to enable the reconstruction of the party which had lost so much ground since August 1980.

Not surprisingly, the most important civilian functions remained in the hands of the military after martial law was lifted and the WRON disbanded itself. The law of 21 November 1983 amended the Law on Universal Military Service, strengthening the powers of the National Defence Committee (KOK). This became independent of the Council of Ministers and its sphere of responsibilities was extended to include security matters in addition to defence. It was empowered to propose the introduction of either martial law or a state of emergency. During such a period it would assume the role of its chief administrator. The KOK's prerogatives with regard to non-military matters have not been clearly defined. Art. 5.7 and 5.9 of the law speak of: 'the co-ordination of the activities of the supreme and local state and economic administrative bodies with regard to national defence' and of fulfilling other tasks with regard to security and defence of the state'.

The law of 21 November 1983 also granted the remodelled KOK wide powers previously belonging to the WRON. These powers concerned not only military matters, but also socio-economic issues. In any future crisis or power struggle resulting in a paralysis of the state administration, the KOK could become its army-based alternative.

A separate Law on the State of Emergency of 5 December 1983 defined the role of the KOK as the administrator of a state of emergency. The remodelled National Defence Committee has thus become a permanent replacement for the Military Council of National Salvation.

The illegality of martial law

Until the law of 20 July 1983 the PPR Constitution, unlike the Polish Constitutions of 1921 and 1935, made no provision for a state of emergency. It referred only to a 'state of war' (Art. 33.1) and 'martial law' (Art. 33.2). The latter article provides that martial law can be declared only 'should this be required by considerations of the defence or security of the state'. Although it was officially said that martial law was introduced on grounds of 'security of the state' no such threat was, in fact, identified.

The martial law authorities themselves gave a number of different reasons for its introduction. Jaruzelski, for instance, spoke of 'the structures of state' which were 'ceasing to function', a 'dying economy' and a 'national catastrophe'. The WRON, in turn, spoke of 'the anti-state, subversive acts of forces hostile to socialism' which had 'pushed the country to the brink of civil war', and 'overt preparations for a reactionary coup'.[3] All the versions stressed the need to ensure and increase protection of the state which was allegedly disintegrating. The state was to be protected at the cost of a 'temporary suspension' of civil rights and trade union freedoms. It is clear that the ruling elite identified its own interests in holding on to power with the well-being of the state. Another often quoted argument was the country's economic collapse. But even if this were true it is difficult to believe that a comprehensive ban on political and trade union activity could be an effective remedy for economic malaise.

As the weeks passed, more formal and legalistic arguments were sought. It was alleged that martial law had been necessary to stop defiance of the PPR's legal order and undermining of its international alliances.[4] Since none of these arguments was really convincing, a twisted interpretation of international law was suggested. It was claimed that the PPR authorities were within their rights in introducing martial law since each state, being sovereign and equal under the UN Charter and the Helsinki Final Act, had the inalienable right to choose its political, economic and social system without any other state being allowed to interfere in any way.[5] This reasoning not only disregarded the rights of the nation but also glossed over the fact that the introduction of martial law, far from being a prerogative of the PPR authorities, was, in fact, evidence of their insovereignty. General Jaruzelski indicated this in his speech of 13 December 1981 when he said: 'It is with our own hands that we must remove the threat. If this chance were to be wasted, history would not forgive the present generation'. In this statement Jaruzelski implied the threat of a second 'liberation' of Poland by the Red Army, this time not from Nazi occupation but from 'counter-revolution'.

The legislation in force in the PPR at the time of the declaration of martial law was deficient in terms of the conditions and consequences of the introduction of martial law. The Law on Universal Military Service only deals with the defence of the country against an external aggressor. The PPR Constitution stipulates only that the Council of State is empowered to declare a general or partial call-up but there is no provision that would empower any body other than the Sejm which, according to Art. 20, is the supreme authority in the country embodying the sovereign rights of the nation, with the right to exercise control over the activities of the state authorities and territorial administration, to pass a law on the conditions necessary for the introduction of martial law and the ensuing consequences.

The Council of State ignored Art. 20 of the PPR Constitution and filled the loopholes in the legal system by issuing the Martial Law Decree. Even if one were to accept that the Council of State was empowered to declare martial law while the Sejm session was in progress, it would not follow that it should possess the authority to abrogate the basic civil rights which would remain in force on the strength of the Constitution itself. Such authority rests exclusively with the Sejm. Having issued the Martial Law Decree in blatant violation of the Sejm's prerogatives, the Council of State introduced martial law on account of the 'security of the state' at the request of an unconstitutional body, the WRON, quoting Art. 33.2 of the PPR Constitution. In this way the Martial Law Decree has, in fact, become an illegally issued ordinance relating to Art. 33.2 of the Constitution.

The power of the Council of State to declare martial law cannot be extended to include the power to issue decrees in this matter. In fact, it may only issue decrees in exceptional and extraordinary circumstances, and only when the Sejm is in recess; this prerogative expires automatically once the Sejm resumes its session. The next plenary sitting was to be held on 15 December 1981. To introduce martial law in accordance with the PPR

Constitution, the authorities would have had to wait three more days, until 15 December 1981, and present the deputies with a bill on the introduction of martial law. If the Sejm had passed the bill, the Council of State would have then been entitled to introduce martial law. Such an approach was, however, out of the question for the architects of martial law who were distrustful even of the Sejm and preferred to act surreptitiously.

The Sejm did not hold its sitting until 25 January 1982 when it voted to ratify the martial law legislation. The ex-post affirmation of extraordinary legislation does not change the basic fact that martial law was not founded on the law but on force.

The introduction of martial law violated not only internal but also international law. Art. 4.1 of the International Covenant on Civil and Political Rights to which Poland is a signatory stipulates as a condition for the derogation of a state from its provisions the existence of 'a public emergency which threatens the life of the nation...'. Art. 4.1 requires also that the threat must be of an extraordinary nature, presenting a real and direct danger and identified before the emergency measures are taken. All the official statements on martial law fail to identify 'a threat to the life of the nation'. Domestic tensions caused by the political opposition are not listed as sufficient grounds on which to conclude that such a threat exists. The sporadic, small-scale acts of violence that did occur in Poland before 13 December 1981 (most of which had, in fact, been provoked by the authorities) were nothing that the courts could not cope with. The opposition was not resorting to organized acts of violence and had no intention of doing so.

The Sejm resolution of 25 January 1982 declared that, 'the developments prior to 13 December 1981 threatened the country with the supreme danger ... the dangers of civil war and of internationalizing the Polish crisis and weakening the sovereignty of the state were becoming real ones'.[6] The Minister of Justice Sylwester Zawadzki said that 'the state of emergency was created in Poland in face of the danger of the social conflict developing into civil war."[7] These statements do not satisfy the substantive prerequisites for the derogation of a state from its obligations under the Covenant since they both mention only a potential danger.

The measure, moreover, in which a state derogates from its obligations must, according to Art. 4.1 of the Covenant be in proportion to the actual danger. The extraordinary legislation passed with the imposition of martial law in Poland went far beyond even the imagined potential danger by suspending virtually all the civil and political rights granted to the citizens of the PPR by the Constitution.

The introduction of martial law also violated Art. 4.2 of the Covenant which provides that under no circumstances may a signatory state derogate from its pledge to observe the right to life, the right to protection against retroactive penal measures, and the right to freedom of conscience and religion (Articles 6, 15 and 18 of the Covenant). Each of these inalienable rights has been violated in the course of martial law.

Finally, the PPR authorities failed to meet one of the formal conditions attached to the Covenant, i.e. properly to notify all the other signatory states of its derogation from certain specific provisions of the Covenant. The PPR authorities did not notify the UN Secretary General until one and a half months after martial law had been declared. In their letter of 29 January 1982 they failed, moreover, to include a number of provisions from which they had derogated.[8] It must, therefore, be stated that on both formal and substantive grounds, derogation by the PPR from its obligations was invalid and martial law was imposed in breach of the International Covenant on Civil and Political Rights. Its primary source was not the law but force.

2. Internment

Imprisonment without trial

The institution of internment is largely unknown in Polish history and did not appear in the PPR criminal law before martial law. It was introduced as a temporary measure on the basis of Art. 42.1 of the Martial Law Decree which states 'Polish citizens over 17 years of age whose past behaviour gives legitimate grounds for suspicion that if they remain at liberty they will not respect the law or will engage in activity which endangers the security or defence interests of the state may be interned in isolation centres for the duration of martial law ...'

Internees were in fact political prisoners deprived of their liberty on the basis of an arbitrary police decision without recourse to legal procedure or the right of appeal. The lawyer Piotr

The Rigours of Martial Law

Andrzejewski described his client Jan Łodyga as 'a civilian imprisoned indefinitely on the strength of the special legal order of martial law, by an inquisitorial and kangaroo court which passed judgement in absentia and without presenting charges'.

The martial law provision is contrary to the principle expressed in Art. 9.1 of the International Covenant on Civil and Political Rights which stipulates that 'everyone has the right to liberty and security of person'. Deprivation of liberty in the form of internment is neither a penalty for a specific infringement of law (i.e. a court sentence) nor a step necessary for the proper course of justice (i.e. a preventative arrest). The criteria for applying this repressive measure are 'legitimate grounds for suspicion'.

The idea behind such an imprecise formula was to give the police a free hand in applying the procedure of internment. Indeed, the procedure was not only instituted ex officio by the security police and carried out in absentia but also enforced immediately. In some cases no reasons were given for the decision to intern; in others, the reasons were so general as to be meaningless. The decision on internment did not, moreover, make any mention of the duration of internment.

In violation of Art. 43.3 of the Martial Law Decree, internees were not served with the decision on internment at the moment of detention. They received it weeks, if not months, after they had been interned.

The decision to intern was taken arbitrarily, on the basis of proscription lists prepared in advance by the voivodship police chiefs and was not subject to control by their superiors. Internees were only entitled to lodge a complaint with the Minister of Internal Affairs. There are no known cases of such a complaint having been successful. The lodging of a complaint, moreover, did not delay execution of the internment decision. Denial of the right to appeal to a court against the arbitrary deprivation of liberty in the form of internment is contrary to Art. 9.4 of the International Covenant on Civil and Political Rights which stipulates that every individual deprived of liberty because of arrest or detention has the right to appeal to a court so that it may without delay consider the grounds for detention and order the liberation of the detainee should his detention be found to be illegal.

The majority of internees were rounded up by special patrols of uniformed and secret policemen in a country-wide sweep on the night of 12/13 December 1981. The patrols, often equipped with crowbars, threatened to break down doors and dragged people out of their beds. The proscription lists included first of all those people who had been active at the turn of 1980 and 1981, i.e. they must have been drawn up well in advance. The aim of interning these people was to remove them from the public scene and deprive them of the possibility of continuing activity which the authorities labelled 'anti-state'. Internment was a penalty imposed on those who had the courage of their convictions and were not afraid to voice them in public.

Internment was applied above all in the first months of martial law. By 10 March 1982, according to official figures, 6,805 people had been interned.[9] Although 10,031 people spent various spells of time in internment prisons.[10] Interment was formally discontinued on 23 December 1982.

Throughout 1982 internment was applied as a repressive measure, largely as a substitute for court proceedings which were lengthier, drew more publicity and did not always guarantee the outcome desired by the authorities. A dissident song writer and singer Jan Kelus, for instance, was detained in connection with the proceedings against Radio Solidarity. During the investigation he kept silent. A search in his flat revealed nothing. Since it was impossible to prove that he had taken part in broadcasting, he was interned. In Szczecin, in the aftermath of 1 and 3 May 1982 demonstrations, 62 people were interned on the basis of photographs taken by police.[11] A number of people were re-interned, after having once been released, for instance Wiesław Matuszewski from the Elwro enterprise in Wrocław who was re-interned shortly after giving an interview to the *Washington Post*.[12]

Ministry of Justice regulations concerning the internees

Order no. 165 issued by the Minister of Justice on 13 December 1981 was of a temporary character and stipulated that internees were to be treated as if they were under temporary arrest. The only difference, which was of little practical significance, was that while internees came under the jurisdiction of the voivodship police chief, those held under temporary arrest were at the disposal of the court or the prosecutor's office.

Another order issued by the Minister of Justice, no. 189 of 31 December 1981, granted wide-ranging authority to internment prison governors. The internees were made totally dependent on their good will. On the basis of undefined 'sanitary or security considerations', the governor was empowered to limit or to revoke the very modest privileges that the internees were allowed. According to this order, internees were entitled to well-ventilated cells at a reasonable temperature, their own food, sufficient personal clothing, three meals a day, eight hours' sleep, medical care, a hot bath once a week, one hour's physical exercise a day, access to books and press, cultural activities and religious practices. The amount of money sent to them could not exceed 990 zloty monthly. In order to be eligible to receive food and clothes parcels up to 3 kg each, each internee had to obtain a special voucher from the camp's governor. Even then, the parcel could not contain articles which because of their wrappings might be difficult to control. Once a month internees were allowed a supervised visit from close relatives or other persons, provided the prison governor agreed. The internee could also talk to his defence lawyer in private but, again, only if he obtained permission from the governor. His private correspondence was censored. In some respects, the situation of the internee was comparable to that of convicts serving their terms of imprisonment under the strict regime.[13]

Apart from granting certain rights, the order of the Minister of Justice also imposed certain duties on the internee. These included carrying out orders issued by the wardens and treating them with respect. The cell was to be kept clean. Internees could not 'disturb the peace', organize themselves or communicate with others from different cells without the warden's permission.

Any infringement of these regulations, such as loud singing, protests against conditions in the camp, or a real or putative disregard of the wardens' orders could resuslt in disciplinary punishment. The penalties most frequently applied were temporary suspension of the right to buy foodstuffs and tobacco in the prison shop and up to seven days' solitary confinement. On some occasions, internees were collectively punished by searches, a ban on contacts between cells, and beatings.

Conditions in internment prisons

These varied according to whether internees were kept in special rest centres (Gołdap, Jaworze, Darłówek), ordinary prisons where a special section was set apart for internment (Białołęka, Załęże, Iława), voivodship police HQs (Lompy St. in Katowice, Mogilska

St. in Kraków) or in other places. Whereas the intellectuals held in government rest homes might be allowed to mix freely, engage in joint activities and go for unsupervised walks, others had to fight for open cells. Internees often complained about overcrowding, insanitary conditions and poor quality food deprived of nutritional value.

Some governors insisted on morning and evening roll-calls, putting out impeccably stacked clothes for the night and even standing to attention when speaking to the wardens. Lying on beds during the day-time was not always allowed.

The Episcopal Committee providing aid to internees points out in a document entitled 'The situation of internees and those arrested under the Martial Law Decree'[14] that internees were under the constant threat of their internment status being changed to arrest. Indeed, the number of internees who were formally charged and tried is by no means small. Apart from the threat of arrest and physical maltreatment two other factors, according to the Episcopal Committee, contributed to the atmosphere of psychological terror prevalent in some of the internment camps. First, the fairly common practice of including hardened criminals among the internees (10 to 15 per cent of the total number of internees) who were suspected, often with good cause, of acting as police informers. Secondly, the internment prison authorities tended to delay and impede hospital treatment recommended by doctors.

The problem of inadequate health care was also raised by a woman doctor interned at Gołdap in a letter of 25 June 1982 addressed to the Sejm Health Commission in which she complained that it was not the doctors but the security police officials who decided on treatment and hospitalization of the internees.

The medical treatment received by internees depended, to a large extent, on whether they landed in a local, municipal or prison hospital.

The Primate's Aid Committee for Prisoners and Their Families, in its report on the health of internees,[15] stated that 620 of the 987 people examined, i.e. over 60 per cent, had developed health problems during internment. Half of that number were already suffering from various lingering diseases before they were interned, and their conditions had become more acute during internment. The remainder had either not suffered from any illness before they were interned or their problems had only come to light during internment. The most frequently recurring diseases were acute disorders affecting the alimentary tract, gastric and duodenal ulceration, joint disorders such as degeneration of the spinal discs, osteoarthritis, respiratory diseases (including four cases of new or reactivated tuberculosis of the lungs and one case (Grażyna Kuroń) of chronic lung congestion resulting in death), hypertension, coronary disease, insomnia, neurosis, transitory and permanent injuries resulting from physical mistreatment or severe beating, viral hepatitis, kidney diseases, mycosis. The report concludes that the very fact of internment reflected significantly and unfavourably on the internees' state of health.

Many of the provisions of the Geneva Convention of 12 August 1949 concerning the protection of civilians in wartime were not respected in relation to internees.[16] For instance, internees were forbidden to elect their own representatives or form committees. Interned families were not held in the same prison. Interned students could not continue their studies. Some of the camps did not have a separate place for religious worship.

A common practice was to encourage the imprisoned people ('you probably will be released sooner...') as well as those who cared about their professional positions ('be careful...') to sign a 'loyalty pledge' prepared in advance which stated that the undersigned would cease all activities which were illegal or detrimental to the PPR's security.

In his statement for the ILO, a former press spokesman of the Solidarity Regional Board in Rzeszów Krzysztof Witoń describes his interrogation:[17]

> I was never physically assaulted in the Załęże prison, but I was threatened verbally during one interrogation. My professional contacts with other Solidarity activists (as with the spokesman of the National Commission, Janusz Onyszkiewicz as well as my appearances in the South–East Region industrial plants and on the local TV before 13 December 1981 were interpreted allegedly by my interrogators as aiming at the overthrow of the Polish government. I was also shown photographs in which I appeared in the company of national Solidarity leaders; my interrogators claimed that these photographs constituted proof that I was responsible for some unspecified 'threats' to national security. Visiting cards of foreign journalists,

which were confiscated from my office in Rzeszów Region Solidarity headquarters, were considered to be a proof of my 'collaboration with the enemies of socialism'.

It was also suggested to Witoń that he appear on national television in Warsaw, or give a written statement to regional newspapers dissociating himself from the union or defaming its leaders.

Internment in penal military centres

At the end of October or beginning of November 1982 at least ten new style military-internment centres were set up under a secret order issued by the General Staff HQ. The places most frequently mentioned in independent reports were Czerwony Bór near Łomża, Chełmno, Rawicz, Unisław, Złocieniec near Koszalin, Węgorzewo, Trzebiatów, Czerwony Dwór near Olecko and a camp near Wrocław. The most active Solidarity members or those whom the authorities perceived as potential 'trouble makers' were 'drafted' into military service in order to remove them from public life, isolate them and subject them to strict military discipline. This was a large-scale preventative operation before the planned general strike proclaimed by the underground Solidarity leadership (TKK) for 10 November 1982 in response to the delegalization of the union.

The military centre in Czerwony Bór was under the direct command of the Ministry of Internal Affairs. The commanding officers were security police officials. Internees were guarded by conscripted soldiers serving their mandatory two-year military duty. They had all been transferred from other military units. Drafted internees wore uniforms but no rank insignia. They were not issued with weapons. They were conscripted at very short notice without regard for age, health or previous military service.

According to Jerzy Las, the chairman of the Solidarity commission in the local communal administration and housing enterprise in Sandomierz who was called up and re-interned in Czerwony Bór, the medical commission from Ełk which was supposed to determine whether a conscript was fit for military service, instead of asking about his state of health asked about his membership in Solidarity. The authorities created a new draft category 'F' to make sure that even ill and handicapped members of the union would not escape the dragnet. This category was:

unfit for military duty, but fit for service within the confines of a military camp.[18] A military doctor was sacked by the officers in charge of Czerwony Bór for issuing too many exemption certificates.

An internee from Lębork serving his military duty at the camp in Chełmno noted in a letter that the internees were thought of as 'a bunch of criminals, bandits and thieves put up in barracks'.[19] They were re-educated by heavy labour including tree-felling or road-building. Should they fail to fulfil the work norms they were punished or threatened with severe punishment.[20] Apart from work, the internees had to take part in indoctrination courses run by political officers. Some of them were periodically subjected to questioning.

It is difficult to assess the numbers involved in this new form of internment. Estimates for the total of those interned in these centres vary from 2,500 to 4,000 people.[21] The advantages of this form of repressive action were very considerable for the authorities. It was a hidden form of internment disguised as a routine draft. Moreover, even after those interned in this way had been released they could still be intimidated and threatened with penalties for 'endangering military secrets'.

* * *

The formal suspension of martial law and the simultaneous discontinuation of internment did not, however, involve a return to normal life for the majority of former internees who were subjected to a whole range of other repressive actions. On their release from internment, many found that they had been dismissed from the jobs they had held before the imposition of martial law. The scale of this practice varied from plant to plant and region to region. In at least one voivodship, the voivod had issued a secret instruction to the effect that any internee attempting to return to work in a militarized plant be fired.[22]

Many former internees were forced to emigrate. Contrary to the Universal Declaration of Human Rights, internees could only apply for one-way passports without the right to return to Poland. This 'offer', which was presented by the Ministry of Internal Affairs for the first time on 3 March 1982, had many features of banishment. Although it formally appeared that internees had agreed to leave the country of their own free will, they were in fact often forced to do so. The alternative was imprisonment, harassment, joblessness, eviction from their flats and living on the bread line.

The institution of internment obviously proved to be a success from the authorities' point of view. Indeed, so much so that it was written into the permanent legislation of the Polish People's Republic as part of the Law on the State of Emergency of 5 December 1983.

3. Military courts

A separate entity

Military jurisdiction, which is distinct from ordinary jurisdiction, comes under the direct control of the Ministry of Defence and is to a large extent managed by the Chief of the Army's Main Political Board which also supervises the military prosecution organs. The distinct character of military courts derives from the specific features of military service.

The purpose of military courts is to strengthen discipline in the armed forces. They try rank-and-file soldiers and officers on active military service, civilians employed by the army and POWs. The appropriate military court to deal with an offence committed by any of these mentioned above (with the exception of POWs) is the one attached to the military unit in which they serve or in which they are employed, whereas in ordinary jurisdiction, the court in whose area an offence has been committed is the one to hear the case.

Only officers on active military service may serve as judges or prosecutors in military courts. Military courts, like ordinary courts, allow for appeal to a higher instance. Regional military courts or garrison military courts are courts of the first instance, while military district courts or courts of the specific branches of the armed forces are courts of the second instance. These are the equivalents of voivodship courts. They also act as courts of the first instance in hearing offences for which the death penalty can be passed. In contrast to ordinary jurisdiction, military district courts or courts of the specific branches of the armed forces do not exercise judicial or administrative supervision over regional or garrison military courts. The Military Chamber of the Supreme Court hears appeals in the second instance.

The Rigours of Martial Law

Offences committed by Soviet soldiers stationed in Poland can be prosecuted by the Polish military prosecutors only with the consent of the Soviet authorities.

Finally, civilian defence lawyers need special permission in order to appear on behalf of a client who is being tried by a military court. A special list of military defence lawyers is compiled and periodically updated by the Chairman of the Military Chamber of the Supreme Court.

The role of the military courts in crushing the anti-Communist opposition

The origins of military courts in the PPR date back to 1943. They were set up in the USSR alongside the Soviet-sponsored Polish First Infantry Division. The personnel of these 'courts', trained by political officers of the Soviet army and largely staffed by Russians, served as an instrument of sovietization after Poland was overrun by the Red Army.

In 1944 the Supreme Military Court was set up as the highest authority in military jurisdiction. A network of 16 military district courts, one for each voivodship, was also established. Their task was to protect 'the people's rule' by investigating the most dangerous 'counter-revolutionary' and 'anti-state' crimes. The members of the Home Army, an underground resistance movement subordinate to the legitimate government of Poland in London, were labelled 'state enemies' who were, according to the Communists' interpretation of recent history, only pretending to fight the Germans while directing their major efforts towards counteracting the influence of the Communist underground.

The most commonly fabricated charges against members of the Home Army included: spying, sabotage, attempting to overthrow the PPR's political system by force, helping the fascists to crush the anti-Communist resistance, treason, etc. To force the suspect to admit to these or similar charges, torture was used as an admissible method of extracting testimony. The NKVD school of interrogation demanded that 'the suspect' himself admit to all the offences imputed to him, incriminate others and beg for mercy.

Only some of the trials were open. There were also show trials which were widely publicized in order 'to educate the public'. The trials themselves were carefully prepared according to a specific scenario. Sometimes the defendant was denounced not only

The Rigours of Martial Law

by the prosecution who played the major role but even by his defence lawyers. Some sentences were kept secret. Some death sentences were not carried out since the authorities hoped to extract further testimonies that might incriminate others who were still to be tried. Between 1944 and 1948 military courts alone passed 22,797 sentences including 2,500 death sentences.[23] Of course, such 'legal measures' were not the only weapon in the fight to eliminate opposition. Secret police terror was used on a wide scale throughout the country.

Repressive legislation that served as the 'legal basis' for trumped-up charges against the anti-Communist resistance fighter was characterized by a wide scope of penalization and severity of penalties. It remained in force for many years and served as a model for future penal legislation.

Documents of the Stalinist period in Poland prove that the courts, especially the military courts, were an integral part of the state-run terror machine. Disregarding the facts of the case, they passed sentences according to directives issued by the party and security apparatus. Were their judges guilty of criminal abuse of the law? According to Aniela Steinsbergowa, a defence lawyer in the Stalinist period, they were. Dr. Mieczysław Szerer, a legal scholar attempted, on the other hand, to exonerate them. In his memorial of 13 May 1957 he tried to justify the sentences passed by blaming the 'atmosphere' and the 'Bolshevik style of work' demanded of the Supreme Military Court judges.[24] The data he quoted prove, however, that military judges were partial, lacking the necessary qualifications, unwilling to resist the pressures exerted on them. Despite the subsequent condemnation of Stalinism by Poland's post-1956 regime, the Stalinist judges did not face disciplinary proceedings and continued in their jobs. A paradoxical situation emerged: the victims of those who had abused the law were rehabilitated, some of them posthumously, whereas those who abused the law were quietly condoned. This had negative repercussions for the judicial system in Poland in subsequent years.

The domination of military courts over ordinary courts came to an end with de-Stalinization. A law of April 1955 stipulated that civilians accused of criminal offences (with the exception of spying) were to be tried by ordinary courts. Regional military courts were abolished. Military courts were to restrict themselves to crime prevention within the armed forces, and trial and punishment of military personnel charged with various offences.

The Rigours of Martial Law

As from 1962 the Supreme Military Court was abolished as a separate entity and it was incorporated into the Supreme Court as its Military Chamber. It became a second instance military appeal court. The chamber also supervises other military courts with regard to personnel matters, financial matters, employment policy, training and organization of work.

Military courts under martial law

During martial law the scope of the jurisdiction of the military courts was considerably increased. On the basis of the Council of State Decree on Military Courts of 12 December 1981 'the most serious infringements of the fundamental political interests of the PPR as well as of the existing legal system' were to be tried by military courts. If a dispute over jurisdiction arose between a military and an ordinary court, the military court decided which of the two courts was empowered to hear the case.

In particular, the military courts were to try offences against:
(i) the fundamental political and economic interests of the PPR listed in Chapter XIX of the Penal Code and including: treason, attempted *coup d'état*, terrorist attack and sabotage;
(ii) the Martial Law Decree, such as Art. 47.1 of the decree ('acting to the advantage of the enemy or to the detriment of the security or defence interests of the PPR or of an allied state'), and Art. 48.1 – 4 (dissemination of 'false information') and other offences under the Martial Law Decree including continuation of trade union activity or leading a strike (Art. 46.1 and 2) should these be committed by employees of militarized enterprises;
(iii) the Law of 21 November 1967 on Universal Military Service which concerned *inter alia* various offences committed by employees of militarized enterprises;
(iv) various infringements of the Penal Code, including homicide, violation of public order, offences involving property and state and professional secrets, setting up of 'an illegal organization', armed robbery, etc. The part of the Penal Code pertaining to members of the armed forces was also applied to employees of militarized enterprises;
(v) the law of 29 December 1950 on the protection of peace, which includes offences such as 'warmongering' and 'war propaganda'.

According to a communiqué issued by the Supreme Military Prosecutor in March 1982, the majority of the 44 per cent of cases heard by the military courts after the imposition of martial law involved 'anti-state activities', 17 per cent concerned the illegal possession of arms, 9 per cent concerned offences committed by employees of militarized enterprises, and 7 per cent involved illegal crossing of state borders. Some 76 per cent of the 'anti-state activities' were supposedly committed by Solidarity members, and 60 per cent of all the defendants were under the age of 30. The majority of cases handled by the military courts involved Art. 46.1 and 2 and Art. 48 of the Martial Law Decree — continuation of trade union activity and organization of strikes in militarized enterprises and establishing an independent information network. Most of these cases were heard under summary procedure.[25]

Although it is difficult to verify these data, their general trend indicates that the role of military courts was political. They were entrusted with the important tasks of 'pacifying' workers employed in key enterprises and breaking the backbone of the uncensored information network.

The very idea of bringing civilians before military courts for 'anti-state offences' is Stalinist in origin. The actual sentences passed by General Jaruzelski's military courts were, however, largely in line with those passed by ordinary courts. There were a few notable exceptions, such as the sentences passed on Ewa Kubasiewicz, Jerzy Kowalczyk and others by the Naval Court in Gdynia or the sentences of up to 25 years' imprisonment passed by the Court of the Warsaw Military District on a group of youths from Grodzisk Mazowiecki accused of membership in an armed gang and of the murder of an uniformed policeman. On the whole, however, the severity of sentences passed by the military courts depended on the moment in time (they were more severe at the beginning of martial law, becoming more lenient as time passed) and on the region in which the trial took place.

Military courts in the post-martial law period

After martial law was officially suspended, the jurisdiction of military courts was limited to some offences stipulated in the Penal Code[26] as well as offences concerning the Law on Universal Military Service of 21 November 1967. According to a law entitled 'Special Regulations for the Period of Suspended Martial Law' of 18 December 1982 (henceforth referred to as the Act of 18 December 1982) proceedings already started were to be continued before the same courts. Summary procedure was limited to the most serious criminal and political offences. In practice, this

The Rigours of Martial Law

meant that military courts would not start any new cases based on Art. 47 and 48 of the Martial Law Decree after 1 January 1983, the day martial law was formally suspended. Ordinary courts regained jurisdiction over offences against public order as stipulated in the Penal Code.

None the less, the jurisdiction of military courts has been permanently extended in comparison with the pre-martial law period. The law of 28 July 1983 introduced amendments to the Code of Criminal Procedure removing offences stipulated under Chapter XIX of the Penal Code 'against the fundamental interests of the PPR' from the jurisdiction of ordinary courts and placing them under the jurisdiction of military courts. In this way some of the provisions of the Council of State Decree on Military Courts of 12 December 1981 have been transferred permanently into the Code of Criminal Procedure. Solidarity activists in the underground had to reckon with being tried by the military courts if caught and charged with treason or sedition, as indeed happened in the cases of Tadeusz Jedynak, Czesław Bielecki, Bogdan Borusewicz, Zbigniew Bujak and Ewa Kulik (see Chapter V), before they were amnestied in September 1986.

4. Militarized enterprises

Universal Military Service extended to key enterprises

Art. 4.2 of the Council of State resolution of 12 December 1981 on martial law reactivated some of the provisions of the Law of 21 November 1967 on Universal Military Service. According to Art. 139 of this Law, in the event of national call-up or during a war, the National Defence Committee (KOK) is empowered to declare some enterprises militarized. The KOK in its resolution no. 9 of 12 December 1981 (unpublished) militarized some 60 per cent of Polish industry including port complexes, some power plants, fire brigades, transport, post, telecommunications, radio and television stations and other related industries and services.

The very idea of militarizing the workforce was not the original invention of the Polish military. Its origin dates back to 'war Communism' in Bolshevik Russia. It was developed by Trotsky in his Theses of December 1919. He believed that labour could be organized on lines parallel to those existing in the army.

The Rigours of Martial Law

Lenin, who was himself fascinated by military organization as a model not only for the new style party but also for the perfect society, backed the idea.[27]

Applied to Poland, the idea of militarizing labour meant that the Labour Code no longer afforded any protection of the work contract and everyone who worked in a militarized enterprise was considered as having been called up, by force of law, for service. Universal military service as expounded in the law of 21 November 1967 was extended to the workplace. Anyone who did not fulfil the duties his job entailed was no longer merely subject to dismissal, but in addition risked charges before a military court. During martial law the provisions of the Law on Universal Military Service were applied as though there were a real war. The management acquired the right arbitrarily to change the conditions of pay and employment. Work discipline was tightened. The employees, in the absence of trade union and self-management organs, could not air their grievances. Militarization was accompanied by the imposition of a strict ban on strikes and protest actions as well as a ban on disseminating independent information.

The employee's position

In militarized enterprises the work contracts of all employees were immediately suspended and they were automatically declared to be on active service like soldiers. Instructions given by superiors to their subordinates were to be carried out as though they were military orders. There was no appeal against a given order. A subordinate refusing to obey instructions could be prosecuted for disobedience.

The employees could not hand in their notice or leave work of their own accord. Anyone doing so risked being declared a deserter. He could be discharged from service only if he was unable to perform it or once he reached retirement age. The management, however, reserved the right to postpone his retirement.

The authorities realized that increased labour discipline alone would not pacify the workforce. It had to be accompanied by sackings. The ruling of the Supreme Court of 27 February 1982 helped the management in this respect. According to this, the dismissal of an employee from his job in a militarized enterprise involved automatic dissolution of his work contract. A discharged employee could only sue his employer for compensation equal to the pay to which he would have been entitled had he been given proper notice. He could not sue for reinstatement. If he was discharged on the basis of Art. 52.1(1) of the Labour Code (being declared the guilty party and dismissed without notice, e.g. on account of participation in a strike or protest action) he was not even entitled to seek compensation.

In another ruling of 11 June 1982, the Supreme Court declared that even one single day's absence from work without approval could justify dissolution of the work contract without notice on the basis of Art. 52.1(1) of the Labour Code.[28] The local appeals commissions which would normally hear labour disputes in the first instance could not examine the grounds on which an 'employee–serviceman' was discharged from service.

The management was no longer obliged to consult the trade unions if they wanted to dismiss an employee. In militarized and non-militarized enterprises, trade union officials and works' council members (workers' self-management) were deprived of the special protection of their work contract stipulated in Art. 39.1 of the Labour Code, which gave former union officials two years' job security. On the basis of this provision local appeals commissions usually reinstated the dismissed Solidarity activists. Management, however, in some cases refused to comply with such decisions, lodging an appeal or simply barring the reinstated employees from entering the enterprise. Such practices were illegal since the martial law regulations themselves obliged management to facilitate a return to work for former trade union officials in their former capacity.[29] At that time, moreover, trade unions were still suspended and not yet formally dissolved.

The Supreme Court stepped in to close this loophole. In its ruling of 4 May 1982, it came to the conclusion that the decision to suspend all trade union activity during martial law nullified all legal provisions concerning the protection of work contracts of trade union officials.

Military commissars or voivods who were the custodians of trade unions' assets dismissed Solidarity's administrative employees under the pretext of protecting these assets from being squandered, in as far as wages diminished assets. The Supreme Court ruling of 15 July 1982 sanctioned this practice.

One of those discharged from service in a militarized enterprise was Ireneusz Kosmahl, a member of the Mazowsze Regional Board of Solidarity, a delegate to the Solidarity

Congress. Before he took up a full-time job as a Solidarity official he was the director of the investment department at the Bus Transport Enterprise (PKS) in Warsaw. Under the provisions of both the Labour Code and the Chairman of the Council of Ministers' order no. 51 of 13 December 1981, he was entitled to return to his previous job. The management, however, fearing his possible influence on the workforce, handed him a notice of dismissal. He was served the notice in March 1982 by the personnel officer in his enterprise while still in hospital. He appealed to the local appeals commission and was reinstated. The commission found it unprecedented that an employee should be served notice while on his hospital bed. The management appealed to court which found the notice justified.

As Kosmahl told the author, over 100 employees in his enterprise (employing some 13,000) were 'discharged from military service' which meant termination of the work contract. This number included virtually all the chairmen of Solidarity commissions in the departments and bus depots, as well as other outspoken members of the union. The decision on dismissal was taken by the management on the basis of blacklists compiled by security officers.

An employee could be allocated different tasks than the ones he usually performed without the need to change his work contract. He could even be transferred from one militarized enterprise to another. He could also be allocated a lower post at his present pay, but should he be disciplinarily moved to a lower post as a punishment for breaching discipline, he would receive the lower pay that went with the job. Local appeals commissions were not empowered to examine whether management was entitled to transfer an employee to different tasks if such a decision were taken because of 'the organizational needs of the enterprise'.

One of the duties of employees in militarized enterprises was to be available at a moment's notice. Other restrictions imposed on the workforce in militarized enterprises involved curtailment of holiday entitlement to one day for each month worked and the extension of working hours. These were determined by a minister or a voivod. The average was a 6-day, 48-hour week, but in certain cases 'determined by the needs of the enterprise', the eight-hour working day could be extended to twelve hours (with the exception of Sundays and employees working in conditions detrimental to their health).

The Rigours of Martial Law

Prosecution of offences

Militarized enterprises were either left under their old managements or made subordinate to military commissars. In the former case, the employees were liable for prosecution only if they committed offences in connection with their service. In the latter case, all offences committed by employees in militarized enterprises were subject to the jurisdiction of military courts, under Chapter XXXVII of the Penal Code, i.e. the part of the Penal Code pertaining to soldiers on active duty. Employees of militarized enterprises could also be prosecuted on the basis of the martial law decree.

In trials involving strikers employed in militarized enterprises, the prosecution usually based charges on Art. 309 of the Penal Code (refusal to carry out orders) and Art. 46.1 or 2 of the Martial Law Decree. A typical example is the case of seven employees of the Transbud transport enterprise in Gdynia who were accused of continuing trade union activity and refusing to carry out their superior's 'instruction-order'. Two of the defendants were additionally charged with organizing and leading the strike which took place in the enterprise between 14 and 18 December 1981.

According to the Naval Court in Gdynia which passed sentences of up to five years' imprisonment, the very fact of membership in the Strike Committee constituted a continuation of trade union activity. The court ruled that two of the defendants, Jerzy Okraj and Antoni Chrzanowski, were de facto members of the Strike Committee since they had participated in talks with the management. Another defendant, Zofia Kwiatkowska, was found guilty of organizing and leading the strike since she had taken the minutes at the strikers' meeting on 14 December and had counted the votes. According to the court, the fact that she, together with another defendant, Aleksander Składanowski, had on several occasions left the striking enterprise and returned with information on strike action in other enterprises, was an incriminating circumstance. The court found that this was tantamount to assisting the chairman of the local works commission of Solidarity, Longin Stojak, in organizing and leading the strike. (His case was excluded for separate proceedings.) At the same time, the court found that Kwiatkowska was not influencing Stojak's decisions. Although the actions of Kwiatkowska and Składanowski were not based on any formal division of labour, by passing on information to the striking workforce in the Transbud enterprise (e.g. on the internment of Solidarity leaders), they had, the court said, created an atmosphere contributing to the continuation of the strike.

The same Naval Court in Gdynia acquitted the defendants of the second charge based on Art. 309 of the Penal Code, arguing that the management could not be said to have issued orders, since they had only ineffectually appealed for calm and informed about the consequences a strike would entail. The workers had been ignorant of their new status as soldiers since they had been issued neither with call-up cards nor with uniforms. The prosecution did not accept this argument and appealed to the Supreme Court. The defence lawyers also submitted a request for a review of the sentence arguing that it was not justified and too severe. The Supreme Court in its ruling of 22 February 1982 lowered the sentences passed against Kwiatkowska and Składanowski from five to three and a half years' imprisonment, conditionally suspended the sentences of the three other defendants, and changed the legal definition of the facts with which two of the defendants had been charged (leading the strike instead of continuing trade union activity).

In the case of Andrzej Szulc, a miner from Knurów coalmine, the Court of the Silesian Military District also found that the management of the coalmine had informed the workforce 'very superficially' about the consequences of militarization. The court passed a lenient sentence of eight months' imprisonment plus one year's loss of public rights.[30]

In another case involving Stanisław Dyląg and Henryk Lewandowski, Deputy Chairmen of the Factory Committee of Solidarity in the Kraków-Czyżyny bus depot, the prosecution presented an additional charge that the accused had made use of a bus which was the property of the Municipal Transport Enterprise in order to establish contact with striking workers in other departments of the enterprise (Art. 46.4 of the Martial Law Decree). They were sentenced under summary procedure to four and three and a half years' imprisonment respectively plus two years' loss of public rights.

Other offences for which the employees in militarized enterprises could be prosecuted included: permanent abandonment of employment (desertion), prolonged avoidance of work (military service), non-execution of a superior's orders, refusal to execute an order or its faulty execution, disrespect to one's superior, etc. Refusal to work under military discipline was treated as a refusal to serve military duty and was punishable by a minimum of six months' and a maximum of five years' imprisonment. Absence from work was considered as unauthorized leave from the military unit and was punished accordingly. Making oneself incapable of service, e.g. as a result of self-mutilation or excessive drinking, was also a punishable offence. The most serious offences such as: desertion, theft, revealing a state or professional secret, organizing or leading a strike, were heard under summary procedure.

Post-martial law restrictions on labour mobility

The militarization of work forces in key enterprises had many features of compulsory labour. The employees were at the mercy of their managements, deprived of the protection of their work contract as stipulated in the provisions of the Labour Code. The rulings of the Supreme Court in labour relations were heavily biased in favour of the management. They contrasted sharply with the decisions of the local appeals commissions which tried on the whole to help employees 'discharged from military service' (dismissed from their jobs).

Military commissars who took up jobs in industry were not prepared for their new assignments. They lacked experience in management and professional skills. They were ignorant of the specific social environment and labour relations in the enterprise to which they were assigned. An anonymous former military commissar bitterly remarked in an interview for the underground *KOS* publication:

> A huge number of top officers have taken up economic management, without being in the least trained for it. They joined a corrupt administration and together they have created a mutual admiration society. In order to keep us from thinking too much we were kept busy with planned and unplanned check-ups, visits and inspections.[31]

Restrictions on labour mobility were retained in those enterprises which had been militarized during martial law. Although the Act of 18 December 1982 formally abolished militarization, it stipulated that the employees of previously militarized enterprises could dissolve work contracts only on the basis of mutual agreement with the management and not unilateral notice. It meant in practice that the management in those enterprises could prevent employees from leaving. An employee could not sue his employer before the local appeals commission or the court for refusing to let him leave. Should he decide to leave after all, he would have to start from the very bottom of the pay scale in his new workplace. The management, on the other hand, was free to dismiss any employee.

The Act of 18 December 1982 stipulated also that working hours could be extended in key enterprises up to 46-hours per week 'should it be necessary for the fulfilment of important economic tasks'. Over-time pay and free Saturdays could be scrapped at a moment's notice. The number of enterprises affected by the Act rose from the 1,372 that had been militarized during martial law to 1,806 since 434 new enterprises classified as fulfilling 'operational plans' or 'government's orders' were added to the list.

The law of 21 July 1983, the so-called 'Special Regulations for the Period of Overcoming the Socio-Economic Crisis' (henceforth referred to as the Act of 21 July 1983) gave the management of enterprises which the Council of Ministers had, in its order of 25 July 1983, declared crucial because of their importance for the national economy, defence or the general public, the right to extend the length of notice of termination of employment handed in by the employee by up to six months.

The Council of Ministers' order of 8 August 1983 introduced mandatory job placement in the 15 most industrialized voivodships. It covered all enterprises, including private and foreign firms, with the exception of some professions and those occupations in which employment was established by appointment. Those categories of employees covered by mandatory job placement (mostly workers) could only be employed on the basis of a recommendation issued by a local department of employment. A person looking for a job was deprived of the possibility of choosing a certain type of work or a specific enterprise. Local departments of employment carried out discriminatory policies with regard to former internees or political prisoners released under the various amnesties. This compulsory labour exchange was used as a means of making the workers still more dependent on their employer – the state, which safeguarded its monopoly on employment.

5. Compulsory labour

The universal obligation to work

One of the priorities of martial law was to exact greater discipline from the workforce by restricting labour mobility and increasing administrative control. What amounted in fact to compulsory labour assumed a variety of disguises. In addition to the militarization of key enterprises which has been discussed in the preceding section, the martial law authorities introduced the so-called 'universal obligation to work'. This idea can be traced back to the Bolshevik 'Declaration of the Working and Exploited Peoples' of 4 January 1918 which recommended it as a means of restructuring society through the elimination of 'the parasitic classes'. The Bolsheviks combined the universal obligation to work with 'the duty to defend the Fatherland'.

The universal obligation to work was set out in Art. 29.1 of the Martial Law Decree. The PPR Constitution, for its part, lacks provisions according to which work could be interpreted as a legal duty. It defines work in moral terms (Art. 19) and speaks of it as a citizen's right (Art. 68). Theorists of law have always interpreted this as implying that citizens were free voluntarily to seek jobs and enter into employment contracts of their own choice. On the other hand the Constitution does not expressly preclude compulsory labour which existed in pre-martial law Poland on a limited scale with regard to prisoners. The Labour Code of 1974, for its part, adheres to ILO Conventions nos. 29 and 105 proscribing compulsory labour.

Art. 29.1 of the Martial Law Decree empowered the Council of Ministers to introduce the universal obligation to work for persons over 15 years of age and who had not yet reached retirement age irrespective of whether they were currently working or unemployed.

The Council of Ministers used these powers to issue an order on 30 December 1981 'on the universal obligation to work in the period of martial law'. It empowered the local administration to summon men between the ages of 18 and 45 with no regular jobs, register them as unemployed and assign them wherever applicable to work in those state enterprises which had staff shortages. The men were obliged to undertake the work to which they were assigned. In addition, the local administration chief (naczelnik) in the locality where an enterprise was operating could ' assign additional tasks to a worker of any enterprise operating within his administrative boundaries or entrust to him tasks of a different type in the same or another locality, even without the worker's consent...' Any worker ordered to undertake different tasks or transferred to another locality could appeal against such a decision but only on the grounds of ill health, personal or family circumstances, and only within three days of receiving the order. The lodging of an appeal with the local appeals commission for labour matters (TKO) did not delay execution of the decision.

Failure to report to the local administration after having been summoned, failure to undertake the work assigned or refusal to perform other tasks or accept a transfer to a different place of employment all qualified as petty offences punishable by fines of up to 5,000 zloty.

In the course of martial law some 268,000 men were registered as unemployed under the 'universal obligation to work'. Their names were drawn from police files, local government files, information supplied by social and political organizations, local residents' committees and places of employment as well as denunciations by informants. Prior to the introduction of martial law 26,277 people had a police record of 'avoiding work' while local government authorities had a list of 31, 275 work shirkers. The police files were officially kept to help with crime prevention. At the end of 1982, some 50,000 work shirkers had been classified as 'hardened'. Of these just under 50 per cent lived off crime, 9.2 per cent off prostitution, and the remaining 40 per cent obtained their means of livelihood in a manner 'contrary to the principles of social co-existence' or from unknown sources.[32]

The practical effects of these measures were negligible. 242,000 of all those registered under the 'universal obligation to work' were assigned to jobs. Of these, 219,000 actually reported for work, though the overwhelming majority subsequently abandoned their jobs. In the Ursus Tractor Factory, for instance, 87 per cent of those assigned to work there left within a short time.[33] The management were in most cases glad to see them go since they were not only unproductive but also had a demoralizing influence on the rest of the workforce.

The Law on Work Shirkers

'The universal obligation to work' was preserved after martial law in a modified form as the law of 26 October 1982 'on Procedure with Regard to Work Shirkers', and was passed as part of a legislative package aimed at fighting social disease. This law marked the first attempt by the military authorities to transfer extraordinary martial law legislation into the permanent post-martial law legislation. The law of 26 October 1982 was, in fact, more stringent than its martial law prototype. First of all, it put the onus of reporting to the local administration office upon the 'shirker' who had to explain of his own accord why he was out of work or not at school and had not registered as a job seeker for over three months. Secondly, those who failed to report, as well as those who ignored an official summons, were subject to three months of 'limitation of personal freedom' or a fine of up to 20,000 zloty. Thirdly, those who did not report to the local administration were deprived of ration cards entitling them to purchase basic foodstuffs which were in short supply on the market.

In the authorities' view the Law on Work Shirkers was not tantamount to compulsory labour but, rather, a new means of putting pressure on those who refused, as the authorities saw it, to work.[34] In fact, this law, inasfar as it was conceived as an instrument of reducing the number of social misfits, turned out to be a failure. Its potential for putting the opposition beyond the pale and its surveillance of non-conformists and those who managed to earn a living without having to rely on the state as an employer, was much more important.

The law of 26 October 1982 was based on three ill-defined concepts: 'the consistent evasion of work', 'socially unjustified reasons' and 'the principles of social co-existence', which were open to arbitrary interpretation and abuse by local officials bent on settling scores with local opposition activists.

In order to pigeonhole those who, in the official view, refused to work, a special, two-stage procedure was devised. The names of all those who were temporarily out of work and not attending school or university were initially entered on a list of unemployed persons. Those who were found consistently to refuse to work were then transferred on to a second register of notorious work shirkers. The dividing line between the two categories was only a thin one. It was up to the local administration to decide that a person listed as unemployed had been out of work or school for too long without 'socially justified reasons' and assign him to a job. Should he fail to report there, his name would automatically be put on the register.³⁵ His finances and sources of income would, moreover, be subject to close scrutiny and, should they prove suspicious, his name would be passed on to the tax authorities. In cases of national emergency, natural disaster or any other 'act of God' those on the register could be called up to join public task forces for up to 60 days in any one year.

Failure to report to the local administration after having been summoned to explain one's finances could be punished either as a petty offence (while on the initial list, under Art. 21.1 of the law) or as a misdemeanour (while on the register, under Art. 21.2). The latter was punishable by up to one year's 'limitation of personal freedom'. Failure to report to work on a task force in cases of natural disaster or an 'act of God' could result in up to two years' 'limitation of personal freedom'.

The law was devised in such a manner as to force people to work one way or another. The penalty of 'limitation of personal freedom' amounted to supervised work for the state with up to a quarter of one's earnings automatically deducted. Failure to serve this penalty (for instance by abandoning the job or changing one's place of residence without permission) could result in the imposition of a fine. Should this prove impossible to exact, the fine could be transformed into a prison term. The idea was that if the local administration did not succeed in forcing a shirker to work then the petty offences tribunal or the court would do so.

In February 1983 General Jaruzelski foreshadowed what the authorities had in store for work shirkers: 'the noose is tightening round the neck of the so-called parasites. If they do not take up employment in the nearest future they will be sent to work on the irrigation and flood preventing front in Żuławy and in the Gdańsk Coastal Region'.³⁶ The Minister of Internal Affairs General Kiszczak deplored the fact that 'only' 39 per cent of the 11,730 people penalized in 1983 under the Law on Work Shirkers had been subjected to 'limitation of personal freedom'³⁷ with the majority being able to escape with no more than a fine.

With the Law on Work Shirkers the authorities equipped themselves with a new means of putting the opposition beyond the pale. Those sacked because of their independent trade union activity, political prisoners released under amnesty, people unable to find jobs in their professions because of their previous records of opposition, could be repeatedly summoned and questioned not only about their sources of income but also about their personal circumstances. This form of de facto interrogation would provide the administration with personal details which in turn could be passed on to the police. The law opened the way to a comprehensive system of keeping tabs on criminals, alcoholics, speculators and other social misfits, on the one hand, and democratic opposition activists, on the other. The police acquired an opportunity to complement their own information networks by exploiting labour ministry channels. They acquired an additional source of information without coming into direct contact with those whom it concerned.[38]

The Law on Work Shirkers could be applied selectively; some of them proved to be more equal than others. People with connections could easily procure false certificates or hand over bribes to ensure that they remained unmolested. On the other hand, the law could be applied rigorously with regard to those whom the authorities wanted to harass.

The extension of compulsory labour

The Act of 21 July 1983 extended the use of compulsory labour set out in the law of 26 October 1982. Compulsory labour was no longer restricted to emergency situations such as natural disasters and 'acts of God'. Henceforth any voivodship people's council could pass a resolution introducing an obligation to work for all those considered work shirkers, 'in order to eliminate obstacles to the proper functioning of the communal and other services of basic importance for the needs of the population'.

The report commissioned by the ILO in May 1984 noted that this legislation was in breach of ILO Conventions nos. 29 and 105 since it introduced an obligation to work for persons 'considered to be inactive for socially unjustified reasons' and made it possible 'to provide for the regular use of non-voluntary labour for carrying out public works that are normally to be done by the workers of communal services'.

The Act of 21 July 1983 also eliminated the distinction between those on the initial list and those on the register of notorious work shirkers. Both these categories could henceforth be assigned to compulsory work on the same basis. Indeed, the whole procedure of dealing with those considered to be work dodgers was made simpler for the authorities and at the same time more rigid. The Act of 21 July 1983 eliminated, for example, the possibility of imposing fines on those who failed to report for compulsory public work, leaving as the sole penalty the 'limitation of personal freedom' for up to two years under Art. 21.2.

Almost immediately, within the last quarter of 1983, compulsory public work was introduced in all but two voivodships. In 28 voivodships there was organized public labour, involving some 3,229 people (11 per cent of those on the records).[39] In most cases the work involved keeping the parks tidy. Many of those assigned to this work failed to show up after the first two or three days and did what they liked for the next three months, unmolested because the law provided a three-month period for 'seeking a new job'. Managements were reluctant to take on such 'blue birds', as they are known, but if they notified vacancies to the department of employment they were under an obligation to do so.[40] This resulted in the ironic situation that when two candidates applied for a vacancy – a regular job-seeker and a registered work shirker – the latter would be given priority, and the management could not refuse to hire him.

In spite of all this, the law was officially acknowledged to be a failure. Even the official party daily observed that, despite the bureaucratic effort put into it, the law in its present form 'failed to promote concerted action by the prosecutor's offices, state administration and social organizations'. It urged different legislation to force people to take jobs.[41]

In early 1986 a legislative bill was proposed and discussed to amend and broaden the Law on Work Shirkers of 26 October 1982. The present law, it was claimed, had failed effectively to curb 'parasitism' and a new act was needed. These moves reflect a style of thinking that was aptly characterized by the late Sejm deputy Karol Małcużyński: 'Passage of laws which only create a semblance of solving an urgent social problem, without reaching to its roots and without seeking proper, non-punitive remedies is, in my opinion, politically harmful and socially demagogic.[42]

6. Special procedures

The Decree on Special Procedures was issued on 12 December 1981 simultaneously with the Martial Law Decree which it was intended to supplement. The Martial Law Decree broadened the scope and severity of penalties and introduced new offences. To enable the courts and the prosecution to cope with the new tasks the Special Procedure Decree reintroduced the summary procedure, and extended the use of, and the maximal penalties under, accelerated and simplified procedures. The prime aim of the Decree on Special Procedures was to enable the courts to pass often very severe sentences as quickly as possible.

Summary procedure

Summary procedure was reintroduced for political not legal considerations. Summary justice is, by its very nature, detrimental to the proper course of justice. Sentences can only be passed speedily at the expense of some of the procedural rights of the defendant. It was applied on a large scale in post-war Poland during the first years of the Communist take-over, on the basis of the decree of 15 November 1946. The procedure persisted until 1970 when the Penal Code of 1969 came into force. For the next 12 years the procedure was kept in cold storage, to be resurrected under martial law for use by ordinary and military courts.

The basic elements of summary procedure in the period of martial law were as follows:

(i) The penalties passed by the court were much more severe than under ordinary procedure. The minimum term of imprisonment was three years. The death penalty could be passed when the minimum penalty under ordinary procedure was eight years' imprisonment (provided all three judges hearing the case were unanimous). A total of 28 various offences described in the Penal Code were liable for the death penalty if tried under summary procedure. The court was obliged automatically to impose the additional penalty of loss of public rights. The court was not empowered conditionally to suspend the penalty of imprisonment. All this meant that the court was much more restricted in its freedom of judgement than under ordinary procedure.

(ii) Some of the procedural rights enjoyed by the defendant under ordinary procedure were eliminated or drastically restricted under summary procedure. The defendant had less time to acquaint himself with the files in the case and prepare his defence. Moreover, the sentence was valid from the moment it was announced and was not subject to appeal. This was contrary to Art. 14.3 (b) and 14.5 of the International Covenant on Civil and Political Rights. The latter stipulated that a person sentenced for an offence by a lower court had the right to appeal to a higher court so that it could reconsider the sentence passed by the lower court, with regard to both guilt and penalty, according to the obtaining legal provisions. The case could be re-examined by the Supreme Court only in exceptional circumstances and only at the request of the First Chairman of the Supreme Court, the Prosecutor General or the Minister of Justice. Such an extraordinary review could also result in an increase in the sentence.

(iii) Summary procedure increased the powers of the prosecutor's office. The prosecutor (or, in fact, the secret police) arbitrarily established 'the degree of social danger' of an offence. If it was found to be high then the case qualified for summary procedure. Such an imprecise term easily lent itself to abuse, and it often served as the sole reason for an unjust arrest or sentence Temporary arrest was routinely applied when a case was investigated under summary procedure. The prosecutor's decision to apply temporary arrest could be appealed by the suspect to court but only within 48 hours. Such an appeal was generally unsuccessful.

(iv) Deadlines under summary procedure were much shorter in comparison with ordinary procedure. The investigation was to be completed within 15 days (30 days in exceptional, complicated cases, subject to approval by the higher prosecutor's office). The defence lawyer had less time to acquaint himself with the files in the case. The court hearing had to be held within five days of the indictment having been filed with the court.

Of the 311 offences described in the Penal Code, 87 could be heard under this procedure, i.e. roughly one quarter of the total. These included offences against the basic political and economic interests of the PPR, offences against public order, common criminal offences, as well as major offences stipulated in the Martial Law Decree.

In its ruling of 22 January 1982 the Supreme Court stated that in cases of cumulative concurrence of legal provisions when one criminal act fulfilled the criteria of criminal liability for more than one offence, for instance, when an offender was liable for prosecution under both the Penal Code and the Martial Law Decree, and if the case could be heard under either ordinary or summary procedure, then summary procedure was to be applied.[43] This ruling was consistent with Art. 5 of the Decree on Special Procedures which read: 'under summary procedure, the provisions of the Penal Code apply only if the regulations of this decree do not state otherwise.' A Supreme Court ruling passed only a few weeks after martial law was declared clearly revealed the official preferences. From the outset, the authorities were determined not only to use extraordinary legislation on a wide scale but to give it preferential treatment over ordinary legislation. The reason was that ordinary legislation could no longer be relied on to achieve the political objectives the authorities had in mind.

Sentences passed under summary procedure were final (not subject to appeal). By the same token, any procedural decisions taken by the court in the course of proceedings could also not be appealed. This fact could actually be turned to the advantage of the defendant in cases where the court ruled that the trial should not be heard under summary procedure and referred the case for hearing under ordinary procedure.

One such case concerned Zenon Nowak and Tadeusz Pacuszka from the Institute of Nuclear Research (IBJ) in Warsaw. The voivodship court in Warsaw decided to hear this case under ordinary procedure and sentenced the defendants to two years' imprisonment. The prosecutor appealed to the Supreme Court demanding that the summary procedure be reinstated and the case heard anew. Defence lawyer Tadeusz de Virion argued that this was no longer possible since the decision to hear the case under ordinary procedure had been taken under summary procedure and, as such, could not be appealed.[44]

The decision to hear a case under ordinary rather than summary procedure required courage on the part of the judges. They had to cast doubt on the prosecutor's assessment of the 'degree of social danger'. Secondly, they had to state that the act imputed to the defendant did not present a significant threat to the order of martial law. Thirdly, a lenient sentence passed under ordinary procedure (i.e. less than three years' imprisonment) might please neither the defendant, who would like to see himself released, nor the prosecutor who had submitted the indictment under summary procedure in the first place. Both of them might lodge an appeal. Of course, not all the judges had such scruples, and some of the most severe sentences were passed under summary procedure.

The courts' heavy reliance on summary procedure was particularly evident in the first two months of martial law. Between 13 December 1981 and 9 January 1982 as many as 394 cases involving 618 people were apparently dealt with under summary procedure, i.e. some 30 cases daily.[45] The Ministry of Justice announced that between 13 December 1981 and the end of 1982 the voivodship courts sentenced 3,700 people under summary procedure. Most of these had been accused of common criminal offences.⁴⁶ According to the PPR's Prosecutor General, Franciszek Rusek, a total of 11,980 people were tried under summary procedure between 13 December and 22 October 1982. Of this total, 2,368 people were tried for political offences.⁴⁷

With regard to political cases summary procedure remained in force until 31 December 1982. The Act of 18 December 1982 limited its use to economic sabotage, arson, offences against the fundamental economic interests of the state, the gravest offences against life, limb and property, as well as some fiscal offences.

The lifting of summary procedure with regard to political offences did not, however, signify that the courts began to pass lighter sentences. In Małopolska region, for instance, nine people were sentenced to various spells of imprisonment in November-December 1982 (five of them had to serve their sentences in prison, four received suspended prison sentences). Between 1 January 1983 and 15 May 1983, 39 people received prison sentences (10 of them were actually sent to prison and 29 received suspended sentences).⁴⁸ Although the sentences passed in the months after the suspension of martial law were less severe than those passed in the early stages of martial law, they were still far from being lenient. The Supreme Court revoked those sentences it considered too lenient. Between 1 January 1983 and 15 May 1983, nine people whose sentences of imprisonment had been conditionally suspended had their suspension clauses revoked and were sent to prison.⁴⁹

Summary procedure before voivodship courts

Offences against public order were from the outset included among those considered most dangerous for the military and they were therefore punished more severely under summary procedure by voivodship courts. Despite the fact that the Martial Law Decree contained no mention of 'leading and organizing a street demonstration', and that it defined 'participating in a demonstration or protest action' (Art. 50) as a petty offence, in practice some demonstrations were dealt with as 'a continuation of trade union activity' under Art. 46.2. This practice was first applied to punish severely 'the organizers and instigators' of street demonstrations in Gdańsk on 30 January 1982.

Certain offences under the Penal Code were investigated under summary procedure by the voivodship prosecutor's office. These usually included: creating a dangerous situation directly threatening life, limb or property (Art. 137), fighting the police with stones or petrol bombs, taking part in a public gathering whose participants jointly committed a violent assault resulting in fatalities, serious bodily injury or considerable loss of property (Art. 275.2), publicly inciting others to break the law (Art. 282), and physical assault on a policeman or other person enforcing law and order (Art. 234.1).

Under summary procedure the defendant could also be charged with offences against the Martial Law Decree in association with criminal offences under the Penal Code. For instance, on 27 September 1982 the Voivodship Court in Katowice sentenced Zbigniew Kieszkowski and Zbigniew Downarowicz to three and a half years in prison each. Both men were accused of leading a protest action in Gliwice on 31 August 1982 by 'inciting other demonstrators to organize protests, chanting hostile slogans and subsequently pointing the direction of the march to demonstrators', as well as 'physically assaulting policemen by throwing stones and instigating others to act likewise'.[50] The offence of 'leading a protest action' was here classified under Art. 46.2 of the Martial Law Decree as 'continuation of trade union activity' in association with Art. 234.1 of the Penal Code — 'physical assault on a policeman in the course of his duties'.

Under summary procedure the voivodship courts tried those participants of independent pro-Solidarity demonstrations whom the prosecution and official propaganda attempted to present as instigators, ring-leaders or organizers. The line drawn between those who were considered 'instigators' and those who only participated passively was drawn thinly and could be redrawn at any time to suit the current version of events.

Apart from blurring the distinction between the offence of participating in a street demonstration and organizing such a demonstration, the prosecution made the offence of chanting anti-regime slogans equal to inciting others to break the law. Instigating could in turn be dealt with as organizing or leading a demonstration.

Among those accused of instigating riots were chance passers-by; the defendants were found guilty on the basis of false or incomplete police testimonies. Incriminating circumstances often sufficed as evidence. The defendant stood a better chance of a lenient sentence if his case was transferred from summary to ordinary procedure. But then the Supreme Court in appeal proceedings sometimes increased the sentence. One such case involved Włodzimierz Paczyński, who was sentenced by the voivodship court in Częstochowa to a two years' suspended prison term for his part in a demonstration on 31 August 1982. The Supreme Court found that the very fact that the defendant took his juvenile son along with him was an incriminating circumstance and revoked the suspension clause.[51]

Accelerated procedure

The Special Procedures Decree also sanctioned and expanded the application of accelerated procedure. This was originally introduced into the Polish legal system on the basis of the law of 22 May 1958 as a means of fighting hooliganism. The idea was that a hooligan caught on the spot or shortly after he committed an offence would be put before a court and punished immediately. The hearing was to take place within 48 hours after an offender had been apprehended and required one judge only. As a rule it took only a few minutes. The police officer who had detained the defendant would make a short oral or written statement informing the court about the offence. No pre-trial investigation was required. Nor was there any need for an indictment. It was only before the court that the defendant learned what he was charged with. A hearing under accelerated procedure commenced immediately after a police officer informed the court about the offence. It was not possible to adjourn the hearing. Only one interval in the proceedings was admissible, provided it did not exceed seven days and the court ordered the defendant to be placed under arrest. Following the sentence, the defendant had only three days to lodge an appeal.

Accelerated procedure at the expense of the defendant's rights favoured the police, who were not required to acquaint him with the 'evidence' they were going to bring before the court. Nor were the police obliged to specify which particular article of the Penal Code had been breached by the defendant's behaviour. The police were, moreover, under no obligation to substantiate the statement which informed the court about an offence.

The privileged position of the police with regard to both the defendant and the court made it difficult for the former to exercise his right to a defence. The defendant usually had to rely on the services of the defence lawyer who happened to be on duty in the regional court at the time his case was brought before the court.

Ever since it was introduced in 1958 accelerated procedure

has been steadily expanded, both in the scope of offences which could be heard under it and with regard to the severity of penalties. Table 1 illustrates this tendency.

Table 1

Date	Number of offences	Maximum penalties	Territorial application
The law of 22 May 1958	11 (hooligan in nature)	6 months' imprisonment	Warsaw, Wrocław plus seven towns in the Warsaw voivodship
The Penal Code of 1969	9 (hooligan in nature)	One year's imprisonment plus up to 25,000 zloty fine	Since 1973 — 43 towns, including all voivodship capitals. Since 1975 — 40 towns
The law on speculation of 25 September 1981	All offences stipulated in this law plus offences under Art. 221–225 of the Penal Code	Two years' imprisonment plus up to 100,000 zloty fine	Throughout the country
Decree on Special Procedures of 12 December 1981	Further 12 offences stipulated in the Penal Code as well as 29 offences stipulated in other laws, not necessarily hooligan in nature. In total 76 offences	Up to two years' imprisonment plus up to 100,000 zloty fine	Throughout the country
The law on State of Emergency of 5 December 1983	39 offences not necessarily hooligan in nature	Two years' imprisonment plus up to 50,000 zloty fine	Throughout the country
The law of 10 May 1985 on Special Criminal Liability (to remain in force till 30 June 1988)	56 offences not necessarily hooligan in nature	Up to three years' imprisonment plus up to 500,000 zloty fine	Throughout the country

The Rigours of Martial Law

From Table 1 we can see that accelerated procedure gradually gained in importance. It is now applied throughout the country to offences not only of a hooligan nature, as originally envisaged, but also to some political ones, as well as to complex criminal cases.

Accelerated procedure which calls for greatly simplified judicial action is applied both before regional courts and petty offences tribunals. Whether a case under accelerated procedure went to a regional court or to a petty offences tribunal was determined by the way in which the charges were formulated by the police. Accelerated justice before petty offences tribunals is discussed elsewhere in this book (Chapter VI/4)

Simplified procedure

Art. 419.1 of the Code of Criminal Procedure stipulated that some offences liable for up to two years' imprisonment, fines or 'limitation of personal freedom' could be heard under simplified procedure by a regional court. Suspects under temporary arrest could not be tried under it. The Decree on Special Procedures stipulated that offences punishable by up to three year's imprisonment and fines could also be heard under simplified procedure.

The main characteristics of this procedure are:
(i) the prosecutor does not issue a decision to present charges (this requirement is satisfied by interrogation of a suspect), open an investigation or terminate it;
(ii) the act of indictment needs no substantiation;
(iii) the defendant is served with a copy of the act of indictment, together with an order to appear in court on a specific date. He may put forward his own evidence within seven days of the act of indictment being served;
(iv) the case can be heard by a single judge who can pass sentence in absentia.[52]

Some 30 per cent of all cases instituted in Poland ex officio by the prosecutor are heard under simplified procedure. In order for a case to be heard under this type of procedure it must be considered 'simple'. The Code of Criminal Procedure does not, however, define what constitutes 'simplicity' as a legal characteristic of admissibility of this procedure. Neither does it stipulate when a simple procedure becomes a complicated one. These loopholes in the law can result in a broader application of this procedure.⁵³ Indeed, the Law on the State of Emergency of 5 December 1983 envisages widespread use of the simplified procedure with some of the offences being punishable by up to five years' imprisonment.

Command procedure

The Law on Special Criminal Liability of 10 May 1985 reanimated a form of simplified procedure, the so-called 'command procedure', which had been in abeyance since 1969. The procedure is applied by the regional court cases when, on the basis of available evidence, the circumstances of an offence have been so thoroughly explained that there is no doubt that the act committed by the defendant is an offence and that he is the offender. Under command procedure a single judge is empowered to rule without holding a court hearing and without seeing the defendant. He can pass a penalty (known as a 'command' and not as a sentence) of up to two years' 'limitation of personal freedom' or a fine of between 20,000 and 50,000 zloty. The penalty of 'limitation of personal freedom' usually involves a duty to undertake work as instructed by the court (it can be unpaid or, if paid, a part of the earnings may be deducted), a ban on changing one's place of residence and a ban on occupying certain posts. Those punished by 'limitation of personal freedom' may not be promoted at their workplace and cannot terminate employment without the court's approval. Those who attempt to dodge serving the penalty can be sentenced in lieu to a fine or – where they are unable to pay it – to a substitute penalty of imprisonment.

Both the defendant and the prosecution can, within seven days after a 'command' has been issued, lodge a protest which results in the case being transferred from 'command' to simplified procedure.

* * *

In the opinion of the Helsinki Committee in Poland, by the end of 1982 the authorities had come to the conclusion that summary procedure was, in fact, inconvenient, too drastic and impractical. The sentences passed under it seemed either too high (ten years, as in the case of Ewa Kubasiewicz) or too low (three years' imprisonment). The procedure was too long in the case of participants in street demonstrations, while it was too short in cases which required careful planning in view of the publicity and protests they might attract.[54] The public rightly considered summary procedure to be unjust and repressive. Not all the judges were convinced that the basic interests of the state needed increased protection and even those who were did not necessarily believe that this protection was to be achieved through summary procedure at the expense of the rights of the defendant. Summary procedure was for some associated with the Stalinist past and the association was not to the authorities' liking.

Accelerated procedure was clearly more advantageous to the authorities as a means of effective and at the same time inconspicuous repression. It passed the test as a convenient device in clearing the streets following anti-government demonstrations. With regard to these demonstrations the procedure gave the police a free hand, for it enabled them to decide whether a case should be brought before a regional court in order to punish an offender more severely or before a petty offences tribunal. While giving the police considerable flexibility, the procedure restricted the judges' freedoms, especially after the Law on Special Criminal Liability of 10 May 1985 which, under the guise of 'strenghtening the protection of the economy, ensuring citizens' well-being and improving the observance of law and order', introduced new emergency measures. These concerned, for instance, tightening of the criteria for extraordinary commutation or suspension of a sentence. Since for quite some time before the Law on Special Criminal Liability was passed, the authorities had been telling everyone (including the judges) that the situation in the country had stabilized, the general increase in the severity of criminal law was greeted with surprise and anxiety. The tendency towards making the laws more stringent continued in the post-martial law period. This was reflected in the widespread application of special procedures.

7. The use of force

Throughout martial law the authorities used force to subdue all forms of protest and to instil fear and the feeling of powerlessness. Force was used to pacify the striking enterprises, to break up peaceful pro-Solidarity demonstrations, to extract confessions from those detained, to pacify the prisoners, to frighten and to

The Rigours of Martial Law

persuade the people that resistance made no sense. Specialized forms of coercion, such as beating, abduction and even death at the hands of unknown perpetrators, were developed and perfected. Force was used indiscriminately and at random.

Beatings administered in order to elicit statements or admissions of guilt and as a method of extracting confessions were not limited to political cases. They were used to improve statistics on unsolved criminal offences and, as such, were the most widespread form of violence in police stations. 'Beatings at police stations were normal practice', declared a policeman in an interview for an underground publication, and added: 'Sure, our superiors officially forbade it, but in practice we administered beatings with their consent.'[55]

In some cases no motive whatsoever could be established for beatings. Severely beaten people were sometimes sent to sobering-up centres for alcoholics and intimidated into keeping quiet about police violence. Few people – victims of arbitrary use of force by police – seek redress for their injuries. They have little faith in winning a case against the police. Experience tells them that in a system which does not operate by the rule of law, incriminating one policeman amounts to challenging the whole system which makes the use of force not only the ultimate but its normal weapon. The higher police echelons (voivodship police HQ) are engaged in the cover-up of arbitrary and excessive use of force by the lower echelons (town and district police stations).

The right to life

The International Covenant on Civil and Political Rights stipulates that the right to life (Art. 6), as the most basic right, cannot be abolished or limited even in an extraordinary national situation, such as a state of emergency (Art. 4.1 and 2). Art. 23 of Chapter 3 of the Martial Law Decree 'Principles of Procedure in Extraordinary Circumstances Connected with the Defence and Security of the State' failed adequately to specify what was meant by 'extraordinary circumstances'. Art. 26.1 allowed the use of firearms: 'In extraordinary circumstances use may be made of direct coercion, including chemical incapacitating agents and water cannon, and in exceptional cases in which a danger, threat, or physical attack cannot otherwise be avoided, firearms may also be used.' Thus 'extraordinary circumstances' involve not only a real danger but also a threat, and not only to public, but also to 'individual or personal property on a large scale' and 'to installations which are important to the defence or security of the state'.

Numerous cases of death can be directly attributed to the imposition of martial law or its maintenance. The list of martial law fatalities includes workers shot during strike actions, people shot in peaceful demonstrations, victims of police patrols and interrogation methods, people who died in suspicious or mysterious circumstances. In some cases suicide followed police harassment or intimidation by 'unknown perpetrators'. A politically motivated murder showing traces of police involvement is sometimes disguised as a suicide. Death as a result of physical mistreatment by the police can be made to appear as though it was caused by an excessive consumption of alcohol. Death certificates are sometimes falsified as some doctors are put under pressure to state false causes of death.[56] In some cases death takes place several months after mistreatment or a beating. The families of those beaten to death are often too frightened of possible police vengeance to lodge a complaint and to reveal what they know.

It is impossible to establish a complete list of martial law victims. The characteristic feature is that a great majority of the several dozen victims were active in Solidarity or other independent organizations or were people known for their independent-minded attitudes.

The official unwillingness to investigate these cases gives rise to the suspicion that the violent intimidation of society, if not directly approved, was at least reckoned with or connived at by the authorities at the highest level.

Notes

1. This particular provision of the Martial Law Decree was the only one changed by the Sejm in its Law of 25 January 1982 'Special Regulations for the Period of Martial Law'. The right of appeal against administrative decisions was restored.
2. The use of firearms was also stipulated under Art. 28.2 of the Martial Law Decree which said: 'The minister of Internal Affairs may direct that members of the Citizens' Militia Voluntary Reserve and of other formations and organizations assigned to the protection of public order or public property shall be provided with equipment for direct coercion and, in especially justified cases, also with firearms'. In fact some of the party apparatchiks had already been issued with

firearms before martial law was declared. This was admitted by the party chief in Poznań voivodship, Edward Skrzypczak, in his interview for the underground press summarized in the *International Herald Tribune,* 4 November 1983.

3. As the most frequently quoted 'proof' of these accusations was a resolution passed by Solidarity's National Commission during its meeting in Gdańsk on 11-12 December 1981 which called for a national referendum on four issues: whether the Poles were in favour of a vote of confidence in General Jaruzelski; establishing a temporary government; free elections with military guarantees to the Soviet Union; and whether the PUWP could be the instrument of such guarantees in the name of the entire population.
4. Maria Regent-Lechowicz, *Rzeczpospolita,* 5 March 1982.
5. Ibid.
6. *Trybuna Ludu,* 26 January 1982.
7. Sylwester Zawadzki during a press conference in the Ministry of Justice Press Centre on 8 March 1982, *Głos Wielkopolski,* 9 March 1982.
8. The letter admitted derogations from obligations stipulated under Articles 9, 12.1 and 2, 14.5, 19.2, 21 and 22 of the Covenant. In fact, the martial law authorities also violated the rights guaranteed under Articles 7, 10, 14.1 and 3, 19.1, 20 and 26 as well as inalienable rights guaranteed under Articles 6, 15 and 18.
9. *Żołnierz Wolności,* 12 March 1982. This figure, quoted by the Minister of Internal Affairs General Czesław Kiszczak, included 3,024 people who had already been released from internment camps by that time and 3,601 who were still being held.
10. *Rzeczpospolita,* 10 December 1982.
11. *Veto* no. 5/1982.
12. *Washington Post,* 24 April 1982 and *Z Dnia na Dzień* no.56.
13. *Solidarność Narodu* no. 5 reprinted in *Kontakt* no 5/6, 1982.
14. Unpublished, prepared in October 1982.
15. *Biuletyn Łódzki* no. 26, 2 November 1983 (extracts).
16. Cf. Helsinki Committee in Poland, Report no. 1 'Human and Civil Rights in Poland in the Period of Martial Law', February 1983.
17. Unpublished, quoted in the ILO Governing Body's Report, 227th Session, Geneva, June 1984. Third item on the agenda.
18. *Serwis Informacyjny RKW NSZZ Solidarność Region Małopolska* no. 42, 13 January 1983; AP New York, 11 March 1983 and the unpublished testimony of Jerzy Las.
19. *Robotnik Lęborka,* 17 December 1982.
20. AP New York, 11 March 1983, quoting Polish refugee Mirosław Domińczyk.
21. AFP Warsaw, 21 December 1982.
22. Dan Fisher in the *Los Angeles Times* of 20 December 1982 quoting a plant manager who said he saw the instruction.
23. *Praworządność* no. 6/7, 10 February 1985 quoting a Polish scholar on criminal law, Dr Lech Falandysz.
24. Cf. *Zeszyty Historyczne* no. 49/1979 and no. 66/1983, Instytut Literacki, Paris.

25. *Żołnierz Wolności*, 12 March 1982.
26. These involved: offences against the PPR's fundamental interests, against public security, illegal possession of arms, manslaughter and murder, armed robbery, as well as offences stipulated in the part of the Penal Code pertaining to members of the armed forces, should they be committed by civilians serving their duty in militarized enterprises or in civil defence units.
27. Cf. Maria Hirszowicz, *The Bureaucratic Leviathan: A study in the Sociology of Communism*. (Martin Robertson, Oxford, 1980).
28. *Żołnierz Wolności*, 11 June 1982.
29. Order no. 51, paragraph 5, of 13 December 1981 signed by the Chairman of the Council of Ministers.
30. *Żołnierz Wolności*, 2 April 1982.
31. *KOS* no. 54, 7 May 1984.
32. *Trybuna Ludu*, 12 May 1982 and *Polityka*, 23 April 1983.
33. *Polityka*, ibid.
34. Ibid. quoting official sources in the Ministry of Labour, Wages and Social Welfare.
35. This decision was subject to appeal to the Supreme Administrative Court. The initial lists were exempted from judicial control of any kind.
36. Radio Warsaw, 27 February 1983, 1805 hours.
37. *Rzeczpospolita*, 14–15 July 1984.
38. Paragraph 5.1 of the Minister of Labour, Wages and Social Welfare order of 30 December 1982 'On Rules and Procedure for Making Entries to the Register of Notorious Work Shirkers' stipulated, for instance, that under certain conditions information contained in the register could be passed on to other state authorities.
39. *Trybuna Ludu*, 26 January 1984.
40. Under Council of Ministers' Order of 6 August 1983.
41. *Trybuna Ludu*, 13 December 1984. The paper noted that in 1983 some 58,200 males between the ages of 18–45 were out of work. This figure corresponded almost exactly to the 57,552 on the files as work shirkers before the introduction of martial law. It was, then, a 'back to square one' situation.
42. *Tygodnik Powszechny*, 7 November 1982.
43. *Państwo i Prawo*, January/February 1982.
44. In spite of its ruling of 12 January 1982 the Supreme Court stated that neither the sentence nor decisions taken by the court in the course of the proceedings could be appealed. See *Prawo i Życie*, 17 July 1982.
45. Radio Warsaw, 12 January 1982, 1300 hours.
46. Radio Warsaw, 21 March 1983, 1700 hours.
47. *Trybuna Ludu*, 27 October 1982.
48. Magdalena Nowakowa, Tadeusz Kowalski and Wacław Majewski, 'Five months of suspended martial law in the Małopolska Region' Kraków, May 1983.
49. Ibid.
50. *Trybuna Robotnicza*, 28 September 1982.
51. *Tygodnik Mazowsze* no. 43, 3 March 1983.

52. If it can be established that the defendant has been notified about the date of the hearing and neither he nor his defence lawyer has appeared.
53. Mikołaj Leonieni, *Palestra*, December 1983.
54. The Helsinki Committee in Poland: 'Memorandum to the Human Rights Commission in the UNO', March 1984.
55. *Veto* no. 8, reprinted in English in *Voice of Solidarność* no. 58, 1 April 1983.
56. For instance, Władysław Lisowski aged 67, beaten in Kraków's Main Square on 13 May 1982. He died two months later. His death caused by a burst liver was described by a doctor as being the result of cancer. *Kronika Małopolska* no. 13, 30 July 1982.

II

THE TRIALS OF DECEMBER 1981 STRIKERS

The Pacification of Striking Enterprises

Although in December 1981 Solidarity did not rule out the possibility of confrontation with the authorities, it did not perceive such a confrontation as being imminent. It expected to be given some notice in the form of legislative measures which would grant new powers to the government. Since the authorities appeared to be having difficulty not only in passing these measures but also in activating those repressive provisions which were already in existence, and believing, in any case, that these provisions were inadequate to suppress Solidarity, the union activists were convinced that the authorities' ability to use extra-legal repression as such was limited. The authorities, however, discarded the existing system of legal repression as no longer affording the social control necessary to ensure their monopoly of power, and replaced it by an entirely new system embodied in the Martial Law Decree. Not only did Solidarity not perceive confrontation with the authorities as imminent, it tended also to disregard the real dangers involved. The union activists mistakenly equated their success in using the essentially negative weapon of strike action with real influence over political developments.

On 2 December 1981, for the first time since the Gdańsk Agreement was signed, the authorities used force against a peaceful sit-in strike at the Firemen's Academy in Warsaw, thereby breaking with the established pattern of settling disputes with Solidarity. This pattern usually started with a working collective or other social group expressing its grievances and seeking satisfaction through strike action. The strikers would present a list of demands. An agreement with the authorities would be signed or negotiations resumed. Sooner or later the agreement would be broken or negotiations result in failure, thus leading to a new strike. After the successful pacification of the strike at the Firemen's Academy, Jaruzelski was able to break with this pattern and use force on a nationwide scale. He was the first Polish Communist leader politically to have survived such a bloody pacification.

Solidarity activists, who had not perceived the union as posing a grave threat to the authorities, were surprised by the sudden show of force, the internment of their colleagues and the incomprehensible regulations. The severance of telephone and telex connections only aggravated the general confusion and lack of understanding about the situation. Local union activists, unable to seek advice from their regional officials, most of whom had been interned, turned to the union statutes which stipulated that, in the case of direct threat to the union, the Factory Committees should transform themselves into Strike Committees. The task of defending the union against martial law thus fell on the shoulders of the chairmen and members of Solidarity enterprise commissions, on those who were most closely involved in the affairs of the workforce. Their primary obligation, as the workers' democratically elected representatives, was to be with the union rank-and-file. The role of Solidarity shop-floor activists in December 1981 was pre-determined by their former record of trade union activity and the functions they had performed before martial law. If they had not supported their colleagues who wanted to protest against martial law, they would have betrayed the mandate entrusted to them and lost their status within a closely-knit working collective.

In fact, many of the strikes against the imposition of martial law began spontaneously and almost immediately after martial law was proclaimed, and the supposed strike leaders were carried along irresistibly. This is well illustrated by the dilemma which faced Ryszard Kowalski, the Chairman of the Factory Committee of Solidarity in workshop no.4 in the Steelworks Repair Enterprise in Katowice. Kowalski was brought to trial on charges of organizing and leading a strike in his workshop on 14 December 1981. The court called two specialists in psychiatry as expert witnesses in order to determine whether he had been fully aware of what he was doing on that day. In their medical report, the two psychiatrists described the sequence of events.[1] Kowalski had learned of martial law on 13 December 1981 from a radio communiqué. The following day, at 6.20, he reported to work. A crowd of workers met him in the corridor of the factory. They said that they could not start work because there was a strike in the steelworks. He explained to them that he did not know what to do because he had not been prepared for martial law. He went to the director's office in the hope that they might issue a joint statement and that some kind of deal could be put to the workforce. The director was unable, however, to make any offers since he did not have a text of the Martial Law Decree. The party secretary Kościelniak was also unable to take any decisions. Both he and the director expected Kowalski to exert a calming influence on the workforce and persuade them to resume work. Kowalski decided, in line with the available information, that he would turn over the union funds and documents to the management and suggested that the local deputies to the Sejm—which he knew was not suspended—be invited to help clarify the situation. He began to transfer the Factory Committee documents to the management. The workers then demanded that the union banner be protected from the ZOMO. He agreed to this and took the banner out of its show-case. In a spontaneous movement, 400 people gathered around the banner and it was carried to the Katowice Steelworks. As they approached the steelworks, the workers sang the hymn 'God Save Poland' and were greeted by representatives of the Strike Committee. It was decided that Kowalski and four other representatives of the Steelworks Repair Enterprise would join the Strike Committee while the rest would disperse and go home. Whoever wished to return to work on the following day would be free to do so.

Kowalski, who was released on 24 January 1983 on the strength of the medical experts' report pending the court's decision on whether to continue the trial, disappeared in unexplained circumstances on 7 February 1983. His body was found in a river on 31 March 1983.

Where the strikes took a more organized form, the leaders understood their task as ensuring that the strike took an orderly and peaceful course. They took steps to protect state property and vital machinery, as well as to prevent sabotage, provocation and damage. They attempted to mediate between the workforce and the management. It was an impossible task. The military commissars assigned to the major enterprises would listen to them but their orders did not include reaching a settlement with the strikers unless it concerned evacuation of the plant. The management staff were for the most part also confused as to what was happening and demanded an unconditional return to work. The majority of the strikers, particularly at the very beginning of martial law, believed that a nationwide workers' response would force the authorities to retreat.

The task of the strike committees was to channel the strikers' emotions into some organized form. They attempted to calm tempers, divide duties, protect property, issue communiqués and passes, establish links with other striking enterprises, put forward their demands and find some common ground with the management or the military who wielded the real power. The key position of the military was underlined by the fact that the management of some enterprises were at a loss as to what to do. At the Promor enterprise in Gdańsk, for instance, both the enterprise director and the party secretary came out in support of the strike. This took a dramatic form when the Chairman of the Solidarity Enterprise Commission, Kazimierz Masiak, asked the managing director Maciej Kucharski, during a meeting with the workforce on 14 December 1981, whether he was with the workforce or against it. The director said that he was with the workforce and resigned his duties. The local party secretary Leszek Jabłoński also declared that his loyalty as a man and a colleague was with the workforce.

The atmosphere of the strikes was tense. In some cases, as in the Katowice Steelworks, the workers warned that they would not hesitate to blow themselves up if the police intervened. In the Ziemowit coalmine dynamite was placed in the underground passages and a high pressure water pump was placed opposite the lift. In some places there was a war of nerves between the strikers who had locked themselves in their enterprises and the riot police surrounding them. The police and the military commanders would try to sap the workers' will to strike by trying to convince them that they had been led astray by extremists within Solidarity, threatening them with severe penalties and repeatedly appealing to them over the internal radio network to surrender. At the Piast coalmine and at the Katowice Steelworks the management or military commissar managed to persuade the wives of some of the strikers to speak to their husbands on the telephone and beg them to discontinue their protest. The conversations between the striking Piast miners and their wives were recorded by the authorities and later broadcast over the national radio network.

Those who participated in the strike action of December 1981

The Trials of December 1981 Strikers

had originally been motivated by their desire to defend their union, Solidarity. As the authorities successfully subdued one striking enterprise after the other, however, the number of those still willing to strike dwindled. Those who remained no longer hoped to bring the authorities to their knees but merely to defend their own dignity. Reason dictated tactics of passive resistance.

The pacification of the striking enterprises was preceded by a concentration of force, street blockades and isolation of the enterprise. In some cases an ultimatum to surrender was presented before the security forces attacked. The ZOMO riot police spearheaded the actual attack and take-over of an enterprise with the military providing the back-up. A tank would mow down the factory gate or wall and the riot police would enter, sometimes under a smokescreen of tear gas. They would then proceed to round up the strikers, pushing them and even beating them with truncheons. In some cases the ZOMO were so violent that they destroyed some of the machinery or equipment in the process. The strikers would be herded together in one place; sometimes they were searched. Some of them had their passes or identity documents confiscated. The members of the strike committee would be identified and separated from the others. In some of the factories, the strikers realized the futility of further resistance and voluntarily discontinued their strike demanding, in exchange, a guarantee of safe conduct and immunity from persecution from the military.

The tragic pacification of the Wujek coalmine, where nine miners were shot dead on 17 December 1981, affected the morale of the strikers throughout the country. With the collapse of the longest strike of martial law, that of the miners in the Piast coalmine, on 28 December 1981, the wave of strikes in protest against the imposition of martial law was finally over.

Retroactive legal measures

The Martial Law Decree was a retroactive legal measure. It changed the existing legal order of the PPR overnight, in so far as it proscribed not only strikes but also trade union activity as such, which was not only legal prior to the introduction of martial law but was actually afforded special protection.

Art. 61 of the Martial Law Decree stated: 'The decree shall

enter into force on the day of its promulgation and take effect on the day of its adoption.' Since the decree was adopted on 12 December but not promulgated in the official publication *Journal of Laws* until 14 December, a major legal dispute developed over whether strike action on 13 December was legal or not. Art. 3.2. of the 1950 Law on the *Journal of Laws* states that laws in the PPR are legally promulgated on the day of their publication in the official *Journal of Laws*. Radio and television are not official organs of promulgation. The question raised in legal circles was, therefore, whether the new regulations could be considered binding as of their announcement on radio and television rather than from the day of their publication. Could the strikers who were not aware of the ban on trade union activity and strikes claim immunity from prosecution on the grounds that they had not been aware of having broken the law?

Before the introduction of martial law the formula used in Art. 61 of the Martial Law Decree had never been used in PPR criminal law. It conflicted with Art. 1 of the Penal Code which stated: 'Only he who commits a socially dangerous act, proscribed under threat of punishment by the law remaining in force at the time such an act is committed, shall be criminally liable.' Since Art. 1 of the Penal Code had not been abrogated by the Martial Law Decree it was fully valid.

In 1977 the PPR authorities, in ratifying the International Covenant on Civil and Political Rights, had pledged to observe the principle *lex retro non agit* expressed in Art. 15.1. Art. 4.2 of the Covenant included this principle among the inalienable human rights. According to Art. 15.1:

> No one shall be held guilty of any criminal offence on account of any act or omission which did not constitute a criminal offence, under national or international law, at the time when it was committed. Nor shall a heavier penalty be imposed than the one that was applicable at the time when the criminal offence was committed...

The principle *lex retro non agit* was also recognized in PPR legal theory. Sylwester Zawadzki, one of the regime's leading legal theorists and subsequent Minister of Justice (in which capacity he also witnessed the imposition of martial law) stated, in a textbook that appeared before his government appointment, 'in extraordinary circumstances it is admissible to pass a law valid retroactively, but not if this law introduces penal sanctions and only exceptionally if it imposes new duties on citizens.'[2]

The *Journal of Laws* no. 29, which contained the valid text of the Martial Law Decree and other extraordinary legal provisions, was, moreover, not so much promulgated on 14 December 1981, as printed with this date. In fact, it was not available for the general public until 18 December and even then some defence lawyers found it difficult to obtain a copy.

From 6.00 to 16.00 hours on 13 December 1981 the people could learn of the introduction of martial law only from radio communiqués. Around 16.00 hours the full text of the Martial Law Decree was read for the first time on television. By that time some of the strikes had already begun. The cases of those Solidarity activists who were subsequently brought to trial for organizing strike action on that day rested on the question of validity of the decree. The prosecution argued that the accused had been or, at least, should have been aware of the fact that they would be criminally liable for their actions since Art. 42.2 of the Penal Code stipulated that non-awareness did not protect an offender from liability if it arose through a misconception on the part of the offender which could have been avoided. The defence, on the other hand, denied this by arguing that, for a long time before the imposition of martial law, it had been public knowledge that Solidarity would strike in the face of a direct threat to its existence, whereas the Martial Law Decree had come as a surprise and the defendants could not have been expected to comprehend all the implications of martial law within a few hours. The defence lawyers emphasized that the promulgation of a law in the *Journal of Laws* was of crucial importance in determining offenders' awareness of the criminal nature of their activity. The distinguished defence lawyers, Tadeusz de Virion and Janusz Kochanowski, argued that Art. 24.2 of the Penal Code could not apply since non-awareness of the illegal character of the defendants' action was not the result of any misconception but of the fact that their action was not yet illegal since the decree had not at that time been formally promulgated.[3] Consequently, nobody could be sentenced under the Martial Law Decree for acts committed on the day of 13 December 1981.

The state of awareness of the average citizen was typified by a witness at the trial of the Polcolor Enterprise strikers. When asked by the prosecutor whether on 13 December 1981 he had heard a radio broadcast on the legal regulations for the period of martial law, he replied: 'Sure, I heard, but nobody really believes what is said on the radio and television. Besides, it was all so muddled.'[4]

The Supreme Court which was asked to rule on awareness of criminal liability went against existing theory and practice and, contrary to Art. 1 of the Penal Code and Art. 3.2 of the Law on the *Journal of Laws,* stated that learning of restrictions on civil rights and public activity through the media was sufficient to determine awareness of criminal liability. In its ruling of 1 March 1982 the Supreme Court stated: 'non-awareness of the illegal character of an act cannot be considered if the various restrictions, bans and duties have been publicly announced, before their promulgation in the *Journal of Laws,* in the media through which the offender learned or could have learned of them.'[5] By issuing such a ruling the Supreme Court overstepped its prerogatives of interpreting legal provisions, and actually took it upon itself to amend the existing norms. Such a usurpation of the Sejm's prerogative was, needless to say, unprecedented even in the PPR. The Supreme Court did not, moreover, address the crux of the matter: the subjective, human factor determining the individual's awareness or non-awareness of criminal liability.

The Supreme Court refused to occupy itself further with the issue and turned down a request from the Łódź Barristers' Chamber for a detailed interpretation of Art. 61 of the Martial Law Decree. The First Chairman of the Supreme Court evaded the issue by stating in his letter of 28 October 1983 that martial law had now been lifted and it was not possible for the Supreme Court to interpret legal provisions that were no longer in force. In line with other apologists of official justice, the First Chairman of the Supreme Court stated that any discussion of the legal aspects of the introduction of martial law was no longer relevant since the Sejm had approved ex post all the provisions of the Martial Law Decree in its law of 25 January 1982.[6]

Even if one were to accept the ruling of the Supreme Court, the sentence passed on Andrzej Słowik and Jerzy Kropiwnicki, the Chairman and Vice-Chairman of the Łódź Regional Board of Solidarity, was a blatant breach of justice. They were both charged under Art. 46.1 and 2 of the Martial Law Decree with continuing trade union activity by organizing a protest action outside the regional union headquarters and calling for a general strike in radio broadcasts and leaflets. The protest action took place on 13 December 1981 between 7 a.m. and 2 p.m. Since the

The Trials of December 1981 Strikers

Martial Law Decree was broadcast in full for the first time at 4 p.m., neither of them could possibly have known its content or been aware of the criminal nature of their action. This action, which was formally within the law at the time it took place, was declared to be illegal one day later, *ex post facto*. Both Słowik and Kropiwnicki were sentenced in breach of the above quoted Art. 1 of the PPR Penal Code and Art. 15.1 of the International Covenant on Civil and Political Rights.

Thus it was that the formal arguments that martial law had been unconstitutionally imposed or that the penal provisions of the Martial Law Decree could not properly be applied to those who had undertaken action on 13 December 1981 were not acceptable to the courts when made in defence of the accused. Any critical remarks on the legal aspects of martial law, moreover, exposed the defence lawyer to the risk of disciplinary proceedings. In the long run only a defence plea based on the merits of each specific case had any chance of being successful in the courtroom.

Strikes and Protest Action

Art. 46 of the Martial Law Decree did not specify which criteria were decisive in classifying a certain action as 'organizing a strike' or 'continuing trade union activity'. The decree did not distinguish between the spontaneous reaction of the workforce and a strike that was planned in advance. This created several practical difficulties for the courts. First, they had to determine whether such diverse actions as wearing an armband, displaying a flysheet in public, or stopping work for several minutes to pay homage to the victims of 'people's rule' were protest actions or not. Secondly, they had to decide whether such an action as organizing a ballot to determine the mood of the workforce, even though no strike was subsequently held, could be considered as 'organizing a strike'. Where was the dividing line between 'organizing a strike' and 'leading it'?

These and other inconsistencies were raised by the defence. Tadeusz de Virion, for instance, said during the trial of strikers from the FSO car factory that the charge of 'leading the strike' must be grounded in concrete evidence. The simple fact that the defendants were on the strike committee was not sufficient proof that they were its 'leaders'. The fact that the strike committee had set up various services to maintain order in the plant proved only that they had performed such services and was not proof of the leading role of the strike committee. What was more — de Virion continued — this was not something to incriminate the defendants; on the contrary, it was a useful and responsible action, ensuring that the plant was not left unprotected. The charge of 'continuing trade union activity' was equally unjustified since only what was established could be continued. The defendants, on the other hand, by becoming members of the strike committee had begun an entirely new activity, since the strike committee was not a part of the already existing Solidarity structures.[7]

The Supreme Court, in its ruling of 25 March 1982 on criminal liability under Art. 46.1 and 2, stated that organizing a ballot on the possibility of protest action constituted continuation of trade union activity. This ruling disregarded the simple fact that a ballot could be organized by anybody, regardless of trade union membership. In the case of Zbigniew Stecki and Jacek Oleksyn, the Chairman and the Vice-Chairman of the Solidarity Committee at the Kórnik branch of the Polish Academy of Sciences, the Voivodship Court in Poznań passed a sentence of one year's imprisonment, suspended for three years. The sentence was upheld by the Supreme Court. The two defendants had organized a ballot among their colleagues and put to them the single question whether Solidarity badges were to be worn as a sign of protest. The ballot did, in fact, give them support for the initiative, although they had, in the meantime, decided not to proceed with it.[8]

In another ruling of 18 February 1982 the Supreme Court stated that 'inciting others to participate in a strike in flysheets that were publicly distributed was a form of strike organizing'.[9] It tried to fill in this way a legal loophole arising from the fact that participation in a strike or protest action qualified as a petty offence ('wykroczenie') and neither the Petty Offences Code nor the Martial Law Decree made provision for 'inciting to a petty offence'. The Supreme Court equated it, therefore, with the more grevous misdemeanour ('występek') of organizing a strike or protest action which was punishable under Art. 46.2 of the decree by up to five year's imprisonment. In doing so it was not only in breach of the Martial Law Decree but also of the Penal Code which, in Art. 18.1, clearly distinguishes between 'inciting', which belongs essentially to a preparatory stage and is directed at unspecified persons, and 'organizing' which requires a much

The Trials of December 1981 Strikers

greater degree of involvement on the part of the offender.

In a ruling of 26 April 1982 the Supreme Court attempted to distinguish between strike 'organizing' and 'leading'. It defined 'organizing' as 'an activity aimed at bringing about a strike or protest action', and 'leading' as 'playing the role of a superior and issuing instructions to the other participants in such an event concerning its course, duration, means of achieving objectives, etc.'[10]

This ruling sanctioned the already prevailing abuse of presenting charges of 'leading' and 'organizing' a strike to those who had shown most initiative in the course of a strike. Needless to say, the facts in such cases were selected and interpreted in such a way as to make the evidence presented against the Solidarity activists fit the criminal provisions of the Martial Law Decree.

The Martial Law Decree treated organizing and leading of a protest action on a par with organizing and leading strikes, and imposed a strict ban on both. In a ruling of 10 May 1982 the Supreme Court defined a protest action by reference to the specific goal which its participants set out to achieve. The Supreme Court ruled that a protest action was 'any behaviour of its participants that tends through various externally manifested forms, to the achievement of a desired goal'. In the specific case of J. Mościcki, Vice-Chairman of the Solidarity Committee at the Ciechanów toy factory, the Supreme Court ruled that the wearing of armbands could be classified as a protest action 'if this particular form of protest were recognized as effective'.[11] J. Mościcki had been sentenced in the first instance to one year's imprisonment for passing round red-and-white armbands to his fellow employees. This symbolic gesture was meant as a protest against the arrest of the chairman of the factory's Solidarity committee. The sentence was upheld by the Supreme Court.

In another case, the Supreme Court was asked to rule on whether the organization of a three-minute work stoppage in order to commemorate the anniversary of the December 1970 worker's riots was liable for penalization under Art. 46.2 of the Martial Law Decree. It refused to give a ruling, justifying this decision by saying that this case required substantive appraisal rather than a formal interpretation of legal provisions.

These two examples show clearly that the Supreme Court found it extremely difficult to work out a legal definition of a 'protest action'. In this situation the legal provision making 'protest action' a punishable offence, since its very content could not be defined, should have been dropped altogether, in keeping with the principle *nullum crimen sine lege*.[12]

Art. 46.1 and 2: A Case Study

The story of the Gdańsk Portworkers' strike well illustrates the use to which Art. 46 of the Martial Law Decree was put. In December 1981 the Gdańsk Port Authority, which has several sectors and is situated next to the Lenin Shipyard, had some 6,500 people in its employ. Only 3 per cent of these did not belong to Solidarity. The relationship between the union and the management was businesslike. Only two members of Solidarity were on the internment list. On 13 December 1981 the Chairman of the Enterprise Solidarity Committee Stanisław Jarosz and two of his colleagues Rudolf Zając and Teofil Wika–Czarnowski met in front of the Sector 1 gate a group of Solidarity leaders who had taken part in the previous night's National Commission meeting in the Shipyard. They decided to go to the chief traffic controller's office since they knew it was vacant on Sundays and that they could hold a meeting there in order to discuss what they might do. There they met the duty controller Bronisław Gniza.

At about 1 p.m. they agreed to set up a National Strike Committee and issued Communiqué no. 1, calling on the workers to stage a general strike from Monday 14 December 1981. Some of them later had lunch in the canteen. All the National Commission members and the representatives from Częstochowa and Wrocław left the grounds of the Gdańsk Port Authority at about 4 p.m. Some time later the riot police, apparently acting on a tip–off that the National Strike Committee was in the port, surrounded the administrative building and detained two traffic controllers and three Solidarity members, mistaking them for the Solidarity National Commission representatives. A duplicating machine was seized in the raid and the door was broken down.

The general mood among the workers reporting for the early shift on the following day, 14 December, was one of bitterness on account of the internment of top Solidarity activists and the sudden and unprovoked ZOMO raid on the port, and strike action was in the air. The managing director Mieczysław Płoski toured the different sectors of the port explaining to the workers what the militarization of the port entailed. The Solidarity Chairman

The Trials of December 1981 Strikers

Jarosz stressed that there would be a strike only if that was the will of the majority. The workers demanded the release of their colleagues who had been detained the previous night, the release of the interned Solidarity leaders, and an end to martial law, and to further these demands they decided to go on strike. A local Strike Committee was set up in the Port Authority.

The Strike Committee issued a leaflet and prepared a list of demands. They distributed tasks in order to ensure discipline and security, secured entrances and prepared points of defence in case of an attack on the enterprise. They also attempted to establish contact with the other striking enterprises in the Gdańsk area.

On 15 December a group of strikers entered the administrative building in order to demand that national flags that had been displayed on the administration building to indicate that a strike was in progress, and which had been removed by the management, be returned. They also told management that they would not comply with the martial law regulations that they abandon their union offices which were to be sealed. Later that same day the strikers held talks with the military commissar assigned to the Gdańsk Port Authority, Commander Swatko, who promised to present the strikers' list of demands to Colonel Molczyk, the Chief of the voivodship military HQ. The workers never received a reply from Colonel Molczyk, and Commander Swatko was shortly replaced.

After the storming of the Gdańsk Refinery on 19 December, the temporary closure of the entire shipyard until 4 January 1982, and the mobilization of ZOMO riot police units in the area, the strikers realized that the odds were against them. The Strike Committee negotiated with the military and agreed to discontinue the strike in exchange for safe conduct for all the strikers. It was agreed that the navy would enter the port at 5 p.m., while the strikers had until 6 p.m. to leave the enterprise. Despite official pledges that the members of the Strike Committee would not be victimized, the police began, however, to hunt for them in the neighbourhood and they were unable to return to work. Some of them, including Jarosz, Andrzej Michałowski and Leszek Świtek, went underground.

Some 24 employees of the Gdańsk Port Authority were tried in 1982–3, most of them during martial law. The biggest single trial involved seven defendants: Rudolf Zając, Treasurer of the Enterprise Solidarity Committee; Eugeniusz Szymecki, Chairman of the Solidarity Committee in Sector 1, Teofil Wika-Czarnowski,

The Trials of December 1981 Strikers

member of the Solidarity Committee in the Marine Services Department; Alicja Sopuszyńska, Secretary to the Chairman of the Solidarity Committee in the Gdańsk Port Authority; Czesław Nowak, a hoist operator; Ginter Erwin Albrecht, a driver; and Marian Podgórski, Deputy Director of the Personnel Department of the Gdańsk Port Authority. The trial took place in March 1982 before the Naval Court in Gdynia.

This trial was typical in so far as it gives an insight into the reasoning of martial law courts, as well as the way they tended to inflate the criteria of criminal liability provided in the Martial Law Decree to fit the arbitrarily selected and interpreted facts. The courts would treat the most insignificant details with the utmost seriousness in order to substantiate the thesis that the strikes had been the work of a few specific troublemakers and not a spontaneous reaction of the mass of workers. The courts were particularly hard on union office holders in order to compromise union activists as 'extremists' in the eyes of the rank-and-file.

Since the Chairman of the Strike Committee Stanisław Jarosz was in hiding, the main burden of responsibility for the strike was placed upon Rudolf Zając, the next most senior Solidarity activist. Zając had originally been charged with the continuation of trade union activity under Art. 46.1 of the Martial Law Decree by:

- requesting the chief traffic controller Bronisław Gniza to hand over the keys to the printing room;

- organizing lunch for the representatives of the National Strike Committee in the canteen of Sector 1 at the request of the Chairman of the Solidarity Committee Stanisław Jarosz;

- performing the role of liaison officer between the strikers in Sectors 1 and 2.

The court, however, went beyond the indictment and in summary procedure found Zając guilty not only of continuing trade union activity but also of strike organizing under Art. 46.2 of the Martial Law Decree by:

- handing over to the Strike Committee instructions concerning action to be taken in the event of the declaration of a state of emergency by the authorities;

The Trials of December 1981 Strikers

- demanding access to the printing room;

- advising the strikers in Sector 1 as to how the strike was to be carried out;

- taking part in a meeting with the military commissar.

He was sentenced on these grounds to six and a half years' imprisonment plus four years' loss of public rights.

Eugeniusz Szymecki was tried under summary procedure for offences under Art. 46.1 and 2 of the Martial Law Decree, and sentenced to five years' imprisonment and four years' loss of public rights for:

- organizing and leading, together with Leszek Świtek (in hiding at the time of the trial — AS), a strike in Sector 1;

- representing the strikers in dealings with the military commissar;

- speaking during the meeting with the military commissar and demanding an end to martial law and the release of those interned;

- reporting on the course of the meeting with the commissar to the strikers;

- consulting decisions concerning the strike in Sector 1 with Rudolf Zając;

- sending a group of 12 strikers from Sector 1 to Sector 2 in order to protect the Strike Committee there.

Czesław Nowak was sentenced under Art. 46.1 and 2 in summary procedure to four and a half years' imprisonment and four years' loss of public rights for:

- informing the chief traffic controller Bronisław Gniza that his office was being taken over for the needs of the National Strike Committee;

- organizing a strike in Sector 1 on 17 and 18 December.

The Trials of December 1981 Strikers

Teofil Wika–Czarnowski was also sentenced under Art. 46.1 and 2 in summary procedure to three years' imprisonment and one year's loss of public rights for:

- leading a strike among the staff of the Marine Services Department of the Gdańsk Port Authority by ensuring order among the strikers and performing telephone duty for two hours in lieu of the Chairman of the Departmental Committee of Solidarity Andrzej Michałowski (in hiding at the time of the trial — AS).

Alicja Sopuszyńska was tried under ordinary procedure. She was found guilty of:

- making, at the request of the Chairman of the Strike Committee, Stanisław Jarosz, a stencil of a flysheet beginning with the words 'The Gdańsk Port is ready for anything' and signed, on behalf of the 'striking portworkers of Gdańsk, by Stanisław Jarosz which called on the public to break the law;

but the court did not sentence her and suspended further proceedings conditionally for two years on the grounds that she had not intended to commit the offence and was only carrying out her secretarial duties at the behest of her superior.

Ginter Erwin Albrecht was sentenced under ordinary procedure to one year's imprisonment and a fine of 3,000 zloty under Art. 46.4 of the Martial Law Decree for:

- using a vehicle belonging to the Gdańsk Port Authority in order to transport members of the Strike Committee as well as to transport the stencil of a flysheet which was duplicated both in Gdańsk and in the area of the Port.

Only one of the defendants, Marian Podgórski, who had been accused under Art. 46.1 of the Martial Law Decree of having been one of the 'armed gang' of workers that invaded the office of the director of the Gdańsk Port Authority and having, under threat of violence, forced Zdzisław Dejewski to return two national flags that had been removed from the building, was acquitted in view of the facts that the witnesses whose testimonies

The Trials of December 1981 Strikers

had incriminated him later withdrew their statements and that his subsequent behaviour indicated that he had not been involved in the strike.

A comparison of the findings of the Naval Court in Gdynia with the description of events as reported by an independent source[13] highlights the distorted perspective of the court which pretended not to see the spontaneous fashion in which the week-long strike evolved and only picked out those specific incidents which could be made out to be premeditated actions constituting criminal offences and included under Art. 46 of the Martial Law Decree. The court, for example, treated the meeting on 13 December of several Solidarity activists in the Gdańsk Port as a pre-planned session of the National Strike Committee. In fact, the several activists met by chance, decided to confer and the National Strike Committee was only set up some hours later, as a result of their deliberations. They decided to go and talk in the office of the chief controller where they could also listen to the radio communiqués. Nowak told the chief traffic controller Bronisław Gniza that they had come to talk in the conference room. Gniza received them in a friendly manner, offered them tea and even told some anti-government jokes. The Solidarity activists did not in any way interfere with or disrupt the work in the controller's office. Their arrival was, however, presented by the court as a brusque invasion of the office, with Nowak made out to be the ring leader who informed Gniza that they were taking over his office and conference room. Apparently Gniza himself had told the Deputy Director M. Bartold that his office had been taken by force. Bartold passed this information on to the civilian and military authorities. This probably was the reason for the unexpected storming of the administrative building by the ZOMO on the night of 13-14 December.

On the morning of 14 December the Solidarity leaders in Sectors 1 and 2 of the port said that they would support strike action only on condition that such was the will of the majority of workers and stressed that anyone who did not wish to strike would be free to do as he pleased. The workers voted in favour of a strike and demanded the release of those who had been interned and an end to martial law. This decision was presented by the court as the result of strike agitation by Stanisław Jarosz, Leszek Świtek and Andrzej Michałowski (all three were in hiding at the time of the trial). The court failed to notice that these three activists were simply responding to rank-and-file pressure. They found, instead, that Jarosz had, by his remarks, frustrated the attempts of the managing director to persuade the workers to return to work.

When the news reached the port that several miners had been shot dead by the ZOMO in the Wujek coalmine, the striking portworkers felt very bitter and they even erected a symbolic shrine to commemorate the victims. The court presented the workers' bitterness in a totally different light. It found that Czesław Nowak had, at a meeting of the workers of Sector 1 with their Director Zbigniew Jackiewicz on 17 or 18 December, by his declaration that because of the events at the Wujek coalmine the workers would not resume work, induced the rest of the workforce to refuse to unload a transport of fruit. The court ignored Nowak's defence that he had simply been expressing his opinion.

When the striking portworkers saw Zdzisław Dejewski taking down the national flags that had been draped outside the administration building a delegation of 30 of them went to the director's office to demand their restoration. There was an angry exchange between the strikers, who warned the management not to try to take over the offices of the enterprise Solidarity Committee, and those present in the director's office. Dejewski himself decided to return the flags to their previous place. The court presented this incident as an intrusion into the building of an 'armed gang, a so-called workers' militia'. The court failed, however, to establish what arms they were supposedly carrying. The court treated the real issue — the removal of the strikers' flags — as a more or less unrelated spin-off. It found that four or five of the 'gang' took Dejewski aside, threatened to 'deprive him of his freedom' and 'using violent means' forced him to replace the flags.

Finally, it is worth mentioning that the court completely ignored the fact that the strikers had barricaded themselves in Sector 2 with containers and heavy vehicles and at regular intervals placed fuses connected to tanks containing liquid fuel. The strikers had also prepared wooden shafts and Molotov cocktails for self-defence. They made no attempt, however, to take over one of the Polish ships that was lying at anchor in Sector 2 loaded with arms. The strikers had threatened to light the fuses if the ZOMO or army units tried to attack them. In the event, however, after six days of strike, they decided to end the strike peacefully in order to protect both lives and national property. One can only speculate that the authorities were unwilling to let it be known that resistance in the Gdańsk Port had been so massive and so desperate, and since the court was unable to find any evidence that would implicate specific individuals as having given orders to build barricades or plant explosives, they preferred not to raise the issue at all.

The Naval Court in assessing the strike considered certain of its elements more important than others. For instance, 'organizing lunch' for members of Solidarity's National Commission or going to the administrative building to warn the management against taking over Solidarity offices was seen as constituting evidence of active involvement in the strike. The material in the case was treated by the court not only selectively, but also arbitrarily. For instance, the public condemnation by Czesław Nowak of the massacre of miners at the Wujek coalmine was evidence of his 'leading role'. A particular twist to the hypothesis that the strike was not a spontaneous reaction of the workforce but a result of the agitation of the few was the court's conviction of Wika–Czarnowski for what was described as 'playing a leading role by the defendant'. The court found that while deputizing for Michałowski he 'had been in a position in which he had a real possibility of controlling developments, and could have changed their course or even discontinued the illegal strike action' but since he had not done so, there could be no doubt as to the fact that he was guilty of strike organizing.

The court also failed to answer Szymecki's line of defence which was that everything he had done was a reflection of the will of the workforce. The court ignored the fact that Szymecki had not called the strike but simply found himself in the midst of one and, as a person enjoying the trust of his fellow–workers, he had tried to represent their interests. The court based its findings on the testimony of the director of Sector 1 Jackiewicz, who said that Szymecki had called on his colleagues to strike 'since the government had declared war on the workers'. It established two other criteria of strike organizing in Szymecki's case: that he had sent a group of workers from Sector 1 to Sector 2 in order to protect the Strike Committee there, and that he had thanked the strikers for participating in the protest action.

Szymecki's own testimony was sufficient to incriminate in the eyes of the court two of his co–defendants: Rudolf Zając and Czesław Nowak. The court found that it was evident from Szymecki's testimony that Zając had been 'something like an adviser' to him in matters concerning the organization of the strike in Sector 1, that he had maintained contact with Sector 2 where Jarosz was based, and that he had participated in talks with the management and the military. Szymecki also testified that during the meeting in the canteen, Nowak had asked the workers assembled there how they were going to react to the events at the Wujek coalmine.

Zając and Nowak were also incriminated by the testimonies of the management employee Dejewski, chief traffic controller Gniza and Sector 1 Director Jackiewicz, although these three prosecution witnesses said that they had not attached particular significance to the wording of their testimonies in the course of the investigation since they had been nervous, and subsequently withdrew the testimonies they had made during the investigation. Jackiewicz even went so far as to suggest that the records of his investigation had been falsified. The court none the less upheld their testimonies and used them as the basis for its own findings. The court was of the opinion that the atmosphere of the courtroom, with the families of the defendants present, was such as to inhibit the witnesses from saying anything that would incriminate the defendants. Jackiewicz had testified that Zając had accompanied Jarosz at 'mass strike rallies'. The same witness had testified that Nowak had on two occasions called on the workers to continue the strike because 'workers had been murdered'. Gniza had testified, for his part, that Nowak had entered his office with a group of Solidarity activists and told him that his office was being taken over by the National Strike Committee. On the basis of these two testimonies the court found that Nowak had displayed 'a high degree of malice ... playing on human emotions, he urged the strikers to continue the strike.'

The court established mitigating circumstances for only two of the defendants—Sopuszyńska and Albrecht. It transferred their cases from summary to ordinary procedure and passed sentences which were relatively lenient by martial law standards. The mitigating circumstances in question were that neither of the two defendants had had the intention of committing an offence and were only carrying out their normal duties.

The trial of the seven strikers from the Gdańsk Port Authority was, in a way, a substitute trial. The Solidarity activists who were most actively involved in the strike, such as Stanisław Jarosz, Andrzej Michałowski, Antoni Grabarczyk, Leszek Świtek, were all in hiding at the time of the trial. In particular, Zając and Szymecki were sentenced in lieu of Jarosz, the Chairman of the Strike Committee.

The Trials of December 1981 Strikers

Jarosz himself was arrested on 30 August 1982 and tried in October 1983 together with Świtek who was arrested in February 1983. For over 13 months he was held in an investigative prison. The military prosecutor charged him on three counts: continuation of trade union activity, organizing and leading a strike in the Gdańsk Port Authority from 14–19 December 1981 (Art. 46.1 and 2 of the Martial Law Decree); disseminating, during the strike in December 1981, printed matter liable to weaken the country's defence readiness (Art. 48.1–3 of the Martial Law Decree); continuation of trade union activity by belonging to an illegal organization — the Regional Co-ordinating Commission — and engaging, in particular, in the dissemination, preparation, collection and storage of various materials containing 'false information' liable to cause public unrest (Art. 46.1 in conjunction with Art. 48.3 of the Martial Law Decree and in conjunction with Art. 276.1 of the Penal Code). Taking into account the amnesty of July 1983, the Naval Court in Gdynia halved the sentences it would otherwise have passed, and gave Świtek a sentence of three years' and Jarosz a sentence of two years' imprisonment.

The great discrepancy in sentences passed by the same court in March 1982 and November 1983 demonstrates that the main function of the trials of the December 1981 strikers which were held in the first months of martial law was to shock and intimidate the rank-and-file members of Solidarity, as well as eliminating from the political scene those Solidarity activists who had held elective posts in the union. The backbone of the union could not be broken without the elimination of those Solidarity activists who enjoyed the confidence of their fellow-workers and had been chosen by them to represent their interests. It was essential that they be removed from their natural environment. That is why they were arrested, discredited by being put on trial and isolated from others who were given to understand that contact with them was dangerous in accordance with the precept: once in trouble with the police, always in trouble. It was not surprising that Zając, Szymecki and Wika-Czarnowski, who held elective union posts, were treated more severely than their co-defendants. The only exception to this rule was Nowak who, although he was only a rank-and-file member of Solidarity, clearly touched an official raw nerve by publicly condemning the massacre at the Wujek coalmine.

This basic function of the trials of December 1981 strikers played a secondary role at the time when Jarosz and Świtek came

The Trials of December 1981 Strikers

to trial. This would account for the discrepancy in the severity of sentences. At this time the authorities were much more concerned with discrediting the defendants as underground Solidarity activists. Świtek's clandestine activity was clearly considered more dangerous than that of Jarosz since he received a heavier sentence. This seems illogical in view of the fact that the charge presented against Jarosz of disseminating 'false information' with the aim of weakening the country's defence readiness was very serious, and was not presented against Świtek.

The case of the Gdańsk portworkers' strike, which was not by any means an isolated incident, shows clearly the important role of martial law courts within the pacification process. The courts were used to achieve the ad hoc political objectives of the ruling regime in blatant disregard of the immanent principle of justice. This tendency is also evidenced by the case of the *Free Unionist*.

The *Free Unionist*

On 5 January 1982 six editors and printers of the *Free Unionist*, a strike bulletin which was published daily during the sit-in strike at the Katowice Steelworks from 13-24 December 1981 were sentenced by the Voivodship Court in Katowice, under summary procedure, to prison terms ranging from three to six and a half years.

The *Free Unionist* (*Wolny Związkowiec*) was one of the most dynamic and interesting independent bulletins to appear in 1980-1. It started appearing at the end of August 1980 and accompanied the union throughout the entire period of its legal existance. At the height of its activity it reached a circulation of between 50,000 and 55,000 copies. Published at first weekly and then fortnightly from January 1981, it reported extensively on all issues of concern to the workers of the Katowice Steelworks. In response to readers' demands the *Free Unionist* later published materials on the history of Poland and Eastern Europe. As a result, two of its editors—Jacek Cieślicki and Zbigniew Kupisiewicz—were summoned in mid-1981 to the prosecutor's office for questioning. No charges, however, were proferred against them.

One of the August 1981 issues of the *Free Unionist* was to have reprinted cartoons portraying the CPSU General Secretary

The Trials of December 1981 Strikers

Brezhnev as a bear. These cartoons had appeared previously in another Solidarity bulletin which had been confiscated by the authorities. While that particular issue of the *Free Unionist* was being printed, the police raided the printing room, damaging the printing equipment. The stencils, however, survived the raid and the cartoons were printed in 250,000 copies. Cieślicki was formally indicted for 'anti-socialist activity harming the interests of the Polish nation'.

When martial law was declared the editors of the *Free Unionist* with the exception of Cieślicki, who had been interned, joined the strike at the steelworks almost from the very beginning. In the early stages of the strike, duplicating and printing equipment was moved for security reasons from the former editorial office to department K32. On the following day, 14 December, the ZOMO riot police broke down the gate and entered the steelworks with the aim of arresting the Strike Committee. They failed to do so since the members of the Strike Committee could not be found. Instead, they detained some 50 steel workers and retreated.

The *Free Unionist* continued to appear as a strike bulletin under the aegis of the Strike Committee. It reported on strike developments and appeared every day; sometimes even twice daily. On 23 December 1981 the strikers, who numbered some 8,000, voluntarily discontinued their sit-in and requested an assurance of safe conduct from the security forces. Although such an assurance was granted ten tanks and some 3,000 ZOMO riot policemen entered the steelworks once the strike was over to remove the strikers. The entire editorial team of the *Free Unionist* was arrested. The investigation and the trial were completed in less than two weeks.

Both the indictment and the sentence relied heavily on an analysis of the contents of several issues of the strike bulletin. They were interpreted as fomenting a strike atmosphere, inciting violence and threatening a stand-still of the entire plant. The court interpreted one of the articles in issue no. 1 of the strike bulletin as calling for the murder of party members: 'The party was called a "purulent ulcer" and its members - "lice" which should be exterminated.' This phrase was used as the basis of both the indictment and the sentence.

The court found the entire editorial team, as well as one of the printers, to be collectively responsible for the contents of this unsigned article. The court went beyond the terms of the indictment, which dealt only with the activities of the *Free Unionist* during the strike, when it noted that the *Free Unionist* had been connected with the most extremist and militant groups within Solidarity. Without any reference to the facts of the case the court stated, 'the call to hang and murder party members did not first appear in the strike issue of the *Free Unionist* of 13 December 1981, but had already been voiced earlier by the most extremist members of Solidarity and other groups hostile to socialist Poland.'

The hearing could not provide any evidence to prove that any of the strikers had, in fact, been influenced by the articles published in the strike bulletin. The court itself, moreover, stated elsewhere that, since the workers had finally, in their wisdom, discontinued strike action, the agitation of the *Free Unionist* had obviously been ineffective.

The severity of the sentences as well as the fact that the editors of the strike bulletin were found guilty not only of continuing trade union activity, but also of organizing a strike, can be explained by the authorities' determination to impose a total blockade on information and stem the flow of uncensored news and opinion.

The PPR's propaganda apparatus seized the opportunity provided by the trial of the *Free Unionist*, which *Trybuna Ludu* described as 'politically of the most extreme orientation',[14] to lash out against the Solidarity press. In particular the case was exploited to justify the introduction of martial law as a means of protecting the country from irresponsible Solidarity extremists.

The Case of the Maritime Academy in Gdynia: Articles 46 and 48 combined

Ewa Kubasiewicz, Jerzy Kowalczyk, Władysław Trzciński, Marek Czachór and five others were accused of 'acting together and in agreement... with the aim of disseminating prepared, collected and stored leaflets containing information liable to weaken the PPR's defence readiness, cause public unrest and disturbances' (Art. 48.1, 2 and 3 of the Martial Law Decree). The defendants Władysław Trzciński, Wiesława Kwiatkowska and Cezary Godziuk were additionally charged with continuing trade union activity (Art. 46.1 of the Martial Law Decree), whereas Jerzy

The Trials of December 1981 Strikers

Kowalczyk and Ewa Kubasiewicz—the Chairman and Deputy Chairman of the Solidarity Committee at the Maritime Academy in Gdynia—were also charged with continuing trade union activity and organizing a strike (Art.46.1 and 2 of the Martial Law Decree).

Ewa Kubasiewicz and Jerzy Kowalczyk admitted to having been among the leaders of the strike by students of the Academy, as well as to having edited one leaflet entitled *Communiqué no.1*. This leaflet provided information about the course of the strike and its termination, and protested against the removal of the democratically elected Rector, Mikołaj Kostecki. The leaflet was the principal piece of evidence in the case. Minutes taken during a meeting at which Kubasiewicz and Kowalczyk reportedly urged the staff and students to strike were also presented as evidence. Kubasiewicz was sentenced to ten and Kowalczyk to nine years in prison for organizing and leading the strike and preparing, duplicating and distributing *Communiqué no. 1* which, according to the Naval Court in Gdynia, contained 'false information' liable to weaken the PPR's defence readiness.

Władysław Trzciński was sentenced to nine years' imprisonment for having on several occasions transported a duplicating machine on which leaflets were printed. Cezary Godziuk received a six-year sentence for storing a duplicating machine and leaflets. Jarosław Skowronek, Sławomir Sadowski and Krzysztof Jankowski were sentenced to five years' imprisonment each for preparing, storing and distributing leaflets.

Apart from Ewa Kubasiewicz and Jerzy Kowalczyk none of the other defendants pleaded guilty to any of the charges brought against them. They were sentenced without evidence since neither the duplicating machine nor the paper on which the leaflets were supposed to have been printed were found. None of the defendants had actually been caught printing or distributing leaflets: most of them were arrested in a private flat in which they were hiding after the strike had already ended. There was no evidence that any leaflets had actually been printed in this flat, which was occupied by one of the defendants, the son of Ewa Kubasiewicz Marek Czachór.

The only evidence against Władysław Trzciński was the discovery of his fingerprints in a student hostel. He admitted to having gone there more than once since he had friends amongst the students and used to play cards with them, but he denied participating in any illegal meetings. The court, nevertheless, upheld the charge that Trzciński had attended an illegal meeting

The Trials of December 1981 Strikers

in a student hostel, although — as Trzciński's defence lawyer pointed out—there was nothing incriminating about the fact that one's fingerprints had been found in the room of one's friend.

The prosecution witnesses testified before the court in favour of the defendants. Some admitted that they had been coerced into making certain statements during the investigation, and withdrew their earlier testimonies. The court nevertheless upheld these testimonies. All motions submitted by the defence lawyers and the defendants themselves were dismissed by the court. Trzciński had intended to call three students as witnesses on his behalf, but the court denied this request on the grounds that there was not enough time and that their testimony would shed no new light on the case.[15]

The court failed to take into account the one significant mitigating circumstance that the strike had lasted only 30 hours and had voluntarily been discontinued by its organizers, who had been promised that they would not be victimized on this account. The plea of the defence to call the newly-appointed Rector, Władysław Rymarz, as a witness in the case was dismissed, in breach of procedural law.

The court also made some factual errors, for instance, by overlooking the purely symbolic nature of the strike since all classes and lectures had been suspended anyway. Secondly, the court's statement that the leaflet *Communiqué no. 1* edited by two of the defendants contained 'false information' liable to weaken the PPR's defence readiness was manifestly inaccurate. As revealed in the course of the trial, the leaflet was a protest against the removal of the incumbent rector, and the court clearly misinterpreted its contents in attributing to it any implications for the PPR's 'defence readiness'. Disregarding the facts revealed during the trial, the court found that certain accidental meetings between some of the defendants constituted an element of 'trade union activity'.

Ewa Kubasiewicz and Jerzy Kowalczyk were sentenced twice for the same offence under Art. 46.1 and 2 of the Martial Law Decree: in the first instance for activities between 14 and 15 December 1981, and on the second, in conjunction with Art. 48.1, 2 and 3, for activities between 14 and 20 December 1981. In this respect the court was in breach of substantive law.

The severity of the sentences passed in the trial of Solidarity activists and students of the Maritime Academy in Gdynia can partly be explained by the fact that at the time of the trial which

The Trials of December 1981 Strikers

took place at the end of January and beginning of February 1982, the authorities were already able to determine the scope of the December 1981 strike action but did not as yet have a clear penal policy. They were, nevertheless, determined to exact severe punishment, and the sentence of 10 years' imprisonment passed on Ewa Kubasiewicz, the heaviest in the entire period of martial law, was designed to give a warning to those who were still eager to resist martial law.

An extraordinary review was finally lodged on behalf of the defendants by the Chairman of the Military Chamber of the Supreme Court only after they refused to apply for pardon. All were released in 1983.

Miners on trial

The sentences passed on the participants of the December 1981 strikes in the Silesian mines were harsh: up to seven years' imprisonment in the case of the Ziemowit coalmine, up to five years' in the case of the Andaluzja coalmine, up to four years' in the case of the Wujek coalmine and two years' in the case of the Julian coalmine. It is clear, however, that the overall severity of sentences passed on the striking miners, all tried by military courts, was in line with those of ordinary courts. In those cases where the sentences handed down by the military courts were not up to their expectations, the authorities attempted to rectify this by lodging an appeal (an extraordinary review if the case had been heard under summary procedure).

This is illustrated by the case of Józef Grembowski and Krzysztof Zaniewski of the Borynia coalmine. The Court of the Silesian Military District was not convinced by the prosecutor's case that inciting others to strike was tantamount to strike organizing. Only one of the 13 defendants, Ryszard Będkowski, was sentenced for strike organizing to four and a half years' imprisonment. The Chief Military Prosecutor, in his request of 3 April 1982 for an extraordinary review of the case by the Supreme Court, argued that although none of the witnesses had actually spoken of Grembowski and Zaniewski as 'organizing' or 'leading' the strike, their actions should still have been defined as such, under Art. 46.2 of the Martial Law Decree, on the basis of a comprehensive analysis of all the circumstances. The Chief

The Trials of December 1981 Strikers

Military Prosecutor requested that the Supreme Court double the sentences passed by the lower court—to nine and seven years' imprisonment respectively, on the grounds that, 'at a time when the will to strike was beginning to flag among the majority of the miners, the [defendants'] appeal to continue with the strike and their success in getting the miners to do so, cannot be regarded merely as incitement'.

Strikers from the Piast coalmine were tried despite the fact that the authorities had pledged that they would be immune from prosecution if they discontinued their strike, the longest of the strikes begun in December 1981 in protest against the imposition of martial law. All nine defendants who were acquitted by the Court of the Silesian Military District were immediately interned.

The case of Jerzy Mnich and the strike in the Manifest Lipcowy coalmine

Jerzy Mnich was one of the founders of the pre-August 1980 Free Trade Unions in Silesia. In August 1980 he organized the strike in the Manifest Lipcowy coalmine in Jastrzębie Zdrój which forced the government to dispatch a commission to negotiate with the strikers and to sign one of the 'social agreements'. Later he exposed links between Jarosław Sienkiewicz, the Chairman of the Inter-Factory Strike Committee in Jastrzębie and the Katowice party dignitary Andrzej Żabiński which contributed to the former's resignation.

As a member of the presidium of the works commission of Solidarity, Mnich considered it his duty to join the striking miners. Only half of the workforce participated in it since a blockade of the streets by the army prevented others from reaching the mine. Two days into the strike Mnich suffered a heart attack and was taken by ambulance to the miners' hospital in Jastrzębie. Soon afterwards the ZOMO stormed and pacified the coalmine. The ZOMO units opened fire and four miners received gunshot wounds.

Some four weeks after the storming of the mine, on 13 January 1982, Jerzy Mnich was visited at his hospital bed by a deputy military prosecutor, Janusz Palus. He was asked to sign a statement admitting to having organized the strike in the coalmine in its early stages. Mnich refused to sign the statement

The Trials of December 1981 Strikers

saying that there had been no strike as such but simply a protest action. The miners had wanted to know for what reason and against whom martial law had been declared. Their protest had resulted in talks between the miners and the military commissar of the Rybnik Mining Region as well as the director of the Manifest Lipcowy coalmine.

The prosecutor, ignoring protests from the doctors, removed Mnich from the hospital. He was first taken to Bytom prison and then to Katowice Police HQ at Lompy Street. His first interrogation took place in a room in the company of soldiers armed with machine guns. After he refused to testify, he was ordered to kneel on a stool and was handcuffed to a radiator. In this position he was administered blows to his heels as a result of which he lost consciousness. During the second interrogation tear gas was sprayed into his eyes from close quarters. For almost six months he was blind in one eye and the doctors could not treat it effectively since they did not know the chemical composition of the gas.

While in investigative prison Mnich was given a distorted version of his testimony to sign. This time he was charged with causing 14 million zlotys' worth of losses as a result of the strike. He reiterated that there had been no strike but only a spontaneous protest on the part of the workforce. Once again he refused to sign.

On 17 January 1982 he submitted a plea for the revocation of his arrest. The Court of the Silesian Military District, having considered his plea, stated that 'the testimonies of witnesses were sufficient to incriminate the defendant of having committed the offences with which he was charged.' The unidentified incriminating testimonies referred to were in fact those of the coalmine director, later the chief of the tenth militarized brigade, Karol Grzywa and a local party secretary Robert Moćko. Both sought revenge on Mnich for his activities in the Free Trade Unions and in Solidarity.

While in investigative prison, Mnich suffered another heart attack and was transferred to a hospital. On 2 February 1982 the court suspended proceedings in the case but did not release him. On 28 April 1982, when Mnich was still in hospital, the Court of the Silesian Military District heard the case of his co-defendants, members of the presidium of the Solidarity works commission in the Manifest Lipcowy coalmine. None of the defendants admitted to having organized a strike. The court ruled that the defendants had only committed petty offences and that therefore they did not come under the jurisdiction of a military court. On grounds of health the case of Jerzy Mnich was excluded for separate proceedings.

He was tried in absentia on 27 January 1983 after martial law was suspended. The offence with which he was charged was no longer found to be 'socially dangerous' and the proceedings against him were finally discontinued. While still in hospital, even before his trial in absentia, Mnich was visited several times by the security officer responsible for the surveillance of the coalmine employees. He offered Mnich a one way passport to leave the country. At first Mnich refused but after his trial and discharge from hospital, with no work prospects, in need of further medical treatment, with a family to support, and threatened with eviction from his flat (in Silesia most flats belong to the coalmine and miners receive them along with the job), he accepted the offer and left for West Germany. Mnich found much to his surprise, that the passport he received was dated September 1982, i.e. long before investigations into his case were concluded.

In his opinion the case against him and his colleagues from the Solidarity works' commission presidium was rigged. The ZOMO riot police would have attacked the Manifest Lipcowy coalmine irrespective of the behaviour of the striking miners. It was the key mine in which one of the 'social agreements' had been signed in August 1980 and a symbol that had to be destroyed to crush the morale of workers still on strike in other parts of the country. Mnich thinks of himself as a victim of secret police and local party dignitaries' vengeance. The tear gas sprayed into his eye was not an act of wanton violence but a calculated act of vengeance. Unable to obtain his conviction in a court case, the security police forced him out of the country.

The real perpetrators of violence in the Manifest Lipcowy coalmine on 15 December 1981, the ZOMO riot police who opened fire on the striking workers, have gone unpunished. An official investigation into the circumstances of this shooting was hastily discontinued barely one month after it was instituted. The military prosecutor found that the firearms had been used by a special platoon of an operational regiment consisting of 16 people who had acted without permission or instruction from their superior officers. They were all, however, found not to be liable for prosecution because of the great haste with which they had been called into action. The prosecutor's reasoning was that since the

The Trials of December 1981 Strikers

policemen had been issued with P-63 pistols in haste, it was impossible to establish which policeman had used which weapons during the action. It is clear that the prosecutor did not try particularly hard to identify the policemen guilty of the unauthorized use of firearms. He was content to accept the police version of the incident, according to which the platoon had acted in self-defence, and to put the blame squarely on the victims.

Some Other Trials

The December strikes were not, in fact, a continuation of trade union activity, but a reaction of the working people to the imposition of martial law. This view expressed by the defence lawyer Władysław Siła-Nowicki at the trial of Anna Walentynowicz was not shared by the prosecution and was not as a rule espoused by the court.

The prosecutor usually charged the most active union officials with leading the strike. Most of the defendants were tried and sentenced under summary procedure within the first few weeks of martial law. Jerzy Kuzian, Chairman of the Solidarity Enterprise Committee at the Stomil Tyre Factory in Sanok, felt personally responsible, after the military commissar refused to talk to the workers, for ensuring that the factory remained intact. He did not call for strike action but the strike broke out during his shift. The Voivodship Court in Krosno sentenced him to one year's imprisonment for strike organizing.[16]

In most cases the prosecutor would base his case on the premise that the defendants had acted as an organized group with each playing his specific part in accordance with the agreed division of labour. The defence, on the other hand, would argue that the protest action had, in fact, been spontaneous and that it was inappropriate to describe it as an organized 'strike'. They would further argue that even if a strike committee had been set up, its role was not an inspirational one but, rather, of a representative nature. The court's assessment of the degree to which the strikers had been organized sometimes differed from that of the prosecutor. At the so-called trial of the Wujek coalmine strike organizers the Court of the Silesian Military District found the prosecutor's evidence that four of the defendants had set up a Strike Committee insufficient and acquitted them of this particular charge.

The Trials of December 1981 Strikers

The dividing line between 'representing' the workforce and 'leading' it was a fluid one. Zenon Nowak and Tadeusz Pacuszka from the Institute of Nuclear Research testified during their trial in December 1981 that they had only represented their colleagues who had taken part in a spontaneous sit-in in one of the buildings. The Voivodship Court in Warsaw found, however, that they had led their colleagues in the protest action, although they had not actually organized it. They were sentenced on 28 December 1981 to two years' imprisonment each.

Agitation to strike was usually treated as strike organizing even though the strike itself may not actually have been held. Wiesław Pyzio, a member of the Solidarity enterprise committee at a machine tool factory in Andrychów, was sentenced to three years' imprisonment for calling on his fellow-workers to strike. None of them followed this call and Pyzio was, in fact, the only striker in the whole enterprise. Marek Karnicki, an executive member of the Solidarity committee at the United Construction Enterprises in Bydgoszcz was sentenced by the Voivodship Court in Bydgoszcz to one year's imprisonment for inciting one person to strike.[17]

The fact of calling a meeting of the staff was usually considered equivalent to organizing a strike. In the case of the Gdańsk Repair Shipyard strike the Naval Court in Gdynia passed sentences of seven years' imprisonment on the Chairman of the Solidarity Enterprise Committee, Wojciech Sychowski, five years each on presidium members Janusz Kucharski and Lech Chmielewski, and four on Lech Sobczak. They had called an informal meeting of the enterprise committee at which it was decided to stage a rally of all the employees of the enterprise and conduct a referendum on whether to strike or not. As a result of the referendum a 24-hour warning strike was staged on 14 December. The workers decided to continue the strike which was finally broken by the ZOMO on 16 December. The court found that,

> although the Solidarity enterprise committee had not formally announced a strike, it decidedly contributed to its staging and continuation... the very fact that they had called a meeting and taken decision in its course proved convincingly that the defendants were continuing trade union activity in breach of the Martial Law Decree... the defendants, who undoubtedly had authority their fellow-

workers, were united in supporting protest action and thereby contributed decidedly not only to the fact that a strike was proclaimed but also to its scale and duration.

Jerzy Dłużniewski from the Marchlewski Textile Works was charged with organizing a general strike in the Łódź region by duplicating *Strike Communiqué no. 1* which he himself had signed.

All these examples show that the vagueness of the martial law regulations with regard to the criteria of strike 'organizing' and 'leading' under Art. 46.2 of the Martial Law Decree gave the prosecutor a free hand in formulating charges. This, however, made the judges' task more difficult. In order to make it still more difficult for the court to be lenient the prosecutor would attempt to establish aggravating circumstances, making the strike in question appear more dangerous than it really was. The Chairman of the Inter-Factory Strike Committee of Western Pomerania, Marian Ustasiak, and ten co-defendants had, according to the indictment, 'acted in order to weaken the country's defences by disseminating information liable to weaken these defences in an appeal to all militarized enterprises in the area, in which they had urged a general occupational strike.' The court was obviously impressed since it passed sentences of up to five years' imprisonment. In the case of Stanisław Handzlik, a member of the Strike Committee in the Lenin Steelworks in Nowa Huta, the prosecutor alleged that his activity had not only 'directly threatened the country's defences' but had also caused production losses totalling 707,592,631 (sic!) złotys. He was sentenced to four years' imprisonment. A group of miners from the Ziemowit coalmine were alleged to have forced their colleagues to strike by using 'illegal threats'. They received sentences of up to seven years' imprisonment. Another frequently presented aggravating circumstance was 'ignoring the attempts of the military and administrative authorities to end the strike'.

The tactics of the defence were in the first place aimed at persuading the court to transfer the case from summary to ordinary procedure. This could happen either at the beginning of the court hearing or when sentence was pronounced.

If the prosecutor failed to convince the court that the defendant had either organized or led a strike he could still argue that the defendant was continuing trade union activity. Such an enforced modification of the charges represented an important breakthrough for the defence. Continuation of trade union activity was a far less serious offence than organizing or leading a strike or a protest action. Also, it gave the defence grounds for submitting a request to transfer the case from summary to ordinary procedure. The defence lawyer Tadeusz de Virion achieved such a victory in the trial of three workers from the FSO car plant in Warsaw: Janusz Pieńkowski, Zygmunt Kamiński and Edward Głowacki. First, the charge of organizing a strike collapsed; secondly, the case was transferred to ordinary procedure; and thirdly, the defendants were tried on the lesser charge of continuing trade union activity. De Virion's next line of defence was that only that can be 'continued' which existed previously and since the Strike Committee was not a part of pre-martial law Solidarity and had undertaken an entirely new type of activity, the defendants could not be said to have continued trade union activity. The Voivodship Court in Warsaw passed sentences of up to two years' imprisonment. Both the prosecution and the defence appealed against the sentences to the Supreme Court which ordered a re-trial. In February 1982 the Voivodship Court in Warsaw suspended the sentences.

The Court of the Silesian Military District hearing the case of four defendants from the Lubin copper mine, Stanisław Chmielewski, Mirosław Demczuk, Edmund Wojewodzic and Jerzy Lipiński, was even more 'lenient'. The four had been accused of organizing and leading a strike between 14 and 15 December 1981. The court found them guilty merely of participating in a strike, a petty offence carrying, under Art. 50.1 of the Martial Law Decree, a maximum penalty of three months' imprisonment.[18]

If the court chose to dismiss the request to transfer the case to ordinary procedure, the defence would concentrate on ensuring that the vague martial law provisions were interpreted by the court in the manner most advantageous to the defendants. Some defence lawyers saw the trials in a wider historical and social perspective. They emphasized that political trials have been a consistent feature of Poland's post-war history or stressed that a conviction would alienate the public and cause widespread bitterness.

Among the witnesses during the martial law trials there was a clear division between those who testified in their official capacity (as directors, party activists, army officers) and the others who were mostly fellow-workers of the defendants. In some cases the 'official' witness testified on behalf of the defendants. Henryk

The Trials of December 1981 Strikers

Wilk, the Managing Director of the Ursus tractor factory, said that despite difficulties it had always been possible to find common ground with the Solidarity union in his enterprise. A similar opinion was expressed by the Gdańsk Port Authority Director, Płoski, and the Director of the Warsaw Steelworks, Żurek. All three were dismissed soon after the introduction of martial law. A PUWP departmental secretary at the Warsaw Steelworks, on the other hand, had no qualms about citing in his testimony reports and denunciations which had reached the PUWP factory organization in order to incriminate the local Solidarity leader Karol Szadurski.[19]

In passing sentence the court should have taken into consideration the duration of the strike, whether it was discontinued voluntarily or as a result of the intervention of the security forces, whether the strike had broken out in a key enterprise or in a small firm, whether the defendants had appealed for calm or had fuelled the strike atmosphere. The trial was not, however, always a fair one. The Naval Court in Gdynia became notorious for its intransigence and severity. In the case of the Hartwig international shipping enterprise, the Naval Court heard the case and passed sentences of up to seven years' imprisonment during one single session lasting from 9 a.m. till 5 p.m. The same court, hearing the case of the Maritime Academy strikers, did not allow the defendants to make final statements. Władysław Trzciński's defence lawyer was told to be brief in his summation.

Although the martial law trials, with a few exceptions, were formally open to the public, access was, in fact, restricted and — in politically sensitive trials — strictly controlled. A special pass was required to gain entry to the courtroom. These passes were issued by the chairman of the court. In Gdańsk passes to the courtroom in which the Lenin Shipyard strikers were being tried were issued only after special applications had been made. As a rule passes were only issued to the members of the immediate family of the defendant and, in some cases, to selected journalists. Plainclothes policemen did not require passes. In some cases even family members had restricted access. During some of the trials the police surrounded the court building and checked handbags, sometimes several times. Władysław Trzciński's 20-year-old daughter Hanka was taken away from the courthouse steps by the police after they had strip-searched her and cut open her shoes, because they were looking, as they said, for illegal publications.[20] Those who gathered outside the courthouse would sometimes have their identity papers checked, they were photographed, detained for several hours, and even tried before the local petty offences tribunal for causing an 'illegal gathering'. Occasionally special precautions were taken to prevent protests against sensitive trials. The management of the Gdańsk Port Authority, for instance, cancelled all leave to make it impossible for the workers to attend the trial of Stanisław Jarosz and Leszek Świtek.

In the cases of the strikers of December 1981 the courts acted swiftly and arbitrarily, passing severe sentences of up to ten years' imprisonment. What mattered was political expediency — Solidarity was to be finally deprived of its strike weapon. Any doubts were interpreted by the Supreme Court in accordance with the political tasks the authorities set out to achieve. The trials created much resentment and bitterness among the general public. It was not the political prisoner who was discredited by being given a severe sentence but a law which showed in practice that it was the very antithesis of individual freedoms.

The trial of Anna Walentynowicz

Lech Wałęsa, speaking in March 1983 outside the courtroom in Grudziądz, described Anna Walentynowicz as a symbol of the Polish workers' struggle and her trials as a political defeat for the authorities. The personal experience of Anna Walentynowicz reflects the transformation of consciousness of the Polish workers. Like the majority of Polish workers, she is of peasant origin, typical of a first generation working class that moved from the countryside to towns. Conscious of her working-class identity she has retained the Polish peasant's deep devotion to the Catholic faith. In the 1950s she was an idealist, a model worker producing up to 270 per cent of the norm and winning the title of a 'Stakhanovite'.

She gradually became disillusioned with the official façade of a workers' state. She discovered officialdom to be corrupt and inefficient. At first, in the 1960s, she campaigned, within the bounds of the official trade union movement, against individual cases of abuse, in particular embezzlement of public funds by union officials. In December 1970 during the strike in Gdańsk Lenin Shipyard she helped in the kitchens. In the late 1970s

The Trials of December 1981 Strikers

Walentynowicz heard for the first time about the free trade union movement. She supported the idea, realizing that if the Polish workers had their independent unions they would not be so defenceless in the face of management. Only a few years earlier she had still been willing to grant the then party chief Edward Gierek the benefit of the doubt pledging 'we will help you' in January 1971 when he met with the workers' delegates. Her involvement with the free trade union movement resulted in a whole series of detentions, searches, disciplinary punishments and other forms of harassment. It was her dismissal from the shipyard on 8 August 1980, after 30 years of employment with only five months to go before retirement that sparked off the strike which led ultimately to the signing of the Gdańsk Agreement on 31 August 1981.

Walentynowicz is an inconspicuous, modest and sturdy woman. Following her recovery from cancer she decided to devote her life to some good cause. She found her cause first in the free trade union movement and, after her release from internment after the introduction of martial law, in the struggle for the release of political prisoners. Her simplicity, honesty, innate desire for justice, passionate nature and habit of setting a personal example without calculating the chances of success have left her open to charges of 'radicalism' and 'mental instability'. Her actions, however, belie these charges. She fights the system on moral grounds as a system breeding injustice, hardship, evil and abuse. Her uncompromising attitude to evil earned her the nicknames 'Woman of Iron' and the 'Pasionaria of Gdańsk'.

On 13 December 1981 Anna Walentynowicz was in Częstochowa and was not interned. On learning of the introduction of martial law she returned to Gdańsk where she joined the occupation strike at the shipyard. This was broken by the security forces on 16 December. She was taken first to the Gdańsk police station and later to Fordon women's prison where she was served an order of internment for allegedly 'undertaking actions whose effect was to bring about anarchy in the life of the people of the Gdańsk voivodship'. On 8 January 1982 she was moved from Fordon to Gołdap from where she was released on 24 July 1982 when internment for women was officially discontinued. She reported to the shipyard on her release, but was not allowed to resume work. She was offered pay without work. After three weeks' holiday she went to Częstochowa where she participated in religious celebrations. On 25 August, together with

The Trials of December 1981 Strikers

15 other people in St Barbara's church in Częstochowa, Walentynowicz began a hunger strike on behalf of political prisoners and in the intention of the Pope's second pilgrimage to Poland. Since the local priest refused his permission to continue the hunger strike, the group left the church after three days and seven people accompanied Anna Walentynowicz to Gdańsk. They decided to continue the hunger strike at her flat. The police raided the flat on 30 August 1982 and detained all those present.

Almost immediately after her detention Walentynowicz was placed under arrest. The Gdańsk Prosecutor's Office suddenly remembered an investigation against her in connection with her presence and activity in the Lenin Shipyard between 14 and 16 December 1981. This investigation was obviously being conducted in secret since Anna Walentynowicz had neither been questioned nor formally presented with charges. The investigation had lain dormant from February 1982 until her arrest. The prosecutor's office had failed to gather any new evidence, with one notable exception: an item based on a Radio Free Europe broadcast on 30 July 1982. The arrest of Anna Walentynowicz was not, therefore, a consequence of the investigation against her, but a preliminary step so that a case against her could be concocted. The arrest was clearly used not as a 'preventative' but a repressive measure. There was no reason why she should not have been arrested earlier, for example, during her internment. The investigation was, moreover, conducted under summary procedure which was inadmissible since the offence with which she was charged had taken place more than eight months before she was arrested. In keeping with Articles 255 and 256.2 of the Code of Criminal Procedure, the authorities should have opened an investigation under summary procedure immediately after they learned of the offence; after so much time had elapsed they no longer had the right to do so.

On 9 September 1982 Roman Mirecki, the prosecutor conducting the investigation, requested a psychiatric opinion in order to establish whether Walentynowicz had been in full control of her mental faculties at the time of committing the offence with which she was charged. Two psychiatrists recommended that she be sent for further hospital examination. The prosecutor had her sent to the Psychiatric Ward of the Central Prison Hospital which is situated within the Rakowiecka investigative prison in Warsaw. Walentynowicz was held there from 21 September to 26 October 1982. She lodged a complaint with the regional court in Gdańsk

The Trials of December 1981 Strikers

against the prosecutor's decision to subject her to psychiatric observation but the complaint was dismissed. From Warsaw, Walentynowicz was not moved back to Gdańsk but to Grudziądz. It was only then, i.e. almost two months after her detention, that summary procedure was lifted. This constituted a blatant violation of the existing regulations which require that investigations conducted under summary procedure must be completed within 15 days or, in exceptional circumstances, within 30 days.

The investigation, now conducted under ordinary procedure, continued to drag. After it entered into its fourth month Walentynowicz was dismissed from her job. No witnesses were called after 6 February 1983 (as evidenced by the dates on the prosecutor's records of investigation).[21] Anna Walentynowicz herself was not questioned until 1 December 1982, when she met the prosecutor who filled out the final sheet concluding the investigation, and brought the files in the case for her to read. The act of indictment was compiled on 6 December. Even then the court rejected her defence lawyer's requests that she be released from prison pending trial. At the same time the regional court in Gdańsk which was to hear the case asked the Supreme Court to transfer the case to a court in Toruń or Grudziądz on the grounds 'that the defendant, as an active member of Solidarity, had made contact with judges and court employees at meetings and, above all, that the inhabitants of Gdańsk might be emotionally involved in the case which would make it more difficult for the court to consider it'. The Supreme Court approved the request and transferred the case to Grudziądz.

The indictment against Anna Walentynowicz differed little from the prosecutor's arrest order which she was served while under arrest on 1 September 1982. She was accused of continuing trade union activity and organizing protest action against martial law on the premises of the Gdańsk Shipyard on 14 and 15 December 1981; inciting workers to remain on shipyard premises despite orders to the contrary from the security forces; and urging the chief of the shipyard fire brigade to put the fire engines, which were equipped with water cannon, at the disposal of the strikers so that they could be used against the riot policemen (i.e. offences under Art. 46.1 and 2 of the Martial Law Decree and Art. 18.1 of the Penal Code, in conjunction with Art. 46.4 of the Martial Law Decree).

The indictment was based on the testimony of firemen who testified in the course of the investigation that Walentynowicz had

The Trials of December 1981 Strikers

made two speeches to the strikers and had come, with other unidentified persons, to the office of the shipyard fire brigade and demanded that the water cannon be handed over to her. The prosecution also managed to compile, as further incriminating 'evidence', two transcripts of Radio Free Europe broadcasts, and a copy with a translation of an article on Anna Walentynowicz that appeared in *Stern* magazine. The use of journalistic material which was not even written by eye-witnesses, and should not have been allowed as evidence, was inadmissible. 'It is a paradoxical situation', said defence lawyer Anna Skowrońska, 'that in the course of a criminal trial where the rules concerning presentation of credible evidence are particularly tight, a representative of the prosecutor's office quotes [as evidence] transcripts monitored from a radio station which is assessed by the official propaganda as mendacious and subversive'. The prosecutor also presented as evidence the report of an unidentified security policeman who had allegedly witnessed Anna Walentynowicz speaking on 15 December 1981 and heard her say to the ZOMO, 'Go on, shoot at the heart of a Polish Mother!' The court did not, however, call the author of this report to the witness stand. One further piece of evidence was a letter from the regional censorship office in Gdańsk, presumably referring to various Solidarity souvenirs seized by the police who had carried out a search in Walentynowicz's flat on 30 August 1982.

The trial opened on 9 March 1983. As usual not all those wishing to be present during the hearing managed to obtain the required pass. There were some hundred people inside the courtroom and as many waiting outside. The managements of state enterprises in Grudziądz and Toruń put a ban on time off for the duration of the trial.

The majority of witnesses testifying before the court could no longer remember the details of what had happened in the shipyard on 14 and 15 December 1981. None of the firemen could confirm that the defendant had insisted that the fire engines be directed at the shipyard gate until they were confronted by the court with the testimonies they had given in the course of the investigation. Only one witness, Ryszard Turowiecki, was able without prompting to reproduce his former testimony. He testified that the defendant had, on 15 December, spoken from the roof of a gate-keepers' lodge and urged the shipyard workers to continue their strike action. He remembered that the defendant had put her hand on her heart and unbuttoned her coat, but he could not remember anything of what she had said. The court was apparently not concerned with establishing whether Turowiecki's testimony corroborated the above-mentioned security policeman's report about shooting at the heart of a Polish mother. Another witness, Stanisław Kowalewski, remembered, for his part, what the defendant had said in her speech to the strikers on 14 December: 'The more numerous we are, the stronger we will be; we will be able to show our strength and we will not be overcome.' In the indictment these words were interpreted as constituting a call on the workers to resist the riot policemen, as well as organization of the protest action. Kowalewski did not actually see the defendant uttering these words. He did not know her personally and only recognized her by her voice since he was familiar with other of her speeches. His testimony was not confirmed by any other witness. The Reverend Henryk Jankowski testified that since the amplifying equipment had been poor it was hard to recognize individual voices. He added that the microphones and amplifying equipment outside gate 2 had been accessible to the general public and that anyone who wished to speak could do so. The simple fact of addressing the people over the microphone did not imply that the speaker was organizing or leading a strike. Another defence witness, Alojzy Szablewski, the Chairman of the Strike Committee at the shipyard, said that Walentynowicz was not a member of the Committee and that he did not issue any instructions to her. She had arrived at the shipyard when the strike was already in progress.

The prosecutor attempted to establish what possible injuries a stream of water from the water cannon might have caused to the riot policemen. Since the water cannon was not used at all, Anna Walentynowicz was tried for something that never happened.

Two of the defence lawyers, Anna Skowrońska and Władysław Siła-Nowicki, stressed that on the strength of the available evidence the defendant could only be charged with a petty offence under Art. 50.1 of the Martial Law Decree, i.e. participating in a strike, and that she could no longer be prosecuted for such a petty offence because more than a year had passed since it had been committed. Anna Skowrońska found the charge of 'continuing trade union activity' (Art. 46.1) unfounded. She said, 'an individual's activity may be described as "union activity" only when it falls within the statutory objectives of the union organization in question. Union activity cannot be undertaken by an individual other than within the framework of the union organization. There is no proof that the defendant did, indeed, undertake such activity.' Skowrońska reiterated that there had been no insistence on the part of the defendant that the fire engines equipped with water cannon be handed over to her and that the charge of inciting the head of the shipyard fire brigade and his subordinates to disobedience was false. Even if the defendant really had said the words ascribed to her by Kowalewski, Skowrońska argued, they still did not prove that she was organizing a protest action. They were only a cry of despair for which she could bear no criminal liability.

Defence lawyer Jacek Taylor drew attention to the abuses of the Code of Criminal Procedure (unjustified application and extension of summary procedure) as well as to the political nature of the charges brought against Anna Walentynowicz.

On 30 March 1983 the court pronounced Anna Walentynowicz guilty of all three charges and sentenced her to 15 months' imprisonment as well as a fine of 15,000 zloty. The sentence was suspended for three years. The court gave credence to the testimonies of all the prosecution witnesses and interpreted them to the detriment of the defendant. The court took no account of what the witnesses had said in the courtroom to the advantage of the defendant. The substantiation of the sentence amounted, in fact, to an expansion of the indictment. The court did not find any of the defence arguments justified, and they were not perturbed by the procedural irregularities of the investigation. In their concluding remarks the court even slipped into the jargon of propaganda, expounding on 'the path to national rebirth'.

The sentence of the Regional Court in Grudziądz was appealed by both the prosecution and the defence. The defence claimed that the court in their findings had gone beyond the testimony of the witnesses and made inadmissible value judgements, thinly disguised as a reconstruction of the events. The prosecutor, for his part, left no doubt as to what Anna Walentynowicz had really been tried for. He presented a new allegation: 'In determining the penalty of imprisonment [much too low, in his opinion], the court did not consider, and did not deliberate in its substantiation, the evidence concerning Anna Walentynowicz's involvement in activities violating the legal and public order at the time of the offence as well as after it was committed, during her subsequent internment and after her release from internment.' According to the prosecutor, Anna Walentynowicz should have been punished

The Trials of December 1981 Strikers

more severely for offences allegedly committed in the first days of martial law on account of her activities during internment and after it. Needless to say, the activities referred to by the prosecutor were not covered in his indictment. The appeal hearing never took place and Walentynowicz's case was covered by the amnesty of July 1983.

The sentence as such was a success for independent public opinion in the sense that Walentynowicz was released from prison the very day it was announced. Whether it was also a political defeat for the authorities, as Lech Wałęsa claimed, is open to discussion. The prosecution, acting in collusion with the political authorities, carried out their instructions, openly violating substantive law, procedural law and even martial law, to harass Anna Walentynowicz, isolate her and make her out to be a person of unsound mind. The court not only failed to bring the prosecutor to order but actively supported him. Thus, from the authorities' point of view, the aim of the trial was achieved: a potential trouble-maker was locked behind bars at a time when Solidarity was being disbanded and martial law 'suspended'. An amnesty which could not be turned down did not afford Anna Walentynowicz the opportunity to clear her name in the appeals court. The authorities came to square accounts with a woman who was quite clearly a symbolic figure. In December 1983, only nine months after she was released, she was once again arrested, charged and tried on a charge of undertaking activities liable to cause public unrest (see Chapter VI / 5). These two trials against Anna Walentynowicz show that there were no 'untouchables' among Solidarity and that the authorities were determined to crush symbols and myths in the same way that they crushed the mass of strikers who tried actively to defend their union. In this sense, Wałęsa was wrong. For the Polish judiciary it would, of course, have been much better had he been right.

* * *

The trial of Anna Walentynowicz is not the only one in which the personal popularity of the defendant among the workers served as an aggravating circumstance. It is also by no means unusual that persons tried for their role in the strikes of December 1981 were sentenced for an activity which had had no negative consequences from the authorities' point of view or had even had positive consequences (such as the protection of public property, eliminating militant tendencies among the strikers, or attempting to bring about the end of the strike through a negotiated settlement). It was understandable and predictable that on hearing about the 'suspension' of their union the workers would want to get together to discuss the situation. Where else could they be together if not in their workplace? It was also natural that they should demand the release of their interned leaders who had mandates to represent them. One of the strikers put it in a nutshell when he stated in the courtroom, 'when war breaks out one defends one's property against the enemy.'

The strikes of December 1981, on account of their character, should more properly be called protest actions. Those who participated in them, in whatever capacities, proved their responsibility not only to their fellow-workers but also to their country as a whole.

What the workers did in the course of their protest actions did not fit the criteria of criminal liability, even as defined in the Martial Law Decree. They were sentenced in violation even of the emergency law the authorities had themselves imposed.

Notes

1. Tadeusz Kowalski, Wacław Majewski, Magdalena Nowakowa, Irmina Piekarska and Artur Sokołowski, 'Five months of suspended martial law in the Małopolska Region', Kraków, May 1983.
2. S. Zawadzki and Z. Jarosz, *Prawo Konstytucyjne* (PWN, Warsaw, 1980), p. 370.
3. *Państwo i Prawo*, September 1982.
4. *Tygodnik Mazowsze* no. 27, 22 September 1982.
5. *Państwo i Prawo*, September 1982.
6. *Palestra* no. 1, 1984.
7. In this case, involving Janusz Pieńkowski, Zygmunt Kamiński and Edward Głowacki, the Voivodship Court in Warsaw sentenced all the defendants to two years' imprisonment. The sentence which was passed under ordinary procedure was appealed to the Supreme Court which ordered re-trial. On 23 February 1982 the defendants received one year's suspended sentences.
8. See Krystyna Daszkiewicz, *Palestra* no. 6-7, 1982.
9. *Państwo i Prawo*, March 1983.
10. Ibid.
11. *Tygodnik Mazowsze* no. 17, 9 June 1982 and *Palestra* no. 1, 1984.
12. *Palestra* no. 1, 1984.
13. A Report by the Clandestine Solidarity Commission in the Gdańsk Port for the period 13 December 1981 — 22 July 1983.

14. *Trybuna Ludu*, 15–16 May 1982.
15. John Darnton, *New York Times*, 6 February 1982.
16. *Fakty* no. 4/5, 1982.
17. Ibid. The sentence was upheld by the Supreme Court on 10 May 1982.
18. *Informacja Solidarności (region Mazowsze)* no. 42, 23 April 1982.
19. *Tygodnik Mazowsze*, nos. 43 and 44, 3 and 10 March 1983, respectively.
20. John Darnton, *New York Times*, 2 February 1982.
21. Jan Prisoner, 'The trial of Anna Walentynowicz' (in Polish), undated manuscript.

III

THE TRIALS OF THE INTERNEES

The practice of internment, oppressive as it was, proved insufficient to break the independent spirit of many Solidarity activists and advisers. A spirit of defiance, born of the certainty that right was morally on their side and fed on the news from outside, mobilised many of the internees to refuse to be subjugated by organizing their time in captivity themselves, turning it to good and common purpose, and consistently demonstrating their independence and solidarity with one another. The authorities retaliated against those who particularly roused their anger and whom they wished to punish by bringing charges against them, placing them formally under arrest and transferring them from internment prisons to prisons proper.

In the case of those with whom the authorities had various old scores to settle the charges brought against them were based on their activities prior to internment. Their trials are discussed elsewhere. In the remaining cases the charges resulted directly from the suspects' attitudes and behaviour in internment. They were for instance charged with and sentenced for 'preparing and possessing, with the aim of distribution, poems, letters and other rhymed verses ... that could seriously harm the political interests of the PPR' (the case of Julian Antończyk, interned in Załęże); 'disseminating false information in a letter addressed to his fellow-internees' (the case of Jerzy Stępień, Łupkowo); 'continuing union activity by issuing honorary Solidarity membership cards' (the case of Krzysztof Goławski, Włodawa) or 'singing songs of anti-state and anti-socialist content' (the case of Bogusław Klich and three others, Załęże).

The Trials of the Internees

'Slandering' the authorities

All these charges were brought under the single most frequently applied provision of the Penal Code, Art. 270.1 which penalizes 'public slander, derision and denigration of the Polish nation, the PPR, its socio-political system or supreme authorities'. Its broad interpretation enabled the prosecution to lump together such diverse actions as passing messages outside the internment prison, criticizing the rigours of martial law in letters to the authorities, or singing songs in order to keep one's spirits up. The wording of the offence stipulated under Art. 270.1 requires that the slander be made in public. In the case of four internees from Załęże, Bogusław Klich, Krzysztof Krzysztofiak, Zbigniew Solak and Jerzy Piekarski, which was heard by the Warsaw Military District Court in Rzeszów, the prosecutor argued that a prison cell was a public place. The defendants emphasized that their cell door was locked and the song they sang could not have been heard outside the prison compound. They added that they had sung in order to pass the time and not to slander the authorities, and that the guitar on which they were accompanying themselves had been given to them by one of the guards. The defence lawyers said that the song in question, 'The Anthem of the Interned Extremists' did not, in fact, slander the supreme authorities of the PPR but only the Military Council of National Salvation — WRON — which was not, according to the PPR Constitution, a supreme state authority. The court in its sentence of 7 October 1982 found that only three of the four defendants had actually sung and that a prison cell was not a public place. All the defendants were acquitted.

In another case involving songs composed by internees, Julian Antończyk from the same Załęże internment prison was sentenced to four years' imprisonment. Antończyk had given his wife the texts of satirical couplets composed and sung by internees when she came to visit him in Załęże. During a subsequent search of their home the police seized the texts and Antończyk was charged with and found guilty of the distribution of satirical couplets which 'could seriously damage the political interests of the PPR'.[1]

Several internees were brought to trial on charges of offending prison guards. The real reason for the 'offence' might, for instance, have been the fact of lodging a complaint with the authorities against a guard who had beaten the internee. This was the case of A. Michalak from the Łowicz internment prison. Michalak had complained to the Ministry of Justice about an incident in January 1982 in which he had been beaten by prison guards. Shortly afterwards, proceedings were instituted against him by the prosecutor's office on the grounds that he had behaved in an offensive manner. Subsequently Michalak was presented with an offer of a deal — the trial would not take place if he were to withdraw his complaint.[2]

Where no better grounds for conviction could be found, internees were charged retroactively with having organized or participated in strikes against the imposition of martial law in December 1981. The Solidarity chairman from the Mining Data Information Centre (COIG) in Katowice, Krystian Konik, had gone into hiding after the declaration of martial law. He was caught and interned in April 1982. Anticipating the closure of internment prisons and preferring to keep Konik inside, the authorities had him formally arrested at the end of November 1982 and charged him with organizing a strike in December 1981. In March 1983 he was released from prison on health grounds. He was re-arrested one month later following a search in his flat under the new charge of appropriating funds belonging to Solidarity. In fact, the money which he had allegedly misused was part of a strike fund that was subsequently used to help colleagues who had been imprisoned or sacked from their jobs for their activities in Solidarity. In October 1983 the Voivodship Court in Katowice acquitted him of this charge but found him guilty of continuing trade union activity, but since this offence was covered by the July 1983 amnesty, he was released. In February 1984, the Minister of Justice asked for and obtained an extraordinary review of the case. The Supreme Court ordered a re-trial of Konik. During the trial a debate ensued between the defence lawyer and the prosecutor as to the legal character of the strike fund. The prosecutor alleged that the strike fund was, in fact, public property; the defence denied this, arguing that the fund had not been set up in accordance with any Solidarity statutes.[3] In November 1984 the Voivodship Court in Katowice upheld the earlier finding and Konik was again acquitted. None the less, he spent some 20 months in prison before he saw justice.

Those who were interned towards the end of 1982 in penal military camps and subjected to military discipline were liable for court martial in the same way as soldiers on active duty. Four internees from the Czerwony Bór military unit no. 3466, Tadeusz

The Trials of the Internees

Balina, Bronisław Kuczer, Józef Bełczewski and Jerzy Las, were tried under Art. 305 of the Military Penal Code for refusing to eat their meal. They were charged with 'failure to carry out a duty resulting from military service'. The alleged 'offence' occurred on 10 November 1982, the day of the ill-fated general strike announced by the Solidarity leadership in protest against the disbandment of the union. According to the indictment, some of the soldiers refused to take their meals while others, who had taken their meals, refused to eat them. The meal was described as 'tasty and in accordance with standards provided for soldiers'. Four internees were singled out for exemplary punishment. They were all arrested and the case was to be heard under summary procedure before the Court of the Warsaw Military District in Białystok. The defendants said that they did not feel hungry since they had eaten in between meals; that they were suffering from various intestinal disorders; and that by failing to consume their lunch they had not intended to demonstrate against anything in particular. Some of them presented medical evidence relating to their intestinal disorders. The court found the defendants' testimony credible and concluded that they had not acted in agreement since they had not known each other before the event, and had not sat together during lunch. Referring to the regulation concerning soldiers on active duty, the court concluded that their basic duty was to observe the programme of the day and that the defendants had not infringed this programme in any way. The court added that there were no provisions to determine physiological matters such as eating meals and that soldiers were not obliged to eat all of their meals. The defendants were acquitted, much to the surprise of their superiors.

The Kwidzyń case

Not one of the cases brought against prison guards for unjustified use of force against internees has been successful. The case of the severely beaten Kwidzyń internees who were made out to be the aggressors and sentenced to penalties of imprisonment is one of the most ignoble episodes of martial law. The roots of the events of 14 August 1982 that led to the pacification of the prison and subsequent trial of some of its victims can be traced to the specific atmosphere that prevailed in the Kwidzyń internment prison. The internees, numbering 148 persons in mid-August, enjoyed privileges denied to inmates held elsewhere. According to Konrad Tatarowski, who was imprisoned in Kwidzyń at the time of the pacification: 'this discrepancy between our de facto imprisonment and the considerable freedoms we enjoyed helped to blur the awareness of some of the internees that here in prison the authorities could make many concessions, even though they were not envisaged in prison regulations, and that they could just as easily withdraw them'.[4]

On 14 August 1982 some of the internees at the Kwidzyń internment prison staged a peaceful protest against the sudden suspension of family visits by the newly-appointed governor. Only six of the families had been allowed in to the prison compound, while the families of some 30 other internees were forced to wait for many hours in the rain outside the prison gate. Many had come long distances. About 100 internees gathered round the fencing dividing the prison courtyard from the administrative buildings, chanting 'let our families in' and making a great noise by banging on metal plates. Some 20 protesters went through a hole in the fencing and sat down on the other side, while others climbed on to the roof of one of the buildings to observe what was going on. Detachments of the ZOMO riot police arrived and removed the families gathered outside the gate, to the resentment of the internees. They became even more disturbed when they learned that a three-man delegation which had tried to persuade the governor to allow the families in had been turned away empty-handed. None the less, their protest was peaceful and although some of them were on the prohibited area outside the fencing they did not provoke the guards who were facing them in full riot gear in any way.

Without any warning, the prison guards started to spray the internees with water from a water pump and proceeded forcibly to disperse them. The guards were reinforced with detachments of the riot police brought in from Sztum and Iława. The internees offered no resistance and only attempted to shield themselves from the stream of water with the help of the stools and tables which they had taken from their cells in anticipation of their family visits. As they retreated to their cells, the internees attempted to barricade the entrance between the two barracks with tables to delay pursuit. This pitiful barricade was no obstacle for the guards with their water pumps. They caught up with the internees in their cells and began 'pacification' even as the internees, drenched and defenceless, were changing clothes in their cells. They were systematically beaten in the cells and some of them were singled out for particularly brutal beating on the corridor where they were forced to 'run the gauntlet'. Altogether 81 internees were beaten, 38 of them severely; 20 required hospitalization. Later in the evening the guards carried out a thorough search of the cells. The personal belongings of the internees were damaged or confiscated. On that same day some of the internees began a hunger strike in support of their demand that the prison's governor be recalled; that the incident be investigated; that those responsible for the pacification be punished; and that the former regulations be restored. The governor responded by ordering personal searches and locking the internees in their cells and not allowing them to communicate.

On the day of the pacification only four internees (including two who were unconscious) were actually taken to hospital. Others were only given a cursory medical check-up. Some of those who had been most severely beaten were not sent to hospital until a few days had passed, as a result of intervention by a delegation of the International Red Cross, whose visit had been arranged before the incident. The prison governor successfully exerted pressure on the medical personnel not to reveal the real extent of the beaten internees' injuries and to discharge those hospitalized as soon as possible.

After the incident of 14 August 1982 the prison officials attempted to isolate the internees from the outside world. Family visits were shortened, Bishop Jan Obłąk of Warmia and the medical team appointed by the Episcopate were not admitted to the prison. It was none the less some time later that the victims were examined by Dr Zofia Kuratowska, one of Poland's leading haematologists and an expert adviser to the Primate's Committee on Aid to Prisoners and their Families. Kuratowska's report, which contained details of the injuries sustained by the internees, could not be hushed up. She herself became the object of a campaign of harassment and her specialist clinic was ultimately closed down.

The Garrison Military Prosecutor's Office in Elbląg announced that investigations into the case would be opened. Those internees who had begun a hunger strike discontinued their protest. The investigation was from the start conducted on the premise that the case involved two separate incidents: an alleged assault on the prison guards by the internees and a retaliatory

The Trials of the Internees

beating of the internees by the prison guards. The former case was entrusted to the voivodship prosecutor's office, while the latter was dealt with by the Garrison Military Prosecutor's Office. The investigation carried out by the civil prosecutor's office was supervised by the Elbląg Voivodship Prosecutor Antoni Dykowski, the protégé and former deputy of Józef Żyta, who was at the time Deputy Prosecutor General.[5] The course of the investigation must have been agreed with the office of the Prosecutor General, whose representatives questioned the internees. It is, moreover, inconceivable that the internees could have been arrested without the consent of Colonel Wincenty Romanowski, who was General Kiszczak's plenipotentiary in charge of internees at the Ministry of Internal Affairs. Indeed, the Investigations Bureau of the Ministry co-ordinated the investigation.

On 6 September 1982 eight of the internees were taken from the Kwidzyń internment prison to the investigative prison in Elbląg and charged with assaulting the guards. They were: Andrzej Goławski (spine damage), Andrzej Bober, Zygmunt Goławski (kidney damage, concussion), Władysław Kałudziński (over 75 per cent loss of sight), Adam Kozaczyński, Mirosław Duszak (coma), Włodzimierz Przybyłka and Stanisław Żygliński. The proceedings against the last two were later discontinued. Another internee Radosław Sarnicki was also included in the proceedings but not placed under arrest on account of his health.

In his speech before the court Zygmunt Goławski described how the investigation was conducted.

> I was taken to the office of the Elbląg voivodship prosecutor who charged me with assaulting a prison guard and building a barricade. After a while the prosecutor called in Gutowski (a prison guard) and asked him what he knew about my participation in the incidents of 14 August. Gutowski said that he had seen me in the yard near the fence. The prosecutor asked him whether I was singing as well. Gutowski replied that various songs had been sung. The prosecutor asked: 'and was Goławski singing?' I asked Gutowski how he could have seen this. He did not reply. Then the prosecutor asked him whether I had built the barricade. Gutowski replied that I had been carrying tables and stools from which the barricade had been built. I said that he could not possibly have seen this because he had been sitting in the guard room the whole time, and the lower

The Trials of the Internees

halves of the guard room windows were painted over; furthermore, Gutowski is small in stature and even I could not have seen what he claimed he had seen. Gutowski did not reply. Then the prosecutor said (to Gutowski) 'you can go', and read me the legal provision under which I was charged.

The indictment against six of the internees was based on the testimony of the prison guards, the alleged victims of the assault. The indictment did not quote any evidence that would have pointed to the fact that any of the prison guards had suffered injuries at the hands of the internees. The evidence quoted in the indictment mentioned that 11 knives had been confiscated from the internees during a search of the cells. There was nothing to incriminate the internees in this circumstance since up to 14 August 1982 there had been no regulations forbidding their possession by the internees. The indictment was, in fact, based on two major distortions of the real course of events. First, it assumed that the internees had organized a protest action and were not, as was in fact the case, acting in self-defence and offering only passive resistance. Secondly, it claimed that the internees had assaulted the guards. To prevent these theses of the indictment from being discredited, all the evidence relating to the beating of the internees, i.e. the testimonies of the beaten internees who should have been the prime defence witnesses, was excluded from the case and passed on to the Garrison Military Prosecutor's Office in Elbląg which was supposedly looking into the case against the prison guards.

Some three weeks before the trumped-up trial of the six internees this same office formally discontinued the investigation against the guards on the grounds that there was 'insufficient evidence that an offence had been committed'. In its report on the reasons for such a decision the Garrison Military Prosecutor's Office absolved the prison governor Captain Juliusz Pobłocki of responsibility by stating, 'it must be understood that he ordered the suppression of the protest action in the name of restoring peace. He had given instructions to the officers who, he assumed, would carry them out in the proper way.' The Garrison Military Prosecutor's Office refused the defence lawyers access to the proceedings. Piotr Andrzejewski, defence lawyer for Jan Łodyga, was not only refused admission but also made to face disciplinary charges shortly after the trial began for 'abusing the freedom of speech'.

The Trials of the Internees

The trial of the six internees opened on 10 March 1983 before the Elbląg Voivodship Court with Judge Alfons Wierzbicki presiding. This former employee of the UB (Stalinist security service) in Poznań had acquired some knowledge of law by attending a special accelerated course. Although he had no degree in law, he was appointed a plenipotentiary judge and it was in this capacity that he supervised the internment of the internees in Kwidzyń.[6] The defence presented a motion excluding him from the case, but it was turned down by both the Chairman of the Voivodship Court in Elbląg, Eugeniusz Walania, and the Supreme Court. Walania is said to have been one of the organizers of the trial; he had assigned the case to Wierzbicki and he followed the course of the proceedings which were broadcast directly to his office. This breach of procedural law was discovered by one of the defence lawyers and was entered in the records of the case.[7]

The atmosphere of the trial was tense. The courthouse resembled a fortress. The public needed as many as three passes to enter the courtroom. During the hearing of 31 March 1983 Lech Wałęsa was not admitted and the chairman of the court was not available to issue a pass. Members of the party apparatus and the police who were present in the courtroom behaved in an aggressive manner.

There was no doubt as to which side the presiding judge Wierzbicki supported. He dismissed the motions of the defence, admonishing them curtly and overruling the questions they put to the prison guards, thereby making it difficult, if not impossible, for them to prove their points. In particular, the defence attempted to prove that the indictment had been based on a false interpretation of what had actually happened, that the pacification of the internment prison had been planned in advance and had been preceded by an organized provocation, and that the evidence quoted in the indictment had been falsified.

Faced with a hostile judge, the defence drew attention to inconsistencies in the testimonies of the prosecution's witnesses, to the lack of evidence that the internees had attacked the guards and to the grave damage to their health that they had suffered as a result of the beating. Defence lawyer Jerzy Woźniak noted that the records concerning the use of force by the prison guards had been falsified by the prosecution conducting the investigation into the case. This fact was admitted in the courtroom by two of the prison guards, Brzezicki and Jórkiewicz, who had signed

The Trials of the Internees

the records in the knowledge that they were not bona fide. Another defence lawyer, Jacek Taylor, said that the testimony of the prison governor, Pobłocki, alleging that the pacification of the prison had not been planned in advance, lacked credibility. Taylor said that Pobłocki, must have called in police reinforcements from Sztum and Iława before he agreed to see the three-man delegation of the internees.

The court did not ask the prosecution witnesses to elucidate these inconsistencies of the indictment, and allowed them instead to describe at length the dirty state of the internees and their lack of discipline. The prison guards' version of the indictment was contrary to what had really happened: they claimed only to have pushed the internees into their cells with the help of their shields (and not truncheons); to have encountered a hail of mess bowls, stools and bottles; to have slipped on the floor polish the internees had spilt on the floor; and to have had to force a barricade.

The defendants, for their part, gave a detailed description of the pacification of the internment prison. Zygmunt Goławski described the provocation which preceded the pacification:

> I could not understand why they [the guards] were letting people go through [the wire fencing] onto the other side. One of the plainclothes policemen was taking photographs. I realized that they would need evidence that the internees were breaking the regulations by going through the fencing. I therefore appealed to my friends not to let themselves be provoked and not to go through the fencing. Those who did go through said that they realized that this was a provocation. During this time the prison gate was opened and closed probably three times. It would not have been difficult for us to have run a few metres and out through the gate. This was also a provocation. I managed to convince some of the internees to come back through the fencing.

Goławski added that the prison governor had deliberately prolonged the talks with the three-man delegation of the internees to allow the police reinforcements from Iława to reach the Kwidzyń prison. According to Goławski, the prison guards who administered the beating to the internees had been drunk.

Another defendant, Mirosław Duszak, stated that some of the internees appeared to have been selected beforehand for particularly harsh treatment. Radosław Sarnicki stated that internees who were beaten in their cells had been photographed. (One can only guess that these photographs were intended to produce evidence of the internees' aggressive behaviour; in the event, however, no such photographs were among the evidence submitted by the prosecution.) Sarnicki added that the internees had been behaving peacefully, a fact which had only served to irritate the guards, and that until the water pump was used no one had called on the internees to disperse. Defendant Kałudziński was chased by a police dog, beaten unconscious by six guards and only regained consciousness in hospital. His denim jacket was stolen. Defendant Bober described the 'barricade' which consisted of three tables. There was no way in which it could have hindered prison guards in riot gear. The 'barricade' was a pitiful and futile attempt at self-defence. The court ignored the testimonies given by the defendants in the courtroom despite the fact that they had all refused to testify in the course of the investigation.

Only two defence witnesses (from a list of over 45) were allowed to present their testimony in the court. They were Krzysztof Zadrąg, a medical practitioner by profession, and himself a Kwidzyń internee, who testified that the prison doctor had given the severely beaten internees nothing more than pain-killers without taking the trouble to examine them properly, and Zenon Szachowicz, whose testimony incriminated Lieutenant Edmund Młotkowski as the prison official in charge of the pacification.

The court failed to elucidate several important details pertaining to the incident. Who had summoned a fire-engine in the absence of any fire in the prison?[8] (The fireman in charge, R. Gołuch, who had refused to drive into the prison yard seeing there was no fire was later degraded to a lower rank.) What was the representative of the local police doing in the internment prison on the morning of 14 August 1982? The court made no attempt to explain these and other questions and based its sentence on its own findings which were contrary to the facts of the case as revealed during the trial. The court established, for instance, that the two prison guards Gutowski and Brzezicki had actually seen the barricade, although at the time of the incident they had been sitting in their duty room with the lower halves of its windows painted over. The court ignored the counter-evidence, such as a medical certificate stating that, following an earlier accident, defendant Kozaczyński was unable to perform certain movements with his arms and could not possibly have thrown a stool.

The Trials of the Internees

Throughout the trial the court consistently resisted all attempts by the defence to prove that, far from having attacked the prison guards, the defendants had, in fact, themselves been the victims of the attack, and insisted that any injuries the internees had suffered did not concern the court since they were the subject of separate proceedings.

On 24 May 1983 the court passed sentences ranging from one to two years' imprisonment plus fines. The 19-year-old Sarnicki received a one-year suspended sentence. Only Andrzej Goławski, who had been beaten so badly that he was unable to walk without crutches, was excluded from the case. All the defendants were released from arrest until the sentence became final.[9] The prosecution objected to their release and lodged a complaint with the Supreme Court which upheld the decision of the voivodship court.

The defendants intended to appeal to the Supreme Court and took the preliminary step of asking for written substantiation of the sentence. The court did not, however, fulfil this duty and adopted delaying tactics. Finally, on 17 July 1983, without presenting the grounds for the sentence, it formally discontinued the proceedings under the terms of the amnesty act of 21 July 1983. The internees were not satisfied with such an outcome and demanded acquittal for themselves as well as punishment for those responsible for the pacification. Defence lawyer Piotr Andrzejewski and others lodged a complaint with the Supreme Court. The Supreme Court upheld the complaint and transferred the case back to the Voivodship Court in Elbląg for further consideration. The Supreme Court observed that the Voivodship Court, having passed a sentence before the act of amnesty took effect and therefore subject to an appeal, was not the proper court to decide whether to grant an amnesty. Therefore a substantiation of the sentence should be written up and sent to the interested parties so that they might exercise their right of appeal.

This time the voivodship court prepared a substantiation, and the former internees appealed against the sentence and demanded a review of their case and acquittal. The hearing took place on 9 February 1984 and on this occasion the Supreme Court overruled the appeal. It stated that, despite the many breaches of criminal procedure by the voivodship court, the guilt of the defendants had been satisfactorily proved. The Supreme Court found that the prison guards had, indeed, abused their authority, which was regrettable, but since no one other than the internees could possibly have thrown stools at the guard, the internees were guilty of the offence imputed to them. The Supreme Court Judge, Kozłowski, expressed his regrets. The victims of the beating were finally amnestied.

The course of the pacification proves that it was devised beforehand. By stopping family visits the prison authorities wanted to provoke the internees to a protest in the anticipation that it would turn into a riot justifying the use of force. In this way they wanted to discipline them. Not all the internees realized this. Their protest, however peaceful, provided the prison authorities with an excuse to use force. On the other hand the internees could not possibly have remained quiet in the face of what was to them an unjustified penalty.

* * *

Internment and imprisonment without a court hearing and without the right of appeal which were intended as means of isolating blacklisted Solidarity activists and other independent-minded people, proved a failure from the authorities' point of view. The internees by and large did not accept their status and did not allow their spirit to be broken. They kept the spirit of resistance alive, they organized themselves to participate in whatever ways they could in the struggle that went on outside their internment prisons. They did not allow the prison authorities to treat them as prisoners.

The criminal proceedings instituted against some of the internees aimed to force them into submission, to subject them to a stricter regime and to punish them for their independent thinking and activity. The majority of the trials against the internees, by virtue of the place of their alleged offences and the charges presented, had a rather grotesque character. In most cases the internees were acquitted and those sentenced were amnestied. Still the worrying fact remains that it proved possible to sentence people to prison terms for what they wrote, sang or said to the guards.

The Trials of the Internees

Notes

1. *Nowiny*, 8 April 1982 and the unpublished testimony of Jerzy Las.
2. *Biuletyn Informacyjny NSZZ Solidarność* no. 32, (Paris) September 1982.
3. *AIS* no. 15, 2–26 November 1983, *Tygodnik Mazowsze* no. 106, 15 November 1984.
4. Report submitted by Konrad Tatarowski to the Polish Episcopate, unpublished, dated 25 August 1982.
5. Deputy Prosecutor General, Żyta had supervised the investigation of the Bydgoszcz incident of 19 March 1981 when three Solidarity activists, Michał Bartoszcze, Jan Rulewski and Mariusz Łabętowicz, were beaten up by the police who broke into the meeting of the voivodship people's council in Bydgoszcz. The investigation into the case was discontinued in September 1981 on the grounds that it had proved impossible to identify the perpetrators. Żyta was promoted to Prosecutor General in June 1984.
6. According to an unpublished manuscript signed by Jan Prisoner of July 1983.
7. Ibid.
8. According to Konrad Tatarowski (unpublished report of 25 August 1982), during the pacification one of the internees attempted to set fire to a mattress on the grass outside a prison block, but it was quickly put out by the internees themselves.
9. Kozaczyński had already been released on 31 March 1983 on account of family circumstances.

IV

THE SEDITION TRIALS

1. KOR and Solidarity's National Commission

The eleven hostages

It is difficult to discuss the indictment against the members of the Social Self-Defence Committee 'KOR' without going into the historical origins of this group and its efforts on behalf of repressed citizens. The offences imputed to them after the imposition of martial law, albeit supposedly limited to their activities in the Solidarity era, must, in fact, appear as a settling of accounts with KOR for their activities from September 1977 to August 1980. The legal argument cannot be distinguished from the tendentious historical interpretation of KOR's activity as presented in the official propaganda.

This same intention lay behind the preparations for the trial of seven members of the Solidarity union's top policy-making body, The National Commission. Although the trial was never held, the preparations for it were well advanced. They give an insight into official thinking which tried to justify the introduction of martial law by claiming that the Solidarity trade union movement was being used to overthrow the existing political system.

The four members of the Social Self-Defence Committee 'KOR' as well as the seven members of Solidarity's National Commission had their status changed from internees to that of suspects under arrest. The very circumstances of the 'formal arrest' of the 'eleven hostages', as they came to be known, were bizarre and the officially stated reason incongruous.

The Sedition Trials

On 1 September 1982, one day after widespread street demonstrations against martial law, the WRON held a meeting under the chairmanship of General Jaruzelski and issued a communiqué in which it asked the Prosecutor General and the Minister of Internal Affairs to 'speed up' the investigation against some of the KOR members, and urged that they be 'charged with offences against the state and society'.[1] The WRON thereby broke its own proclamation of 13 December 1981 in which it stated that 'it did not violate the jurisdiction of nor did it remove responsibility from any cell of the people's authorities'. In this particular case it was clearly telling the Prosecutor General, as well as the Minister of Internal Affairs, what to do.

The four KOR members: Jacek Kuroń, Jan Lityński, Adam Michnik and Henryk Wujec, were accordingly transferred from the Białołęka internment centre to the Mokotów investigative prison in Warsaw. Two other KOR members, Mirosław Chojecki and Jan Józef Lipski, who were abroad, were also covered by the investigation — in absentia. They had all been active in the pre-Solidarity democratic opposition movement, defending and supporting repressed workers, and helping to establish free trade unions, uncensored publications, independent academic programmes, etc. They had all served as Solidarity advisers on the national or regional level. The reference to 'speeding up' the investigation implied that the KOR members were already being investigated and, since they had not been presented with charges, that this investigation was being conducted in secret. Adam Michnik had no illusions about the nature of the whole charade. In an appeal to international public opinion written just before his transfer from Białołęka to Mokotów he wrote 'In any normal trial generals do not evaluate the evidence and decide what can only be the province of an independent court ... No one can have confidence in a judiciary that functions according to the dictates of generals wielding power.'[2]

The second group of hostages, seven members of Solidarity's National Commission, Andrzej Gwiazda, Seweryn Jaworski, Marian Jurczyk, Karol Modzelewski, Grzegorz Palka, Andrzej Rozpłochowski and Jan Rulewski, had also been interned following the imposition of martial law. They were not formally arrested until 22 December 1982 when it was decided to 'suspend' martial law and terminate the practice of internment. All of them had held elective posts during Solidarity's legal existence. Three of them had challenged Lech Wałęsa for the chairmanship of the

National Commission during the Solidarity Congress in October 1981, others had been entrusted with conducting negotiations with the government on behalf of the union.

The eleven Solidarity leaders and advisers who were to stand trial were people with whom the Communist authorities had 'unfinished business'. Although investigations into the activities of KOR had continued under differing charges throughout almost the entire period of the Committee's existence, the authorities had not been able to devise a scenario for the trial. With regard to the Solidarity leaders, the authorities wanted revenge for the 16 months during which they had been forced on to the defensive by the very workers whose 'avant garde' they purported to be.

Both groups of 'suspects' were charged with crimes against the basic interests of the state as listed in Chapter XIX of the Penal Code. These were not covered by the Act of Abolition issued by the Council of State on 12 December 1981. The investigation in both cases was carried out by the Supreme Military Prosecutor's Office in Warsaw.

The charges against the 'Solidarity Seven'

The seven National Commission members were at first charged under Art. 123 of the Penal Code in conjunction with Art. 128.1, i.e. attempting a coup d'état. The charge was later slightly modified to preparing such a crime, i.e. Art. 128.1 of the Penal Code in conjunction with Art. 123.

Art. 123 of the Penal Code says: 'whoever, aiming to deprive the PPR of its independence, secede part of its territory, overthrow the socio-political system by force or weaken its defence capability, undertakes in agreement with others activity leading to the fulfilment of this aim shall be subject to the penalty of imprisonment for at least five years or the death penalty'.

This article protects the four basic interests of the state: independence, territorial integrity, socio-political system and defence capability. It must be emphasized, however, that Art. 123 of the Penal Code is a vague legal formula. Any form of activity, not necessarily involving the use of force, can be interpreted as leading to an offence under this article. Only the content of this activity is more narrowly defined in so far as it must lead directly to fulfilment of one of the four aims defined under Art. 123. But even this restriction can be by-passed by reference to Art. 128.1, of the Penal Code which stipulates as an offence any activity

The Sedition Trials

leading indirectly to one of the aims mentioned under Art. 123.

One of the elements of the offence under Art. 123 is what is known in PPR legal theory as a 'criminal agreement'. It is defined as 'a conspiracy in a loose form, not organized, not durable and therefore not requiring for its existence any kind of permanent structure, internal discipline or organizational ties. Nor is there any need for statutes, a specific organizational structure, a leadership, orders or instructions, meetings, discussions, etc.'[3] All the prosecution would have had to prove was that the seven members of the National Commission had concluded such an 'agreement' in order to commit an offence under Art. 123.

A second necessary element for a coup d'état is the use of violence. This element of the offence is also defined very broadly. It has been argued, for instance, that it is not necessary for a member of a conspiracy to have actually used violence himself; it sufficed that violence was envisaged as a means of action by the conspirators who aimed to overthrow the PPR's socio-political system.[4]

This interpretation of Art. 123 of the Penal Code reflects a totalitarian philosophy which can be summarised as follows: since the existing order cannot be changed because it is the best, and as 'the final stage in history' can only be perfected, it is socially dangerous to advocate change and seek an alternative to it. The nonconformists — the reasoning goes — are sooner or later bound to realize that it is unrealistic to hope for peaceful change in order to make the system more representative, and those still seeking it must, at least secretly, in their thoughts, envisage the use of force. The totalitarian mind explains reality, especially those developments which it cannot control or foresee, in terms of plots or provocations hatched by 'the enemy'. This aberration is often accompanied by the fear of having to face the real issues. To avoid the real issue, i.e. the existence of a trade union movement free of party control, the authorities preferred to think that a handful of people had created and led astray a huge social movement. Reassured by this thinking they could then generously 'forgive' the masses and reimpose upon them the familiar formula of social activism.

Last but not least, the offence imputed to the 'Seven' involved 'overthrowing the socio-political system'. This term is, in fact, no more than a façade to cover the monopolistic rule of the Communist party. Thus, the interests of state are identified with those of one party. This was made formally possible by writing into the PPR Constitution in 1976 the doctrinal principle of 'the leading political role of the Communist party in society in the construction of socialism'. Since then the two notions: 'the sociopolitical system' and 'the leading role' have become inseparable. Judges in sedition trials did not as a rule attempt to separate them. 'The leading role' implies in practice not only a monopoly on always being in the right, but also a monopoly on representing the Polish *raison d'état*.

Although under Art. 123 an offence may be considered to have been committed even if the alleged plot failed to materialize, the prosecution would still have had to prove that the activity of the conspirators was of such gravity that it would have resulted in the violent overthrow of the socio–political system, i.e. that the forms of activity undertaken by the conspirators must have led to their intended result. In the case of the 'Solidarity Seven', this would clearly have presented logistic problems for the prosecution, unless, of course, the authorities had been willing to stage a regular Stalinist–type show trial.

To make the task of the prosecution somewhat easier, the charges against the 'Seven' were finally modified on 7 November 1983, ten months after the investigation began. The emphasis was now laid on Art. 128.1 of the Penal Code which made not the deed itself, but preparations for it, an offence. Admittedly, the suspects were now liable for lesser penalties (from one to ten years' imprisonment). The prosecution would still have had to demonstrate that the activity of the conspirators did, indeed, constitute preparations for the deed itself, but this would have presented fewer problems since the legal concept of 'preparing to overthrow' was vague enough to admit a number of interpretations.

The prosecutor's order on the presentation of charges to the suspects revealed the prosecuting authorities' train of thought and indicated the direction which the trial might have been expected to take. Andrzej Gwiazda, for example, was charged with having undertaken 'with the aim of overthrowing by force the socialist system of the PPR and weakening its defence capabilities, and in agreement with other Solidarity activists, as well as members of other illegal political groups, activities leading directly to the fulfilment of the intended aim'.[5] The order went on to detail six separate charges: (1) by disseminating false information and slandering the socio–political system, he aimed to set the masses against the constitutional government and organs of state

The Sedition Trials

administration; (2) during meetings and rallies, as well as by various other forms, he advocated the forceful abolition of the governing role of the PUWP in the state and its leading role in society, and the removal of party committees from state enterprises; (3) in a direct and indirect manner he incited to acts directed against the unity of the PPR and its allies ... ; (4) he participated in preparations for a general strike, for para-military formations, tribunals whose verdicts were to terrorize the supporters of socialism in the PPR, and new central and local government bodies code-named the Social Council for National Economy, the Provisional Government, the Clubs for a Self-Governing Republic — 'Freedom Justice Independence' (WSN) — which were to replace the constitutional state authorities in a violent turnover; (5) he organized (sic) plans for violent assaults on public officials; (6) he prepared plans to transform mass demonstrations into a so-called 'national uprising'.

The official argument was that Andrzej Gwiazda, in agreement with his six colleagues, was involved in an illegal conspiracy in addition to and behind the façade of statutory union activity. The basic element of this charge — a conspiracy — was maintained even after the original charge was modified.

A prosecutor's order on the presentation of charges issued to Seweryn Jaworski after the charges were modified, was formulated as follows: 'as a member of the Mazowsze Regional Board of Solidarity, from the second half of 1980 until 12 December 1981 ... , exploiting the legal status of this organization for illegal activity aimed at overthrowing by force the socialist system of the PPR and weakening its defence capabilities, he undertook, in agreement with other Solidarity activists as well as with members of other illegal political groups, preparatory actions leading to the fulfilment of the intended aim...'[6]

The specific acts with which Jaworski was charged were identical to those imputed to Gwiazda before the charge was altered. Modification of the legal basis for the charges changed the emphasis from 'activity' to 'preparation', but not their substance.

The investigation into the case of the seven Solidarity National Commission members dragged on. Their fate was clearly dependent on the outcome of the proceedings against KOR. In fact, the indictment was never completed. The authorities found it too difficult to decide upon a plausible scenario for the trial. A Stalinist-type show trial to demobilize the masses proved too costly to stage, since the very fact of the Solidarity leaders' imprisonment mobilized the people to protest, providing a focal point for many independent initiatives both at home and abroad.

The Seven, instead of providing the authorities with a justification for the introduction of martial law, were becoming a troublesome symbol of repressive policies. Their imprisonment without trial was vivid evidence of the abnormality of the situation after 13 December, contradicting the official claim that everything was back to normal.

The investigation into the activities of KOR

Following their 'arrest' in early September 1982, the members of KOR were charged, under Art. 128.1 of the Penal Code, with preparing, in their guise of Solidarity advisers, a coup d'état that the Solidarity leaders were to have implemented.

In the course of the investigation, the proceedings against Jan Józef Lipski and Mirosław Chojecki were discontinued, Jan Lityński could not be brought to trial because he had failed to return to prison after he was temporarily released on compassionate grounds and gone underground (it turned out that his arrest warrant had expired while he was on leave of absence from prison) and Zbigniew Romaszewski, who had already been sentenced in the Radio Solidarity trial in January 1983, was included in the case in place of Lityński 'to make up the numbers'.

The investigation did not involve all the members of KOR. The group whose 35 members always acted in concert was split for the purpose of the trial into the alleged 'ring-leaders' and the others. The 'leaders' were to be the defendants and some of the others were to act as 'witnesses'. The writings and statements of the four arrested KOR members, for which they had always taken personal responsibility, were interpreted as being representative of the whole of KOR.

The aim of the investigation was to procure 'evidence' to confirm the pre-conceived image of KOR as a subversive force and make the trial credible. According to this concept, KOR was an organization implementing a subversive political programme. To justify the exclusion from the proceedings of the overwhelming majority of the members of KOR, a theory was devised that only a handful of KOR members constituted 'a decision-making centre'. To facilitate the prosecution's task still further, this 'centre' was described in the indictment as 'informal'.

The Sedition Trials

The investigation clearly gathered momentum at the beginning of 1983. In January of that year the police searched the homes of four writers. They claimed to be looking for printing ink and a copying machine but, finding nothing, they took away a number of books and documents published in Poland and abroad and not cleared by the PPR censors. The four writers: Marek Nowakowski, Kazimierz Orłoś, Piotr Wierzbicki and Wiktor Woroszylski were subsequently questioned as witnesses 'in connection with the illegal KOR organization'.[7] In February 1983 the Supreme Military Prosecutor's Office in Warsaw questioned a senior member of KOR, Father Jan Zieja, and Lech Wałęsa, in the same connection. In March, at the Łęczyca prison, the recently sentenced underground Solidarity leader Władysław Frasyniuk was questioned and offered an immediate release should he agree to testify against Jacek Kuroń and Karol Modzelewski.[8]

Apart from putting pressure on some of the potential witnesses in the case, the military prosecution tried to eliminate any positive evidence of the suspects' innocence. For example, documents pertaining to the activities of KOR's Intervention Bureau (responsible for documenting the help given by KOR between September 1976 and September 1977 to workers from Radom and Ursus who had been victimized by the authorities for their participation in the June 1976 food riots) were excluded as evidence under the excuse that these materials were to be investigated separately. These documents would have clearly shown that KOR had been set up in order to help the victims of official repression and not as a conspiratorial organization with political ambitions. The Intervention Bureau was the *raison d'être* of KOR and without taking its activities into consideration the truth about KOR could not but be distorted.

The prosecution were intent on producing evidence to suggest that some of the KOR members had ties with foreign intelligence units. Going through the files in his case after the investigation was closed, Michnik found among the evidence the testimony of a witness who had said that Michnik's trip to Italy in 1977 had been financed by unidentified centres of American espionage. Michnik wrote a letter to the Chairman of the Italian Socialist Party, Bettino Craxi, asking him to confirm publicly that he had made the trip to Italy at the invitation of his party. Craxi complied with this request. Michnik was for some time held in one cell with a certain Zenon Celegrat, a convicted spy who enjoyed privileges denied to other prisoners. This same Celegrat alleged in a televised propaganda programme entitled 'To be continued' that Romaszewski had contacts with the US Embassy in Warsaw.

The files in KOR's case also quoted a forged document published by the leftist Spanish weekly *El Tiempo*, according to which KOR was an integral part of an American intelligence plot devised by the National Security Adviser to former US President Jimmy Carter, Zbigniew Brzezinski in order to destabilize the political situation in Poland. Brzezinski himself publicly denied this allegation stating that neither KOR nor Solidarity had any ties with US intelligence and that 'the leaders of both groups fought for freedom on their own'.[9]

The defence lawyers representing the suspects were prevented from taking part in the investigative proceedings despite the fact that the Supreme Military Prosecutor's Office had not issued any order to exclude them. Several formal requests put forward by the defence lawyers, that certain documents pertaining to the activities of KOR and its members be included in the files of the case, were dismissed.[10]

The indictment against KOR

The indictment against KOR, signed by the military prosecutor Colonel Włodzimierz Kubala on 27 September 1983, gained widespread publicity both in Poland's independent press and in the West. Its vagueness, inconsistency, lack of logic and imprecision prompted the defence lawyers for Kuroń and Romaszewski to submit a request demanding that the court return the files in the case to the prosecution for completion as failing to satisfy the requirements stipulated in the Code of Criminal Procedure. The indictment was based on the prosecution's concept that the four KOR members were in an anti-state conspiracy. Its main thesis was political not legal in character. It said: 'with the aim of overthrowing the socio-political system by force and weakening the defence capability of the PPR by breaking its alliance with the USSR, and in agreement with people subject to other proceedings [the Solidarity Seven — AS], the suspects undertook preparatory activities aimed at fulfilling this objective.'

Apparently finding it difficult to substantiate the claim that the suspects intended to commit the crime with which they were charged, the prosecution alleged that the suspects were camouflaging 'their real intentions with the help of statements and slogans whose external editorial form was not associated with legally forbidden or criminal activity'.

The indictment did not specifically define the charges against the individual suspects but simply charged joint responsibility on the grounds that all the suspects were supposedly joined in a conspiracy involving activity over a certain period of time.

The act of indictment described the history of KOR without much regard for the truth. Different events were mentioned selectively in order to illustrate specific charges. Romaszewski, for instance, was said to have taken part during the Solidarity period in meetings with workers in Płock and Rzeszów, a circumstance obviously taken by the prosecution as evidence of his subversive intent. The fact that he had acted as an expert for the Solidarity branch in Radom in negotiations with the government concerning responsibility for the police pacification of Radom in June 1976 and compensation to the victims was, however, omitted since it would have required acknowledging the existence and the achievements of the Intervention Bureau as well as the positive role played by Romaszewski.

The prosecutor condemned the views held by the suspects, who 'took as their starting point the assertion that the existing socio-political system in Poland was totalitarian in nature, supposedly subjugating society and the individual, depriving them of political freedoms, civil rights and liberties. They constantly declared that the Polish state was not sovereign, that the nation was not free, and that the actions of the authorities served the imperialist interests of the USSR.' With regard to Romaszewski the prosecutor claimed that 'the suspect described the existing system in Poland as a system of power based on "horrifying lawlessness"'.

The indictment was full of unfounded allegations such as: 'the motive for the suspects' behaviour was contempt for and hatred of the socialist system' and speculation or even sweeping generalizations such as 'the suspects also influenced social consciousness, attitudes and behaviour through their writings and interviews.'

As evidence the prosecutor quoted a compilation of articles and interviews, some of which had never been published, and others that had been published in the pre-Solidarity independent press, or in the West, and in the case of Kuroń two interviews that had appeared in the official, censored dailies *Dziennik Bałtycki* and *Sztandar Młodych* in 1981. It added, as a further incriminating circumstance, that some of those publications had been broadcast to Poland by Radio Free Europe and charged that its authors had co-operated with and been financed by RFE, the Paris-based Instytut Literacki which publishes the monthly *Kultura* and the Polish Government in Exile in London.[11]

The indictment was not based on a strictly legal course of argument. Instead it abounded with propagandistic formulae suggesting that the prosecutor was seeking to substantiate questions such as 'who stood to gain from KOR's activity?' and 'who stood behind them?' Rather than establishing the facts, the indictment consistently imputed anti-state motives to the suspects, but failed totally to demonstrate any criminal intent on their part.

The indictment was unable to quote a single KOR document propagating the use of force or the violent overthrow of the socio-political system. Instead, it concentrated its attention on the founding declaration of the Clubs for a Self-Governing Republic which had been signed at a meeting in Kuroń's flat on 30 November 1981 by some 50 people, several of them former KOR members or sympathizers. The prosecutor charged that this declaration was a programmatic document and that the role of the Clubs was 'to engage in the preparation of a socio-political platform for the approaching elections to the local people's councils and future elections to the Sejm'. In this respect, the prosecutor claimed, the Clubs were also to fulfil an organizational role. The electoral platform of the 'Clubs' was to ensure the success of political forces opposed to the PUWP, who would 'work out a new arrangement with the USSR'. In this passage from the indictment we find the totalitarian rulers' fear of the opposition's participation in the electoral process. Still the indictment fails to convince that such participation or, more precisely, the demand for it would have been tantamount to the violent overthrow of the socio-political system. On the contrary, it would rather seem to suggest a desire for gradual change by peaceful, democratic methods. Indeed, the founding declaration of the Clubs was described by the Polish defence lawyer, Aniela Steinsbergowa, herself a founder member of KOR, as 'positive proof of the suspects' innocence'.[12]

By sentencing the members of KOR on the basis of the indictment described above, the authorities would, in fact, have admitted that the struggle for the observance of law and order in the PPR was incompatible with the existing socio-political system. Secondly, they would have admitted that the system could

The Sedition Trials

guarantee neither human nor social nor economic rights. Thirdly, a sentence of guilty would have confirmed the totalitarian and ideological nature of the system.

The indictment itself tells much about the system under which the Poles have to live. The views for which the KOR members were indicted closely resemble those of the majority of the population. By accusing them, the authorities have, in fact, accused themselves: 'With particular passion, the suspects attacked the basic values and principles of the ideological system, accusing it of having supposedly "nationalized" not only the individual but also all forms of social life, and of having degraded the individual, reducing him to being an enslaved object of manipulations on the part of the power apparatus and the bureaucracy'.

Negotiations to secure the hostages' release

For ideological reasons the authorities would have liked to have brought both the Solidarity leaders and advisers to trial, but practical considerations prevailed against such an option. Unable to build a convincing case against the Eleven, and unwilling to pay the political cost of show trials, the authorities procrastinated. The resulting impasse was in itself a major embarrassment to them. Asked by reporters when the trial of KOR would be held, the government spokesman Jerzy Urban replied: 'most likely at the beginning of next month' (15 February 1983); 'it depends when the suspects will finish reading the files in the case' (20 September 1983); 'as soon as possible' (11 October 1983); 'they still have not finished reading the files' (25 October 1983); 'on 13 July 1984' (12 June 1984).

The sceptical reaction, both at home and abroad, to the terms of the July 1983 amnesty, which did not cover the Eleven, may have influenced the authorities' thinking about further developments in their case. Still unable to work out a concept of the trial the authorities decided to look for another solution which would enable them to save face and strike a blow at the opposition at the same time. This proved to be difficult and several different approaches were tried before the Eleven were finally released.

On 29 September 1983, when the indictment against KOR had already been sent to court, the Minister of Justice Sylwester Zawadzki, speaking in the Sejm, suggested that the Eleven might be released under the terms of the July 1983 amnesty, at the discretion of the Supreme Court, if the Solidarity underground leaders came out of hiding. This was tantamount to using the Eleven as hostages to force the hand of the underground leaders, saddling them with moral responsibility for the fate of their imprisoned colleagues.

One month later Jerzy Urban floated the idea, through the foreign journalists accredited in Warsaw, that the 'professional organizers of conflicts, political trouble-makers' might leave the country for a certain period of time. This suggestion, described as 'immoral' and 'illegal' by Edward Lipiński, the most senior member of KOR, would have amounted to forced exile and, as such, was not taken up by any of the Western governments.

In the autumn of 1983 an attempt was made to solve the problem by Church mediation. The Church representatives put down two conditions for any agreement on the release of the Eleven: that the case of the seven leaders of Solidarity not be separated from that of the four members of KOR, and secondly, that the solution be accepted by all those concerned.[13] In December 1983 the authorities broke off the talks, claiming that the Church was violating confidentiality rules. The negotiations with the Church were resumed a few months later. They resulted in a meeting on 20 April 1983, Good Friday, at a government villa in Otwock. Nine of the eleven prisoners (one was ill, the other refused to attend) met with ten Solidarity advisers appointed by the Church to act as intermediaries. The prisoners were presented with a modified version of an earlier offer that they would be released under the terms of the July 1983 amnesty provided that they renounced political activity for two and a half years. An appropriate pledge to this effect would be made to the Church leadership. In exchange some 472 political prisoners would be released. The offer gave rise to serious doubts. For instance, the meaning of 'political activity' was so broad that it could well be interpreted by the authorities as including the expression of personal views on political matters. Further, it constituted a crude attempt at moral blackmail.

The authorities also put forward an alternative that the Eleven be tried behind closed doors and receive sentences effectively limited to the time they had already spent in prison. These offers were also rejected by the Eleven.

The authorities also took the unusual step of seeking the help of the United Nations Organization. In February 1984 UN Secretary General Javier Pérez de Cuellar visited Warsaw and was

The Sedition Trials

promised the release of Alicja Wesołowska, a UN employee sentenced in March 1980 by the PPR authorities for spying, in return for UN mediation. At the beginning of May, the UN envoy Emilio de Olivarez visited ten of the prisoners at the Rakowiecka investigative prison. He presented them with the offer outlined by Urban in October 1983, suggesting that they go into temporary exile, at the cost of the UN, for a period of six months to one year, with a guaranteed right of return.

The negotiations concerning the three offers took place under highly unusual conditions. The prisoners could not communicate directly with the authorities nor among themselves. There were attempts to break their united front by striking bargains with each of them individually. In this atmosphere of threats, bizarre offers, blackmail and confidentiality, the Eleven were unanimous in their rejection of any deal. Being innocent they demanded either unconditional release or a fair trial. By rejecting the freedom offered to them under certain conditions, they remained truly free, although at the cost of further imprisonment. By refusing to compromise on their principles they unmasked the deceitful intentions of the authorities who wanted both revenge and impunity.

What these peculiar negotiations between the gaolers and their prisoners, or terrorists and their hostages, revealed was that it was not the province of the court of law to decide the fate of the Eleven. Adam Michnik, in a letter to the Minister of Internal Affairs of 10 December 1983, commented on the negotiations to release the Eleven: 'to admit to such open disregard of the law one has to be an idiot; to offer a man, held in prison for two years, the Côte d'Azur in exchange for his moral suicide, one has to be a swine; and to believe that I could accept such a proposal is to consider every individual to be a police henchman'.

The trial of KOR

Faced with the failure of negotiations and strong pressure to decide the prisoners' fate one way or another, the authorities finally decided to bring them to court. The trial of the four KOR members opened on Friday, 13 July 1984, before the Court of the Warsaw Military District. Even at this late stage the authorities seemed undecided how to proceed with it and procrastinated. The trial was supposed to last till the end of October, but during the

The Sedition Trials

second session, on Wednesday 18 July 1984, the proceedings were adjourned indefinitely. A few days later the Eleven were 'amnestied'.

Security outside the courthouse was tight; the hearing was closed to Western journalists. Solidarity leader Lech Wałęsa and the union's advisers were barred from attending the proceedings. A total of 17 out of 28 seats for the public were occupied by employees of the Ministry of Internal Affairs. There were also seven relatives of the defendants, eight defence lawyers and three representatives of the official media.

When the hearing began Jacek Kuroń suggested that the Western journalists be allowed to follow the proceedings over loudspeakers in the adjoining rooms. His defence lawyer Jerzy Woźniak said that his client's right to a defence had been limited. Woźniak had been allowed to see Kuroń only in the investigative block at the Rakowiecka prison and not privately in the rooms normally used for meetings between a defence lawyer and his client. For fear of bugging devices Kuroń had to communicate with his lawyer by writing on pieces of paper that were later destroyed. Woźniak complained that copies of the letters sent by Kuroń to the court or other official institutions had not been forwarded to him by the prison administration.

Adam Michnik challenged the legitimacy of the trial. He said that his right to prepare a defence had been denied to him. He said that until he was presented with the legal grounds for this denial he would not consider the three judges a legitimate court but a sorry lot of three individuals who did not have enough courage to refuse to participate in such a case. Michnik was threatened with removal from the courtroom for contempt of court.

The defence lawyers raised motions that the defendants be granted access to documents which they needed to prepare their defence and that former Solidarity advisers be admitted to the trial as observers. The trial was adjourned to allow the court to consider these motions and the complaints of the defendants.

The second session, which was to hear the testimony of Kuroń, was indefinitely adjourned after only five minutes. The presiding judge said that since PRON had appealed to the Sejm for an amnesty, the court decided to defer the trial pending the Sejm's decision.

Adam Michnik was unrepentant till the end. Even before the trial opened he said that he would be satisfied only with an acquittal and that he would not accept an amnesty because this would imply that he was guilty. He also insisted that the authorities apologize for jailing him unjustly for two and a half years and that he would refuse to leave his cell, even if the warders had to carry him to freedom from his cell. In the event he was not carried but jostled to freedom.

Postscript to the trial of KOR

Seven KOR members were charged and four of them tried not because they had committed a specific offence but because of the very essence of KOR, a human rights movement operating within the law but independently of the authorities and resisting the totalitarian system with peaceful means. The main charge against KOR was that it had engaged in political activity which had culminated in its hijacking of Solidarity. In fact KOR, being a citizens' committee, was not aiming for political objectives. Its mission was to resist totalitarian attempts to atomize society and make it function according to the rules characteristic of the party itself: uniformity, anonymity, hierarchy, centralism. As Marek Tarniewski put it, the party by nationalizing information, economy and culture was aiming at nationalizing society itself.[14] KOR, together with other democratic opposition movements, tried to resist this trend. KOR was a movement of self-organization understood as society's defence against the totalitarian drive of the party. Self-organization was to restore the natural social bonds which were being systematically destroyed, alienating individuals from one another. These bonds were to be reconstructed through the struggle for independent culture, uncensored information, social thought, aid to the victims of repression, self-help groups, a free trade union movement. As Jan Józef Lipski wrote:

> The struggle against totalitarianism becomes a fight for the most essential human values. A man deprived of these values is but a shadow of a man. Such a struggle can be undertaken in any domain of life. Resistance to totalitarianism in nonpolitical areas, that appeals to nonpolitical motives is particularly threatening to it, even when not immediately successful.[15]

KOR was an attempt to persuade society to organize itself in defence of values threatened by the totalitarian system, such as freedom of thought and expression, the rule of law, tolerance, diversity of culture, dignity of labour.

Since the authorities could not openly attack the ideals for which KOR stood, they sought recourse to deceit and distortion. The language of the indictment set the stage for the trial which was to seal the image of KOR as the 'enemy of the people' and impose a false interpretation of reality. The prosecutor attempted to twist the meaning of words and to present a human rights group or a civic initiative as an organization directed by mafia-style masterminds. KOR's goal of reactivating independent social bonds was presented as a political programme threatening the life of the nation and the state. Peaceful attempts to influence public opinion were presented as promoting the use of force. Moderation was equalled with extremism and the open admission of aims with a treacherous conspiracy. As if all this were not enough, the official propaganda reserved for itself the exclusive right to know 'the real intentions' of the indicted members of KOR. The propagandists' aim was not to convince anybody but to impose the conceptual framework within which KOR was to be discussed and spell out the language in which its activities were to be evaluated. The ritual language helped the party to reclaim the past. KOR was finally exorcised.

2. The trial of the Confederation of Independent Poland (KPN)

KOR and KPN

The basic difference between KOR and KPN was that KOR was a social movement and KPN aspired to be a political party. KOR were against the establishment of political parties at that stage of Polish developments. They thought that only a society which regained its self-awareness and organized itself in movements and institutions representative of its members and independent of the authorities would be able to resist the encroachments of the totalitarian system and violation of the law as practised by the PPR authorities. KOR's ideal of a society organized in social self--defence movements was to be achieved evolutionally.

The founder of KPN, Leszek Moczulski, for his part, put forward the idea of 'constructive revolution'. In his political

The Sedition Trials

manifesto 'Revolution Without a Revolution' he foresaw that this process would have five phases one of which would involve the emergence of independence-orientated political parties subsequently confederated in the 'Polish Political System' (PSP), which would eventually take over power and proclaim the Third Republic. Moczulski, who was writing in mid-1979, anticipated an outbreak of social unrest. He hoped that a political struggle would follow and that the Communists would be the losers. He believed that independence-orientated political parties had to be in existence in order to be ready for the struggle when it came.

Moczulski, an historian and journalist originally associated with the independent Movement for the Defence of Human and Civil Rights (ROPCiO) founded a new group, the Confederation of Independent Poland (KPN), on 1 September 1979 following conceptual differences in the Movement. According to Moczulski, KPN was eventually to constitute the authorities of the Polish Political System. KPN operated semi-publicly. It was headed by a policy-making body, the Political Council, with Moczulski as Chairman and an executive board, the Current Action Directorate—KAB. It was divided into regions and operational groups and provided for three levels of membership. This internal structure was intended to give KPN a dynamic character, though it only really gathered momentum in the Solidarity period. At the beginning of October 1980, i.e. at the time of the arrest of its leading activists, the KPN counted 1,472 members, candidate members and participants. By the end of 1981 the group, which was more successful in recruitment among the workers than among the intelligentsia, claimed to have 100,000 members.

The KPN considered the restoration of independence to Poland as the supreme objective for the democratic opposition movement. It was against any dialogue with the PUWP since it considered such dialogue tantamount to legitimizing Communist rule. The PUWP was, according to the KPN, a totalitarian instrument of Soviet domination over Poland, hence Poland could rid itself of this domination by eliminating the country's ruling Communist party.[16] This aim was to be achieved, without bloodshed or destruction, through political struggle. At the beginning of 1980 the KPN put forward eight candidates for election to the Sejm but they were predictably refused registration on the ballot. The action was a symbolic one—it was intended to demonstrate to the public that there could be an alternative to rule by the PUWP.

The Sedition Trials

Although none of the KPN members acted as adviser to the strikers in August 1980, at least two of its members, Krzysztof Bzdyl and Tadeusz Jandziszak, were involved in setting up branches of the independent trade union movement. Bzdyl organized the strike in his enterprise in Kraków and Jandziszak was one of the organizers of the Inter-Factory Strike Committee (MKS) in Wrocław.

Proceedings against KPN during the Solidarity period

Shortly after the Gdańsk Agreement was signed seven members of KPN were arrested. The arrests took place between September 1980 and January 1981. Those arrested were: Krzysztof Bzdyl (an economist from Kraków), Zygmunt Goławski (a farmer from Siedlce), Tadeusz Jandziszak (an historian from Wrocław), Leszek Moczulski, Tadeusz Stański (a lawyer, former Chairman of the PAX branch in Siedlce), Jerzy Sychut (an electrician from Szczecin) and Romuald Szeremietiew (a lawyer, former Chairman of the PAX branch in Leszno). The institution of formal proceedings against the KPN so soon after the Gdańsk Agreement cast doubts on the authorities' intentions. It signified an attempt to distinguish between the workers' 'just anger' and the subversive dealings of 'political troublemakers'.[17]

Moczulski himself was arrested on 23 September 1980 under the charge of slandering the supreme authorities of the PPR. This charge referred to an interview he had given to the West German weekly *Der Spiegel*.[18] The investigation was not, however, limited to the circumstances and the contents of the interview, but was expanded to cover the period 1977-80. According to the official communiqué, the investigation had shown that Moczulski 'was guilty of other crimes against the interests and security of Poland'. In this way he was arrested under one charge and investigated for another.

The case against the KPN was to be based on two sources. First, the private correspondence of Leszek Moczulski, which had been seized and read by the police without his knowledge. Some of the letters sent to Moczulski by Maciej Pstrąg-Bieleński, a KPN representative who had been living in the West since the end of 1979, apparently mentioned anti-Communist organizations with which he was in contact.[19] These included National Alliance of Russian Solidarists (NTS), an anti-Communist Russian emigré group and 'Free Poland', a little known and somewhat dubious group set up in America. Some of the telephone conversations between Pstrąg-Bieleński and Moczulski and the latter's wife Maria were secretly tape-recorded and forged to portray Pstrąg-Bieleński as a person allied to groups in the West which would like to reopen the question of Poland's post-war Western borders. Excerpts from the tapes were broadcast on television.[20]

The second source of incriminating evidence against the KPN was the testimony of Marian Skuza, an activist of the Free Democrats Movement which had been active within ROPCiO before the latter split into several groups including the KPN. There has been speculation that Skuza had been co-operating with the secret police and reporting on the activities of ROPCiO.

The indictment against the KPN signed on 6 March 1981 charged Moczulski, Stański, Szeremietiew and Jandziszak with 'undertaking preparatory activities aimed at weakening the country's defence capability, breaking allied unity with the USSR, and overthrowing by force the socio-political system of the PPR by setting up an illegal association, the KPN, which was financed, supported and inspired by centres of political subversion hostile to the PPR' (Art. 123 in conjunction with Art. 128.1 of the Penal Code). Moczulski was charged in particular with 'devising the suggestion, which was false and harmful to the interests of the PPR, that the socio-economic and political system in Poland could be neither improved nor reformed'.

The Voivodship Court in Warsaw to which the indictment was sent decided to refer the case back to the prosecutor's office for completion. The prosecutor, however, considered the investigation closed and lodged a complaint with the Supreme Court, which upheld the complaint and ordered the Voivodship Court in Warsaw to proceed with the case on the basis of the indictment as it stood.

The imprisonment and impending trial of four KPN members (the other three were released pending further inquiries), led to widespread public protests. On 10 December 1980, a Committee for the Defence of People Imprisoned for Their Convictions was set up by Solidarity's national leadership, the National Consultative Commission (KKP). The Committee sent a letter dated 20 December 1980 to the Chairman of the State Council protesting the use of criminal law as an instrument of political struggle.[21] Stating that they did not share the views of the prisoners, the signatories of the petition declared that they found imprisonment of people for their political beliefs unacceptable and contrary to the Gdańsk Agreement. The pressure to release the imprisoned KPN members was partially successful and on 4 June 1981 they were released pending trial.

Soon after the trial opened on 15 June 1981, the prosecution (Wiesława Bardonowa and Tadeusz Gonciarz) did their best to have the four re-arrested. The court dismissed two requests to this effect, but the Supreme Court took the side of the prosecution, initially ordering police supervision of the defendants and later, just before the Extraordinary IXth PUWP Congress, reinstituting arrest.

The defence lawyer Zdzisław Węgliński, characterizing the indictment, said that it did not contain a precise description of the offences imputed to the defendants. Both the means with which they were supposed to have committed these offences, as well as the circumstances of the acts of which they were accused, were unclear. The defendants were supposed to have had contacts with people whose names the indictment failed to mention. Under these conditions—concluded Węgliński—both the defence and the defendants found it difficult to exercise their right to a defence. The court, however, dismissed the defence lawyer's request to refer the indictment back to the prosecution to correct its omissions.

The court upheld, however, the request of another defence lawyer Tadeusz de Virion to adjourn the hearing for one month to enable the defendants to acquaint themselves with the evidence assembled by the prosecutor's office. Since the files in the case, following termination of the investigation, had been either with the voivodship court or with the Supreme Court, the defendants had had no opportunity to study them.

When the hearing resumed Moczulski argued that the prosecution had used false documents during preliminary proceedings, concealed pertinent evidence and failed to include all the relevant material in the court record, as well as including some documents of 'doubtful origin'.

The prosecutor Bardonowa attempted to present Moczulski's pamphlet 'Revolution Without a Revolution' as the KPN's programme despite the defence's convincing counterevidence in the form of policy statements by the KPN's Political Council. 'The political programme of the KPN', said Bardonowa, 'was the emanation of an obsessive hatred of the socialist socio-political system and the PPR's supreme authorities'.

Moczulski used the hearing to deliver a damning indictment of the system of government in Poland and drew attention to Poland's lack of sovereignty.

The Sedition Trials

The trial progressed at a slow pace. When it was in its fourth month the prosecution began to run out of patience and accused the defendants of procrastinating with their testimonies and, in this way, abusing their right to a defence. On 28 October 1981, the court warned the defendants that it would not tolerate statements not relevant to the indictment and that it would consider concerted attacks on the indictment as an attempt to exert pressure on the court.

The imposition of martial law brought the proceedings to a halt. They were re-started a few months later with a new trial before a military court.

The case re-started

The second KPN trial opened before the Court of the Warsaw Military District on 22 February 1982. The charges were largely the same as those presented to the defendants in the course of earlier proceedings.

The defendants refused to testify for most of the trial, saying that they had already done so before the voivodship court and requesting that their testimony be read out. The defence argued that the means of exercising power which the defendants had criticized could not be identified with the socio-political system of the PPR as such, and that there was nothing to suggest that they had reckoned with the use of force as a means of achieving their political objectives. In his closing remarks Leszek Moczulski said that he was being tried for his views, which were opposed to those of the PUWP, and that the sentence, as politically motivated, could not have any legal justification. Stański said that the judges and the prosecutors, by virtue of their membership in the PUWP, ought to be excluded from the proceedings since their impartiality was in doubt.

On 8 October 1982 the court handed down sentences finding all the defendants guilty and sentenced Moczulski to seven years' imprisonment, Stański and Szeremietiew to five years' each and Jandziszak to two years' imprisonment, suspended for five.

In the substantiation of the sentences the court found that setting up an illegal association, the KPN, constituted preparation to overthrow the socio-political system of the PPR by force, and weaken its defence capability through breaking allied unity with the USSR.[22] The defendants were also found guilty of 'exploiting the current political and economic situation for a propaganda

The Sedition Trials

campaign aimed at frustrating the constitutional activity of the supreme state and administrative authorities'. The court implied that they were guilty not so much of specific criminal acts, as of dangerous misconceptions pertaining to the essence of the pre-Solidarity crisis. According to the court 'they exploited irregularities undoubtedly existing in the political and economic life of the country, brought about by individuals who identified themselves with the system as such and shifted the burden of responsibility for this state of affairs onto the PUWP as a whole, as well as on the PPR's allies, particularly the USSR'. In this way the socio-political system in force in the PPR was endowed with the prerogative of infallibility and its critics who attempted to fight it with political means were sentenced as criminals.

The court interpreted very widely the key element of the offence under Art. 123 of the Penal Code, i.e. force, and ruled that 'in criminal law [in the PPR] the notion of force is not confined to any activity that renders the state defenceless by the use of physical force and military structures, but involves also any actions which de facto paralyse the operating forces [of the state] by rendering them defenceless or incapable of resisting the enemy. Under the notion of force, the threat of immediate coercion is also to be understood if the conditions to implement such a threat exist'. The words 'de facto' were here deliberately used incorrectly. The words 'could possibly' would have been more exact. Since a criminal court should be concerned with specific criminal acts and not possibilities, the words 'de facto' were used as a camouflage.

The four defendants appealed and in June 1983 the Supreme Court upheld the sentences passed against Moczulski, Stański and Szeremietiew and excluded the case of Jandziszak for separate appeal proceedings on account of his poor health. The KPN members were released under the July 1984 amnesty. In March 1985 Moczulski was rearrested. The investigation against Bzdyl, Goławski and Sychut, who had been arrested in September 1980 and subsequently released pending further investigation, was discontinued by the Prosecutor's Office of the Warsaw Military District on 31 January 1983. With regard to 39 other KPN members, the prosecutor's office decided not to open investigations.

The Sedition Trials

The right to set up political parties in the PPR

During the KPN trial the court was not concerned with determining whether the KPN was a political party. It simply described the KPN as an illegal organization. Moczulski for his part argued that nothing in the PPR Constitution forbade the formation of opposition parties. On the other hand, there is no provision in the PPR Constitution specifically allowing the formation of political parties. The PPR Constitution allows only for the activity of 'organizations of working people' (Art. 84.2), but fails to mention political parties specifically. No ordinances relevant to this provision have, in any case, ever been issued. The International Covenant on Civil and Political Rights grants the right to set up political parties (Art. 22), but this provision is not expressed in PPR domestic law, which contains many loopholes with regard to the procedure for setting up a political party, its registration and delegalization.

In the case of KPN, the court failed to establish whether the group could be classified under Art. 84.2 of the PPR Constitution as an 'organization of working people'. Instead, the court stated that the KPN was illegal on the basis of Art. 84.3 of the PPR Constitution which forbids associations whose programme is incompatible with the basic tenets of the system. Since the KPN was not an association but a political party, it remains open to doubt whether the criminal court was right to apply this provision. It is, moreover, inadmissible for a criminal court to interpret and apply the provisions of the Constitution to a case in which it should properly have applied the provisions of the Code of Criminal Procedure. The proper procedure to follow would have been to transfer the case to a civil court to determine whether the KPN was acting legally or not. The notion of legality is derived in PPR law from legal status which only a civil court can grant by formally registering a group of people as an association, a society or a political party.

In the KPN's case the criminal court took it upon itself to determine the scope of the right to associate by applying the provisions of the PPR Constitution instead of transferring the case to a civil court. It described a political party as a criminal association and its activities as a threat to the system. The ruling elite was simply not prepared to engage in political struggle with its opponents.

The Sedition Trials

3. The Bałuka trial

The KPN trial served in many respects as a prototype for proceedings against Edmund Bałuka, a shipyard worker of leftist orientation. He had been the chairman of the Strike Committee in the Szczecin Shipyard in December 1970 and January 1971. Fearing for his life, he had fled to the West in 1973. Having settled in France, Bałuka cooperated with the Force Ouvrière trade union and later set up a leftist-orientated political group which published its own journal *Szerszeń* ('The Hornet'). In 1979 Bałuka formed a body called the Permanent Liaison Committee for the Defence of Free Trade Unions in Eastern Europe and the USSR.

After August 1980 Bałuka felt that his place was more than ever among the Polish workers, in particular at the Szczecin Shipyard, where he had worked for many years. He returned to Poland illegally in April 1981 and went directly to the Szczecin Shipyard where he explained the motives for his return to the representatives of the workers. He was received with a certain degree of reserve but the workers nonetheless agreed to protect him and vouched for him at the prosecutor's office. Bałuka was later re-employed at the shipyard and joined Solidarity.

On 14 September 1981 he drafted the founding declaration of the Polska Socjalistyczna Partia Pracy (Polish Socialist Labour Party — PSPP). He never applied for its registration and the party was soon banned by the Szczecin voivod. In its programme the PSPP stated that the Communists in Poland were using the word socialism as a smokescreen to conceal their bureaucratic practices. To restore the real meaning of the word 'socialism' was the principal aim of the PSPP. The party was committed to pluralism in public life. In its declaration it stated that no political party should claim for itself the constitutional status of 'a leading force', and that the PUWP could not enjoy a monopoly of power. The PSPP demanded that neither the army nor the riot police be used against workers exercising their right to demonstrate peacefully. It proposed the disbanding of the repressive forces of the Ministry of Internal Affairs (SB, ZOMO, ORMO). The PSPP advocated reform of the economy through setting up workers' councils in state enterprises and giving them a decisive say in matters pertaining to production and finance. With regard to Poland's international situation Bałuka's PSPP demanded the invalidation of the Teheran, Yalta and Potsdam accords as unjust to Poles and forcing them into the Soviet sphere of influence.

Following the introduction of martial law Baluka was interned. On 3 June 1982 he was formally placed under arrest. His trial opened on 11 June 1983 before the Court of the Pomeranian Military District in Bydgoszcz.

The charges against Baluka were listed in ten points. Similarly to the members of the KPN, he was charged under Art. 123 of the Penal Code with undertaking activity, both abroad and following his return to Poland, with the aim of overthrowing by force the socio-political system of the PPR and weakening the country's defence capability. According to the indictment,

> Edmund Baluka's fundamental political activities were aimed above all at the de facto elimination of the PUWP which he considered 'the source of all evil in Poland'. In his publications and public statements he attacked the party in an openly hostile fashion and with undisguised hatred. His statements contained words calling for 'the elimination and destruction of renegades' by which he meant the members of the PUWP. His activities were, therefore, aimed against the party as the governing political force in the state.

In the concluding passage of the indictment the prosecutor presented Poland's subjugation to the USSR, expressed in military terms as compulsory membership in the Warsaw Pact, as crucial to the country's defence potential. The accords of Teheran, Yalta and Potsdam which deprived Poland of its sovereignty were presented in the indictment as affording the country its territorial and defence guarantees. The passage read,

> It cannot be doubted that the PPR's defence potential is greatly enhanced by the stationing on PPR territory of the allied armies, that is, the units of the Soviet army. The territorial and defence guarantees enjoyed by our state obviously also derive from the fact that the political treaties of Teheran, Yalta and Potsdam are in force. Any political activities disavowing those treaties, as well as any activities aimed at breaking the alliance with the USSR, may be unequivocally described as weakening the PPR's defence capability.

The prosecutor's office intended to link Baluka's activity with

The Sedition Trials

the Trotskyists in France. The material quoted as 'evidence' in the indictment failed to establish such a connection. The material included among others: copies of *Szerszeń* which had been smuggled to Poland, as well as quotations from this publication which were supposed to demonstrate that Bałuka had propagated a forceful overthrow of the PPR's socio-political system, tapes recorded secretly during Bałuka's public appearances, the founding declaration of the PSPP, fly-sheets, transcripts of an interview given by Bałuka to Radio Free Europe, items confiscated during a search in Bałuka's flat, etc. Experts from the Ministry of Internal Affairs were charged with identifying Bałuka's voice on tapes recorded during his public meetings. This task was entrusted to Lt Colonel Stanisław Błasikiewicz, who has frequently participated in sensitive political trials and been summoned to render similar services in the Radio Solidarity trial, as well as the Gdańsk trial of Frasyniuk, Lis and Michnik.

The trial against Edmund Bałuka was held behind closed doors. The prosecutor, comparing his activity to that of the members of the KPN, said: 'The difference between him [Bałuka] and Moczulski was that he directly and quite openly acknowledged violence as the only means of overthrowing the people's rule. They differed in their choice of political instruments which were to serve the fulfilment of their aims. In Bałuka's case this instrument was soon to be bloodied.'[23] These remarks went even further than the charges presented against Bałuka in the indictment. The absence of any legal argumentation and recourse to insinuation were characteristic of the prosecutor's position throughout the hearing. In his attempt to prove that Bałuka was undertaking activity with the aim of weakening the PPR's defence capability, the prosecutor said: 'The country's potential here and now is dependent on its international political and military alliances; he who attacks them and propagates their alteration is acting with the aim of weakening the PPR's defence capability.'[24]

The conclusion which the prosecutor wanted drawn from this passage was that the Poles could not demand national sovereignty since such a demand, irrespective of whether action was actually taken, was in itself tantamount to weakening the PPR's defence capability, i.e. the PPR could maintain its military capacity only at the expense of its sovereignty. No criticism of Poland's 'military and political alliances', i.e. repudiation of the country's subservience to the USSR and the Warsaw Pact, would be tolerated by the authorities in political thinking.

The Sedition Trials

Bałuka himself said that 'it is the PPR citizens' right to express their personal or collective opinions concerning the way the country is governed regardless of whether these opinions are negative or positive'. He added that 'the demand for a change in the system of government is not a crime but the right of the ruled, the right of citizens'.

On 30 June 1983 Bałuka was sentenced to five years' imprisonment. The court found him guilty, not of undertaking any activity but of making preparations to 'overthrow the socio-political system of the PPR by force, and weakening the PPR's military alliances' (Art. 128.1 of the Penal Code instead of Art. 123 under which he had originally been charged). He was released under the terms of the July 1984 amnesty.

* * *

Charges of sedition are the most serious that can be brought by the authorities against those who engage in independent political reflection or who endeavour to reform the system. The trials discussed in this chapter took place at a time when, as a result of martial law, the authorities had regained the initiative in public affairs and organized opposition had been disrupted. All these trials can be described as a 'squaring of accounts' between the Communist party and its opponents.

Sedition charges and trials are a signal of how far the authorities are prepared to tolerate independent social initiatives (KOR), trade union movements (the Solidarity Seven) or political activity (KPN, Bałuka). The indictments against KOR and Bałuka, and the sentences passed on the KPN, show clearly that there still exist taboo subjects about which the authorities are particularly sensitive. These refer to the vital issues of Poland's political and military dependence on the USSR, and the lack of sovereignty of the nation vis-à-vis the Communist party. Imposing a blanket of silence on these issues goes hand in hand with denying the Poles their political rights.

In sedition trials the prosecution presents the motives and the activities of the defendants in a distorted light as criminal and politically irresponsible. By contrast, the Communist party is presented as a guardian of the status quo, the constitutional order, socialist legality, etc. These sedition trials give a telling insight into the arguments, legal and political, which the Communist party uses to justify its monopoly of power.

The Sedition Trials

Notes

1. *Trybuna Ludu*, 2 September 1982.
2. *Information Bulletin Solidarity Abroad*, no. 34, 15 September 1982.
3. Kazimierz Kalita, *Nowe Prawo*, January 1983.
4. Ibid.
5. Quoted by the Polish Helsinki Committee in its second report.
6. *KOS* no. 46, 2 January 1984.
7. Reuter, Warsaw, 18 January 1983 quoting W. Woroszylski.
8. *Financial Times*, 21 September 1983 and Polish Helsinki Committee Report no. 2.
9. Statement made in New York on 22 October 1983 in an address at a banquet given in honour of Lech Wałęsa who had been awarded the Nobel Peace Prize.
10. For instance, the publication *Radom 1976*, describing workers' protests of that year and KOR's efforts to help them; the Polish Helsinki Committee's report of October 1980 documenting the non-compliance of the PPR authorities with the provisions of the Helsinki Final Act; and Jan Józef Lipski's book on KOR published in London by Aneks.
11. In fact, both *Kultura* and the Polish Government in Exile administer funds to support independent social initiatives in Poland. The money comes from donations contributed by members of the Polish emigré community in the West. Both centres publish accounts of the aid they sent to Poland. KOR was not the only group to receive money through these centres.
12. *KOS* no. 27, 14 March 1983.
13. *Tygodnik Mazowsze* no. 87, 10 May 1984.
14. *Głos* no 1/2, 1980.
15. *Philadelphia Inquirer*, 13 July 1984.
16. In its resolution of 17 September 1979 the Political Council of the KPN put forward four conditions for normalizing Polish–Soviet relations. These were: sincere condemnation of all crimes committed by the Soviet authorities against the Polish nation, compensation for grievances, repudiation of Soviet imperialist policy with regard to Poland, and withdrawal of Soviet troops from Poland.
17. *Polityka*, 20 September 1980.
18. 'Die Sowjets sollen Abziehen', *Der Spiegel*, 15 September 1980.
19. There is some confusion as to whether Pstrąg–Bieleński was acting in the name of KPN or on his own initiative, as suggested by Władysław Gauza and Tomasz Strzyżewski in a letter to the editor of *Kultura*, published in May 1981. The Political Council of the KPN later withdrew Gauza's and Strzyżewski's authorization to represent the KPN abroad.

20. According to Maciej Pstrąg-Bieleński, *Kultura*, April 1981.
21. *Kultura*, March 1981.
22. Marian Reniak: *KPN: Kulisy Fakty Dokumenty*, (Książka i Wiedza, Warszawa, 1982).
23. *W służbie narodu* reprinted by *Głos Szczeciński;* 3-4 September 1983.
24. Ibid.

V

THE TRIALS OF THE UNDERGROUND SOLIDARITY ACTIVISTS

The emergence of the underground

It was never the aim of Solidarity to be an underground movement. On the contrary, their very *raison d'être* was their acceptance of the existing political and legal framework. Even after Solidarity regrouped underground, their structures were not meant to be either permanent or illegal. They emerged because the people at large did not recognize martial law, the suspension of Solidarity and the official policy of 'normalization' as legal or justified. As a peaceful movement committed to dialogue with the authorities, the union could not have prepared itself to resist martial law even if it had known about it beforehand. Although the rigours of martial law, the police raids on Solidarity offices, and the confiscation of the union's assets largely destroyed Solidarity as an organization it did not extinguish it as an idea or stop people from manifesting their support for it.

The spontaneous grass-roots resistance movement showed that although technically the authorities were in control, politically they had suffered a defeat. Those Solidarity activists who publicly recanted their trade union activity and decried its 'politicization' were treated as renegades, and they constituted a tiny minority in comparison with those who believed that their prime responsibility was to the rank-and-file who had entrusted their mandate to them. It was these latter who, having evaded the police dragnet on the night of 12 to 13 December 1981, strove to rebuild Solidarity under the new conditions and preserve its continuity as an organization. They went underground because they knew that they risked internment or arrest if they were caught. Others

The Trials of the Underground Solidarity Activists

went into hiding in order to regroup and re-establish contacts, to give expression to the free word or simply to wait and see. Those who went into hiding were only a part of the clandestine effort. Others who led a normal professional or family life 'on the surface' attended secret meetings, printed clandestine publications or distributed them. Others provided safe addresses and contact points, or acted as couriers to those who were in hiding.

From the authorities' point of view the emergence of the underground was an 'accident'. In their ideal model there ought to have been no independent trade union activity following the successful military crackdown. Solidarity activists ought to have been sitting either in internment camps or prisons, if they had taken part in the strikes of December 1981. A considerable number of people had, however, gone underground and this fact presented a challenge to the security forces. There were no specific provisions penalizing underground trade union activity. As far as criminal liability was concerned it was irrelevant whether the offender was acting in the open or underground. Hiding from the police was not in itself an offence. Thus, the martial law authorities initially treated clandestine activity as 'continuation of trade union activity'. As time wore on and the underground proved to be more resilient than the authorities had bargained for, other legal formulae had to be sought.

The underground, then, emerged in an ad hoc fashion. From the very beginning, however, there were doubts as to the idea of setting up a political underground in a Communist dictatorship. Writing in the Białołęka internment prison Adam Michnik expressed these doubts in the following way:

> No underground has ever been effective in a Communist system. The Communists have not achieved much but they were [always] able to destroy popular resistance, especially any form of clandestine resistance ... The destruction of social bonds was a precondition for Communist dictatorship — the apparatus of power and its institutions which served to destroy human solidarity and keep the people in line were the only [admissible] forms of social organization.[1]

Despite these reservations, Michnik accepted that under martial law the Poles had no choice since Jaruzelski had chosen for them.

The inherent dangers of clandestine underground activity

could, nevertheless, not be underestimated. There were three principal dangers: police infiltration resulting in provocation and arrests; loss of contact with the general public as it slid progressively into passivity and apathy and became increasingly preoccupied with trying to make ends meet as the economy stagnated; and the temptation to use terrorist means. These dangers have, in fact, largely been avoided. To prevent police infiltration the underground Solidarity activists did not hide behind pseudonyms but revealed their real names. To counteract apathy and passivity, the resistance movement was based not on actions inspired from above but on broad, spontaneous grass-root initiatives that were simply co-ordinated on the regional and national levels. Finally, the Solidarity leaders underground actively campaigned against the use of violence and armed struggle, advocating instead various peaceful forms of exerting pressure on the authorities in the hope of forcing the authorities into a compromise with society.

The conditions in which Solidarity were forced to act clandestinely were inevitably much more difficult than those they had known during their legal existence. Their means were limited, their activists were hunted by the police, they had to evolve a new programme, plan of action and organizational structure. They had no previous experience on which to draw, and, above all, the union had to fight for the right to exist. Their tasks were, according to Zbigniew Bujak, governed by four considerations. First, Solidarity was a trade union forced to act clandestinely; secondly, it was acting in a situation of deteriorating economic crisis; thirdly, the state was not founded on the rule of law; and finally, it was not a fully sovereign state. In such a situation, Bujak had no doubts as to where the union's priorities lay:

> In view of the tragic economic situation our primary task is to defend those with the smallest incomes and force the authorities to use their reserve resources, for example by limiting the funds available for military purposes, as well as the police and security apparatus. The lack of justice in our country forces us to take up the struggle for the release of political prisoners, for an independent judiciary, social arbitration, freedom of the press. Last, but not least, the lack of sovereignty. The imposition of martial law has finally proved that it is impossible for an independent trade union to function in an undemocratic state. In order to rebuild

The Trials of the Underground Solidarity Activists

an independent union movement we must first, through our struggle, ensure that the state is founded on democratic principles.[2]

These tasks were to be achieved through such forms of resistance as street demonstrations, boycott of the pro-regime trade unions, refusal to participate in regime-sponsored activities such as elections, creation of an independent information and publishing network, work stoppages, wearing certain emblems, boycott of the official propaganda (press, television), and revealing the names of those who exhibited excessive zeal in carrying out unpopular, officially-inspired decisions. This list shows that the Solidarity underground were primarily a social resistance movement using boycott and protest as their major weapons in their struggle for recognition and reform of the system. At the beginning of martial law, the Solidarity underground lacked a realistic assessment of the balance of strength between the authorities, on the one hand, and society, on the other. Solidarity's tactics were based on the assumption that the authorities would be damaged, weakened and isolated by the various forms of boycott and that they would eventually be forced to negotiate and compromise with the representatives of society. This assumption proved, however, to have been a false one since the authorities were determined to destroy the independent union at any cost. In fact, open resistance to martial law only raised the cost of the 'normalization' exercise.

The tactics of boycott put the Solidarity underground on the defensive, depriving them of the initiative. Solidarity called for protests on various occasions, usually as a reaction against decisions considered unacceptable to society at large, or on a national anniversary. In the first months of martial law they succeeded in mobilizing the masses against the regime, but, as time wore on, found it more difficult to present them with the vision of goals in the name of which they were to participate in protest actions. A positive programme was unrealistically expected of the union which was struggling even to survive in a skeleton form. Above all the Solidarity underground needed success to reassert themselves. This was not easy in the face of the unprecedented mobilization of police, security forces and the military. Solidarity, a reform movement by definition, were never allowed to proceed with reform. Their only chance of working out a meaningful programme of reforms was a compromise with the authorities.

The Trials of the Underground Solidarity Activists

The latter, however, expected nothing but surrender. Solidarity were caught in the dilemma of reconciling a programme of an evolutionary change in the system with tactics of effective, strong pressure on the authorities. Their programme called for compromise with the authorities while their tactics called for boycott and confrontation. The underground leadership gradually came to realize that the struggle would be a long one and that it would require something more constructive and long term than protest and boycott.

The tactics of the 'long march' towards a 'self-governing society', were spelled out in the TKK programme 'Solidarity Today' of 22 January 1983, and endorsed by Wałęsa in his proposals of 16 December 1983 which also called on all Solidarity members to campaign on behalf of union pluralism, the rule of law and self-management.

Solidarity began to re-organize in the underground within a few weeks of the declaration of martial law. The National Resistance Committee (OKO) was formed in early January 1982 by some 20 Solidarity activists who had not been interned. Their aim was to coordinate Solidarity activities until martial law was lifted. On 22 April 1982 representatives of the four most active and best organized regional Solidarity organizations — Mazowsze (Warsaw), Gdańsk, Małopolska (Kraków) and Lower Silesia (Wrocław) — came together to form the Provisional Co-ordinating Commission (TKK). The TKK was conceived, as the very name suggests, as a temporary body, co-ordinating the diverse Solidarity efforts throughout the country until such time as the suspended National Commission of Solidarity were able to resume their proper functions. The TKK did not aspire to be a central command centre. Regional Solidarity structures recognizing the TKK soon began to be formed. Those that were already in existence also recognized the authority of the TKK. By August 1982, 14 regional Solidarity centres of resistance were in existence (in comparison with the 38 regions and 4 independent districts that had existed before 13 December 1981). The main role of these clandestine regional bodies was to follow events and give a lead in social resistance activities, co-ordinate various local protest actions, maintain contacts with the workers of the key enterprises in the region, support independent publications, prepare factories for a general strike and popularize independent initiatives such as unofficial educational schemes and cultural events.

The establishment and development of Clandestine Factory

The Trials of the Underground Solidarity Activists

Commissions (TKZ) was of great importance for the Solidarity underground movement. These constituted the fundamental link with grass-roots workers' opinion. Their activities involved collecting information and passing it on to the regional Solidarity structures, as well as disseminating information among the workforce and keeping the Solidarity spirit and ideas alive. They issued statements on matters of vital interest to the workforce, organized self-help actions, in particular for the victims of repression and their families, organized and co-ordinated factory-level protest actions, prepared the general strike and maintained contact with the regional union authorities. The Clandestine Factory Commissions continued to collect union dues and published detailed accounts of income and expenditure. They promoted the boycott of the new pro-regime unions and denounced official policy on the trade union movement, self-management or the labour law.

The Clandestine Factory Commissions became the prime object of the authorities' repression. Sackings, police surveillance, emigration, as well as the fluctuation of the workforce and the benefits offered by the regime-sponsored 'Wron-unions' took their toll, weakening the position of the Clandestine Factory Commissions. Both the authorities and the Provisional Co-ordinating Commission realized that it was in the factories, and especially the key enterprises, that the fate of Solidarity would, in the long run, be decided. In the fifth year of Solidarity's existence the TKK member Zbigniew Bujak called, in a Radio Solidarity broadcast, for the reconstruction of union cells on the factory level: 'We cannot be satisfied with Solidarity in our hearts', he said, 'We have to maintain real organizations in the enterprises'.[3]

The influence of the Clandestine Factory Commissions has, understandably, been limited by several factors: they could not operate openly or canvass for support, they needed to be constantly on their guard in case they were caught by the police or management, they had to challenge the official unions, and counteract the widespread despondency among the workers. These factors led to a situation which Jacek Kuroń described as follows:

> When the workers start arguing over something in their department, work team, or in the factory as a whole, then [the authorities] usually give in. But if these matters are raised in the name of Solidarity, then the chances [of success]

are considerably reduced and the affair is considered a political one. The struggle by Solidarity on the economic front is incomparably more difficult when it is carried out en masse than in a single factory or work team. And people prefer to engage in an activity that is effective...[4]

There were other forms of clandestine activity in addition to the Provisional Co-ordinating Commission, Regional Executive Commissions and Clandestine Factory Commissions. There were several inter-factory organizations (e.g. the Inter-Factory Workers' Solidarity Committee — MRKS — which brought together clandestine Solidarity activists from several key enterprises in Warsaw), independent groups not integrated into the regional Solidarity structure (such as 'Fighting Solidarity') as well as occupational and professional bodies (such as the Social Committee for Science — SKN, the Council of National Education — REN, or the National Farmers' Resistance Committee — OKOR). Apart from trade union opposition stemming directly from the experience of Solidarity, there emerged an openly political opposition in the form of political parties orientated to the reconquest of Poland's independence. A major weakness of this last form of opposition was the difficulty of formulating a programme which could be translated into everyday actions that would lead eventually to the desired goal.

To assess the scope of underground Solidarity's influence one must take into account the fact that it was unable to perform a strictly trade union role on account of the repressive conditions in which it had to operate. Still, with its protest actions and boycott, Solidarity managed to isolate the authorities in society, making them aware of how deeply unpopular, unrepresentative and fundamentally unlawful their rule was. The trend, characteristic of Soviet-style Communism, towards merging state and society was arrested. In this way, martial law and the emergence of the underground freed social consciousness of years of systematic indoctrination. The underground movement, moreover, inspired many independent cultural, social, economic, publishing, educational and political initiatives whose aim was to counter the one-party monopoly. On the other hand, the Solidarity underground failed to change the course of martial law policies and restore even the limited civil liberties of the Solidarity heyday. Since it was unable to use its only weapon — the strike — its ability to influence events could not have been other than

The Trials of the Underground Solidarity Activists

limited. On the whole, however, the existence of the Solidarity underground complicated the authorities' task by raising the political cost of their repressive policies and demonstrating, both at home and abroad, that the Communists in Poland, in an attempt to re-animate their dead utopia, had had to re-conquer civil society.

Zbigniew Bujak gave a somewhat pessimistic, but none the less realistic, assessment of Solidarity's influence when he said 'Solidarity is weak, but it is the strongest organization that could be created in this situation. If we had abandoned Solidarity when it was banned, we would have been more divided as a society.'[5] The underground movement, although undoubtedly weaker since the amnesty of September 1986, still poses a potential threat to the authorities. In the event of another socio-political crisis for the Communist regime, the veterans of the underground movement constitute a group of people ready to provide the workers with leadership and a sense of direction. Much as they would like to disregard Solidarity and treat them as outlaws, the authorities have to acknowledge the de facto existence of a political opposition. Secondly, the underground actions of Solidarity strengthen the hand of those Solidarity activists who attempt to act openly within the confines of the system. Thirdly, the existence of the underground makes the official trade union movement more radical than it would otherwise have been. Finally, the underground symbolizes the popular refusal to accept force as a means of solving social conflicts, reaffirms the values shared by the vast majority of the people, provides a skeleton organization and an independent network of information and, last but not least, does not stop at protest actions but actually puts forward alternatives to official policies.

The defendants

Only the trials of those Solidarity activists who had actually gone into hiding to continue the fight for their union's right to exist and who were on the police wanted lists are discussed below. The most important cases referred to in this chapter are those of the Warsaw-based Inter-Factory Workers' Solidarity Committee (MRKS); Władysław Frasyniuk, Piotr Bednarz and Józef Pinior,

The Trials of the Underground Solidarity Activists

the three successive Chairmen of the underground Regional Strike Committee in Wrocław and members of the Provisional Co-ordinating Commission (TKK); Zbigniew Romaszewski, KOR member and Solidarity activist involved in the setting up of Radio Solidarity; Janusz Pałubicki, Chairman of the clandestine Provisional Board of the Wielkopolska Region (Poznań) and member of the TKK; Tadeusz Jedynak, Chairman of the underground Regional Executive Commission in the Śląsko-Dąbrowski Region (Katowice) and member of the TKK; Bogdan Lis and Bogdan Borusewicz, successive Chairmen of the Regional Co-ordinating Commission in the Gdańsk Region and members of the TKK; Czesław Bielecki, underground publisher and writer; and Zbigniew Bujak, Chairman of the Mazowsze Regional Executive Commission and member of the TKK.

Most of the defendants in the trials of the underground activists were workers. But there were also intellectuals — a librarian, a physicist and an architect. Some of them were active in the underground from the beginning of martial law, others went through spells of internment or imprisonment before they went into hiding. Since there was no penalty for simply going underground, clandestine Solidarity activists were tried for their role in the strikes of December 1981, various protest actions, activity in the underground Solidarity information network or their part in specific initiatives such as independent publishing or radio broadcasting.

Intense police surveillance usually preceded the arrest of the underground Solidarity activists. Most of the arrests resulted from carelessness on the part of the activists in hiding or a tip-off to the police by an informer. Police activity usually intensified before nationwide actions planned by the union, such as demonstrations, protest actions against price rises or the election boycott, as well as before important official events such as the delegalization of Solidarity or the party congress.

Any arrests were exploited for their propaganda value. The authorities were not content simply to arrest an underground activist, they usually attempted to induce the captive to recant in public and show repentance in front of the television cameras. In the case of Tadeusz Jedynak they made clear that the reward for recanting would be an immediate release and, to make the argument more convincing, they even arranged for his wife to visit him so that she might try to persuade him to take part in the television programme. Another Solidarity underground activist,

The Trials of the Underground Solidarity Activists

Piotr Bednarz, was filmed from a hidden camera while at Wrocław Police HQ after he refused to give a television interview and a snippet of this film was shown on television. After Józef Pinior was arrested the authorities broadcast a television programme entitled 'The Last Payoff' that included photos of stacks of Polish zlotys and American dollars said to have been in Pinior's possession at the time of his arrest. Radio Warsaw aired a special half-hour broadcast based on what purported to be a secretly taped conversation between two women who were alleged to have had close ties to the Wrocław underground. The two women, who used somewhat vulgar language, described how Pinior enjoyed his life on the run from the law, spending union funds on wine, women and merry-making. The message was clear to everyone: the workers put their lives in danger while the underground leaders of Solidarity were living it up at the workers' expense. After the arrest of the most wanted Solidarity fugitive, TKK member Zbigniew Bujak, the authorities insinuated that his hiding place had been known to the US Embassy in Warsaw.

With the passage of time the authorities no longer attempted to lure those arrested in front of television cameras, choosing, instead, to present them as people linked to 'centres of foreign subversion'. On 10 May 1985, during a Sejm debate, the Minister of Internal Affairs Czesław Kiszczak slandered the underground political writer and publisher Czesław Bielecki by saying that he was 'an agent of long standing of foreign centres of political subversion who was to have been illegally sprung to Paris in order to take over from Giedroyć, at the behest of the CIA, as the director of the Paris *Kultura',* and that he had engaged in 'activities hostile [to the PPR] on the instructions of his Western taskmasters'.

In the case of the Inter–Factory Workers' Solidarity Committee (MRKS) official propaganda attempted to create the impression that their actions were akin to the terrorism of the Red Brigades.

The investigation

The aim of the police was not only to arrest the leading underground Solidarity activists, but also to round up their back-up men, neutralize contacts and safe addresses, and seize printing and broadcasting equipment, in other words, render ineffective the whole unofficial network. With this aim in view the police would always arrest not only the underground leader, but also a number of other people whose testimony could possibly lead to still further arrests. In the case of Józef Pinior, the police arrested some 30 people, many of them involved in underground publishing. In the case of Janusz Pałubicki the police originally arrested six people and later, as a result of the testimony of one of the suspects, Marek Zierhoffer, a further ten.

The aim of the investigation was not so much to establish the objective truth as to work out a political as well as legal concept of the trial and, secondly, to obtain detailed testimony and a confession from at least one of the suspects. A suspect whom the investigative authorities managed to soften up and consequently to win his co-operation could be used as the principal witness incriminating others who refused to testify in the course of the investigation. Investigations involving underground Solidarity activists were formally supervised by the prosecutor's office, but it was General Kiszczak's Ministry of Internal Affairs, specifically its Investigations Bureau, which indicated the direction of the investigation, charted its course and decided on its termination. The Investigations Bureau of the Ministry acted as a party in the proceedings, actively working towards incriminating the suspects or offering them deals involving their release at the price of self-incrimination.

In the course of the investigation the authorities might change their original concept of the trial. A suspect might be questioned in connection with a specific charge and subsequently be accused of another offence. Józef Pinior, for instance, who was arrested in April 1983 was questioned intensively about his alleged embezzlement of union funds just before the imposition of martial law. Lech Wałęsa, who was summoned as a witness to the regional police office in Gdańsk, was also questioned on the same subject. As the investigation progressed the investigative authorities came to be more interested in Pinior's membership in Solidarity's regional and national underground structures.[6] Another TKK member, Tadeusz Jedynak, who was arrested in June 1985, was investigated under the charge of treason but accused in May 1986 of preparing a coup d'état, and in July of that year tried under this charge. In the case of Bogdan Lis and Piotr Mierzewski, a research scientist from Gdańsk who was at one stage included in the proceedings against Lis, the authorities clumsily

The Trials of the Underground Solidarity Activists

attempted to explain a similar manipulation of the charges:

> The suspects were charged with having held as of April 1982 posts in the illegal, so-called Provisional Co-ordinating Commission and having taken part in the activities of foreign organizations serving the interests of foreign countries including the so-called Solidarity Co-ordination Bureau in Brussels, the aim of which was to abolish by force the PPR's socio-political system and weaken its defence potential. The evidence gathered during the investigation does not leave any doubt that the suspects aimed at abolishing by force the PPR's socio-political system; it has not been confirmed, however, that their action constituted the crime of treason.[7]

Such a modification of charges was sufficient to release the two activists under the terms of the July 1984 amnesty.

To make the preconceived scenario for the trial appear credible the investigative officers would attempt to impose a specific frame of reference by using certain propagandistic expressions. In this way they managed to present a spontaneous grass-root protest or independent initiative as a highly organized conspiracy inspired by subversive ring-leaders, motivated by anti-state considerations and, therefore, socially harmful. In the case of the Inter-Factory Workers' Solidarity Committee, whose leading activists were arrested in July 1982, the investigative officer put on record expressions such as 'the supreme Five', 'special task forces' and 'the bosses'.

Various methods were used to soften up the suspect. The investigative officers strove above all psychologically to break a suspect by creating a feeling that he was at the complete mercy of the officer, that he had no recourse other than the investigative officer, that the law could be stretched to suit the needs of the investigative officer, that the fate of the suspect was predetermined and that the courts were bound to do their part and convict the suspect when he was brought to trial. As a second step the investigative officer would suggest that it was in the suspect's interest to say what he knew and sign what he was given to sign, otherwise he might be tried for a still more serious offence. To make it easier for the suspect to take up this 'suggestion' the investigative officer would try to assuage possible pangs of conscience on the part of the suspect. He would be told that the

The Trials of the Underground Solidarity Activists

case was already solved, that the police already knew everything and that all that was required of the suspect was mere confirmation of some secondary details. At this stage the suspect might be confronted with evidence gathered by police through 'operational means', or with the testimony of a fellow-suspect. Those who still refused to testify might be blackmailed. They might be told that members of their families might suffer for their stubbornness, that they might be included in the case of 'a dangerous psychopath', or 'an armed gang', and that, in this case, the court would punish them more severely. Blackmail was usually accompanied by the offer of a 'deal'. Andrzej Michałowski, a member of the Regional Co-ordinating Commission of the Gdańsk Region, who was arrested in September 1985, was offered a one-way passport to join his wife in Norway provided he revealed where another underground Solidarity activist, Bogdan Borusewicz, was hiding.[8] Bogdan Lis was told that he would not be released under the amnesty unless he co-operated with the investigative authorities. He rejected the 'offer' and was still released, albeit six months later, after the authorities were unable to find sufficient grounds for a charge of treason. Suspects in political cases were lined up by the investigative authorities according to the pre-conceived concept of the trial; if the concept changed they might be re-grouped. Some of the suspects might be excluded from the investigation altogether, others might have the proceedings against them suspended or dropped. In the case of Janusz Pałubicki, who was arrested in December 1982, all of his co-suspects — 16 in all — were amnestied in July 1983. Another TKK member Bogdan Borusewicz, who was arrested in January 1986, was linked to the case of Andrzej Michałowski who had been arrested previously, and was charged with leading and participating in the activities of an illegal organization (i.e. the Regional Co-ordinating Commission of the Gdańsk Region — RKK) whose aim it was to cause public unrest. Later Borusewicz's case was separated from that of Michałowski and he was charged with preparing a coup d'état.

The investigative authorities' method of working on one particular suspect in order to win his co-operation and incriminate others with his testimony proved a success in some of the important trials of underground Solidarity activists. It is well illustrated by the case of Radio Solidarity. The two main defendants in this trial, which opened in January 1983 before the Court of the Warsaw Military District, Zbigniew Romaszewski

The Trials of the Underground Solidarity Activists

and his wife Zofia, were incriminated by the testimony of Roger Noël, a Belgian who was arrested in Warsaw on 5 July 1982 while passing radio equipment smuggled into Poland for Radio Solidarity. Romaszewski himself was arrested on 30 August 1982. Noël was questioned between 5 and 13 October 1982 as a witness in the case of Radio Solidarity. At this time he was serving a three-year prison term to which he had been sentenced for smuggling a radio transmitter to Poland. In his detailed testimony he incriminated Romaszewski by admitting, for instance, that during one of his visits to Warsaw he had agreed to take a letter from Romaszewski to Mirosław Chojecki in Paris. He also described his contacts with the opposition in Poland. His testimony was also shown to another of the suspects, Anna Owczarska, who broke down and incriminated others. Noël, who had been tried under summary procedure, was given the option of paying a fine of $10,000 and leaving the country. He did so shortly after he had given his testimony. In this way he was not available to testify in person before the court at the trial of Radio Solidarity. His testimony was read out in court and, since he was not there, he did not have the opportunity to retract or clarify it.

In the MRKS case all five leading activists were arrested. Subsequently four of them were charged, tried and sentenced and one of them, Edward Piotrowski, testified as the principal witness for the prosecution. Piotrowski had signed everything he had been asked to sign by the investigative officers in the course of the investigation. The MRKS case was perhaps all too easy for the police since they had not only a model witness but also their own 'agent provocateur', a certain Sławomir Miastowski, who had also romanced with another MRKS activist, Elżbieta Stobbe.

The latter only realized his police connections during the pre-trial detention. The main suspect Adam Borowski did not realize Miastowski's connections until after the investigation was over. He had worded his pre-trial testimony in such a way as to protect Miastowski and only revealed Miastowski's real role in the MRKS activities at the trial. The advantage of having both a model witness and an 'agent provocateur' was that the prosecution could cover the evidence collected by the latter with the testimony of the former. Thus the methods used by the police needed not come to light.

To break down a suspect, and render him defenceless and susceptible to persuasion, it was necessary for the investigating officer to break his bonds with the outside world, and to destroy

The Trials of the Underground Solidarity Activists

his faith in the people with whom he had been working, his hopes for the future and his conviction that continuation of the struggle for freedom or trade union rights made sense. Although the very fact of isolation and the passage of time helped the police to soften up some of the suspects, most of the underground Solidarity activists remained true to the Solidarity ideals and only a handful reneged. One of those who did was Władysław Hardek, head of the Małopolska Regional Executive Commission and member of the TKK, who was arrested in August 1983. According to unconfirmed reports, he was found in a situation that was personally compromising and a pistol was found on him. During the investigation he was questioned not only by a security officer but also by specialists in law, psychology and history. They talked him into letting his arrest be presented as a voluntary surrender under the terms of the government amnesty of July 1983. On 23 August 1983 he was shown on television repenting for his underground trade union activity. Discredited in this way among the opposition, Hardek was released. After the arrest of his fellow TKK member Bogdan Lis, in July 1984, Hardek was taken by police helicopter from Kraków to the Gdańsk investigative prison, where Lis was being held, in an attempt to persuade Lis to recant. Lis refused, however, to enter into conversation with Hardek and the ploy ended in failure.

To make the task of softening up the suspect easier for the police he was frequently isolated from the outside world and from his co-suspects. Czesław Bielecki, who was arrested in April 1985, was not allowed to see his lawyer in private for several months and it was only as a result of a long hunger strike that he was allowed to see his two sons. If the suspect is being held on charges of sedition, contacts with defence lawyers are strictly limited. Only those defence lawyers whose names are to be found on a special list, compiled by military courts and periodically revised, are allowed to take up the case and even then they are frequently denied access to the suspect and excluded from the proceedings.

Lawyers who agree to represent underground Solidarity activists are often subject to police harassment. Zofia Adamowicz, who acted for Adam Borowski, the main defendant in the MRKS trial, had her flat searched in April 1983. The police looked through her files on the case of the MRKS, violating professional secrecy. In September 1983 several burglaries occurred in Wrocław in various group legal practices. Some documents pertaining to the case of Józef Pinior went missing and were never found.

The Trials of the Underground Solidarity Activists

Among the missing documents were signed statements from Solidarity members authorizing Pinior to manage the trade union funds which he was alleged to have embezzled.

Messages smuggled out from prison by the suspects could also be used against them in so far as they might provide the investigative officer with new clues. Such messages were, as a rule, included in the police files on the case.

On completion of the investigation, the preconceived scenario was expressed in the thesis of the indictment. This was in turn corroborated by the evidence that the investigative authorities had managed to gather. The fact that there was all too often a glaring discrepancy between the thesis and the evidence did not seem to give the prosecution authorities much cause for concern.

The charges

The choice of charges presented to underground Solidarity activists seems to have been determined not so much by what they actually did nor even by the sum of evidence collected, as by the stage in time at which the trial itself was held. Generally speaking, the early trials of underground activists were based, with few exceptions, on the Martial Law Decree and were modelled on the trials of the December 1981 strikers. With the formal suspension of martial law the charges, while still based on the Martial Law Decree, were supplemented by the provisions of the Penal Code. With the formal lifting of martial law and the abrogation of the Martial Law Decree in July 1983, the charges were based solely on the Penal Code. This had, of course, in the meantime been amended to accommodate certain of the martial law provisions.

The martial law model

Underground leaders who were brought to trial in the first year of martial law were as a rule charged either with the continuation of trade union activity(Art. 46.1 of the Martial Law Decree) or with organizing or leading strikes or illegal protest actions in December 1981(Art. 46.2 of the Martial Law Decree). Some were charged under both these provisions.

The principal charge against Stanisław Handzlik, a member of the Regional Executive Commission of the Małopolska Region

The Trials of the Underground Solidarity Activists

(Kraków), was that of strike organizing and it was only supplemented by the charge of continuing trade union activity. The indictment was for the greater part concerned with his role during the strike at the Lenin Steelworks in Nowa Huta in December 1981 while his underground activity was treated more cursorily. Handzlik, who was arrested on 24 June 1982, was sentenced to four years' imprisonment in July 1982.

In the case of Patrycjusz Kosmowski, who was arrested on 19 January 1982, the charge of strike organizing could not be made since Kosmowski had been away when the strike took place. Kosmowski, as Chairman of Solidarity's Beskidy Region (Bielsko-Biała), had prepared, at a meeting of his regional executive on 9 December 1981, contingency arrangements in anticipation of the military crackdown about which they had been tipped off. He was accused of continuing trade union activity by organizing clandestine structures which were to prepare protest actions against martial law. He was sentenced on 9 March 1982 to six years' imprisonment.

In the case of Władysław Frasyniuk who was arrested on 5 October 1982, various specific offences, such as his activity within the Regional Strike Committee in Wrocław, participation in the TKK, inspiring and organizing street demonstrations, protest actions, leading the activities of clandestine groups responsible for printing and distribution of illegal publications, fly-sheets as well as Radio Solidarity broadcasts in Wrocław were subsumed under the offence of continuation of trade union activity.

In order to make the offence appear more grievous the authorities sought to link the arrested Solidarity activists to independent publishing activities: editing, printing or distributing underground publications and fly-sheets. A Solidarity activist from Łódź, Jerzy Dłużniewski, who was arrested on 20 February 1982 was, for instance, charged with 'organizing on 14 December 1981 in the enterprises of the Łódź region a general strike', as well as 'having, with the aim of disseminating false information liable to cause public unrest or disturbances, written a text signed with his name which was to appear in issue no. 10 of the illegally published bulletin *Solidarność Walczy* ('Solidarity Fights On')'. He was, moreover, charged with preparing and signing an open letter addressed to workers in the Marchlewski Textile Enterprise (i.e. offences under Art. 46.2 and 48.3 of the Martial Law Decree). Dłużniewski was sentenced to four years' imprisonment by the Court of the Pomeranian Military District in Bydgoszcz.

The Trials of the Underground Solidarity Activists

The charge of continuing trade union activity under Art. 46.1 of the Martial Law Decree was regularly presented to suspects who were members of Solidarity, even though the activity for which they were charged was not of a strictly trade union nature. In the case of Zbigniew Romaszewski and others associated with Radio Solidarity the indictment specified that 'after the introduction of martial law the suspects did not cease their activity in the suspended trade union Solidarity whose members and activists they were, but continued it by disseminating, in illegal Radio Solidarity broadcasts, false information about the social and political situation in the country that was liable to cause unrest and disturbances, and incited others, moreover, to resist the laws and legal ordinances of the state authorities'. While it was true that Romaszewski and other co-defendants were activists and supporters of Solidarity, the fact of setting up Radio Solidarity was not, strictly speaking, a continuation of trade union activity since it was a new initiative that had only begun after the imposition of martial law. On the other hand, there was no mention in the trial of Romaszewski's membership in the clandestine Mazowsze Regional Executive Commission which should logically have constituted the prime argument in the prosecution's case against him. This argument was reserved for the trial of several members of the Social Self-Defence Committee 'KOR' in which Romaszewski was also to have appeared as one of the four co-accused. In this way the investigative authorities devised a singular way of trying Romaszewski for the same activities under two different hats. A comparison of the two indictments shows that the same activities were simply called by different names: they were legally qualified in one case as 'continuation of trade union activity' and, in the other, as 'preparation of a coup d'état'. Romaszewski was sentenced to four and a half years' imprisonment for his involvement in Radio Solidarity.

Mixed model

From the suspension of martial law as of 31 December 1982 until its formal lifting in July 1983 the charges presented to underground Solidarity activists tended to be based on both the Martial Law Decree and the Penal Code. The charge of continuing trade union activity under Art. 46.1 of the decree was, in the majority of cases, presented in conjunction with Art. 276.1 and

The Trials of the Underground Solidarity Activists

3 (participating in or founding a criminal association), Art. 278.1 and 2 (participating in or setting up a secret association), or Art. 278.3 (leading an association which had either been disbanded by the authorities or refused legalization). The aims of the secret association were invariably presented as subversive. In the case of 19 clandestine Solidarity activists from Opole, the main defendant Stanisław Jałowiecki was charged with

> having, together with others, set up an association whose aim it was to commit an offence and whose existence, internal structure and aim were to remain unknown to the state authorities; having subsequently led this association; having, moreover, as a member of the suspended trade union Solidarity, failed to desist from trade union activity and continued it, disseminating by print false information liable to cause public unrest or disturbances.

During the trial, which was held before the Court of the Silesian Military District in January 1983, the defendants were acquitted of charges under Arts. 276 and 278. The court found that there was no evidence that the defendants had set up a new secret association, nor that they had had the intention of doing so. The defendants, for their part, claimed that, although they had been active in the underground and engaged in publishing the bulletin *Sygnały Wojenne,* they had only done so in order to preserve the trade union of which they were members. They said that they had done so in the hope that the authorities would one day lift the ban on Solidarity and that the union structures they had preserved would be able to resume open activity. 'The very fact of maintaining certain, even far reaching forms of clandestine activity could not', in the court's view, 'lead to the erroneous conclusion that a new secret association had been set up'. The court passed remarkably lenient sentences of up to one year's imprisonment.

Faced with charges under both the Martial Law Decree and the Penal Code, the defence lawyers would try to present the activities of the underground Solidarity activists as constituting simply a continuation of trade union activity which was a lesser offence. The prosecution would, on the other hand, insist that the defendants had led or taken part in the activities of a criminal or secret association. A major dispute between the prosecution and the defence concerning the legal assessment of the underground activity of the Solidarity leader Janusz Pałubicki was

The Trials of the Underground Solidarity Activists

decided by the Air Force Court in Poznań in October 1983 in favour of the defence. Pałubicki was accused of leading an illegal association known as the Provisional Board of Solidarity (TZR) for the Wielkopolska Region and of participating in the activities of the Provisional Co-ordinating Commission (TKK), distributing underground bulletins and using a falsified identity document. According to the prosecutor the aims of both the TZR and the TKK were criminal. The defence lawyer Aleksander Berger argued that it was incorrect to speak of the TZR and the TKK as being two separate organizations. They were, in fact, two levels of one and the same organization which was a continuation of the Solidarity union that was officially recognised prior to the introduction of martial law. Both the TZR and the TKK had the same statutes, programme and aims. They could not be described as criminal since all they wanted was to persuade the authorities to allow trade union pluralism. The charges under Art. 276.1 and 3, continued Berger, were not justified; Pałubicki ought rather to have been charged with continuing trade union activity (until the Trade Union Act came into force i.e. 11 October 1982) and leading an organization which had been dissolved (after 11 October 1982). The point of this exercise in legal finesse was to persuade the court to accept a legal assessment of Pałubicki's activities which would enable him to be freed under the terms of the amnesty of 21 July 1983. The court, although accepting the legal argument of the defence that the defendant was guilty only of continuing trade union activity none the less passed a relatively high sentence of four years' imprisonment which meant that Pałubicki would still have to serve time since the amnesty halved the sentence. Had he been sentenced to three years' imprisonment he would have been freed forthwith.

Józef Pinior, like Pałubicki, was not originally charged with continuation of trade union activity but eventually found guilty of this particular offence. The Voivodship Court in Wrocław passing sentence in May 1984 found, moreover, that Pinior had organized strikes and protest actions, led an illegal association, been involved in the production of underground publications whose content incited people to commit offences and undertaken other activities with the aim of causing public unrest or disturbances. Pinior was also sentenced to four years' imprisonment halved under the amnesty of July 1983.

The authorities would also attempt to hide the political character of underground activity by presenting charges under Art.

The Trials of the Underground Solidarity Activists

276 of the Penal Code, i.e. taking part in setting up or leading a criminal association. Such charges were originally presented, in conjunction with Art. 278, in the trial of nine activists of the Inter-Factory Workers' Solidarity Committee (MKRS) which was held before the Court of the Warsaw Military District in May 1983. The MRKS was, according to the prosecution, both criminal and secret. In the indictment the main defendant Adam Borowski was accused of

> having, together with others, founded after 13 December 1981 an association called CDN ('To Be Continued'), which in April 1982 was transformed into the Inter-Factory Workers' Solidarity Committee, whose existence and internal structure were to remain secret from the state authorities, and whose aim it was to violate the legal order of martial law in a criminal manner, in particular through printing and distributing anti-state propaganda publications, containing false information liable to cause public unrest or disturbances, as well as through organizing strikes and protest actions; in addition, having led this association.

The prosecutor refused to recognize the MRKS as a Solidarity structure. In his indictment he alleged that the activities of the MRKS constituted 'a serious attempt to dismantle the state in the period of martial law'.

The absurdity of this charge is best seen when one considers the forms of activity of the MRKS. The indictment stated that one of the basic forms of the MRKS's activity was the printing and distribution of various publications, including the periodical *CDN — Voice of the Free Worker*. The prosecutor went on to analyze the contents of various MRKS publications and described them as false, slanderous and aiming to 'create a psychosis of fear among the people'. The indictment also listed other forms of MRKS activity including organizing of and inciting to street demonstrations, inciting others to organize strikes, carrying out various actions which had 'terrorist features', and organizing underground cells among the workforce of Warsaw and the Warsaw voivodship.

The defence lawyer Władysław Siła-Nowicki argued that the trial was based on a false legal premise. The defendants, he said, had only continued trade union activity which had been declared illegal by the martial law authorities. Since their activity had taken

The Trials of the Underground Solidarity Activists

place during martial law they ought to be tried under the Martial Law Decree. The MRKS was not a new, illegal and secret organization but a continuation of Solidarity. The restoration of this union's right to exist was the MRKS' sole objective. Alluding to one of the points in the indictment, the spilling of a stinking substance in the Komedia Theatre, which the prosecutor had described as terrorist in nature, Władysław Siła-Nowicki said that terrorism involved the spilling of blood and not of stinking substances. Siła-Nowicki concluded that neither Art.276 of the Penal Code nor Art. 278 were appropriate to the activities of the MRKS. Art. 276 was unjustified since the MRKS activists had not set up a criminal association. The aim of the MRKS was not criminal; the group had simply wanted to continue the traditions of Solidarity. The application of Art. 278 of the Penal Code was equally inappropriate since the defendants had not attempted to hide the aims or the existence of the MRKS. Only the internal organization of the MRKS was secret. The main defendant Adam Borowski had been in hiding, and could not have made his name and address public. The proper legal solution, according to Siła-Nowicki, would be to apply Art. 46 of the Martial Law Decree, the more so since the decree, by virtue of its extraordinary character, took precedence over the Penal Code.

The Court pronouncing on 19 May 1983 passed sentences of up to three and a half years' imprisonment finding the defendants guilty, as the defence had argued, of continuing trade union activity. The prosecutor appealed, however, to the Supreme Court arguing that his original legal assessment of the offences committed by the defendants, based on Art. 276 and 278 of the Penal Code, was correct. The Supreme Court hearing the case on 12 August 1983 increased the sentence passed on the main defendant Borowski assessing his activity, as demanded by the prosecutor, on the basis of the Penal Code. The Supreme Court sentenced Borowski on two separate counts to five and two years' imprisonment passing a joint penalty of six years' imprisonment. The penalty was halved as a result of the amnesty of 21 July 1983. The charges against Borowski's co-defendants were not re-evaluated by the Supreme Court and since they had all been sentenced under Art. 46.1 of the Martial Law Decree they were all covered by the amnesty. Since the prosecutor had claimed that all the defendants had performed leading roles in the MRKS, it is clear that Borowski, as the 'ringleader', was singled out for more severe punishment.

The Trials of the Underground Solidarity Activists

The Penal Code model

With the lifting of martial law underground Solidarity activists faced charges under the Penal Code of participating in or leading a criminal association (Art. 276.1 and 3); participating in, setting up or leading a secret association (Art. 278. 1, 2 and 3); treason (Art. 122); and sedition (Art. 128.1). Although the charges were formally based on the Penal Code, it was clear that the spirit of the Martial Law Decree was far from dead. In particular Art. 278.1 of the Penal Code, as amended by the law of 28 July 1983, served as a substitute for Art. 46.1 of the Martial Law Decree. It read: 'Whoever takes part in the activities of an association whose existence, internal organization or purpose is kept secret from the state authorities shall be subject to a penalty of imprisonment of up to three years'. Those who set up or led such a clandestine association were subject to a penalty of up to five years' imprisonment. Leading an association that had been dissolved or refused legalization (e.g. the human rights committees set up after the murder of Fr. Jerzy Popiełuszko) was treated on a par with leading a secret association and made the offender liable for up to five years' imprisonment (Art. 278.3). Charges based on Art. 278.1 or 278.3 were often supplemented by Art. 282a (inciting unrest — see Chapter VI/5), a modified version of Art. 48.3 of the Martial Law Decree. In this way, the prosecution was able to impute a subversive aim to any independent activity that was neither inspired nor controlled by the authorities.

To make the charge of subversive activity more convincing the authorities attempted to portray underground Solidarity activists and organizations as maintaining ties with foreign intelligence services or centres of hostile propaganda abroad. This attempt at making underground trade union activists into foreign agents was as much necessary for ideological and propaganda reasons as the charge was impossible to prove. In order to blackmail and intimidate Solidarity supporters at home and abroad, the authorities insinuated that the Solidarity Co-ordination Bureau in Brussels was financed by foreign intelligence centres which were willing to pay underground activists handsomely for a successful boycott of elections to the people's councils in June 1984 (the case of Bogdan Lis). The Brussels based bureau was also named in the indictment against Tadeusz Jedynak, alongside other 'centres of political subversion in the West' with which he was allegedly co-operating.

The Trials of the Underground Solidarity Activists

The authorities went even further in the case of Zbigniew Bujak who was arrested on 31 May 1986 in so far as they implied not only that he had co-operated with 'foreign centres', but also that 'his activity was directed and inspired by Western special services and centres of ideological diversion'.[9]

Although treason charges might seem better suited to a scenario portraying the underground as an instrument of foreign agencies, the authorities were apparently reluctant to risk a trial on these charges. In the cases of both Lis and Jedynak the treason charges that were originally presented were later changed to sedition.

All the major trials of the underground Solidarity activists that were being prepared in mid 1986 were based on sedition charges under Art. 128.1 in conjunction with Art. 123 of the Penal Code (the cases of Czesław Bielecki, Tadeusz Jedynak, Bogdan Borusewicz, Ewa Kulik and Zbigniew Bujak), i.e. making preparations to overthrow by force the political system of the PPR. Jedynak, for instance, was accused of having intended to achieve this by 'inciting public unrest and organizing a general strike'. This charge referred to protests that were planned by underground Solidarity in response to the food price increases of February 1985. He was alleged to have 'co-ordinated his activities with foreign centres of political subversion in the West and the so-called Solidarity Co-ordination Bureau in Brussels'.[10] Bujak who was, contrary to the facts, presented as the head of the TKK was supposed to have prepared the overthrow of the Communist socio-political system by 'inspiring illegal nationwide publishing activities, strikes, ... street clashes and other excesses'.[11]

From the authorities' point of view presenting sedition charges to the captured Solidarity activists offered several advantages. The charge of sedition, while not quite as sinister as treason, was none the less sufficiently serious to frighten Solidarity supporters, discredit the underground and shift the blame for the authorities' own policy failures on to the captured union activists. Secondly, the charges allowed the authorities much room for manoeuvre as far as fixing the penalty of imprisonment was concerned — from as little as one to as much as ten years' imprisonment. Thirdly, the cases of those charged with sedition were since December 1982 being heard by the military courts which allowed for greater secrecy and limited the suspects' choice of lawyers.

In political cases of a lesser calibre the authorities would often present the charge of participating in, setting up or leading a secret association under Art. 278. This charge was, for instance, presented to Andrzej Michałowski, a Solidarity activist from the Gdańsk Port Authority who had replaced Lis in the Gdańsk Regional Co-ordinating Commission following the latter's arrest in June 1984 and was himself arrested in September 1985, as well as Konrad Bieliński, a member of the Mazowsze Regional Executive Commission, who was arrested alongside Bujak.

On 11 September 1986 the authorities announced their decision to release on the strength of the 'Special Procedure Act' of 17 July 1986 most of the political prisoners, including the six underground Solidarity leaders (Bielecki, Bieliński, Borusewicz, Bujak, Jedynak, Kulik) whose cases were still pending. The move which initially awoke hopes for a new political opening on the part of the authorities did not, however, signal any change in their refusal to make allowance for society's needs and aspirations. It was a spectacular gesture designed, on the one hand, to impress Western governments and induce them to end the economic sanctions and the political isolation imposed upon Jaruzelski's regime after the declaration of martial law and, on the other, to deprive the opposition of the common cause that had hitherto served as their one unquestioned and overriding objective. It was also prompted, perhaps, by the realization that it would anyway be too costly and impractical to stage so many political trials within such a short space of time. Thus, the Special Procedure Act of 17 July 1986 cleared the backlog of cases pending trial and marked the transition from a policy of penal repression to a more subtle one involving greater emphasis on psychological warfare, infiltration of the opposition, misinformation, threat of prosecution, blackmail and political intrigue. It forced underground union activists on to the defensive, embroiling them in a difficult and time-consuming discussion on the new strategy to be adopted in the new situation.

The release of almost all political prisoners in mid-September 1986 was followed up by broader changes in penal policy misleadingly described by government officials as 'depenalization'. The effect of amendments to the Petty Offences Code passed on 24 October 1986 was that some of the most frequently applied political charges could henceforth be tried by petty offences tribunals (see chapter VI/4), which involves lesser penalties. At the same time all the major political provisions of the Penal Code remained in force — but in cold storage, as it were. This means that one and the same act can be treated either severely as an offence or leniently as a petty offence. It is the police who decide. In this ambiguous situation the Penal Code model remains at least a hypothetical possibility in trials of underground activists.

Case Study I: The Trial of Władysław Frasyniuk

The trial of Władysław Frasyniuk, a bus driver who emerged as a workers' leader during the strikes of 1980, was significant as much for its omissions as for what it included. The trial, which took place before the Wrocław Voivodship Court in November 1982 was significant because it concerned the very essence of the agreements signed in August 1980 between the striking workers and the authorities. It was also a major dispute about the legality of martial law. Frasyniuk was the first member of the TKK to stand trial. He was charged under Art. 46.1 and 2 of the Martial Law Decree with organizing strikes and protest actions and continuing trade union activity. According to the indictment he was supposed to have committed this offence by '... being an initiator of many actions, and, in his capacity as the Chairman of the Regional Strike Committee (RKS), directing their course. In the name of the RKS he issued appeals, open letters and communiqués, published them in the underground press, appealed to others to participate in RKS managed protest actions, and gave interviews to the illegal trade union press. The *views* [my italics — AS] he expressed, as well as his statements urging further, active participation in the activities of underground Solidarity, incited unrest'.[12] Frasyniuk was further charged with having 'inspired and organized street protest actions and manifestations whose participants attacked the forces of law and order, caused injuries and damage to property; organized and led the activities of underground trade union cells whose task was to prepare and distribute illegal publications and fly-sheets and broadcast illegal radio programmes; participated, moreover, within the so-called TKK in organizing illegal trade union activities and protest actions throughout the country'.[13]

A brief look at the main issues in Frasyniuk's trial gives an insight into the way the investigative authorities arrive at their preconceived scenarios for political trials.

The Trials of the Underground Solidarity Activists

His role during the December 1981 strikes

According to the prosecutor the very fact that Frasyniuk was present among the striking workers and addressed them had the effect of giving the strikes an organized and co-ordinated character. The prosecutor also said that Frasyniuk was directly responsible for the institution of the RKS. The defendant refuted these charges saying that it was as a result of his appeals and those of the other members of the RKS that the striking workers had only resorted to passive resistance and not tried to make a stand against the pacification forces. It was not true that he had set up the RKS since, according to trade union resolutions, all the regional boards of Solidarity were automatically to transform themselves into regional strike committees in case of a direct threat to the union.

His alleged militancy

According to the prosecutor, 'the activities of Frasyniuk have resulted in the fact that Wrocław has, since the introduction of martial law, been a focal point of social unrest'. The defendant argued that he had always believed that the future of Solidarity would be decided by the workforces in their individual enterprises and not by street riots. It was for this reason that he had striven for Solidarity cells to be maintained and rebuilt in factories. He had supported underground trade union structures since he understood this form of organization as society's self-defence in the face of the repressive and unpopular policies pursued by the authorities. His activity was compatible with the union statutes.

His motives for pursuing activity in the underground

According to the prosecutor, Frasyniuk had come to the fore on the crest of the wave of workers' protest. He had been trusted by the workers and he had abused this trust. Frasyniuk responded that he was duty bound to represent those who had entrusted their mandates to him, i.e. the rank-and-file trade union members. He had taken an oath pledging that he would ensure that both the agreements of August 1980 and the trade union statutes were observed. He emphasized that martial law had been imposed in an unlawful manner and that the police state was unlawful. His activities were lawful; it was the authorities who were responsible for the lawlessness of martial law.

The Trials of the Underground Solidarity Activists

His role in the underground
According to the indictment, Frasyniuk's role as 'organiser' involved not only announcing and inspiring various protest actions, but also influencing the minds of many members of former Solidarity who still considered him one of their leaders. The prosecutor presented him as one of the initiators of the idea of setting-up the TKK, (incorrectly) referred to as 'the chief decision-making centre', and one of their founding members who had, until his arrest, taken part in all their meetings. The defendant explained that both the RKS and the TKK had campaigned for trade union rights through peaceful means, mostly by various forms of boycott. It was their aim to bring about a meaningful compromise with the authorities. Frasyniuk pointed out that the prosecutor had in his indictment presented the activity of the TKK selectively, omitting their constructive proposals for a social compact with the authorities and appeals to the workers for restraint. As the Chairman of the RKS Frasyniuk had co-ordinated the activities of various groups in the region, and neither inspired nor organized street riots. In extending the scope of activities of the underground cells in his region he had taken account of the wishes expressed by the rank-and-file Solidarity members and the specific needs of individual enterprises.

His responsibility for the street disturbances on 31 August 1982
According to the prosecutor, Frasyniuk had, in signing appeals calling for street demonstrations on the second anniversary of the Gdańsk Agreement, behaved 'in a morally ambiguous way'. The prosecutor alleged that the defendant, while calling for a peaceful demonstration, well knew that it could not remain peaceful. Frasyniuk responded that the TKK's decision to call on Solidarity supporters to take part in street demonstrations on 31 August 1982 had been consulted with the regional executive commissions which had themselves consulted with the union members in various enterprises. Secondly, the decision to stage a protest had been taken only when it became clear that the authorities would not respond to a major good-will gesture made by the TKK in its appeal entitled 'Five Times Yes'. Thirdly, the TKK was under strong pressure from the rank-and-file union members to commemorate the second anniversary of the Gdańsk Agreement. The TKK had considered the demonstrations of 31 August 1982 as constituting 'a peaceful form of pressure on the authorities'. They had counted on the authorities' restraint and common sense.

The Trials of the Underground Solidarity Activists

His role as tactician
The prosecutor charged that the TKK's concept of an underground society, to which Frasyniuk subscribed, involved rejection of the law, dialogue and agreement. The very fact of organizing and living outside of official public life implied, in the prosecutor's opinion, an attempt to inject new divisions into society and put the majority of people (who, according to the prosecutor, accepted the socio-political system as well as the government) beyond the pale. Frasyniuk countered that he was in favour of a 'self-governing society', i.e. a society which was not merged with the state under a single, all-encompassing totalitarian power, but enjoyed the right of self-determination. In his open letter dated 25 September 1982 on Solidarity's programme of action he had said that although full self-determination was Solidarity's ultimate objective, the struggle for this objective did not preclude talks with the authorities with regard to partial objectives. To persuade the authorities to enter into dialogue it was necessary to exercise peaceful pressure. This involved the struggle for freedom under the law, denunciation of official abuses of the law, spreading the free word, refusal to comply with those of the authorities' decisions which were not in the public interest, condemnation of the regime's henchmen, and helping the oppressed.

Frasyniuk's defence lawyer Stanisław Affenda tried to discredit the prosecutor's case by showing that the image of the defendant as a demagogic and irresponsible trouble-maker was a distorted one. He emphasized that Frasyniuk had not organized strikes, and that it was thanks to his activities in the enterprises of Wrocław that there had been no uncontrolled outbreaks of workers' anger after the imposition of martial law. Affenda also argued that Frasyniuk had not founded the RKS, that the forms of protest advocated by the RKS were peaceful and that, since the introduction of martial law was unconstitutional, Frasyniuk had not perceived his actions as being unlawful.

In the course of the trial a number of witnesses were brought from prisons or other places of internment. Many of them were unable to recall the incidents in which they were said to have taken part, and many questions went unanswered. Other witnesses withdrew the testimonies they had given under investigation saying that they had been beaten, pressured or blackmailed into testifying as requested by the investigative officers. None of the witnesses confirmed the prosecutor's charge that the defendant had incited others to strike or organized the strikes; on the contrary, they all stated that he had appealed for passive resistance.

The defence protested against the prosecutor's attempts to include as evidence various materials of doubtful origin, such as forged publications purporting to issue from the RKS; a draft letter to the miners of Upper Silesia which Frasyniuk had, in fact, never sent; another letter signed 'Władysław Frasyniuk', but which the defendant denied having written; as well as a newspaper cutting from the Polish-language emigré weekly *Czas* published in Canada. The prosecutor argued that since this weekly had published the text of Frasyniuk's open letter of 25 September 1982, it was obvious that the defendant had written it in order for it to be exploited by Western propaganda. One of the witnesses presented by the prosecutor, a certain Rzeszowski, posed as Frasyniuk's courier and driver. The defendant denied that he had ever come into contact with this witness.

The court found that Frasyniuk had, indeed, played a significant role in the strikes of December 1981. The court also rejected the argument that the demonstrations which Frasyniuk had helped to organize were intended to be peaceful. The court found that the defendant should have been able to foresee the results of his actions. It found that Frasyniuk, as the Chairman of the RKS and member of the TKK had 'taken decisions, prepared organizationally and appealed to people to participate en masse in street demonstrations on 31 August 1982' and was therefore responsible for the ensuing material losses, injuries and even fatalities in Lubin and Wrocław. This clearly constituted an inadmissible attempt on the part of the court to re-write the causes, course and results of developments in Poland during martial law with a view to clearing the ZOMO riot police of responsibility for the use of force against the people. As far as the activities of the RKS and Frasyniuk were concerned, the court failed to perceive any extenuating circumstances and declared in their sentence that the defendant's activities were 'directed against the state authorities, martial law provisions and public order'.

The court, characteristically, failed to confront the delicate question of the legality of martial law, saying simply that 'the legal basis for the introduction of martial law and other acts of law passed at that time were generally known since they had been publicly explained by reliable representatives of the state authorities'.

The attitude of the court can best be summarized by quoting the following exchange that took place between the defendant and one of the judges, Marian Mizio, on the third day of the trial:

Frasyniuk: I would not be able to give up civil freedoms, to live with a gag.
Mizio: Habit becomes man's second nature.

Although Władysław Frasyniuk was punished with six years' imprisonment for his faith in and support for the ideals of Solidarity, the trial as such was popularly seen as a defeat for the authorities. It was absurd to present the December 1981 strikes and the spontaneous underground Solidarity movement that developed in their wake as an outcome of activity directly led or inspired by the defendant. The sentence was seen as harsh and unjustified, and further proof of the fundamentally unlawful nature of martial law.

Frasyniuk's trial served as a model for the trial of his successor in both the RKS and the TKK Piotr Bednarz. By the time of Bednarz's trial in December 1982 the authorities felt much more in control of the general situation. Bednarz was sentenced to four years' imprisonment. The court emphasized that the sentence was relatively mild because 'the current situation in the country was characterized by a strenuous striving for national agreement and conciliation'.[14]

Case Study II: The Świebodzin Case

On 17 June 1982 the Court of the Silesian Military District sitting in Zielona Góra passed sentences of up to six years' imprisonment in the case of 16 people who were accused of setting up, belonging to and leading a 'criminal association' — 'Underground Solidarity of the Świebodzin Region'. The group was active in the first three months of martial law. Its basic forms of activity were the printing and distributing of communiqués, leaflets and posters. The defendants were sentenced not only for continuing trade union activity through the dissemination of 'false information' liable to provoke public unrest and disturbances, and preparing and storing such publications (Art. 46.1 in conjunction with Art. 48.2,3 and 4 of the Martial Law Decree), but also for participating in setting up and leading a 'criminal association whose aim it was to slander the state authorities' (Art. 276.1 and 3 in conjunction

The Trials of the Underground Solidarity Activists

with Art. 270.1 of the Penal Code).

Five of the co-defendants were singled out for particularly harsh sentences.

Czesław Stasiak was sentenced to six years' imprisonment for setting up and leading an illegal association with the aim of violating the provisions of the Martial Law Decree; organizing cells of this association; and preparing posters and fly-sheets slandering the socio-political system of the PPR and liable to provoke public unrest or disturbances.

Tadeusz Rzeszótko was sentenced to five years' imprisonment for the same offences as Stasiak and, in addition, for sheltering Stasiak in the full knowledge that he was wanted by the police.

Paweł Zalisz was sentenced to five years' imprisonment for setting up an illegal association, leading it and preparing, with the aim of dissemination, slanderous material liable to provoke unrest.

Ryszard Nogajewski was sentenced to four years' imprisonment for performing a leading role in an illegal association, transporting and disseminating posters and fly-sheets of a slanderous content liable to provoke unrest.

Hubert Błaszczyk was sentenced to four years' imprisonment for performing a leading role in an illegal association and preparing, with the aim of dissemination, fly-sheets of slanderous content liable to provoke unrest.

Others were sentenced for joining an illegal association, transporting slanderous materials, distributing them and, in the case of Romuald Mackaniec, preparing stencils for slanderous posters.

The sentences seem particularly harsh in the light of the defendants' actual activity. While the defendants had, indeed, prepared and distributed posters and fly-sheets, their contents were critical of the authorities, but certainly not subversive and they do not seem to have provoked any large-scale anti-regime demonstrations of the kind the authorities might have labelled 'socially harmful'. Stasiak, for instance, had prepared in January 1982 a message to Solidarity members calling on them to light candles in the windows of houses as a token of support for Solidarity. In a 'special communiqué' prepared by Stasiak and Rzeszótko, and addressed to military commissars, directors and other decision–makers in Świebodzin, the rigours of martial law were criticized. Communiqué no. 11 criticized the PUWP CC plenum and accused the party of 'bad faith' with regard to the

The Trials of the Underground Solidarity Activists

future of the trade union movement in Poland. Another publication entitled 'An Open Letter' explained the reasons for continuing trade union activity despite martial law. As far as other forms of 'criminal activity' were concerned, the court was able to establish nothing more than two instances of leafleting in apartment blocks in Świebodzin and in local enterprises.

None the less the court presented the activities of the defendants as being highly organized, hostile to the state and terrorist in nature. This finding was based on the unwarranted assumption that outward forms and nomenclature are synonymous with real actions and that the mere mention of explosives is tantamount to the intention of using them. According to the court, 'Underground Solidarity of the Świebodzin Region' was supposed to have had not only two main organizers (Stasiak, Rzeszótko), but also 'chiefs of staff' (Stasiak, Rzeszótko, Zalisz, Nogajewski, Błaszczyk and Rajmont-Proch). Its members had to swear an oath in the presence of a priest on the basis of a special text prepared by Stasiak. The court was not concerned with establishing the nature of the functions of these para-military sounding 'chiefs of staff' nor the practical significance of the purely ceremonial oath. The court found, moreover, that the creation of a terrorist group had been discussed at the initiative of the defendant Zalisz and that 'certain actions were undertaken in this regard'. Andrzej Blek was supposed to have been detailed to supply incendiary and explosive materials. The facts that the group neither actually procured nor planned to use any explosives did not shake the court in its conviction that they were dealing with dangerous criminals.

The case was made easier for the prosecutor by the fact that two of the witnesses gave detailed testimonies, including one — Ryszard Nogajewski — who revealed the substance of one of the conversations during which the use of incendiary and explosive materials was supposed to have been discussed. Nogajewski, who became the chief witness for the prosecution, did try, in the course of the trial, to withdraw or at least to qualify some of the things he had said under interrogation, but the court chose to uphold them, claiming that Nogajewski was being influenced by the 'atmosphere in the courtroom'. Thus, the supposition that the defendants had planned terrorist-style actions in the future was established on the basis of this one, inconclusive piece of incriminating evidence. Secondly, the prosecutor's case against the defendants was strengthened by the fact that the police had

The Trials of the Underground Solidarity Activists

found copies of the afore-mentioned fly-sheets and posters during house searches. Thirdly, the two main defendants, Stasiak and Rzeszótko, admitted to having prepared the fly-sheets and violated the provisions of the Martial Law Decree, since, as they said, they had acted out of conviction.

Barely seven months later, in January 1983, the same Court of the Silesian Military District passed relatively lenient sentences of up to one year's imprisonment on 19 underground activists from Opole who had been charged with the same offences. The discrepancy in the severity of the two sentences can be explained partly by the fact that the latter trial took place shortly after the formal suspension of martial law and the authorities were interested in showing their magnanimity now that the situation was supposedly stabilizing, and partly by the fact that the Świebodzin group not only broke the martial law provisions but, worse still, insulted the Communists and their political system. The posters distributed by this group included a five-armed red star with claws; the words 'Polish United Workers' Party' dripping with blood and accompanied by the slogan 'Free the people and Wałęsa'; the name of the party arranged in the form of a skull and crossbones; a symbolic obituary for the PUWP; and the Fighting Poland anchor sign, a symbol of the 1944 Warsaw Uprising.

The court established that the 'slanderous content' of such posters constituted an aggravating circumstance. The fact that these posters were printed and distributed in the form of booklets, enabling their broader dissemination, was also mentioned. Finally, the court emphasized the social danger of distributing such material in the factories and enterprises.

The Świebodzin case was characteristic in that both the court and the prosecutor attempted to establish a connection between independently organized group activity and a criminal association, as well as between dissemination of independent information and provoking public unrest or disturbances. All the defendants were sentenced on the basis of fragmentary and inconsistent evidence.

* * *

The aim of the trials against the underground Solidarity activists was to disarm those who refused to resign themselves to the imposition of martial law. Politically, the trials can be seen as the ruling elite's attempt to win a legitimacy based on force.

The Trials of the Underground Solidarity Activists

The message conveyed through these trials was: 'We have the right to rule, because we are stronger, and there is no alternative to us'. The authorities would have had greater cause for satisfaction had the captured Solidarity activists agreed publicly to renounce their activity, but they could not boast many successes in this respect. Legally, the trials discussed in this chapter can be seen as the extension of the trials against the strikers of December 1981, a kind of 'mopping up operation' of those who had escaped the police and military dragnet at that time.

Contrary to official wishes the trials demonstrated that Solidarity continued to operate even under martial law, that the Solidarity underground was a continuation of the independent movement born of the workers' dissatisfaction with official policies in August 1980, and that the authorities were guilty of breaking the agreements they had voluntarily entered into. The moderate policies pursued by most of the captured underground Solidarity activists, with their appeals for dialogue and compromise, showed up the authorities' bad faith and their unrepresentative policies. Staging trials in these conditions was an awkward task. How was it possible to keep bringing underground activists to trial and claim, at the same time, that the Solidarity underground was a spent force, with nothing to offer, and not worth bothering about? A way out of this official dilemma was, after a fashion, offered by the three successive amnesties of July 1983, 1984 and 1986.

These three amnesties did not, however, stop the underground Solidarity activists from continuing their activities and complicating the authorities' task of winning at least a measure of acceptance. On the other hand, the regime gradually learned to live with its political prisoners, in the hope that with time they would not generate the same interest as at the beginning of martial law.

The activists of the underground Solidarity groups continued their activities, in spite of the fact that the odds were overwhelmingly against them, out of conviction, faithfulness to their oath or mandate, or a desire not to let down those who had trusted them. In doing so, they also fought for freedom under the law. Speaking during his trial in September 1983 Janusz Pałubicki expressed this ideal in the following words:

> The laws made in a burst of legislative enthusiasm have for
> a long time now fallen short of the socially accepted ethical

norms. All this intensifies social instability and impels the people to seek fairer, more transcendent laws. I perceive these laws not only in man's inalienable right to freedom and freedom of convictions but also in the right to express these convictions, not only within the family circle; in the right to create institutions giving expression to these convictions until they can be realized ... I perceive these laws in the recognition of the people's will as the supreme value ... Whoever would place his own merits or the opinions of his allies above the nation's will publicly proclaims the limited sovereignty of the state.

The trials of the underground Solidarity activists reflected in the national dimension the lack of sovereignty of the PPR, and the repressive methods applied to hide this fact. In a Western-style democracy these activists would have been a recognized element of the political landscape as its moderate opposition. In the PPR they are its political prisoners.

Notes

1. Adam Michnik, 'O oporze', *Krytyka,* 13/14, 1982.
2. *Tygodnik Mazowsze,* no. 69, 24 November 1983.
3. AP, Warsaw, 30 August 1984.
4. *Wola,* no. 173, 13 February 1986.
5. *Tygodnik Mazowsze,* no. 117, 14 February 1985.
6. Although Pinior was subsequently sentenced for his underground union activity, the 'evidence' gathered in the earlier stage of the investigation did not go to waste. After he had served his sentence (reduced to two years by the amnesty of July 1984), the authorities brought a civil suit against him. He was ordered by the Voivodship Court in Wrocław in February 1985 to 'repay' the money to the state, as well as paying legal costs.
7. Radio Warsaw, 7 December 1984, 2300 hours. Lis was released largely as a result of international pressure. In particular, the US government insisted on the fullest possible implementation of the July 1984 amnesty act and made it clear that it considered such an implementation a precondition to lifting the remaining sanctions imposed after 13 December 1981.
8. *Przegląd Wiadomości Agencyjnych,* no. 2/1986.
9. *Trybuna Ludu,* 2 June 1985.
10. Radio Warsaw, 17 May 1986, 1430 hours.
11. *Trybuna Ludu,* 2 June 1986.
12. Dobrochna Kędzierska, *Polityka,* 4 December 1982.
13. Ibid.
14. *Gazeta Robotnicza,* 28 December 1982.

VI
THE BASIC FREEDOMS AND THE COURTROOM

1. The right to a defence

Allowed to live but not breathe freely

'The Bar in Poland has for many years been like the man who had one of his lungs removed: able to live but not breathe freely.'[1] This opinion, expressed by Juliusz Leszczyński, a barrister from Łódź, is an accurate description of the current state of the barristers' profession: it is tolerated, but it is denied real autonomy and its opinions are very seldom taken into account. Indeed, the right to a defence in a political trial is incompatible with the dogmas of Communist state theory which claim that the Communist state has abolished 'class exploitation', vested all power in the 'working people of towns and villages', and aims to create the 'perfect' socio-political system under the 'infallible' leadership of the party. It follows, therefore, that the citizens do not need any protection against the state since this would be tantamount to protecting them against themselves. This theory, applied to the Bar, has meant its 'socialization' and reduction to the role of a state office. This process of 'socialization' began in 1952 and was completed in 1973 when the last private barrister's bureau was closed. Since then group legal practices have become the established norm.

Both the 1950 and 1963 laws on the Bar were passed out of political considerations. The latter in particular aimed to deprive the profession of its independence, which was considered dangerous to the state.[2] Barristers were no longer allowed to practise their profession individually and the supervisory powers

The Basic Freedoms and the Courtroom

of the Minister of Justice were extended. One of the essential features of the process of 'socialization' was the elimination of the barrister's financial independence. He was no longer free to agree his fees with his client but was bound by the mandatory official charges which were set artificially low. This made barristers potentially more susceptible to bribery and to the temptation illegally to accept money above the official limit. It also created for the authorities an opportunity to exert pressure on barristers: it was easy to stage a provocation and then prove charges of financial misappropriation.

The Bar in Poland is organized in 24 district chambers presided over by elected and formally appointed deans, and 397 barristers' group practices, which serve at the same time as the basic level of barristers' self-government. The highest authorities are the National Congress and the Chief Barristers' Council. The barristers' organization enjoys much greater prestige than other Polish lawyers' organizations, such as the Polish Lawyers' Association (the umbrella organization for the entire legal profession) and the National Council of Legal Advisers. The Association of Barristers and Trainee Barristers which was set up in September 1980 and was associated with Solidarity did not survive martial law.

One of the reasons for the high esteem enjoyed by the barristers' profession in Poland is its relatively low level of party membership. Out of a total of 5,797 registered barristers, as of 31 December 1984, 3,528 were practising their profession full or part time; 747 belonged to the PUWP, 173 to the United Peasants Party and 237 to the Democratic Party, i.e. more than two-thirds of practising barristers had no party allegiance.[3] The average age for the profession was over 50 and a considerable number of barristers could remember the independent Republic of Poland. Although the Bar is considered an elitist profession, the earnings fixed by the Minister of Justice (the employer) are low even by Polish standards. Needless to say the conditions of employment are much worse than in the West. In particular there is a desperate shortage of office space; it is not uncommon for an 18-member legal practice to occupy 30 sq metres of office space. The rate of mortality among Polish barristers is equal to that of Polish miners.

The Basic Freedoms and the Courtroom

Defending one's client but not at any cost

The position of defence lawyer in a political trial is a difficult one. The barrister knows that the law is treated instrumentally, that it is not applied equally, and that it allows for discrimination between state or party officials and ordinary citizens. Defence lawyers operate in a system in which there is no rule of law and yet they have to behave as though there were rule of law. Occasionally, the Minister of Justice will remind them that 'they must also realize that they operate within the law which has political contents'.[4] Speaking about the duties of a barrister, the minister, Lech Domeracki, left no doubt as to the limits imposed upon them.

> *Question:* Defence lawyers are above all bound to defend the interests of their client?
> *Domeracki*: But should they do this irrespective of the cost, should they use any means available?
> *Question:* And which means would be inadmissible?
> *Domeracki*: That would be for the disciplinary commissions to decide.

Barristers under martial law

According to an estimate by the independent Polish Helsinki Committee about 20 defence lawyers were interned during martial law.[5] They were denied the right to present their views before disciplinary commissions.

Ryszard Piotrowski was interned at the outset of martial law because he had participated in court proceedings against police Colonel Jerzy Gruba, the Chief of Police in Katowice. Two barristers from Łódź, Karol Głogowski and Lech Grabowski, were both interned in mid-January 1982. Głogowski, who had defended a Solidarity activist Ryszard Kostrzewa, was alleged by the Chief of Police in Łódź to have 'exacerbated the situation by publicly questioning before the court, as well as in other places, the validity of the Martial Law Decree, thereby making it more difficult for the Council of National Salvation to implement its tasks, that is, he was sowing defeatism'. Another defence lawyer from Łódź, Andrzej Kern, was interned in May 1982, two days before the court sentenced his client Jerzy Dłużniewski, a well-known Solidarity activist from the Marchlewski Textile Enterprise. Jan

Piątkowski from Opole, who was representing Mariusz Przybylski from Częstochowa, was interned in June 1982 before his client's appeal could be heard by the Supreme Court.

In March 1982 the Ministry of Justice issued a secret circular requesting that all judges inform their court chairmen about any case in which the defence lawyers criticized or questioned the validity of martial law.[6] This secret circular was soon supplemented by open threats. On 9 June 1982, during a session of the PUWP Central Committee's Commission on Law and Order chaired by Politburo member Mirosław Milewski, it was stated that: 'barristers could and should, to a greater extent than before, fulfil the important mission of stabilizing and normalizing the situation in the country. There are still too many signs of passivity and a low level of activity in this respect.'[7] This meant that the barristers should gloss over the legal nuances of martial law and not complicate the tasks of the prosecution and the judges who stood 'in the front line' in the implementation of martial law tasks.

Defending in a political trial

In a political trial 'it is impossible to defend a client without touching on the ideas he represents'.[8] Any barrister who, like Piotr Andrzejewski, who was suspended in December 1983 from practising at the Bar, holds such a view is sooner or later likely to come into conflict with the authorities since it is precisely the ideas that are persecuted.

The old school of Polish defence lawyers, represented by such names as Władysław Siła-Nowicki, Jan Olszewski and Witold Lis-Olszewski, believed it was better to tone down the rhetoric in the courtroom in order to obtain the best possible outcome for their clients. This line of defence was characterized in the following way by Władysław Siła-Nowicki: 'A defence lawyer [in a political trial], must have a cool assessment of realities in the country. The point is to get the whole truth before the court, but at the same time avoid turning the defence into an act of political propagandizing.'[9]

Some defence lawyers adopted an attitude of 'playing naive'. They took the authorities' declarations at face value, treating the court as a bona fide one or, tongue in cheek, they addressed the court as if it were genuinely independent. During the trial of eight Radom workers who had been accused of distributing anti-government leaflets, Władysław Siła-Nowicki asked the court whether the real aim of the trial was to mete out severe repressive penalties or to make a step forward towards 'national reconciliation'. Everything pointed to the conclusion, he continued, that the court was motivated by the second consideration. Consequently, he argued, the court ought to take account of the martial law provision for cases where 'the degree of social danger' resulting from the offence was not high, and hear the case under ordinary, and not summary, procedure.[10]

Other defence lawyers, however, drew attention to the political character of the trials. For instance Andrzej Grabiński, defending in the trial of workers from the Warsaw Steelworks, said that the 'history of social movements has in recent years been enacted in the courtrooms'. Tadeusz de Virion, defending in the same trial, said: 'After having enjoyed broad civil rights for one and a half years, the people were surprised by their limitation to an unprecedented degree'. Jerzy Woźniak, defending in the Ursus trial, said: 'We have reached yet another political turning point'.[11]

Some of the defence lawyers tried to defend Solidarity activists by questioning the validity of the Martial Law Decree on the basis of which charges had been brought. Such a line of defence was unacceptable to the authorities who took decisive steps to stifle the argument of invalidity. At least four defence lawyers (Krystyna Skalecka, Andrzej Kern, Karol Głogowski and Władysław Grabowski) were interned for using this argument.[12] Others, such as Piotr Andrzejewski and Tadeusz de Virion, had to face disciplinary proceedings. Among the finest speeches made in the courtroom by Polish defence lawyers at this time were those of Władysław Siła-Nowicki (at the Ursus trial) and Stanisław Affenda (at the Frasyniuk trial). Both argued that martial law was not only unconstitutional but also unjustified and that, as a result, the workers who were being tried for their role in the strikes of December 1981 had been unaware that they were acting contrary to the law.

Some of the more uncompromising defence lawyers were verbally abused in the courtroom. Ryszard Szczęsny, prosecuting in the trial of Marta Walter who had been accused of distributing the underground publication *Tygodnik Mazowsze,* described the attitude of the defence lawyers as 'constituting peculiar support for the offence, and deriding the judicial system'. Judge Alfons Wierzbicki, presiding at the Kwidzyń trial, told the defence lawyers not to behave 'as though they were speaking into the microphones of Radio Free Europe'. A judge of the Naval Court in Gdynia told the defence lawyer defending Władysław Trzciński to be brief in his summation 'because the facts of the case were already on file'.

The more the authorities are concerned with creating an appearance of a fair trial and hiding its political character, the greater is the role of the defence lawyer. By his knowledge, arguments and attitude he is able not only to embarrass those who, acting behind the scenes, attempt to pre-determine the sentence, but also to provide legal grounds for an appeal.

A defence lawyer who happened to be in the authorities' bad books was not, as a rule, allowed to represent a client before a military court (for the case of Piotr Andrzejewski see below). Eugeniusz Szymala, a reserve major who had been acting on behalf of internees beaten up in the Wierzchowo Pomorskie internment prison and other people charged by local petty offences tribunals, was actually removed from the Szczecin Garrison Military Court's list of defence lawyers allowed to defend those whose cases are tried before this court. Such lists are kept by all military courts and are subject to periodical verification.

Repressions against independent-minded defence lawyers

The independent-minded defence lawyer also has to reckon with the possibility of harassment outside the courtroom. The range of repressions open to the authorities is a broad one.

Violation of the secrecy of a defence lawyer's personal files
In flagrant violation of the Code of Criminal Procedure which states that personal files are a professional secret, prosecution officials or secret police officers penetrated the files of several defence lawyers. The most drastic case occurred in Warsaw on 11 January 1984 and involved Maciej Bednarkiewicz, a legal representative of Mrs. Barbara Sadowska (since deceased), mother of the murdered schoolboy Grzegorz Przemyk. During a search of Bednarkiewicz's flat, his files and notes were confiscated and taken to the Warsaw prosecutor's office. They were returned to Bednarkiewicz's legal practice only after they had been examined at the prosecutor's office.

On 29 April 1983, during a search in her flat, a security police officer looked through the files of Zofia Adamowicz who was acting on behalf of Adam Borowski, the main defendant in the case against the Inter-Factory Workers' Solidarity Committee (MRKS).

A number of documents were seized in a series of mysterious burglaries that occurred in legal practices in Warsaw and Wrocław in 1983.

Disciplinary proceedings
These were instituted against a number of barristers. The use of this repressive measure was particularly widespread in 1982 and 1983. It was used against Tadeusz de Virion and Piotr Andrzejewski for their speeches during the trial of Solidarity activists from the Institute of Nuclear Research (IBJ), in particular for the latter's apt description of the procedure of internment (see below); and Andrzej Rozmarynowicz from Kraków for questioning the findings of the official investigations into the death of Bogdan Włosik, who was shot dead in Nowa Huta during street disturbances on 13 October 1982. The most frequently quoted grounds for disciplinary proceedings were neglect of professional duties, 'the abuse of the freedom of speech' in the courtroom, contempt of court and breach of professional ethics. This last charge was presented to Wiesław Johann from Warsaw for offering tea and three sandwiches to one of his clients, Andrzej Rozpłochowski, who was awaiting trial on sedition charges.[13]

The defence lawyer's right to freedom of speech in the courtroom in the PPR is not the barrister's inalienable right, but a kind of concession reluctantly granted to the profession and grudgingly tolerated by the authorities. In this respect barristers are no better off than the rest of the people. Their freedom of speech in the courtroom is circcumscribed, under Art.8.1 of the Law on the Bar of 26 May 1982, not only by the provisions of the law itself but also by 'the tasks of the Bar'. These are determined by several factors, including 'the current socio-political situation'.[14]

Disciplinary proceedings can be instituted by an elected representative of the district barristers' chamber who is called 'the spokesman'. His role was greatly enhanced by an order of the Minister of Justice, dated 19 November 1983, which excluded the prosecutor from disciplinary proceedings.

Disciplinary proceedings can be instituted by the spokesman on the basis of a resolution of the district barristers' chamber, a request presented by the Minister of Justice, or a notification that a disciplinary offence has been committed. The provisions do not specify who is to issue such a notification. The spokesman presents charges against the barrister in question if he decides that there are sufficient grounds to continue with the proceedings. He then decides whether disciplinary punishment by the dean of the district barristers' chamber is sufficient or whether to file an indictment with a barristers' disciplinary court.

If the Minister of Justice requests that disciplinary proceedings be instituted, the spokesman is under an obligation to inform him if and when they were started, and send him copies of his decisions. Should the spokesman decide to discontinue the proceedings the Minister can appeal to a disciplinary court.

The Minister may temporarily suspend a barrister or barrister trainee from practising his profession without waiting for the outcome of disciplinary proceedings, albeit not less than 30 days after he first submitted the request for proceedings and only after having acquainted himself with the barrister's explanations. The period of suspension can be from three months to three years. An appeal against ministerial suspension can be lodged by the barrister concerned with the Supreme Court or the district barristers' chamber. The previous Law on the Bar of 19 December 1963 made no provision for appeal but at that time a barrister could be suspended for no more than two years. The barristers' disciplinary court can overrule a ministerial suspension and impose the lesser penalties of a reprimand, a warning, a fine or even acquit the defendant. A barrister who has been punished with a fine cannot be elected to the Bar's self-government authorities for a period of three years, while a barrister who has been punished with a transfer to another locality forfeits the right to election for six years. The ultimate penalty is expulsion from the profession.

Spurious criminal charges against defence lawyers
Early in 1984 Maciej Bednarkiewicz, representing Mrs Barbara Sadowska whose son Grzegorz Przemyk had been murdered by the police, was arrested following a search of his flat. Documents pertaining to the case were seized and he himself was charged with having offered a man who claimed to be a deserter from the ZOMO riot police money in exchange for a police radio transmitter. Some time before this incident, Bednarkiewicz told another lawyer, Władysław Siła-Nowicki, that he had been approached by a man who claimed to be a ZOMO deserter but

that he did not believe the man's story and had declined to take on his case. One month after Bednarkiewicz was arrested, on 16 February 1984, Siła-Nowicki wrote an open letter to General Wojciech Jaruzelski asserting 'that Maciej Bednarkiewicz was the victim of a cynical provocation'. Siła-Nowicki was in turn himself interrogated, his flat was searched and he was charged with 'degrading the PPR's supreme authorities and causing a harmful propaganda campaign abroad'. That very same day the government spokesman Jerzy Urban, writing under one of his pseudonyms in *Trybuna Ludu*, engaged in a personal polemic with Władysław Siła-Nowicki in an attempt to discredit his letter to General Jaruzelski.[15]

Another barrister Edward Wende was charged with 'profaning the national flag'. He was seen picking up a flag which was lying on the pavement.

Detention for up to 48 hours
This means of intimidation is applied either as a repressive or a 'preventative' measure. Stanisław Affenda, for instance, was taken from his office for two hours' questioning immediately after he had delivered a speech during the trial of Władysław Frasyniuk. In May 1983 he was again detained — this time for 48 hours. Henryk Rossa was detained for 48 hours on 29 April 1983, as part of a preventative police operation in anticipation of anti-regime demonstrations on 1 May 1983. On 6 May 1983 Jan Olszewski and Władysław Siła-Nowicki were detained shortly after they had taken part in a trade unionists' meeting in a private apartment in Warsaw.

Attempts to drive a wedge between the defence lawyer and his client
The secret police in Lublin tried to intimidate the families of the defendants represented by Tomasz Przeciechowski by spreading rumours that he was active in the underground and that any contact with him was dangerous. Przeciechowski and his clients were conspicuously followed by plain-clothes policemen.

Selective auditing of books
The financial provisions governing barristers' legal practices contain many loopholes which can easily be exploited in order to present any barrister with unfounded accusations. It is, moreover, easy to manipulate witnesses or set up a provocation

by sending the barrister a client who offers a bribe. In 1983–4 the authorities tried to catch out some of the more outspoken barristers by auditing their books. Only the most courageous defence lawyers were selected for this auditing campaign: Andrzej Grabiński, Jerzy Woźniak, Zofia Adamowicz and Jolanta Zabarnik-Nowakowska from Warsaw, Jerzy Kurcyusz and his daughter Teresa Kurcyusz-Hoffmanowa from Katowice, Leszek Piotrowski from Wodzisław, Jerzy Chmura and Roman Łyczywek from Szczecin and Tomasz Przeciechowski from Lµblin. The auditors studied the books in secret. After a few days some of the clients of these barristers received summonses to fiscal offices where they were told that they had overpaid the standard fees for legal services. The barristers of those clients who, caught unawares, might have admitted that they had indeed given a small gratuity, would have become liable for proceedings under suspicion of having accepted extra money.[16] This auditing campaign did not yield the desired results since these barristers usually adhere strictly to the code of professional ethics and agree as a rule to take on the defence in political as well as other trials for reasons of principle and not financial gain.

Blackmail and misinformation
The authorities have even on occasion resorted to blackmail in order to neutralize a barrister who is prepared to act on behalf of opposition activists. Such a barrister may be threatened with the institution or continuation of disciplinary proceedings or the publication of certain details of his private life, in order to discredit him. Shortly after Stanisław Affenda was elected Dean of the District Barristers' Chamber in Wrocław he was given the choice of resigning from this post or facing disciplinary proceedings that had already been instituted against him for alleged abuse of the freedom of speech during the trial of Władysław Frasyniuk. Pressure on barristers not to take up certain cases has on some occasions been exerted through the heads of the legal group practices.

Misinformation is another tested weapon in the Communists' arsenal for dealing with political opponents. In the case of Władysław Siła-Nowicki, a plot was devised to discredit not only him but also Lech Wałęsa, whose adviser he was during the Solidarity period. A false transcript of an interview he gave to Radio Moderata in Sweden, in which he was to have said that Wałęsa had donated his Freedom Prize to Radio Free Europe in

Munich, a regular target of the regime's propaganda offensive, was circulated in the West.

The case of Piotr Andrzejewski

This 42-year-old barrister from Warsaw took part in several trials during martial law. He was a defence lawyer in the Institute of Nuclear Research (IBJ) trial, the Inter-Factory Workers' Solidarity Committee (MRKS) trial, the Elbląg trial of the Kwidzyń internees and the KOR trial. He soon became known as an uncompromising and courageous defender of his clients, and found himself in conflict with the authorities.

During the IBJ trial on 16 January 1982 he described the night of 12–13 December 1981 as 'a headhunt', and martial law as reverting the country to its sad past. He emphasized that the defendants Zenon Nowak and Tadeusz Pacuszka had been morally right in defending their colleagues and that they had acted in accordance with International Covenants on Human Rights. The judge, Chłopecka-Pszczółkowska reported that Piotr Andrzejewski and another defence lawyer, Tadeusz de Virion, had questioned the legality of martial law in the courtroom. A few days later, on 22 January 1982, the Minister of Justice requested that disciplinary proceedings be instituted against the two barristers. Proceedings were started but were subsequently discontinued. Soon afterwards Andrzejewski's house in Władysławowo was burnt down in mysterious circumstances.

On 16 March 1983, the Minister of Justice suspended him from his legal practice for writing a letter to the Naval Court in Gdynia on behalf of his client Jan Łodyga, one of the internees who had been beaten up by guards in the Kwidzyń internment prison on 14 August 1982. In his letter, dated 1 November 1982, he described the procedure of internment as 'an inquisitorial kangaroo court which passed judgement in absentia and without presenting any charges'. The Minister justified the suspension by stating that Andrzejewski had 'abused the freedom of speech'.

Andrzejewski wrote to the disciplinary spokesman on 15 January 1983 refuting the charge and saying that in his speech he had used technical legal terms corresponding to the institutional characteristics of the procedure of internment. At the disciplinary hearing Jan Olszewski representing Andrzejewski took a similar view and stated emphatically that his colleague had simply called things by their correct names.

The Basic Freedoms and the Courtroom

On 9 April 1983 the disciplinary court of the Warsaw Barristers' Chamber found Andrzejewski guilty of having used without 'substantive need ... an ambiguous expression ... containing also a pejorative content'. Andrzejewski was reprimanded for breach of professional duties, but the ministerial suspension was revoked. This sentence was appealed on behalf of Andrzejewski by Olszewski who argued that 'the ambiguity of an expression cannot constitute a proof of guilt'. He added that no lawyer could consider the expression 'inquisitorial kangaroo court' pejorative and still less contemptuous.

A higher disciplinary court at a hearing on 16 July 1983 changed the punishment to a warning. On 2 September 1983 the Minister of Justice submitted an extraordinary review to the Supreme Court demanding that Andrzejewski be suspended in his practice for two years. The hearing before the Supreme Court was held on 14 December 1983. Carefully selected judges, known for their attitude of subservience to the authorities, found that Andrzejewski had degraded one of the elements of the legal order of the PPR (i.e., internment). He was suspended for one year.

In this way the uncompromising defence lawyer was eliminated from the two important political trials which were in preparation at that time: the trials of KOR and the seven Solidarity leaders.

The new Law on the Bar

Although the new law of 26 May 1982 formally described the Bar as 'a professional self-governing body', it did not, in fact, do justice to the aspirations of the profession and fell short of the demands made at the First Barristers' Convention in Poznań on 3–4 January 1981. These proposals involved an overall reform of the PPR's legal system as well as specific provisions on the Bar itself. The Poznań Convention set up a legislative commission to prepare a draft of the new Law on the Bar which was presented to the Sejm in May 1981. This draft unequivocally proclaimed the independence of the Bar in performing its tasks. It was generally well received at its first reading on 29 July 1981. The Sejm set up a sub-commission to study the draft in greater detail but the second reading never took place. After the imposition of martial law many deputies withdrew their support for the draft. During the debate on a new draft, the PUWP Sejm deputy Adam Łopatka criticized the earlier draft as being 'excessively prejudiced in favour of the principle of self-government and saturated with lack of confidence in the government'.[17] The then Minister of Justice Sylwester Zawadzki made clear the intention of the authorities: 'We expect that the provisions of the new law ... will contribute to strengthening the Bar's co-responsibility for the proper functioning of the socialist judicial system.'[18] The profession none the less fought for each provision of the new law on principle, even though they knew that practice mattered more than the provisions of the law itself.

The basic objections with regard to the law of 26 May 1982 can be summed up in four points: (i) the law extended ministerial supervision of the Bar to personnel policy; (ii) the law made it all too easy for legal advisers to enter the barristers' profession without proper qualifications; (iii) barristers over 70 could no longer practise their profession; (iv) other ministerial prerogatives which had been criticized in 1980-1 were maintained.

Ministerial supervision over personnel policy
The Minister of Justice is empowered to veto within 30 days a decision of the district barristers' chamber to take on a trainee barrister and enter his name on the barristers' register. Any candidate who belonged to Solidarity or, worse still, was active in the union is liable to be refused as 'not warranting proper fulfilment of the barrister's profession in the PPR' (Art.65 of the Law on the Bar). The vagueness of this provision, needless to say, gives the Minister a free hand in blacklisting those he wants to eliminate from the profession. A candidate vetoed by the Minister can appeal to the Supreme Court, but practice shows that as a rule the Supreme Court upholds the ministerial veto. In 1983, in the case of three trainee barrister candidates from Łódź (Krystyna Ostrowska-Kasprzyk, Piotr Czarnecki and Marek Markiewicz), the Supreme Court upheld the Minister's view that the very fact of belonging to Solidarity was an obstacle for a candidate wishing to enter the profession.[19] During the first year that the new law was in force, the Minister vetoed 20 candidates who had been placed on the register.

Admission of legal advisers to the profession
Despite the fact that the barrister's and legal adviser's professions are very different, Art.66.4 of the new law allows qualified legal advisers who have worked full time in their profession for at least three years to enter the barrister's profession without serving the

mandatory three-year barrister traineeship and without taking the examination which any barrister trainee must pass in order to qualify for the profession.

By potentially opening the profession to an influx of underqualified amateurs, the authorities doubtless hoped to abolish the exclusiveness of the Bar and undermine its prestige, make the barristers compete for clients and put legal advisers in a position of even greater dependence on state patronage.

The several district barristers' chambers were reluctant, however, to put aspiring legal advisers on the register of barristers. They were supported in this by the Chief Barristers' Council which argued that the requirements that legal advisers had to satisfy in order to qualify before the Law on Legal Advisers of 6 July 1982 came into force were lower in comparison with those stipulated by this law. Since most of the legal advisers who wanted to enter the barrister's profession had qualified under the Council of Ministers' resolution no. 533 of 1961, and not the new law, their qualifications were insufficient and Art. 66.4 of the Law on the Bar should not be applied in their case.

The Minister of Justice objected to this argument and asked the Supreme Court for a legal interpretation of Art.66.4 of the Law on the Bar. The Labour and Social Insurance Chamber of the Supreme Court ruled on 11 August 1983 that the ministerial objection was justified and legal advisers who had qualified before 1 October 1982 (i.e. before the law of 6 July 1982 came into force) could be considered for entry into the barrister's profession under Art. 66.4 of the Law on the Bar.

The age limit
The new Law on the Bar stipulated in Art. 19.1.(3) that barristers over 70 years of age would be automatically disqualified from practising the profession. Those who had already passed the age of 70 on 1 October 1982, the day the law came into force, were allowed to remain in practice during a transitional period up to 31 December 1983. The law did not, however, stipulate whether a similar privilege applied to barristers who reached the age of 70 between 1 October 1982 and 31 December 1983. This loophole gave rise to a dispute between the Chief Barristers' Council and the Minister of Justice.

On 11 December 1982 the Council passed a resolution stating that all barristers who turned 70 years of age between 1 October 1982 and 31 December 1983 could continue as members of legal practices until 31 December 1983. The Minister appealed to the Supreme Court which overruled the resolution on 14 April 1983. The barristers affected by the resolution were given three months' notice to wind up their affairs. The issue was an important one since the age limit meant that as many as 415 barristers would have had to leave the profession by the end of 1983 and a further 60 by the end of 1984.[20] These numbers included some of the best-known champions of human rights such as Władysław Siła-Nowicki who was born on 22 June 1913 and ceased practising his profession in late 1983. In this way Siła-Nowicki was excluded from the two key political trials of four members of the Social Self-Defence Committee 'KOR' and seven members of Solidarity's National Commission. The best those who had passed the age limit could hope for was to become low-paid copy clerks.

Having ignored the wishes of the profession and violated previous arrangements,[21] the authorities allowed only one exception to the 70-year rule. On the basis of Art. 4.3 and Art. 37 of the Law on the Bar in exceptional cases the Minister of Justice, at the request of the district barristers' chamber, could at his own discretion grant special licence to a barrister aged over 70 to continue practising his profession.

Other ministerial prerogatives maintained
Although the new law formally placed the Chief Barristers' Council under the supervision of the Council of State, the Minister of Justice has retained many prerogatives which enable him to interfere in the affairs of the profession and severely restrict its autonomy. He may, for instance, request the profession's highest authorities (the National Congress or the Chief Barristers' Council) to adopt a resolution in a specific matter pertaining to their sphere of competence.[22] Conversely, he may ask the Supreme Court to overrule any resolution of these two bodies that he considers contrary to the law.

Last but not least, the Minister of Justice has been placed in the position of an employer with regard to barristers, in so far as he retains a decisive say in determining the fees that barristers charge for their services.

The Pacification of the Bar

The Congress that put the authorities in the dock
The First National Congress of Barristers attended by 315 elected

delegates was held in Warsaw on 1–3 October 1983; it was, in fact, the third such gathering in post–war Poland. The first was held in Warsaw in 1959 and the second in Poznań in January 1981 but the official argument was that the first of these could not be considered as having been fully empowered to act as a supreme authority of the Bar, while the second, held during the Solidarity days, was labelled 'informal', there being no legal provisions at that time for its convocation.

Even before the congress was held, the authorities applied psychological and police pressures on the profession. The Politburo member, CC Secretary and Chairman of the CC Commission on Law and Order, Mirosław Milewski, issued a warning during talks with the then Chairman of the Chief Barristers' Council Kazimierz Buchała. He in turn relayed 'official concern' to the representatives of the district barristers' chambers in a series of 'talks'. The idea of these 'talks' was to persuade the profession to elect delegates acceptable to the authorities. Police pressure included house searches, interrogations and even anonymous burglaries at legal practices with the aim of confiscating some of the documents.

These pressures proved largely ineffective. Barristers known for their independent attitudes, such as Maciej Bednarkiewicz, Karol Głogowski and Władysław Siła–Nowicki, were elected to the Chief Barristers' Council. Maria Budzanowska, who was actively involved in reforming the Polish legal system during the Solidarity period and subsequently voted against the martial law provisions in the Sejm, was elected chairman. The Higher Auditing Commission included Anna Skowrońska, Aranka Kiszyna and Andrzej Grabiński.

The congress resolutions entitled 'Guidelines for Self-Government in the Barristers' Profession' and 'Motions and Demands on the Substance of Laws and Their Application' prove that the Bar wanted actively to participate in the legislative process, as well as in the application of the law. The second of these resolutions lucidly lists the main inadequacies of the Polish legal system. A resolution entitled 'Position of the Bar on Socio-Political Matters' urged the authorities to solve the problem of political prisoners by broadening the scope of the Act of Abolition of 12 December 1981 and the amnesty law of 21 July 1983. Two other resolutions 'expressed deep concern over the dismissal of many workers from their jobs ... for their membership in Solidarity' and 'expressed regret at the dissolution of the

Association of Barristers and Trainee Barristers'.

The authorities, surprised by these signs of independence, responded swiftly and unequivocally. *Trybuna Ludu* lambasted the delegates and stated that some of the speeches had been made 'from hostile positions'. The delegates spoke 'not from positions of a profession whose role was to serve law, but from positions of an imaginary historical mission'.[23] The attack was echoed by the lawyers' weekly *Prawo i Życie*. It accused the barristers of having tried to stage an opposition political party congress.[24]

The authorities step up pressure on the profession
An unprecedented propaganda campaign against some of the representatives of the Polish Bar was staged in the aftermath of the congress. It was most intense between February and April 1984 and was followed by a request from the Minister of Justice to the Supreme Court to revoke the major resolutions adopted by the congress. The aim of this campaign was two-fold: to divide the profession and to force the convocation of an extraordinary National Barristers' Congress which would express its lack of confidence in the incumbent presidium of the Chief Barristers' Council and its Chairman Maria Budzanowska.

The propaganda campaign was preceded by an intensification of judicial and police actions (see above). Four barristers were singled out for particular criticism: Władysław Siła-Nowicki, Maciej Bednarkiewicz, Piotr Andrzejewski and Jan Olszewski,[25] although the propaganda campaign as a whole was aimed against some 20 to 30 defence lawyers known for their vigorous and effective defence of clients in political trials.

The Chief Barristers' Council was attacked by the weekly *Argumenty*. The author of the article charged that 'the law and the judicial system have in recent years become one of the platforms of more or less open political struggle against our socio-political system.'[26]

Pressure was applied on district barristers' chambers, through the voivodship party committees and the 'faithful' party members in the profession, to prod them into expressing their lack of confidence in the Presidium of the Chief Barristers' Council and its policy. Three smaller chambers (in Suwałki, Koszalin and Wałbrzych) yielded to the pressures and passed votes of no confidence. Two other chambers (in Częstochowa and Katowice) went still further and demanded the convocation of an extraordinary National Congress.

The Basic Freedoms and the Courtroom

The Sejm Commission on Internal Affairs and the Judicial System signalled a further tightening of the screw. In its 'opinion' addressed to the Chairman of the Council of State and the Minister of Justice it called for 'the indispensable strengthening of ministerial supervision over the activities of barristers' self-government ... with special reference to disciplinary proceedings'.[27]

At the same time the selective auditing of books was combined with attempts to procure 'evidence' against defence lawyers participating in political trials. False rumours were spread about the barristers who were soon to be blacklisted.[28]

In this way the ground was prepared for a ministerial request to declare illegal some of the provisions adopted by the First National Barristers' Congress. On 22 June 1984, eight and a half months after the resolutions were adopted, the Minister of Justice asked the Supreme Court to revoke the two main resolutions, as well as 15 specific provisions pertaining to the functioning of the Chief Barristers' Council, the District Barristers' Chambers and the Barristers' Congress.

The Minister wins his case as usual

The case brought before the Supreme Court by the Minister of Justice had wider implications. It concerned the prerogatives of the Bar as an autonomous profession as well as its role in public matters.

Art. 1 of the Law on the Bar of 26 May 1982 states that the members of the Bar 'co-operate in the protection of civil rights as well as in the formulation of laws and their application'. This article clearly lacks precision and raises a number of fundamental questions: With whom are the Bar to co-operate and on what basis? What is meant by 'co-operation' — rubber stamping decisions imposed from above or putting forward their own proposals? Are the Bar to wait passively until they are consulted? Are the Bar to co-operate in the protection of all civil rights or only some of them? Where can a catalogue of these rights be found? In other words, is Art. 1 of the Law on the Bar just a legislative façade or has it got a substantive meaning, and if so, what does this imply?

The Communist authorities preferred a narrow interpretation of Art. 1 of the law: the very fact of the Bar's participation in the application of law ensured their co-operation in protecting civil rights. The barristers, on the other hand, argued that protection of civil rights should take the form of specific initiatives by the barristers' self-governing body and that the Chief Barristers' Council should, therefore, be included in the legislative process as such.

The Chairman of the Council Maria Budzanowska understood Art. 1 of the Law on the Bar to mean 'regular verification of the obtaining legal provisions in order to ascertain the extent to which the law and the way it is applied provide adequate protection of civil rights'.[29] The Minister of Justice, Lech Domeracki, argued however, that Art. 1 applied only to the barristers' professional practice and not to the legislative process. The Supreme Court shared the Minister's point of view and ruled that Art. 1 of the Law on the Bar was only in the nature of a declaration and was not reflected in any specific provisions of this law. The interests of the barristers' self-government, according to the Supreme Court, could not clash with the interests of the state.[30]

Having established that Art. 1 of the law was only a façade, the Supreme Court judge Stefan Perestaj ruled that the Barristers' National Congress could not pass resolutions on the dissolution of associations and acts of amnesty, since these matters were outside its sphere of competence as defined in the law. On the basis of this ruling, two of the congress resolutions, 'Guidelines for Self-Government in the Barristers' Profession' and an appeal to the authorities to end discrimination against former Solidarity members, were pronounced null and void. The latter was described by the Minister in his request to the Supreme Court as 'containing insinuations and calumnies with regard to state authorities'.[31]

Apart from these two resolutions, the Supreme Court repealed 10 other legal provisions voted by the congress and pertaining to the convening of the National Congress, the functioning of the district barristers' councils, procedures for electing candidates to these bodies, the organization of plenary sessions, income-sharing among barristers, membership of a legal practice, and rules for practising the profession individually or in partnership with another barrister.

A 'palace revolution' removes Maria Budzanowska
An important provision repealed by the Supreme Court stipulated that in the event of an extraordinary congress, all the delegates elected for the previous congress would automatically participate.

The Basic Freedoms and the Courtroom

This provision was part of the regulations adopted by the Warsaw Congress and was in accordance with Art. 11 of the Law on the Bar which stipulated a three-year term of office for elected officers of the Bar's self-governing bodies. The authorities knew that an extraordinary congress had no hope of passing resolutions to the authorities' liking unless a new set of barristers, loyal to the regime, were elected as delegates. This meant that those who had been elected to the Warsaw Congress and could not be intimidated into subservience had to be removed.

Considering the Law on the Bar of 26 May 1982 as a mistake, the authorities moved to have it replaced by a new one. At the end of 1984 the CC Commission on Law and Order headed by General Milewski circulated draft amendments to the law. These would have given the Minister of Justice important new powers including the prerogatives of calling an extraordinary National Congress and repealing resolutions as well as the subjection of internal regulations to his approval. Under the proposed provisions, the Minister would have been entitled not only to suspend barristers but also to control appointments to self-governing bodies.[32]

These threats of 'legal' reprisals were soon to be supplemented by political action. General Jaruzelski, speaking at the eighteenth PUWP plenum, encouraged barristers who were also party members to exercise greater influence within their profession and act to stop any adverse trends, both political and personal.[33]

In response to this signal for the party faithful to mobilize against the enemy, the PUWP cell at the Warsaw Barristers' Chamber adopted a resolution supported by PUWP organizations in all 24 district chambers. It was tantamount to a vote of no confidence in the presidium of the Chief Barristers' Council, which, as the party loyalists claimed, '... has to date still not achieved a proper platform for co-operation with the state and administrative authorities and the supreme bodies of social and political organizations ... We demand that the administrative department of the PUWP organize a national conference of the party activists within the profession with a view to analyzing the work of its supreme authorities and taking joint political steps.'[34]

The resolution reflected official attempts to exploit divisions within the profession. The course of confrontation with the independently minded barristers had been charted. It focused on the Chairman of the Chief Barristers' Council Maria Budzanowska, who was to be removed in the course of a 'palace revolution'. The authorities had obviously come to the conclusion that the cost of removing Budzanowska would be lower than that of passing still another law on the Bar or staging an extraordinary congress. A few hours before the next scheduled Chief Barristers' Council presidium meeting selected chairmen of district barristers' chambers, as well as certain other members of the Chief Barristers' Council, were called to a special meeting with the Minister of Justice and CC representatives. During the meeting they were told to take a vote of no confidence in Budzanowska. The authorities promised in exchange to introduce a new pay tariff for the profession, discontinue auditing of books and retain the Law on the Bar as it stood.

At the meeting of the Chief Barristers' Council presidium on 16 March 1985 the Chairman of the District Barristers' Chamber in Zielona Góra, Czesław Dużyński, appealed to Budzanowska to resign her post. In the course of a secret ballot forced on her, 24 votes were cast against her and 16 in favour. Budzanowska said she would consider the outcome of the ballot and would announce her decision later. In the course of the next presidium meeting on 28 March 1985 she was asked by a former Chief Barristers' Council Chairman Kazimierz Buchała to desist from exercising her functions until a new barristers' congress could be held. Budzanowska replied that she would make a statement on this subject during the plenary session of the Chief Barristers' Council which she proposed to hold on 14 April 1985. Three members of the Chief Barristers' Council presidium then threatened to resign. Faced with internal revolt within the presidium, Budzanowska agreed not to perform her functions until the Chief Barristers' Council plenary session which was set for 14 April. At that meeting, following a stormy discussion, she finally gave way under pressure, stating only that it was the National Barristers' Congress that had entrusted the post to her. Kazimierz Łojewski became the new chairman. The authorities could be sure that he would not pose any problems for them. He declared that 'barristers' self-government was an extension of the authority of the state with regard to matters of interest to the profession'.[35] In this way, the aspirations to autonomy of the barristers' profession which had been expressed, however inadequately, in the new Law on the Bar were effectively contained. The case of Maria Budzanowska illustrates the fact

The Basic Freedoms and the Courtroom

that in the Communist system it is people who decide how the law is applied rather than specific legal provisions. With her departure it was no longer necessary to amend the Law on the Bar. The barristers also received the new tariff as promised. Too much autonomy in one section of the legal profession might have proved contagious and affected the other sections. The barristers were not allowed to forget who was really in charge.

There are people in high places, as one of the Polish defence lawyers remarked, 'who would like to see us short-sighted, half-deaf and impeccably behaved.'

2. The right to freedom of association

Nationalizing all forms of social life

The right of association is perhaps the most illusory of all the rights discussed in this chapter and, at the same time, the one whose lack is the most keenly felt by the Poles.

The PPR Constitution guarantees its citizens the right of association (Art. 84.1), making it clear, however, that this is not a natural right but one that exists only because of and through the PPR which ensures it. This implies that the state may withdraw this right from the people if it so wishes. The aims which a particular association is to fulfil are not determined by its members but are imposed from above. Under Art. 84.1 the PPR ensures the right of association to its citizens in order that 'the working people of towns and villages may be politically, socially, economically and culturally active'. The scope of activity is further circumscribed under Art. 84.2 of the PPR Constitution which, while enumerating the admissible forms of 'social organizations of the working people', fails specifically to mention political parties, citizens' committees, foundations, charities or interest groups. Art. 84.3 forbids the formation of and participation in the activities of those associations whose aims or activities are contrary to the socio-political or legal system of the PPR. In effect this means that only those associations that are set up or, at best, inspired by the authorities are able to operate.

Art. 84, which is written in heavy, ideological phraseology, has remained in force, unchanged, since 1952. Some pro-regime lawyers argue that Art. 84.3 of the PPR Constitution formally conforms with Art. 22.2 of the International Covenant on Civil and Political Rights[36] which admits certain restrictions on the exercise of the right to associate with others but only 'those which are prescribed by law and which are necessary in a democratic society in the interests of national security or public safety, public order, the protection of public health or morals or the protection of the rights and freedoms of others'. These substantive conditions are not, however, met by the PPR legal system which has placed various restrictions on the freedom of association not in order to protect democracy but to prevent it.

The Law on Associations in force in the PPR dates back to 1932. This law, which was already authoritarian in spirit when it was enacted, has since then been repeatedly amended by the Communists in power to suit the needs of totalitarian despotism, bent not only on exercising control over all forms of organized social life, but also destroying these forms in order to remodel society. Leszek Kołakowski considers the right to associate freely with others as incompatible with the very principle of monopolistic power. Discussing the regime's 'sustained efforts towards destruction of all forms of social life other than those sponsored by the authorities', he concludes:

> Since social conflicts are certainly not removed but suppressed with repression and concealed with ideological phraseology, they seek various forms of expression with the result that most forms of social organization, unless they are under strict police supervision, may indeed become transformed into opposition groups. This results in the desire to 'nationalize' all forms of social life and in constant pressure aimed at the destruction of all spontaneously created social bonds in order to promote compulsory pseudo associations whose sole objectives are negative and destructive and which represent the interests of the ruling class. For, although the system needs enemies, it none the less fears any form of organized opposition ... It is a natural need of despotism to intimidate individuals by depriving them of the means of organized resistance.[37]

In the PPR it is the party–controlled administration which decides whether an association can exist by conferring or withholding legal status. Such a legalization is based on an administrative decision that is not subject to any control by the court. In the case of a refusal to grant legal status, those concerned can appeal only to the Minister of Internal Affairs whose decision is then final. In some cases the procedure of legalization is begun ex officio by the administrative body concerned despite no formal request having been presented. Legalization is refused on the basis of stock arguments.

There are three categories of associations in the PPR: ordinary, registered and 'of greater public benefit'. The state's powers with regard to registered associations include supervision of their finances, dissolving and determining the use of their assets, a deciding say in the establishment of local branches, and reprimanding the governing body as well as suspending it for a period of up to two months.

As far as associations 'of greater public benefit' are concerned, the authorities can suspend the governing body and impose a compulsory management. Although these associations which are set up on the basis of an order of the Council of Ministers usually enjoy certain privileges, they are, in fact, subject to the strictest controls. They are not even allowed to change their own statutes.

The activists of the pre-Solidarity democratic opposition had no illusions about the purely formal character of the right to freedom of association and did not attempt to win legal recognition for their activities. They knew that their ventures, which had been set up freely and were not sponsored by the party apparatus, had no chance of being legalized, not because they were anti-state, but because they were independent.

In the Solidarity period the right to freedom of association for a short time became a reality and many independent interest groups came into being. This was not caused by any changes in the law but was a direct result of the fact that the political monopoly of the authorities had been broken. The many-sided conflict between the authorities and civil society became institutionalized both through the newly-founded independent organizations and existing organizations which attempted to become more representative of their members. Solidarity became the essence and the symbol of this institutionalized conflict which the authorities wanted to suppress in order to return to their former monopolistic practices. The price that had to be paid for the restoration of the myth of unity between the party and the masses was the dissolution of the social bonds that had been restored through the independent organizations. Martial law was

The right to freedom of association and the Penal Code

The Penal Code of the PPR distinguishes between an association 'which has a criminal purpose' (Art. 276.1); a secret association (Art. 278.1); and an association which has either been disbanded or refused legalization (Art. 278.3).

An association 'which has a criminal purpose' can assume the form of either a conspiracy or a gang (depending on whether it has in mind one specific offence or several offences), while a secret association is one whose existence, organizational structure or aim are intended to remain unknown to the authorities. Offences involving both these types of associations, i.e. under both Art. 276.1 and Art. 278.1 of the Penal Code, are described as 'formal'. This means that in order to establish criminal liability it is sufficient to prove that the suspect joined the association in question in full awareness of its aim and forms of activity, even though he subsequently did nothing to further these aims. Membership in such an association can be established on circumstantial evidence such as the fact that the suspect allowed a meeting to be held at his home. The members of an association 'which has a criminal purpose' need not have planned to commit a specific criminal act; the essence of their offence is in the fact that they were aware that they had joined together with general criminal intent.[38] Similarly, under Art. 278.1 the very fact that three or more people have joined together in a secret association outside the official structures, although they may not actually have done anything, is sufficient criterion of criminal liability. The founding and leadership of an association 'which has a criminal purpose', or whose character is secret, is punished more severely than membership in such an association (up to ten years' imprisonment under Art. 276.3 or five years' under Art. 278.2).

Membership in an association which has either been disbanded or refused legalization was not initially penalized and only leadership of such an association was an offence (Art. 278.3). On 28 July 1983, however, an amendment to Art. 278.1 made membership in a disbanded or outlawed association punishable on a par with membership in a secret association. This amendment was introduced primarily in order to ensure that continued adherence to Solidarity remained a punishable offence after Art.

The Basic Freedoms and the Courtroom

46.1 of the Martial Law Decree, which had penalized continuation of trade union activity, became invalid with the abrogation of martial law. In this way those members of Solidarity who did not accept the disbanding of their union and continued to support it in various ways, in particular by paying their union dues, became liable for criminal prosecution.

Cases brought under Art. 276.1 and 3 or 278.1 and 3 during martial law were investigated by the military prosecutors' offices under summary procedure. Most of these cases involved youths or students and could not be classified under Art. 46.1 of the Martial Law Decree as continuing trade union activity. An analysis of the charges in such cases proves that illegal youth organizations were invariably set up in protest against martial law.

In February 1982 the Court of the Pomeranian Military District sentenced under summary procedure Zbigniew Zieliński, a student at the Agricultural Academy, and Jacek Koza, a secondary school pupil from Brodnica, to four years' imprisonment each, as well as three years' loss of public rights. They were accused of founding and leading an illegal organization — 'The Union of Struggle for Independence'. This organization was, according to the prosecution, involved in preparing and distributing leaflets, painting anti-regime slogans in public places, and disseminating 'false information' liable to cause public unrest or disturbances. A group of four youths from Gdańsk allegedly belonging to the Young Poland Movement were also charged with belonging to an association which had a criminal purpose. Their offence was to have printed some 1,000 leaflets (describing the WRON as 'the junta of national destruction') and distributed them. They received sentences of between three and four and a half years' imprisonment. Four other activists who founded an organization called 'The Underground Movement of National Rebirth — Granite', whose existence and aims were to be kept secret from the authorities, were sentenced to penalties of between three and four years' imprisonment for distributing anti-regime posters in Dębno Lubuskie and in Gorzów voivodship.

A group of 27 students from the Poznań Technical University who belonged to 'The Academic Resistance Movement' (ARO) and were engaged in independent publishing activity were charged with belonging to and leading an association which had a criminal purpose. The ARO was supposed, according to the indictment, to have organized publishing activity and steered various kinds of protest actions and demonstrations in order to foment unrest and disseminate 'false information' in the academic community. At the trial which took place between March and May 1983, the military prosecutor Cpt. Jacek Jatczak, interpreted Art. 276.1 formally, stating that since the accused students had met with the intention of committing an offence, the fact that they did not actually undertake any activity did not remove their criminal liability.[39] This proves that the students were tried not for any specific criminal activity, but for their independent aspirations. The young people whose hopes had been awakened after August 1980 found it difficult to accept the inevitable disappointments of martial law. They resented the tightening of discipline at schools and colleges, repudiated the return of the discredited 'youth activism' of the bygone era, and balked at the reintroduction of ideologically slanted curricula which were particularly offensive in the courses of History and Polish Literature.

Art. 276.1: the case of Wojciech Ziembiński

Wojciech Ziembiński has long been a thorn in the flesh for successive PPR regimes. He was born in 1925 in a family traditionally committed to fighting for Poland's independence. He has cultivated the memory of the Polish army's heroic traditions. These preoccupations, as well as his deep attachment to the Catholic faith, have been the recurring themes of his post-war activity. He was a member of the famous Crooked Circle discussion club which arose in 1956 on the wave of de-Stalinization and continued its activity for several years, albeit unofficially, since it was soon outlawed by the new regime. He was a member of the first Catholic Intelligentsia Club, one of the founder members of KOR and, later, of ROPCiO.

Ziembiński has always refused to acknowledge the Communists' right to rule Poland and has demanded that the sovereignty of the Polish nation be expressed in political life, in particular through free elections. He considered the Yalta agreements an infamy. Poland's future social and political system was to be based on the ideals of social justice and Christian morality. Ziembiński was the first to organize rallies at the monument to the unknown soldier in Warsaw and other independent commemorations of patriotic anniversaries. For his activities and opinions he received a suspended sentence of one year's imprisonment in 1970, as well as being subjected to official harassment and repeatedly sentenced by petty offences tribunals.

The Basic Freedoms and the Courtroom

Following the introduction of martial law, Ziembiński went into hiding, but was arrested on 25 April 1982. The investigation focused at first on the 'Clubs in the Service of Independence' which Ziembiński had set up in co-operation with other 'independence orientated groups of the centre' on 27 September 1981. The prosecutor's thesis was that the clubs were an association whose purpose was criminal, involving the offence of public slandering, deriding and degrading of the Polish nation, the PPR, its socio-political system or its supreme authorities (Art. 276.1 and 276.3 in conjunction with Art. 270.1 of the Penal Code).

In the course of the investigation the prosecutor Lt. Col. Włodzimierz Kubala was replaced by Second Lieutenant Tadeusz Gonciarz and the charge pertaining to foundation and leadership of the 'Clubs in the Service of Independence' was dropped. The investigation continued, however, under the very same Art. 276.1, only this time it concerned Ziembiński's part in another association, the 'Committee of the National Self-Determination Compact' (KPSN), which was set up on 10 February 1979 and ceased activities after August 1980. The indictment was completed at the end of October 1982, but Ziembiński was released on the recommendation of his doctors who drew attention to his serious heart condition and deteriorating sight, and in December 1982, the Court of the Warsaw Military District suspended the proceedings against Ziembiński.

The indictment against the KPSN gives an insight into the authorities' understanding of the legality of an association which is, in principle, to be determined by an association's 'aims, programme, principles, and actual activities'. Those organizations whose programmes are not approved by the ruling elite are declared to be against the principles of the PPR's political system. As evidence to support his charge, the prosecutor supplied quotations from various issues of the KPSN publication *Rzeczpospolita*. The indictment was brought against Ziembiński retroactively, i.e. it concerned activities which had taken place over two years earlier, in spite of the Act of Abolition of 12 December 1981. The indictment which attempted to prove that Ziembiński was aiming to undermine the sovereignty of the PPR, ironically only proved that the Polish nation was in fact deprived of its sovereignty.

The Basic Freedoms and the Courtroom

The right to freedom of association under martial law

The Martial Law Decree empowered the authorities to raze virtually all organized forms of social life to the ground. According to Art. 15 of the decree: 'If the activity of a society, trade union, association, or social or professional organization strikes at the political and social system or the legal order of the PPR or otherwise endangers the interests of the security or defence of the state, and also for other valid reason, such activity may be suspended ...' The Chairman of the Council of Ministers or the voivod, in the case of locally-based associations, were empowered to decide which associations would be tolerated and which would be suspended. In other words, they were to review the different social organizations, and suspend those where they found 'valid reason' to do so, and, in addition, determine how to deal with their assets (Art. 15.3). Art. 16 provided for a separate order of the Council of Ministers suspending self-management in state enterprises and entrusting its functions to the enterprise director.

The associations suspended included not only those which, like the Polish Writers' Union, had signed a co-operation agreement with Solidarity, but also many associations which had remained loyal to the authorities during the Solidarity period. Some of the suspended associations were subsequently dissolved within the first few months of martial law (including the Independent Students' Association, the Conference of Rectors, the Joint Committee of Creative and Scientific Associations and the Association of Polish Journalists); others resumed activity following personnel changes (PAX); still others were put under pressure to revoke some of their resolutions, introduce amendments to their statutes, or dismiss their governing bodies and elect new officers who would be loyal to the regime (the Polish Writers' Union, the Film-makers' Association). The blacklisted associations were dissolved without much regard for propriety. The Association of Polish Journalists (SDP) was dissolved on 20 March 1982. A new pro-regime journalists' association (SDPRL) was set up the very same day and registered only two days later. Although the Chairman of the SDP Stefan Bratkowski appealed against the decision to the mayor of Warsaw, his appeal had no chance of success since the SDPRL had already been registered.

Three other important national associations were dissolved in the months that followed: ZASP (actors), ZPAP (artists) and

ZLP (writers). 'Patronat', an association helping prisoners and their families [40] and the Association of Barristers and Trainee Barristers, both of which had arisen in September 1980, largely as a result of the efforts of the legal profession, and had subsequently been registered by the authorities, did not survive the military purge. The latter had aimed to become a platform through which the barristers could speak on public affairs, specifically on matters referring to the observance of law and order.

New professional associations were formed to replace some of those disbanded. Many of them bore the same names in order to create a semblance of continuity but they were headed by individuals enjoying official approval. The extent of party supervision over the professional associations increased. The SDPRL, for instance, became totally subordinated to the PUWP CC's Press Radio and Television Department.

The authorities enforced changes in the statutes of some of the professional associations. For instance, under the statutes of the revamped Polish Writers' Union, those writers whose works are published underground or by any of the emigré publishers are barred from membership.

Dissolution was, as usual, accompanied by a campaign of propaganda and misinformation. With regard to the writers' union the media were at pains to impress upon the public that it was the writers themselves and not the authorities who had made it impossible to maintain the somewhat fragile modus vivendi. The ultimatum presented to the writers by the authorities was described as 'patient and generous discussions and attempts to find a compromise'. A forged letter, allegedly written by the Chairman of the ZLP Jan Józef Szczepański and rejecting, in a brusque and truculent manner, any compromise with the authorities, was circulated at home and abroad.

Virtually all unofficial associations, organizations, unions of youth, discussion clubs and societies were dissolved in the course of martial law and in its aftermath. Under the terms of the Act of 18 December 1982 suspending martial law, the authorities were bound to determine within six months the fate of those associations still suspended at the time the Act was passed,[41] and, within four months, the fate of the workers' self-management councils in state enterprises. Those self-management councils that were allowed to continue saw their scope of activity significantly reduced. In those state enterprises that had been militarized the self-management councils lost the right to appoint the director — a key provision of the Law on Workers' Self-Management — and they could not even veto the candidate imposed by the authorities. In addition, self-management councils became liable for up to six months' suspension if they impaired the legal order or basic social interests. Appeal against the Minister's or voivod's decision by the workers' self-management council did not delay its implementation. These provisions effectively neutralized the Law on Workers' Self-Management passed during the Solidarity period. The workers' self-management, which made the enterprise independent of the central and local bureaucracy, was to have been one of the instruments of economic reform. Trade union activity itself was allowed to recommence with the suspension of martial law, albeit within the limits imposed upon it by the Trade Union Act of 8 October 1982.

The formal lifting of martial law in July 1983 marked a further attempt to extend the prerogatives of the administration over associations. Under Art. 15 of the Act of 21 July 1983, 'in cases when the governing body of an association acts in a way that is contrary to the law or its own statutes', the administrative organ supervising its activities may suspend or dissolve it. A temporary management may be appointed for the interim period. This provision, extending the scope of administrative interference into the internal affairs of an association at the expense of its members, opened the possibility of carrying out less conspicuous purges of non-conformists elected to the governing body. To eliminate those who did not enjoy official approval it was no longer necessary to dissolve the whole association. The result was the same: election of a governing body by members of an association became a gesture devoid of meaning.

The provision was applied to dissolve the governing body of the Polish PEN Club on 19 August 1983, and the governing body of the Szczecin Catholics' Club in March 1984. The latter were accused of propagating 'an anti-socialist orientation'. As examples of such 'orientation', necessitating official reaction, the authorities mentioned meetings to which Solidarity advisers Tadeusz Mazowiecki and Władysław Siła-Nowicki had been invited as guest speakers. They were also accused of having endorsed the boycott of elections in July 1984.[42]

The same Act of 21 July 1983 placed similar restrictions on workers' self-management. Should the authorities consider that the activity of a self-management council 'impaired the legal order or basic social interests' it could be suspended for a period of up to six months; and 'should the circumstances so demand', the authorities could request a special commission recently established by and attached to the Council of State to dissolve it. The council affected had no right of appeal to a court of law.

The Act of 21 July 1983 also affected academic freedoms. Government ministers were empowered to suspend for a period of six months the prerogatives of the departmental councils and senate of any university or institute within their sphere of responsibility. The Chairman of the Council of Ministers was empowered to annul, at the simple request of the relevant minister, the resolutions of a university's elective bodies.

All these repressive measures remained officially in force until the end of 1985. By this time the authorities had been able to ensure that the governing boards of all the associations and self-management bodies had been taken over by trusted people and that there would be no surprise stirrings of independence. Some of the repressive measures had also in the meantime been incorporated into the permanent law. They can be seen as part of the authorities' attempts to institutionalize repression in the post-martial law period. Their effect has been to restrict the scope of independent activity, i.e. not officially sponsored or inspired, that is permitted under the PPR law.

The right to form and join a trade union of one's choice

Under the Gdańsk Agreement of August 1980, the PPR authorities pledged to observe the provisions of the International Covenants on Human Rights, as well as the ILO Conventions no. 87 and 98 guaranteeing the workers' rights to form and join a trade union of their choice and to strike. These conventions, although ratified by the PPR authorities, were not, in fact, observed before August 1980. Trade union pluralism really existed in Poland throughout the Solidarity period, with the official branch and quasi-independent autonomous trade unions existing alongside Solidarity.

With the declaration of martial law, independent trade union activity became a punishable offence. Solidarity members were pressed to renounce their membership, discriminated against at work, interned, imprisoned for 'continuing trade union activity', blacklisted, forced to emigrate and even, in a few cases, assassinated.

The Basic Freedoms and the Courtroom

On 8 October 1982 the Sejm rubber-stamped the new Trade Union Act which eliminated the most important freedoms guaranteed to the Polish workers under the Gdańsk Agreement of August 1980. The Act disbanded Solidarity, Rural Solidarity, the Polish Teachers' Union and two other union organizations, allowing only for weak and fragmented trade unions, operating exclusively at the level of a single workplace to be set up in the foreseeable future. The new unions' dependence upon the PUWP was written into the Act which stipulated that every trade union must recognize the leading role of the Communist party and support the 'socialist system' as well as 'the constitutional principles of the PPR's foreign policy'. A number of occupational groups were not allowed to form their own trade unions, including private farmers, artisans and certain groups of state employees (the judiciary and employees of the central government, state arbitration, control and inspection agencies). Finally, not only soldiers, policemen and prison guards, who are excluded under Art. 9 of ILO Convention no. 87, but also civil employees of military and Ministry of Internal Affairs establishments were banned from unionizing.

The Act restricted the right to strike in such a way as to make it meaningless. Trade union pluralism, although not openly denied, was left to the discretion of the authorities. It was finally ruled out on 24 July 1985 with the passage of an amendment to the Act stipulating that the single trade union in each enterprise formally 'represented the professional interests of all the employees' regardless of whether they were members of the union or not. The Act also disposed of the property of the trade unions that existed prior to its passage by placing all union assets under the temporary management of government commissioners who later transferred them to the new unions (Art. 54).

The Trade Union Act of 8 October 1982 was contrary to the basic provisions of ILO Convention no. 87 since

- the workers were denied the right 'to establish and ... join organizations of their own choosing';
- the stipulations that all newly set-up trade unions must be formally registered by a court of law and must receive Council of State permission to operate on the national level were tantamount to the 'previous authorization' precluded by Art. 2 of ILO Convention no. 87;

- the previously existing workers' organizations were dissolved by administrative authority;
- the new trade unions were denied the right to draw up their own statutes and rules, they were presented with 'model statutes' on which to base their own versions, while certain provisions, such as the branch structure (unionization by occupations and not by regions), were imposed from above.

The manner in which the new unions were promoted among the workforce following the adoption of the Trade Union Act breached ILO Convention no. 98 which forbids interference by the management in the establishment of trade unions by promoting or supporting with financial or other means certain trade unions 'with the object of placing such organizations under the control of employers or employers' organizations'. A confidential PUWP CC report made it clear that 'the creation of the new trade unions was politically guided and inspired by party agencies and organizations'.[43]

The newly set up trade unions were dependent on and inspired by management despite the fact that the act declared them to be independent of the factory or enterprise administration. The example of Szczecin's Warski Shipyard, where the managing director Stanisław Ozimek requested all departmental chiefs, managers, foremen and master craftsmen to join the new unions or face dismissal, was not, by any means, an isolated one.[44] What can only be described as an Orwellian situation occurred at the Hortex enterprise in Warsaw where the managing director himself actually asked the workforce to 'organize yourselves into an independent and self-governing union so that we may discuss the proposed new pay tariffs'.[45] Various kinds of material incentives and bribery were used to boost the membership of the new unions. It is worth noting that, however they may have lacked authenticity, the new unions indirectly paid tribute to Solidarity. The expressions 'independent' and 'self-governing' had, after all, been a major bone of contention between the authorities and the Inter-Factory Strike Committee (MKS) during the negotiations of August 1980 at the Gdańsk Shipyard. Aware of the popular appeal of these ideals, the Communists paid them at least lip service as they set up their new trade union structure.

The Act of 8 October 1982, together with the fact that Solidarity had been forced underground, meant that a great majority of the Polish workers were deprived of their representation. Those who wished to remain active in the name of their union could only do so clandestinely, i.e. illegally.

The right to freedom of association after martial law: the case of the Citizens' Care Movement

Despite the suspension of martial law as of 31 December 1982, Poland was still a country of political prisoners. At that time a group of former internees from Strzebielinek took steps to initiate a Citizens' Care Movement (ORO) to aid political prisoners and their families. The 'Gdańsk Appeal of former internees of Strzebielinek' of 31 January 1983 signed by some 50 signatories stated the initiators' aims: 'to undertake efforts towards the release of all political prisoners in the PPR and a stop to all other repressive measures against independent socio-political, cultural, scientific and trade union activities' and 'to provide constant and comprehensive care for those who are imprisoned and their families, and, as far as possible, to those who are victimised in other ways and their families'. To perform these tasks the signatories proposed the formation of a Regional Care group in each voivodship. Representatives from each of these groups would come together as a national assembly to elect a National Care Council which would co-ordinate regional activities. The movement would not provide direct material help, but would rather act as spokesman for the interests of political prisoners and their families, presenting their cases to the public and local government offices in the light of national and international law.

In February 1983 the initiators of ORO appealed in a letter to the Sejm to declare an immediate and unconditional end to martial law, an amnesty for political prisoners, the restoration of withdrawn or suspended rights to workers and students, and an end to repressions against independent socio-political, cultural, scientific and union activities. At the same time the letter announced the formation of ORO.

The response of the authorities was swift and decisive. At the end of March some of the signatories of the letter addressed to the Sejm were requested to give testimony at the Gdańsk Voivod's Office. Those requested to appear were at the same time handed a written order prohibiting participation in the activities of 'an organization threatening public security'. Their appeal against this order to the Ministry of Internal Affairs was turned down.

The Basic Freedoms and the Courtroom

The case of the Citizens' Care Movement is fairly typical. It illustrates the basic mechanism used by the Communists to stifle all unofficial attempts to set up associations not directly inspired or controlled by the ruling apparatus. The mechanism starts with a negative political assessment of the proposed venture, followed by an administrative decision to ban it. This decision is tantamount to a warning: since no licence has been obtained, the initiators of the venture make themselves liable for criminal proceedings if they pursue their activities.

The administration usually know about the independent venture and its initiators not from their application for registration but from other sources (the police, the local party committee, denunciations, etc.) They gather 'evidence' or are supplied with it. The 'evidence' gathered concerns not only the venture itself, but also its promoters ('who is behind it?') and it is gathered in order to corroborate the stock charges that the proposed venture 'constitutes a potential threat to public security, peace or order'. A detailed substantiation of these charges is not provided, the sources of the information that constitutes the 'evidence' are not revealed. A written prohibition is, as a rule, with immediate effect.

In order to make a specific case fit the ready-made legal formulae, various independent ventures such as a citizens' movement, initiative group or citizens' committee are treated as though they were associations or even organizations. This practice infringes even the 1932 Law on Associations since the regulations governing the procedure for founding associations state clearly that the institution of legal proceedings towards registration may only take place at the request of the association concerned and not ex officio by the state administration.

As a result of these practices an association that was not actually in existence, the Citizens' Care Movement, was banned from pursuing activities. One of the venture's initiators, Józef Wyszyński observed in his appeal against the decision of the Minister of Internal Affairs that the decision banning ORO had been issued without any factual or legal basis. Another initiator, Zygmunt Kędzierski, remarked in his appeal: 'Surely, the wish to give unselfish aid to prisoners in dire need, which is in keeping with the principles of socialist morality, does not threaten the systemic principles of our state? If that is, however, the case then on what grounds and on what evidence has such a threat been established?'

The Basic Freedoms and the Courtroom

The right to exercise social control: the case of The Social Association for the Defence of Human Rights (Toruń)

Under Art. 86 of the PPR Constitution, 'the citizens participate in the exercise of social control, in consultations and discussions on key issues of the country's development, and put forward their suggestions'. This provision, ostensibly 'creating an opportunity for grass-root criticism of the shortcomings and inefficiency of the administration, as well as developing a channel for social initiative'[46] is meaningless without the right to freedom of association. This is illustrated by the case of the human rights committees set up spontaneously in many parts of the country after the kidnapping and murder of Father Jerzy Popiełuszko in order to monitor and publicize cases of official abuse of the law. Such committees were set up in Wrocław, Kraków, Toruń, Wałbrzych, Szczecin and in the village of Ciepłowody in Wałbrzych voivodship, to act as pressure groups to force the authorities to abide by their own as well as international laws. Asked about aims and methods of action, a member of the Warsaw committee, Jan Józef Lipski, replied:

> It will be very difficult to halt the violence. That would require the involvement of immense social forces. We simply want to show that opposition is possible. We shall gather material on acts of violence, we shall publish it, and bring it to the attention both of society and of the authorities. I do not think we are capable of doing anything more or even that we want to do anything more. We would lack the strength. Anyway, we believe that the committee should restrict itself to this single problem... of combatting the use of violence, by which we mean beatings, abductions, and also psychological terror. Respect for the law is an immeasurably greater problem and we are unable to cover it all.[47]

Another founder of the Warsaw committee, Jacek Szymanderski, said that 'society must overcome its fear of open activity'.[48]

The committees were loose civic groups, not formally structured organizations; they took various names and acted independently of one another. An exception to this pattern was the Social Association for the Defence of Human Rights in Toruń whose members, as the very name indicates, considered themselves an association and, as such, submitted a formal application for registration with the local voivod's office. In their founding declaration, the 32 signatories, including scholars of the Mikołaj Kopernik University, doctors, workers and a priest, announced that they were particularly concerned and outraged by abductions, assassinations and other acts of terrorism in the Toruń area. The declared objectives of the signatories were to collect and publicize detailed information about abuses of the law, draw the attention of the authorities to these abuses, provide legal aid to their victims, campaign for political prisoner status for the imprisoned opposition activists, and co-operate with other bodies whose aims were similar.

Their application for registration was turned down. The document detailing the decision of the voivodship authorities in Toruń totally lacked substantiation. It failed to set out the facts as established by the voivod, the evidence which he had taken into consideration and reasons for which he had rejected other evidence. The document also failed to explain the legal basis on which the decision had been taken. The voivod did not attempt to explain how public law and order might have been threatened had the association undertaken activity in keeping with its stated objectives. These and other points were raised in the appeal against the decision sent by the founder members of the association to the Minister of Internal Affairs. The latter upheld the voivod's decision, however, forbidding the establishment and activity of the association. The Minister's decision stated that 'the aims of the proposed association, as well as the reasons for its establishment ... undermine the credibility of the state prosecution bodies and the administration of justice,... insinuate that facts [such as torture and other forms of cruel, inhumane and degrading treatment or punishment] have been tolerated by the PPR authorities'.

The Minister's decision left unanswered the fundamental question raised in the founder members' appeal: 'If the decision forbidding the activity of the Social Association for the Defence of Human Rights in Toruń were to be upheld, this might create the impression that the authorities were not concerned with establishing legal forms for citizens' social activity'.

The case of the Toruń association was fairly atypical, since most committees were banned outright and threatened with prosecution. Jacek Szymanderski of the Warsaw committee described what seems to have been the standard procedure:

> First, we were summoned by the municipal authorities the very day after we had announced our formation. Here we were handed decisions that referred, among other things, to a previous questioning which had not, of course, taken place. The decisions and orders for our immediate disbanding had been prepared in advance ... on the grounds that it was contrary to both binding legal provisions and the PPR Constitution for society to organize itself against political banditry. At the prosecutor's office we were threatened with imprisonment.[49]

In the case of the Regional Social Citizens' Committee for the Defence of the Rule of Law formed in Szczecin on 23 November 1984, the authorities' reaction seems to have been particularly harsh. Legal proceedings were instituted against two of the 13 founding members, Edmund Bałuka and Jan Kostecki. The prosecutor's office alleged that Kostecki had,

> between November 1984 and February 1985, in Szczecin, as the Deputy Chairman of an association called 'The Regional Social Citizens' Committee for the Defence of the Rule of Law of the Western Pomerania Region' which was refused legalization by decision of the Socio-Administrative Department of the Voivodship Office in Szczecin dated 30 November 1984, sent letters, statements and appeals whose contents slandered the legal order and undermined social confidence in the authorities of the PPR, to the authorities, state offices and organizations outside of Poland, as well as publishing them in a periodical entitled *Obraz* which was produced and distributed without permission (Art. 278.3 of the Penal Code).

On 25 January 1985 Kostecki was sentenced to two years' imprisonment for playing a leading role in an illegal organization. The regional court, handing down the sentence at the end of a one-day trial, found the defendant guilty of damaging the interests of the PPR and slandering the state authorities. Bałuka, who was in France at the time of the trial, was fined for failing to appear. Kostecki's defence lawyer appealed against the sentence and the voivodship court acquitted him. The Minister of Justice then demanded an extraordinary review of the case on the grounds that the court of the second instance had erred in its factual findings. The Supreme Court repealed the acquittal sending the case back to the voivodship court for review. This time Kostecki was sentenced to one and a half year's imprisonment. At the same time he was not sentenced under Art. 278.3 for 'playing a leading role' but for 'membership' in an illegal association which had been refused legalization under Art. 278.1. In this way the court breached substantive law on at least two counts: first, the Regional Social Citizens' Committee for the Defence of the Rule of Law of the Western Pomerania Region had never applied for registration (legalization) with the authorities and was refused legalization ex officio contrary to the provisions of the Law on Associations of 1932; secondly, the Committee, lacking in internal structure, division of roles and leadership, was not an association but a citizens' initiative.

Jacek Kuroń has said that independent activities undertaken in defence of human and civil rights could be regarded as 'illegal' only by a government that was itself based on 'lawlessness'.[50] Kuroń, who was not a member of any of the committees himself, added,'organizing people in order to investigate acts of political terrorism and inform the public about them is supported by the law in any country where there is law and by any government which is based on law'.

'Public unrest': the second KPN trial

In the post-martial law period Arts. 276.1 and 278.3 have increasingly been used in conjunction with Art. 282.1 of the Penal Code (fomenting public unrest or disturbances) in order to nip in the bud any attempts to devise independent action programmes. In this way, by prosecuting not only for illegal association but also for offences against the public peace, the authorities aimed to exacerbate the offences imputed to those who engaged in any independent activity, be it charitable, publishing, trade union or party political. The Gdańsk trial of Frasyniuk, Lis and Michnik, which is discussed elsewhere in this book, was brought under these joint provisions. Although the nature of their activity was quite different, the charges were the same and the Gdańsk trial served as a model for the second trial of the Confederation of Independent Poland (KPN) which opened in Warsaw on 3 March and ended on 22 April 1986.

The defendants, Leszek Moczulski, Krzysztof Król, Andrzej Szomański, Adam Słomka and Dariusz Wójcik, were charged with 'having, between August 1984 and March 1985, with the aim of causing public unrest, undertaken activities which reactivated an illegal association, the Confederation of Independent Poland, by calling in December 1984 the second KPN Congress, setting up its Political Council and forming branches of this association throughout the country and, acting in this way, they performed leading roles'. They were further accused of having in publications of the KPN, 'degraded the socio-political system and its supreme authorities by presenting and publishing slanderous charges about the totalitarian nature and anti-democratic character of the state authorities'.[51] These charges were very similar to those presented to Frasyniuk, Lis and Michnik during the Gdańsk trial. In both trials the major piece of evidence was a heavily doctored tape (in the KPN case, seven tapes containing recordings from the second KPN Congress that had allegedly been sent to Sweden and impounded by PPR customs officials). The tape was authenticated by the same expert witness, Colonel Stanisław Błasikiewicz, whose dubious methods of identifying human voices had been used by the authorities in previous political trials. Also the judges adjudicating in the case had been carefully selected to ensure the conviction of the defendants.

The prosecution charged that the KPN had failed to register with the authorities as required of all associations and that, in this light, the resumption of activity by Moczulski in August 1984, following his release under the terms of the 21 July 1984 amnesty, was a criminal offence. According to the prosecutor Wiesława Bardonowa, the KPN's stated aims, i.e. the struggle for Poland's independence, were no more than a 'mystification'. She alleged that the defendants were a group of people inspired from abroad.

The defence lawyer Edward Wende answered that the KPN had all the characteristics of a political party and that political parties in the PPR were not required to register. The PUWP, he argued, was not registered either. The PPR Constitution, the International Covenants on Human Rights and the Human Rights Charter all guaranteed PPR citizens the use of political rights, including the right to set up and join political parties of their own choosing. Another defence lawyer, Tadeusz de Virion, said that the prosecution had failed to prove that the party was illegal. The defendants had a right to take an active part in political life and did not have to accept the PPR system, he added.

The main defendant, Leszek Moczulski, invoking the PPR's Constitution and international accords ratified by the PPR, insisted that the KPN was legally entitled to work for the peaceful transformation of the current system. He demanded that the authorities permit 'the free elections Poland was promised at Yalta'.

The court was unconvinced and, calling the KPN an 'anti-socialist organization' working against the stabilization encouraged by the authorities, passed sentences ranging from two to four years' imprisonment.

The trial was held because the PPR authorities regard the KPN as a potential threat. The KPN demands an end to both the interference of the Soviet Union in Polish affairs and the PUWP's monopoly on power. The PPR authorities are anxious to suppress these ideas and are not willing to risk political pluralism. The KPN trial was, in fact, a trial against Polish aspirations for political independence and democratic freedoms. To discredit both the defendants and these aspirations they were presented with a criminal charge and the real aims of their activity were ridiculed as a 'mystification'.

Activists of other nascent independence-orientated political parties were tried under less conspicuously political provisions of the Penal Code. In February 1985 Stanisław Kotowski and Andrzej Karpiński of the Liberal-Democratic Party 'Independence' were sentenced to two and a half and one and a half years' imprisonment respectively for disseminating uncensored publications. Kotowski's sentence was subsequently increased to three and a half years as a result of the prosecutor's appeal against what he considered too lenient a sentence.

* * *

In the course of a political trial the aims which have led people to organize outside the official structures are declared illegitimate by definition. The courts tend to disregard the motivation of the defendants and use the existing legal provisions to protect the Communist authorities' monopoly on political initiative. The regime is well aware that once the people acquire the habit of setting up their own associations in response to specific needs for which the system does not provide, its monopolistic and despotic nature will be exposed and its very foundations will be at risk.

The Basic Freedoms and the Courtroom

3. The right to freedom of expression

Administrative control over the free word

Before any publication, performance, exhibition, poster, poetry reading or other cultural activity is released for public consumption it must first be approved and its contents checked by the appropriate censors — this is called preventative censorship. It is exercised by the Main Office for Control of the Press, Publications and Performances (GUKPPiW). This office was set up on the basis of the decree of the Council of Ministers subsequently ratified by the Polish National Council (KRN) on 5 July 1946. Since then it has become an irrecusable part of the post-war political landscape in Poland. The censors' basic duty has always been to implement the current political line of the party. But even the censors cannot be infallible and the party line, although maintaining a pretence of constancy, is subject to periodical changes. A second level of censorship has therefore been evolved. It is exercised by the Central Committee's Department of Press, Radio and Television, as well as the culture departments of the party's voivodship committees — this is political censorship. It is a less conspicuous form of censorship, being largely informal and functioning without any legal basis whatsoever. The CC Press Department also has a decisive say in determining personnel policy in the media.

The essence of the censor's prohibitions has remained unchanged over the years. It involves certain taboo topics which may not be mentioned at all, and other topics which may only be mentioned in a specific manner (for instance in ritualised terminology where official doctrine is involved) or in certain restricted circles. Politically important topics which concern the current party line have to be handled with the utmost care. Whenever in doubt, the censor should consult his superiors for directives.

The main function of institutionalized censorship is to shape public opinion by prohibiting some material and encouraging others. The mass media are a major political instrument in the hands of the party elite. They are used to fight impermissible thoughts, ensure secrecy, impose uniformity. The preventative censor whom Joseph Conrad compared to a *magot chinois* acts, in a spirit of asiatic barbarity, as an arbitrary administrator of creative work in science and culture. In this capacity institutionalized censorship co-operates with the prosecutor's office and secret police. This is well illustrated by an exchange of correspondence between two employees of the Investigative Department of the Warsaw Police HQ and a representative of the Main Office for the Control of Press, Publications and Performances, Kazimierz Garnys. The subject of this exchange of letters were two sermons pronounced by Fr. Jerzy Popiełuszko on 28 August 1982 and 28 September 1983. The second of these sermons was found to contain 'praise for unregistered organizations and unions, and also for persons whose activities are contrary to the law'. Both sermons were secretly recorded by the police and used in the course of an investigation into the activities of Fr. Jerzy Popiełuszko.

Another function of the censor is to ensure that the party has sufficient room for manoeuvre. Censorship ensures that the authorities' mistakes in planning, investment, social policy, etc. do not become public knowledge. An agent of centralism and autocracy, censorship petrifies the existing structures of power and contributes to the unaccountability of the authorities to society. Censorship is coherent with the fundamental philosophy of a Communist state, with its emphasis on collective interests which the party alone claims to be able to represent, because of its ideological legacy. Stanisław Barańczak, one of the editors in the late 1970s of the unofficial literary quarterly *Zapis*, described the paradox of censorship: 'it undermines the very state power whose interests it is supposed to protect. For in an atmosphere of mistrust, corruption and disinformation, the machinery of state cannot function smoothly. It becomes a victim of the various fantasies and deceits which it has itself created.'[52]

Mirosław Chojecki, the head of the unofficial publishing house NOWA, blamed censorship for the lack of authority in public life. During his trial in June 1980 he said that 'the public has become accustomed to the fact that officialdom never asks straight questions or gives straight answers'. Such an abnormal situation results in duality of life, double standards and profound demoralization. The nation must be allowed to know its own culture with its two most important elements — history and literature. This knowledge cannot be placed at the authorities' discretion. For it is in its treatment of history that the Orwellian nature of the PPR's censorship is most evident. One of the instructions reprinted in the Black Book of Polish censorship, smuggled to the West by a former censor, stated that one and only one line of assessment of the past was permissible.[53]

The Penal Code and the rulers' self-image

Criticism of the ruling party and its methods of wielding power can be classified as an offence under Art. 270.1 of the Penal Code as: 'public slander, derision or denigration of the Polish nation, the PPR, its socio-political system or its supreme authorities'. The penalty is six months' to eight years' imprisonment. Art. 271.1 of the Penal Code forbids the 'dissemination of false information if it is liable to cause serious harm to the PPR's interests'. The penalty for this is up to three years' imprisonment. It can be as high as five years' imprisonment if the offence of 'dissemination of false information' is committed abroad or if 'false information' is passed on to foreign centres engaged in activity directed against the PPR's political interests (Art. 271.2). An offence committed 'by using a medium of mass communication' (Art. 273.1 of the Penal Code) can be penalized by up to ten years' imprisonment. In the age of telecommunications satellites, 'a medium of mass communication' can in the PPR include carbon copy paper and a manual typewriter. Art. 273.2 prohibits both the preparation and the dissemination of uncensored publications.

A broad interpretation of offences under Art. 270.1 of the Penal Code makes any criticism of the Polish United Workers' Party (PUWP) and its methods of wielding power synonymous with 'slandering and deriding the socio-political system of the PPR'. In this way the Penal Code is used to sanction an undemocratic constitution which states in its Art. 3.1 that the PUWP is 'the leading force of society in the construction of socialism'.

Solidarity's fight for access to the state controlled media

Dissatisfaction with the mass media and official information policy was expressed in point 3 of the Gdańsk Agreement of 31 August 1980: 'Radio and television, as well as the press and publishing houses, must offer the possibility of expressing different points of view. They must be subject to social control'. During their 16 months of legal existence, Solidarity only succeeded in putting forward their own 'different point of view' because they created their own network of information and not because they had any access to the state controlled media. In fact, the authorities did all they could to hamper such access. Indeed, it may well be said that had it not been for the emergence of free and uncensored publications, bulletins and news sheets, some of them, like *Robotnik*, associated with the movement towards free trade unions, there might have been no Solidarity. After August 1980 the free press was one of the foundations of Solidarity.

During the Solidarity period access to the media, especially radio and television, was one of the most important issues. Without such access Solidarity could not achieve complete openness in public life and generate a genuine public discussion on ways out of the Polish crisis. The authorities made it clear, however, that he who pays the fiddler calls the tune. The Radio and Television Committee (RTVC) which managed the affairs of both radio and television could not be subject to social control, they argued, since it was an agency of state. The successive chairmen of the RTVC effectively obstructed Solidarity's attempts to gain access to radio and television. Under the direct supervision of the Central Committee, television news became, in late 1981, the symbol of aggressive, mendacious and even provocative propaganda. The talks on the subject of Solidarity's access to the media were used as a smokescreen while preparations for a 'state of emergency' were already under way in June 1981. One month later a new 'contingency' television studio was secretly built on the premises of an air force institute. Those on a restricted list of RTVC employees with access to the studio were issued with military uniforms. It was from this studio that General Jaruzelski made his declaration of martial law in the early hours of 13 December 1981.

The law on censorship

During the Solidarity period few people went as far as advocating the abolition of censorship. Instead, there was general support for a law to establish clearer criteria of censorship. Up to that time censorship had been a secret procedure which the authorities had attempted to conceal from public view. The Solidarity idea was to make censorship open. On the basis of the law of 31 July 1981, passages removed by the censor were to be clearly marked as such. The law granted the publisher the right to appeal against the censor's decision to the Supreme Administrative Court. The passage of the law proved, however, to be no guarantee of real liberalization.

The Basic Freedoms and the Courtroom

On 13 December 1981 the *magot chinois* struck back. The Martial Law Decree suspended the provisions of the Law on Censorship. It imposed censorship of private mail and telephone conversations. It is worth mentioning, as a bureaucratic curiosity, that some censored letters at the beginning of martial law were stamped with the words 'exempted from censorship'. Before martial law private mail, as well as parcels from abroad, were opened and read secretly at the Office for Control and Exchange of Post identified on censored letters by the seal 'Warszawa 3'. The censorship of private mail, which had always been done selectively and in secret, turned for a few months, with the imposition of martial law, into a full-scale and open practice.

In order to restore their monopoly over information which was threatened by Solidarity's publications, the authorities decided to tighten the provisions of the Law on Censorship. On the basis of amendments passed on 28 July 1983, internal circulation trade union bulletins — the main bastion of freedom of expression during the Solidarity period — were subjected to preliminary administrative censorship. The censor's control was also applied to reprints of literary works which had already been censored, bibliographical publications, the visual arts and photographic exhibitions. The criteria applied by the censor for refusing permission to publish once again became nebulous and full of newspeak jargon: the censors were, for instance, empowered to confiscate any material that 'presented a threat to state security or defence' or whose content 'clearly constituted an offence'. Previously the law allowed only for confiscation of material that 'praised an offence'. Censorship based on such criteria could be applied arbitrarily. To by-pass the provisions of the Law on Censorship, the censor could refuse to give the legal grounds for his decision to prohibit publication of a text or to issue his decision in writing, thus preventing appeal against it to the Supreme Administrative Court.

Another proposed amendment to the Law on Censorship would have provided for up to five years' imprisonment for the 'dissemination of false information abroad' if such information was liable seriously to damage the interests of the PPR. This provision would have seriously jeopardized the work of foreign journalists in Poland and hampered contacts between Poles and foreign nationals. It was later withdrawn on the grounds that 'the obtaining legal provisions were sufficient defence against the dissemination of false information harmful to the PPR's interests'.[54]

The Basic Freedoms and the Courtroom

The Law on Censorship itself was supplemented by the Press Law of 26 January 1984. This stipulated that in order to publish a newspaper or a journal permission must be obtained from the Main Office for Control of the Press, Publications and Performances. The prospective publisher must specify the political line of his intended publication as well as the 'social need' for it. Any journalist could be dismissed for failing to follow the ideological line as set out by his editor-in-chief. Publishing without permission became a punishable offence.

The party maintains its monopoly over the distribution of the printed word through a state concern known as 'RSW Prasa--Książka-Ruch'. The allocation of paper is not regulated by the law and is used as a means of delaying certain publications or forcing them greatly to reduce their circulation or number of pages. The Catholic monthlies *Więź* and *Znak* and the publication of the Chief Barristers' Council — *Palestra* — are among those which regularly appear with several months' delay.

To vanquish the free word

Under martial law trade union bulletins and information sheets became one of the prime targets of police operations and prosecutions. They provided tangible evidence that Solidarity continued to function despite the military crackdown. Independent publications defended the union against official propaganda and provided information when information was deliberately blocked. The need for free unbiased reporting and an uncensored press, aroused among broad sections of the population during the Solidarity period, became even more pronounced after the imposition of martial law. Despite the seizure and destruction of numerous printing presses during police raids on Solidarity offices, and the internment of union printers and editors, more than 100 titles appeared in the underground within the first four months of martial law. This was soon to become only a small proportion of the total number of underground publications appearing throughout the country.

Article 48 of the Martial Law Decree

One of the charges frequently presented by the prosecution in political trials during martial law was the dissemination of 'false information'. To counteract criticism of the regime among the general public, and possible agitation in the armed forces, the Martial Law Decree included an updated version of Art. 22 of the infamous Small Penal Code (m.k.k.) of 1946. As Art. 48, it greatly broadened the scope of penalization of free speech. The distinction between legitimate criticism and private opinions on the one hand, and the dissemination of 'false information' on the other, was very fluid. Even a personal opinion could be classified as 'false information' for 'a piece of information can be hidden under the guise of an opinion'.[55] The court did not, as a rule, bother to examine specific pieces of information to establish whether they were true or false. Information printed underground was usually viewed as false simply because it came not from official but independent sources.

Art. 48.1 penalized the distribution of any information which was deemed liable to weaken the PPR's military readiness, irrespective of whether it was true or false. It carried penalties of imprisonment of no less than three years. What mattered was not the content of the information disseminated but the intent of the offender ('whoever disseminates information ... with the aim of weakening...'). This provision was clearly designed to prevent any fraternization between the public (especially striking workers) and the military who, together with the ZOMO riot police, were entrusted with the task of breaking resistance to military rule.

Criminal intent did not matter, on the other hand, when the charge was based on Art. 48.2 of the Martial Law Decree. Dissemination of 'false information liable to provoke unrest or disturbances' was punished even though the offender had not intended to provoke any unrest. In theory, the prosecution had simply to prove that information disseminated by the defendant was false, since it was taken for granted that there was an inherent risk of public unrest in the dissemination of false information. In practice, however, information was simply described as 'false' without being analyzed on its merits. Under Art. 48.2 of the Martial Law Decree it was thus possible to bring to trial and sentence anyone who spread rumours or wrote graffiti on walls.

Art. 48.3 penalized 'preparations' for the offences covered by Art. 48.1 and 2: 'Whoever, with the aim of dissemination, produces, collects, stores, carries, transports or sends, written or printed matter, tape recordings or film containing information liable to weaken the PPR's defence readiness or to provoke public unrest or disturbances' is liable for up to five years' imprisonment.

The author of a private letter critical of official policies could easily be charged and sentenced under this article. Art. 48.3, which treated printed, written and recorded matter equally, served as a model for the subsequently amended Art. 273.2 of the Penal Code.

Art. 48.4 recognized printed matter as 'a medium of mass communication'. This provision of the Martial Law Decree was formulated as follows: 'any person who commits the offences defined in points 1 or 2 with the aid of print or other medium of mass communication shall be liable to imprisonment of not less than one year and not more than ten years.'

The Supreme Court rules on false information

Art. 48.2 of the Martial Law Decree was used so frequently to bring to trial critics of the martial law regime, and the definition of 'false information' that was at the heart of this provision led to such controversy that the Supreme Court had to issue its own interpretation. Its ruling of 10 March 1982 did little, however, to clarify the meaning of this formula. According to the Supreme Court 'false information' was 'all information about facts, regardless of their outward form, concerning past, present or future events, whether these are completely invented (fictitious) or whether they are deliberately distorted by the introduction of untrue elements or by the omission of circumstances having a real bearing on the actual picture of the given fact (event)'.[56]

Two distinct terms, 'facts' and 'events', are confused here and used synonymously. The ruling opens up the possibility of taking as fact an event which may or may not occur in the future. The anticipation of future events which is not subsequently confirmed in real life cannot be considered as 'false information' but, at most, an error of judgement. On the basis of this ruling it would be possible, for instance, to sentence a science fiction writer. An individual's failure to perceive 'the best intentions' of the regime can, on the basis of this ruling, be presented as the 'omission of circumstances having a real bearing on the actual picture'.

The Supreme Court in the independent Republic of Poland was more precise. In its ruling of 13 August 1934 it stressed that a causal connection had to exist between the dissemination of false information and the provoking of public unrest. This causal connection was to be established on the basis of the real situation and information was to be judged true or false according to both objective and subjective criteria. The 'public' element of this offence was stressed, together with its legal characteristics. According to the 1934 ruling, only that kind of false information was dangerous which might provoke unrest among people at large.

The discrepancy between these two rulings can be explained by the fact that the pre-war criminal law grew largely out of a liberal democratic tradition, whereas the post-1945 criminal law clearly shows the mark of totalitarianism.

The ruling of 10 March 1982 also purported to explain the meaning of 'social danger' which the courts are obliged to take into account, as constituting the substance of an offence, in evaluating its gravity. According to the Supreme Court, 'the degree of social danger of the offence defined under Art. 48.2 of the Martial Law Decree is determined by such objective-subjective elements as: content, form, quantity, significance, impact of the false information, its actual scope and the type of potential negative social repercussions which might result from this information, as well as the motives and aims of the offender'.[57]

The Supreme Court recommended that the courts took action against the alleged offenders in view of the probability of 'potential negative social repercussions' and not in consideration of any real damage caused. According to the Supreme Court's reasoning, the public has to be protected from the impact that 'false information' might have on it, and freedom of expression must be considered socially dangerous for fear of 'potential negative social repercussions'.

Application of Art. 48 of the Martial Law Decree

Art. 48 of the Martial Law Decree was probably its most abused provision. The Naval Court in Gdynia, hearing the case of Ryszard Jagodziński, found criticism by the defendant of the following facts as constituting the dissemination of 'false information'.

— the fact that the local petty offences tribunals had sentenced the participants of street demonstrations in Gdańsk on 31 January 1982 without any evidence;
— the fact that the activities of the Polish military regime were being directed by political centres in the USSR;
— the fact that the Polish nation was deprived of its rights and

liberties;
— the fact that trade union freedoms had been limited by the military regime in Poland;
— the fact that students of the pro-regime students' union had jumped the housing queue.

It transpires from this incomplete list that the prime target of prosecution under Art. 48.2 of the Martial Law Decree was information concerning the real scope of repression, Poland's lack of sovereignty and cases of social inequality. These subjects once more became taboo issues.

During the investigation the prosecutor's office and, during the trial, the courts, often availed themselves of the services of the censor who authoritatively determined and assessed what constituted 'anti-state content' in independent publications. At the trial of Stanisław Danielewicz, a 35-year-old critic of popular music, an expert witness from the Institute of Press Research was requested to evaluate the music reviews he had written for *Dziennik Bałtycki* after August 1980. The expert, Dr Maciej Chrzanowski from Kraków, declared that Danielewicz had displayed 'a hostile attitude towards socialism and the PPR'. Danielewicz had written, in February 1982, a column on Amanda Lear's long-playing record 'Incognito',[58] in which the first letter of each paragraph, read from top to bottom, gave the slogan 'WRONA SKONA' (THE CROW WILL DIE).[59] He was arrested and held at an investigative prison in Gdańsk. The prosecutor charged him with an offence under Art. 48.2 of the Martial Law Decree — 'disseminating false information liable to provoke public unrest or disturbances'. During the trial Danielewicz was neither sentenced nor freed. He was held in the investigative prison until 20 December 1982. His case was first transferred from summary to ordinary procedure and later discontinued.[60]

'False information' under Art. 48.2 of the Martial Law Decree could also be disseminated by word of mouth.

Possession of underground Solidarity publications or making public criticism of the regime was often linked to membership in Solidarity, enabling the prosecutor to charge the offender with continuing trade union activity by disseminating 'false information'. This was the case of Wacław Kiciński, the Chairman of the Solidarity Commission in the Communal Construction Enterprise in Sopot.

The Basic Freedoms and the Courtroom

According to the indictment, Kiciński said that General Jaruzelski was 'a prime minister of doubtful qualities'. He was supposed to have said this in the director's office, on 14 December 1981, in the presence of the director and nine other employees. He was also supposed to have said that the decisions taken by the military could not concern either him or Solidarity since they were illegal. He was charged not only under Art. 48.2 of the Martial Law Decree, but also under Art. 46.1 and 2 — for continuing trade union activity and organizing a strike — and, additionally, under Art. 270.1 of the Penal Code which speaks of 'public slander, derision or denigration of the Polish nation, the PPR, its socio-political system or its supreme authorities'.

During the trial the defendant testified that the meeting at the director's office was a discussion. He denied having made the incriminating statements imputed to him in the indictment. Kiciński said that on the day in question he had thought he was on holiday since he had asked for time off even before 13 December 1981, and he had gone to work simply to collect some of his belongings.

The Naval Court in Gdynia acquitted Kiciński of the charge under Art. 46.1 and 2 but found that the meeting in the director's office was not a discussion since it concerned the introduction of martial law and the suspension of trade union activity. 'Under these circumstances', the court declared, 'the claim of the defendant that he was only expressing his own opinions was unjustified since these opinions were derisive in character'. The defendant was sentenced to four years' imprisonment and three years' loss of public rights.[61]

In a similar case, Kazimierz Masiak was charged with having

> ...organized a strike; ...at strike meetings, incited the workforce, including Solidarity members, not to desist from strike action; described WRON as a council of extermination and national dishonour; stated that the government had harassed and arrested the leaders of Solidarity by which he was guilty of disseminating false information which might have caused public unrest among those who were listening to him at the strike meeting; as well as leading a strike in the Promor Enterprise in Gdańsk, a strike which was ended against his intentions in view of the attitude of the majority of the workforce who were in favour of ending the strike and returning to work.

The Basic Freedoms and the Courtroom

The Naval Court in Gdynia did not find the fact that the workforce had voted against strike action as justifying a decision not to mete out a penalty or, at least, to pronounce a lesser penalty, and sentenced Masiak on 26 July 1982 to four and a half years' imprisonment and three years' loss of public rights.

Mariusz Hinz, the chairman of the Solidarity commission in the international freight enterprise 'Hartwig', received a seven-year sentence on identical charges (organizing a strike, continuing trade union activity, disseminating false information liable to cause public unrest or disturbances and publicly slandering the supreme state authorities). During a staff meeting he had described the highest PPR authorities as 'a fascist military dictatorship' and had written on a notice board in his workplace the slogans 'treason', 'down with dictatorship' and 'the nation will win'.[62]

The seizure of more than one copy of an underground publication during a house or body search often resulted in the suspect's being charged with 'collecting, with the aim of dissemination', under Art. 48.3 of the Martial Law Decree. Wojciech Kazior, a student at the Department of Navigation in the Maritime Academy in Gdynia, was detained at a railway station in Gdynia on 24 February 1982. A considerable number of copies of various underground and pre-martial law publications were found on him. The prosecutor's office charged him with 'collecting and transporting printed matter containing false information about mass arrests of Solidarity activists and leaders, the legality of trade union activity during martial law and other information liable to cause public unrest and disturbances'. Kazior's membership in the Independent Student Association (NZS) was held against him as an incriminating circumstance.

During the trial Kazior admitted to possessing and transporting the publications but denied that he had intended to disseminate them. He claimed that he had found the publications by chance in the student hostel where he lived and decided to take them home to Rzeszów as a souvenir.

According to the court, Kazior was not in possession of the incriminating materials by accident and he must have placed a value on them since he had decided to take them home when leaving Gdynia for good. Explaining any doubts to the disadvantage of the defendant, the Naval Court in Gdynia sentenced Wojciech Kazior, on 9 April 1982, to three years' imprisonment. Clearly, Kazior was sentenced without any evidence to contradict his own explanations about the origins of

The Basic Freedoms and the Courtroom

the publications found on his person. Moreover, it had not been proved that the defendant had intended to disseminate the publications either himself or in agreement with any other person.

Leaflets and posters

During the legal existence of Solidarity, leaflets aimed at discrediting the union or its leaders appeared occasionally but, as a rule, the prosecution pretended not to notice them, even though they were duly informed. Leaflets purporting to be from the 'revanchist' *Landesmannschaft* organization Aktion Oder-Neisse, but written in bad German, promising financial support for Solidarity, were found in Gdańsk, Elbląg and Chorzów in March 1981. Anti-semitic leaflets whose apparent aim was to present the union as being manipulated by Jews also made an appearance. These leaflets unquestionably violated the provisions of the Penal Code, but the prosecutor's office was reluctant to pursue such matters and establish their origin.

Not so, however, during martial law. In its early stages, particularly during the strikes of December 1981, almost everyone caught with a leaflet was questioned and often brought to trial. Those who were suspected of maintaining the information network between striking workforces in different factories, or between union cells, were subject to particularly severe sentences. If the charge was based on Art. 48 of the Martial Law Decree, the case was invariably tried by a military court.

What was treated as a leaflet in court could often not technically be described as such. Sometimes the evidence presented in the court involved hand-written notes or posters which were neither mass produced nor printed. Ewa and Wiesław Szwed, for instance, were tried and sentenced for displaying a note on a notice board in an enterprise in which they were employed.[63] The decisive factor in convicting a suspect was not so much the appearance or the form of the leaflet but its anti-regime content. This was variously interpreted as 'slandering the social and political system of the PPR and its supreme authorities', 'a public call for a general strike', or 'inciting the public to break the law'. Roman Bukowski, an inhabitant of Piła, was sentenced on this last charge by the voivodship court under summary procedure to three and a half years' imprisonment for displaying on the premises of the Margomin furniture factory a note which read: 'death to the reds'. Leaflets supporting strikes or demonstrations planned by Solidarity were classified in the case of Zdzisław Paczko from Katowice as 'acclaim for criminal acts planned by the union'.[64] He was sentenced to three and a half years' imprisonment.

The preparation, printing and distribution of leaflets was often made out to be much more dangerous than it really was by linking it to wider 'anti-state activity' such as participating in or setting up an 'illegal organization' or 'continuing trade union activity'. Needless to say such charges carried stiffer penalties.

The seizure of a larger quantity of leaflets usually resulted in the suspect's being accused of acting 'with the aim of disseminating'. In the case of Stefan Sadkowski, the Voivodship Court in Łódź found that the defendant 'passively agreed' to disseminate about 1,000 leaflets by accepting them from an unknown individual at his place of work and subsequently passing them on to his 17-year-old son and his son's 18-year-old friend. The court found him guilty of continuing trade union activity and sentenced him under summary procedure to three years' imprisonment.[65] In a similar case Bogusław Choina from Gliwice was charged with 'continuation of trade union activity' by 'collecting and storing, with the aim of distributing, Solidarity and KPN leaflets containing false information liable to cause public unrest', as well as with 'having passed, with the aim of distributing, several dozen of these leaflets to two other people', who subsequently disseminated them by sticking them up on the walls in the staircases of blocks of flats in Gliwice. Choina's sentence of two years' imprisonment passed by the Garrison Military Court in Katowice on 11 January 1982 was appealed by the Military Prosecutor General's Office to the Supreme Court which on 25 February 1982 increased the sentence to five years' imprisonment.

In some cases the prosecution attempted to establish connections between leaflets and anti-regime protest actions. These, according to official propaganda, simply could not take place spontaneously but had to be organized by 'ring-leaders'. The task of the prosecutor's office was to find these ring-leaders. A group of four students from Toruń apprehended by the police while carrying leaflets were later charged not only with disseminating the leaflets but also with organizing a protest action. According to the prosecution, the street demonstrations that had taken place in Toruń on 1 and 3 May 1982 and had resulted in the brutal intervention of the ZOMO riot police were a direct result of the dissemination of the leaflets by the defendants. During the trial the prosecution was unable to prove that the four defendants — all students —' Marianna Błaszczyk, Grzegorz Jędryczka, Krzysztof Łęgowski and Jacek Bonek, were familiar with the contents of the leaflets which did not, in any case, contain any statements contrary to the law. Eye-witnesses testified that it was the ZOMO riot police who had provoked the disturbances by beating up some of the demonstrators.[66]

Many trials for possession and dissemination of underground leaflets involved students and secondary school pupils. A student from Toruń, Marek Dębiński, was sentenced by the Pomeranian Military District Court on 21 April 1982 to one year in prison for possessing and 'disseminating' one single leaflet.[67]

The trials of printers and distributors of underground publications

The printing and distributing of underground bulletins and information sheets was also penalized even if the publications in question were still only in a preparatory stage.

Possible intent to distribute or possess underground publications, if proved by the prosecutor, could also result in a conviction. In a case involving the underground publication *Biuletyn Małopolski,* the three defendants Tadeusz Świdziński, Adam Kramarczyk and Edward Kubisowski were apprehended by the police in a flat in which large quantities of this publication were seized. None of them lived in that flat and the prosecutor was unable to prove that they had actually distributed or possessed the publication. They were none the less sentenced to three years in prison for 'possible intent' to possess the publication.[68]

The printing and distribution of underground publications were readily linked with other offences, most commonly with the continuation of trade union activity. After the lifting of martial law it was usually linked with participating in or setting up an 'illegal organization' or 'slandering and deriding the socio-political system of the PPR and its supreme authorities'.

At the trial before the Naval Court in Gdynia of Krzysztof Kapica and others accused of publishing the underground bulletin *Krzyk,* the defendants testified that they had not considered the publication of their bulletin as a union activity. The court, however, found that publishing an underground bulletin actually constituted 'active continuation of membership in Solidarity', especially in view of the fact that so many of the articles published in *Krzyk* had appealed for 'trade union solidarity'. Other articles openly mentioned the union authorities and some issues of the bulletin even contained statements by Solidarity members. The court concluded that: 'trade union activity involves not only holding office and discharging one's duties ... it also involves working for the trade union, acting on its behalf and under its aegis ... Any previous trade union activity, and the extent of involvement in such activity before 13 December 1981, is irrelevant'.[69]

Even the typing of underground publications was penalized. The Garrison Military Court in Łódź sentenced Marek Kapuściński and his wife Elżbieta to a suspended sentence of one and a half years' imprisonment for helping to type an independent bulletin.[70] Another resident of Łódź, Wojciech Skłodkowski, was sentenced by the very same court to three years' imprisonment for typing a stencil of issue no. 10 of an underground bulletin *Solidarność Walcząca*. The issue contained a letter addressed to Solidarity activists written by Jerzy Dłużniewski who had gone into hiding after the declaration of martial law, as well as an item written by Skłodkowski himself. Kapuściński and Skłodkowski were charged with preparing, with the aim of distribution, texts liable to cause public unrest or disturbances, under Art. 48.3 and 4 of the Martial Law Decree. Skłodkowski's co-defendant, Klemens Zbroński, received a sentence of one and a half years' imprisonment for 'storing in his flat a considerable number of copies of an illegal bulletin and for passing it round to others'.

Persecuting graffiti and cartoons

The martial law authorities took themselves very seriously and could not bear the sight of Solidarity slogans and anti-regime graffiti scribbled on the walls. The Voivodship Court in Bielsko-Biała sentenced 27-year-old Władysław Dyrcz and 23-year-old Kazimierz Jasernik to three years' imprisonment under summary procedure for scribbling graffiti on 1 October 1982 in villages in Bielsko-Biała and Tarnobrzeg voivodships, as well as drawing cartoons in the village of Sopotnia Mała in the commune of Jaselnia. The court found that the graffiti and cartoons had been aimed against the interests of the state.[71]

On 5 April 1982 the Garrison Military Court in Katowice handed down a sentence of one year's imprisonment suspended for three years in the case of Stanisław Łaski. He was found guilty

The Basic Freedoms and the Courtroom

of calumniation of Leonid Brezhnev and threatening the PPR's alliances. Laski, a worker turned cartoonist, had a remarkable talent for portraying party dignitaries, policemen, prison guards and other 'functionaries of the system', as they are seen through the eyes of the working class, prisoners and 'socially maladjusted people'. His cartoons never appeared in the censored press and it was not until the emergence of Solidarity bulletins that he began to publish his drawings, mostly in *Wolny Związkowiec* (Free Unionist), an uncensored Solidarity publication in the Katowice Steelworks. In July 1981 he drew two cartoons which served as the pretext for instigating proceedings against him — but not until after the declaration of martial law. One showed Leonid Brezhnev in a policeman's uniform armed with a truncheon and holding a bird-cage with Solidarity inside. The second showed a meeting between Brezhnev and Jaruzelski during which they were discussing whether to hang Wałęsa or behead him with a hatchet. The relatively mild sentence can be explained by the fact that the court came to the conclusion that the defendant had been suffering from a persecution complex.

Post-martial law amendments to the Penal Code

After the suspension of martial law, the Act of 18 December 1982 increased the maximum penalties for offences under Art. 271.1 (dissemination of false information), Art. 282 (inciting public unrest) and Art. 287 (illegal manufacture or possession of a radio transmitter) of the Penal Code to five years' imprisonment from three, two and three years respectively. At the same time, the scope of penalization for the offences of public slander and dissemination of false information was broadened under Art. 273.2 to incorporate new legal characteristics. The new wording, which was modelled on Art. 48.3 of the Martial Law Decree, made it illegal not only to prepare, store, transport, carry or send written and printed matter liable to be interpreted as subversive but also to collect such materials, as well as tape recordings and films. It provided penalties of six months' to five years' imprisonment. On the basis of this amendment one might ask whether there is any difference between 'storing' and 'collecting'? The authors of this amendment were clearly wary of leaving possible loopholes and wanted to provide for all conceivable situations.

The Supreme Court, in its interpretation of this article ruled that an offence is also committed when the offender does not personally intend to distribute the materials but is aware that they are meant for distribution by some other person and he stores them for this purpose.[72] In such a way, the direct intent required by the Penal Code ('with the aim of distribution') has been superseded by an awareness that the materials are meant for distribution. This broadened interpretation is to the disadvantage of the defendant in so far as the establishment of his guilt is concerned.

The trend towards a further limitation of the freedom of expression was also reflected in Art. 282a.1 of the Penal Code which stipulates that: 'whoever undertakes an action with the aim of causing public unrest or disturbances is liable for up to three years' imprisonment'. This provision was frequently applied as an additional charge against publishers, printers and distributors of unofficial publications, and the organizers of Radio Solidarity.

Under Art. 282a.1 of the Penal Code the prosecution no longer had to provide evidence that information distributed unofficially was false. It was sufficient to prove that the offender had acted 'with the aim of causing public unrest or disturbances'; it was also irrelevant whether this had actually been caused.

Privacy of mail and telephone conversations has never been sacrosanct to the regime, but until 18 December 1982 it was only used as background information to supplement other evidence gathered by the police. Since 18 December 1982 information obtained by the police through monitoring private telephone conversations or censoring private mail has become admissible as evidence in court. An amendment to Art. 198 of the Code of Criminal Procedure, in the Act of 18 December 1982, made it incumbent upon post or telecommunications offices to hand over at the order of the court or prosecutor personal letters and tapes of private telephone conversations. The wording of this provision is singular in that it tries to conceal the role of the secret police who are actually engaged in tapping telephone conversations and censoring mail.

A telephone subscriber can lodge a complaint against the court or prosecutor's order. In order to do so, however, he needs to know that his telephone has been tapped. On the other hand, if telephone tapping and the censorship of private correspondence is to yield results the police must keep it secret. Being aware of this the PPR legislators added paragraph 2 to Art. 198 of the Code of Criminal Procedure. It stipulates that information about telephone tapping can be withheld from a telephone subscriber 'if the good of the case demands it'. In this way, like Franz Kafka's hero Joseph K., he becomes a suspect without being aware of it.

* * *

It would have been naive to suppose that freedom of expression would be restored with the formal ending of martial law. Indeed, printers, publishers and distributors of independent publications now became prime targets for repression, constituting the single most numerous group of opposition activists brought to trial. Independent publishing continued to be regarded as dissemination of 'false information' (Art. 271.1 of the Penal Code), or 'public slander' (Art. 270.1 of the Penal Code). A charge of disseminating, printing or even possessing uncensored publications was often presented in conjunction with Art. 282a.1 of the Penal Code, i.e. 'undertaking an activity liable to cause public unrest or disturbances', a legal formula closely modelled on Art. 48 of the Martial Law Decree. Alternatively, charges under Art. 282a.1 of the Penal Code were presented in conjunction with Art. 45 of the Press Law. Marek Mickiewicz, for instance, was charged with 'having printed, between 1983 and 12 September 1984, in Warsaw, with the intention of dissemination, with the aim of causing public unrest, without proper permission, publications such as *Tygodnik Mazowsze, Biuletyn Międzywydawniczy, Biuletyn Uniwersytetu Warszawskiego* and others'. His offence was to have allowed his house near Warsaw to be used by others to print and store uncensored publications. He was sentenced in March 1985 to two years' imprisonment and heavy fines.

Freedom of expression, necessary for scientific research and creative work, as defined in the International Covenant on Civil and Political Rights, has never been observed in Poland and still remains an unfulfilled aspiration. Without it there can be no openness in public life. The actual extent of freedom of expression depends on social pressures and varies according to political expediency. The monopoly on information is a jealously guarded instrument of power: the ruling elite which wields it establishes the criteria of true and false.

4. The right to peaceful assembly

In Poland demonstrations may not be organized without the consent of the authorities. Plans for any rallies, marches or demonstrations must be submitted in advance for approval by the local administration. As a rule, all demonstrations other than those which are organized, supported or inspired by the party are refused permission. Any independent demonstration organized on the occasion of a national anniversary or in support of a trade union or other democratic cause is labelled anti-state. In this way, the PPR authorities deny their citizens something that is a fundamental right in any free society. They are afraid of the popular will which has repeatedly been expressed on the streets as a vote of no confidence in the authorities. Street riots, in some cases involving loss of lives, usually forced changes in the party leadership and resulted in concessions offered by the new leadership to the people in general.

The PPR's Penal Code contains provisions which can be and have been applied against those who try to exercise their right to peaceful assembly. They can be charged with numerous offences. 'Taking part in a public gathering whose participants jointly commit a violent assault on persons or property' (Art. 275.1), can be punished by up to five years' imprisonment. If the result of a violent assault is 'death, serious bodily injury or considerable damage to property' (Art. 275.2), then the penalty can be as high as 10 years' imprisonment. 'An assault on a police officer, or other representative of law and order, in the course of his official duties' (Art. 234.1) can be punished by up to eight years' imprisonment, and 'inciting others to commit an offence or praising an offence' (Art. 280.1) can be punished by up to five years' imprisonment. Shouting slogans can be punished either as 'verbal abuse of a police officer in the course of his duties' (Art. 236) or 'verbal abuse of a political organization [e.g. the PUWP] or other nationwide social organization' (Art. 237) and may result in up to two years' imprisonment.

Those who are refused permission to hold an assembly can appeal to the Supreme Administrative Court. The court, however, is empowered only to examine whether a decision to ban a specific demonstration has been taken in accordance with the obtaining provisions and not whether it was justified on substantive grounds.

The Basic Freedoms and the Courtroom

The Petty Offences Code and the right to peaceful assembly

The PPR's Petty Offences Code distinguishes between gatherings (Art. 50) and assemblies (Art. 52). Anyone who participates in a gathering and does not comply with a police order to disperse is liable only to be fined or reprimanded. During martial law, many of those who participated in pro-Solidarity marches, rallies and demonstrations were sentenced under Art. 50, although these meetings should technically have been classified not as gatherings but assemblies. This abuse served as a legal device to impose heavier penalties on participants in independent street demonstrations. As of 1 July 1985, this device has no longer been necessary since amendments of 10 May 1985 brought the penalties for illegal assemblies in line with those for gatherings.

Art. 52 of the Petty Offences Code imposes tight controls over public assemblies, their convention, course and specific details. The description 'assembly' includes not only events such as congresses, rallies, demonstrations and marches but also lectures, processions and pilgrimages. Social meetings and family reunions are also classified as assemblies but they can be organized without notifying the authorities or obtaining their permission. At the same time, however, they can be dissolved by the authorities at any moment.

Under Art. 52 of the Petty Offences Code the very fact of calling upon people to join an illegal assembly is a petty offence even though the assembly may subsequently not be held at all. A last-minute change in the location or agenda can be interpreted as a breach of the conditions under which permission to hold an assembly was granted. An assembly can be dissolved by the local administration official responsible or the police even though permission to hold it was duly obtained. Police decisions to dissolve an assembly are announced verbally. It is sufficient in such a situation for the police to declare that the course of the assembly was not compatible with its purpose or with the provisions of the Penal Code. All participants are then required to disperse immediately; delay in complying with an order to disperse constitutes a separate offence (Art. 52.1(iv)).

Art. 52.1 of the Petty Offences Code defines inter alia the following acts as petty offences:[73]

— calling an assembly
    a. without the required notification or permission,

b. in breach of conditions under which permission had been granted;

— leading an assembly
   a. convened without the required notification or permission,
   b. in breach of conditions under which permission had been granted,
   c. after it was dissolved;

— using technical equipment in order to organize or conduct an assembly without permission or in defiance of a prohibition;

— occupying a place or trespassing on premises where another person or organization is legally responsible for convening an assembly or presiding over it;

— remaining on the site of an assembly
   a. in defiance of a call to disperse by an authorised person or other representative of the authorities,
   b. after an assembly has been dissolved;

— allowing the use of:
   a. premises for the purpose of convening an assembly called without the required notification or permission,
   b. a place designated for religious practices for an assembly which is not connected with these practices.

Art. 52.2 provides penalties for anyone who incites or aids others to commit any of the aforementioned petty offences. Separate permission is required to set up loudspeakers, microphones and amplifiers. Should these be used without permission or in breach of the conditions under which permission to use them was granted, they can be confiscated even if the offender is not their owner (Art. 63.1 and 2). The manufacture and possession of radio broadcasting equipment is a separate offence punishable under Art. 287 of the Penal Code with a maximum penalty of three years' imprisonment.

Other provisions of the Petty Offences Code can also be used in purely political cases against demonstrators. Art. 56.1 requires that permission be obtained for fund collecting in public in order to pay fines imposed by a court or a petty offences tribunal. Any breach of this provision is punishable with a fine or imprisonment.

The Basic Freedoms and the Courtroom

Art. 61.2 forbids the manufacture, use or wearing of officially banned emblems, insignia or uniforms. It was frequently applied during martial law to punish people for wearing Solidarity badges, despite the fact that Solidarity had never had any official emblem or insignia. Art. 63a forbids the display in public places of posters, announcements and drawings which have not been approved by the appropriate authorities. This new provision, introduced as a result of an amendment of 28 July 1983, enables the authorities to punish those who were detained while putting up posters, drawing graffiti or sticking up leaflets, when the evidence against them is too slim to charge them with distributing 'false information', 'slandering the supreme authorities' or other activity 'liable to cause public unrest'. Before this new provision was introduced, putting up unofficial posters or slogans was treated as the littering of public places and the penalty was not too severe. The offender can now be ordered to pay a higher fine or to restore the public place to its original state.

Although demonstrating against the PUWP is nowhere specifically forbidden, the interests of the party are, in fact, well protected. The Petty Offences Code lists among 'official and social institutions' that must be treated with respect 'other social organizations of working people', a transparent euphemism for the party and its apparatus (Art. 47.4). Art. 49 of the Petty Offences Code forbids public manifestations of anti-regime political sentiments and penalizes those who 'ostentatiously demonstrate a lack of respect towards the Polish nation, the PPR, its socio-political order and its supreme authorities'. Although this provision does not actually mention the PUWP, it is common knowledge that the 'socio-political order' is founded on exclusive rule by the party. The reputation of the PUWP is also protected from 'hostile criticism' by Art. 270.1 of the Penal Code which penalizes 'public slander, derision and degrading of the Polish nation, the PPR, its socio-political order and its supreme authorities'.

The previous Petty Offences Code which was passed in 1932 included only 47 offences divided into five chapters. The present one, dating back to 1971, listed well over 100 and divided them into twelve chapters. This number has since grown as a result of subsequent amendments.

The Basic Freedoms and the Courtroom

Petty Offences Tribunals

The local petty offences tribunals which dealt with over 700,000 cases in 1982 (in comparison with an average of some 500,000 cases annually) are not even formally independent courts but semi-judicial organs attached to and dependent upon the local administration, as well as the Ministry of Internal Affairs. The local petty offences tribunals have often been criticised for their unprofessional character, their lack of experience, the ease with which they pass severe sentences, their arbitrary interpretation of the Petty Offences Code and their procedural irregularities. After August 1980 reformist-minded lawyers proposed that they be deprived of the right to pass prison sentences.

Members of petty offences tribunals are selected by local people's councils from a list of candidates submitted by various official organizations. The term of office is four years and the jurors can at any time be recalled by the people's council. Each case is heard by a panel of three jurors: a chairman and two others. Only the chairman of the tribunal is required to have a degree in law or in administrative studies.[74] A legal adviser is appointed to each tribunal in order to provide professional legal services. One of his tasks is to see that the tribunal complies with the guidelines set down by the people's council, the voivodship prosecutor's office and the police. In fact, the adviser, as a professional and an appointed official knowing which strings to pull, exercises considerable influence over his less experienced colleagues and it is he who, to a large if not decisive extent, determines the verdicts passed. He acts as the link between the administrative authorities and the tribunal.

Overall political supervision over petty offences tribunals is exercised by the Minister of Internal Affairs who is also in charge of the police. In the vast majority of cases heard before tribunals police officers perform the functions of public prosecutor and witness simultaneously. According to the Ministry of Internal Affairs, 87 per cent of all the cases heard by petty offences tribunals in the first one and a half years after their reorganization at the end of 1982 were submitted by the police.[75]

Direct supervision over tribunals is exercised by the people's councils which are empowered to issue guidelines on verdicts. The tribunal chairman's duties include preparing periodical reports on the state of law and order for the people's councils. Control over the tribunals is also exercised by the Prosecutor General and his subordinates. The verdicts passed by the lower level regional tribunals can be overruled ex officio if they are found 'to have been passed without legal basis or to be evidently wrong' by special supervisory commissions attached to voivods or city mayors. No official data are published about the number of verdicts overruled by these commissions.

Higher level tribunals hearing appeals against verdicts passed by regional tribunals are also attached to voivods or city mayors. Approximately 60 per cent of the verdicts passed by the regional tribunals are either changed or overruled.[76] This figure alone bears witness to the fact that poor legal standards are the norm in regional tribunals.

There were 51,588 jurors of regional petty offences tribunals in the 1983-6 term of office. Only 2,219 of that number had a degree in law or administrative studies; 25,330 belonged to the PUWP; and 19,113 had been re-selected,[77] i.e. they had served during the previous term, which began in 1977, ended in late 1980 and was extended until October 1982.[78] A similar trend was apparent in the higher level petty offences tribunals. The degree to which the tribunals are dependent on the local administration is evident from the fact that approximately 50 per cent of jurors are local administration officials. This is, in fact, the largest single profession from which jurors are recruited.

The authorities took the opportunity presented by the extension of the 1977-80 term of office to reorganize the local petty offences tribunals. On the basis of the law of 20 December 1982 several lower level tribunals which were attached to rural communities and city districts were amalgamated to cover a larger area corresponding to the regional divisions of the courts, the prosecution and the police. In this way they were integrated still further into the police system of repression. The previously existing 2,383 tribunals were replaced by only 376 tribunals. This increased the difficulties already felt by tribunals situated in larger urban centres; in particular, they were unable to cope with the increased workload.[79]

Local petty offences tribunals are the most common and, at the same time, the crudest form of administering justice. In 1982 the number of cases heard by them reached 732,042. This was undoubtedly a record year, equivalent to an annual growth of 57 per cent on 1981. According to official figures, in that year 196,586 cases involved various violations of martial law regulations; in 1983 the overall number of cases heard fell to 530,000.[80]

The Basic Freedoms and the Courtroom

The weekly *Życie Literackie* published a report on the work of a petty offences tribunal in one of the Warsaw districts. This tribunal was said to have heard 5,778 cases during the first half of 1982. 61 per cent of all these cases concerned petty offences under the Martial Law Decree. The majority of them — 2,809 — were curfew violations, 425 involved unauthorized residence in Warsaw without the required residence permit, 172 were brought against people who were unable to produce their personal identity documents on demand, and 248 involved participation in various protest actions and street demonstrations. The remainder concerned such petty offences as work dodging and taking pictures without permission. 94 per cent of the cases heard during martial law were brought under accelerated procedure, i.e. within 48 hours of the offender's apprehension by the police. In 3,393 of the cases heard under the Martial Law Decree the tribunal returned a verdict of guilty and acquitted the defendants in only 67 cases.[81]

Such data, although it is presented in a censored publication, reveals a great increase in police activity on the streets. Secondly, the application of accelerated procedure which greatly reduces the defendant's right to a proper defence was widespread. Thirdly, the number of cases in which the jurors' panel returned the verdict of guilty was very high.

The real extent of repression as practised by the local petty offences tribunals is difficult, if not impossible, to ascertain. In some cases the details were deliberately concealed; some hearings took place behind closed doors while in other cases the defendant's family were not informed about the date of the hearing.

Tribunals and the penalty of imprisonment

The two penalties most frequently applied by the petty offences tribunals during martial law were fines and imprisonment. Fines (up to 20,000 zloty) were imposed in some 93 per cent of cases.[82] In 1983, for instance, 17 per cent of the fines imposed by the petty offences tribunals exceeded 10,000 zloty. In nine out of ten cases the fines could not be exacted from those on whom they had been imposed because they did not possess such sums of money.[83] In such a situation the tribunal can impose a substitute penalty of imprisonment or allow a few days to complete the payment. One of the consequences of the widespread practice of substitute imprisonment was a growth in the prison population: some 40,000 people annually were serving various spells of imprisonment as a result of a verdict passed by a petty offences tribunal.

The defendant can appeal to a court only when sentenced to imprisonment or 'limitation of personal freedom'. There is no appeal against fines or decisions concerning the confiscation of property. It is interesting that regional courts hearing appeals tend to overrule verdicts of imprisonment. The verdict is, on average, upheld by the regional court only in every third case. Most commonly the verdict is either suspended conditionally or lowered. Full acquittals are none the less rare: 5.5 per cent of the cases heard under ordinary procedure and 11.2 per cent under accelerated procedure.[84]

Accelerated procedure before petty offences tribunals

Cases can be heard by petty offences tribunals under accelerated procedure on the basis of an administrative decision by the appropriate national authorities or individual voivods, whenever 'a specific offence appears to be widespread in a given area'. The tribunals then deal exclusively with this offence (Art. 70.3 of the Petty Offences Procedure Code). Accelerated procedure is also commonly applied with regard to people who have no fixed employment or address, or if the jurors' panel is of the opinion that it would be impossible or much more difficult to hear the case under ordinary procedure.

Under this procedure the alleged offender is taken from a police station to a tribunal within 48 hours of being detained. The hearing is usually reduced to the reading of a police request to punish the defendant. This request is prepared by the police officer who originally detained the offender. It is usually presented in general terms, stating that the person in question participated on such and such a date in a street demonstration, shouted anti-state slogans or did not heed the call to disperse. The jurors' panel listens to explanations by the defendant but bases its verdict on the testimony of the policeman. The vast majority of defendants do not plead guilty. Some of them might have been detained although they were innocent by-standers or happened to be in the area of a demonstration as it was coming to an end. The cases resemble one another closely and each jurors' panel hears several cases during the course of a day. The defendant is seldom informed of his rights and his family or friends are not informed about his detention. He himself has no possibility of choosing his own defence lawyer.

The Basic Freedoms and the Courtroom

The jurors' panel can order immediate imprisonment or demand on-the-spot payment of a fine. In the latter case, if the defendant is unable to pay up immediately he might be sentenced to substitute imprisonment. He may then appeal to a court, but only within three days. Whether he appeals or not, he still has to serve his sentence in prison as there is no provision for release pending appeal. In many cases it takes longer for the regional court to process an appeal than the actual term of imprisonment. Even if the regional court subsequently orders the defendant's immediate release, he is not entitled to claim any compensation for unfair deprivation of freedom. Appeal proceedings do, however, give the defendant certain procedural guarantees of which he was deprived in the first instance before the tribunal. First, he can avail himself of the services of a defence lawyer. Secondly, his case is heard by a professional judge and two lay adjudicators (people's jurors), who are, at least formally, independent. Thirdly, the police have to present conclusive evidence against him. In practice, however, the procedural guarantee of judicial control over tribunals' prison sentences is largely illusory since by the time the regional court passes its sentence in appeal proceedings, the penalty of imprisonment is largely served.

The cost of demonstrating

The extent of independent pro-Solidarity demonstrations after the imposition of martial law took the authorities by surprise. In Gdańsk voivodship, for example, various hard-line party activists demanded that people detained in the aftermath of demonstrations on 30 January 1982 should be severely punished.[85] Local petty offences tribunals complied with these demands; out of a total of 205 persons detained, 101 received prison sentences of between one and three months and 33 people were fined between 2,000 and 5,000 zloty.[86]

Demonstrations staged throughout the country on 1, 3 and 13 May 1982 showed the extent of popular opposition to the martial law authorities. The demonstrations led to the detention or arrest of 2,269 people and the internment of 211 people; 1,139 appeared before petty offences tribunals; 24 of those who were tried by regional courts received sentences in excess of three months' imprisonment. On 20 May, a Justice Ministry spokesman said that 99 people had been sentenced for up to three years and a further 164 for longer periods. The authorities raised four-fold the maximum fines that petty offences tribunals could impose on participants of anti-regime demonstrations, and introduced accelerated procedure in cases brought before regional courts.

These moves did not, however, frighten people off the streets. On 13 June 1982 pro-Solidarity demonstrations took place in Wrocław and Nowa Huta. Six weeks later, on the second anniversary of the August 1980 agreements, demonstrations were staged in 66 towns and there were 25 serious disturbances. In the words of Władysław Frasyniuk, this was a 'great moral victory' for Solidarity while the authorities were politically confounded. But moral victories also have their price. The Provisional Co-ordinating Commission (TKK) had hoped that these demonstrations would 'force the authorities to compromise', but this was not to be. Not only were the authorities still unwilling to sit at the negotiating table, they also responded with large-scale repressions: 5,131 people were detained or arrested, 3,023 out of the total of 3,277 people who were hauled up before petty offences tribunals under accelerated procedure were sentenced to fines or imprisonment; the courts also tried 111 cases involving 126 people under accelerated procedure, 189 people were interned; there were at least four fatalities, as well as numerous injuries and widespread dismissals from jobs.[87]

This time the regional and voivodship courts made much more frequent use of their special powers to mete out severe punishment. Apart from the aforementioned 111 cases submitted to the regional courts under accelerated procedure, the prosecution submitted to the voivodship courts a further 236 cases involving 354 people to be heard under summary procedure.

The authorities were determined to impose severe punishments. In a letter to the chairmen of voivodship courts the Deputy Minister of Justice, Tadeusz Skóra, recommended the 'necessary organizational decisions' to be taken to ensure that cases submitted under accelerated and summary procedures, as well as appeals against verdicts passed by petty offences tribunals, were dealt with 'as quickly and effectively as possible'. In his letter, Skóra also made it clear that he would rather have the defendants sentenced than acquitted. If the court had insufficient evidence against the defendant it should place its trust in the prosecutor, who would supplement it once the case had been returned to him for completion. In a clear indication of his impatience, Skóra stated in his letter that: 'the penal policy applied hitherto must be essentially verified with regard to those who committed offences which were political in character'.[88] So much for the judicial independence of judges who were bluntly told what the authorities expected of them. On 6 October 1982, the authorities held a conference in Warsaw for judges adjudicating in penal cases. The judges were told to 'increase punishment, especially in the cases under summary procedure of the organizers and most aggressive participants [of demonstrations] who were guilty of violating public order'.[89]

The third call for nationwide street demonstrations announced by the TKK to coincide with the anniversary of the union's registration, in protest against the delegalization of Solidarity, was ill-timed. The authorities felt stronger after having regained the initiative. The police scored a number of successes, such as capturing Władysław Frasyniuk and breaking the October 1982 strike in the Lenin Shipyard. After disbanding the union, the authorities released Lech Wałęsa from internment. In places where strikes and demonstrations did occur, they were easily broken, according to a well-established pattern of force and repressive judicial action.

During martial law the police perfected their methods of preventing politically-motivated demonstrations. Mass searches and short-term detentions for up to 48 hours proved quite effective in this respect. In Wrocław, for example, as many as 700 people were detained for 48-hour spells between 29 April and 1 May 1983. Photographs taken by police during demonstrations were used on a wide scale to detain and institute proceedings against those whom police could identify. In Wrocław approximately 300 people identified from pictures taken on 1 May 1983 were detained by the police the following day.

The authorities also increasingly used dismissal from work, or the threat of dismissal, to ensure that the streets remained calm. Art. 5 of the Act of 18 December 1982 qualified participation in a street demonstration as a severe breach of the employee's basic duties and, as such, punishable by dismissal without notice. Similar measures were introduced to prevent students from taking part in street demonstrations. Those who had proceedings instituted against them after being detained in connection with a street demonstration were automatically suspended and struck from the register on conviction (Council of Ministers' Resolution no. 189 of 30 August 1982).

The Basic Freedoms and the Courtroom

Crowd-dispersing techniques and their results

The main task of breaking up demonstrations was entrusted to the ZOMO riot police who were equipped with helmets, visors, truncheons and shields. They fired tear gas canisters and concussion grenades in order to break up peaceful demonstrations. They indiscriminately beat smaller groups of demonstrators or individuals who attempted to flee from the scene of violent clashes. The ZOMO were backed up by water cannon, armoured carriers, police vans and, occasionally, helicopters. Demonstrators were filmed or sprayed with coloured water to facilitate their identification once the pacification was over. Laundries were encouraged to inform the police when they received colour-stained clothes for cleaning. Plainclothes policemen mingled with the crowd and observed what was happening in order to identify the most active participants, incite the crowd to shout provocative anti-regime slogans, and destroy property in view of discrediting the protest.

Such random and excessive use of force resulted in injuries, permanent physical handicaps and the loss of life. According to the Committee of Social Resistance (KOS) active in the Health Services in Kraków, the injuries suffered by the population in Kraków and Nowa Huta from 3 May to 11 November 1982, can be classified as follows:[90]

(i) Injuries requiring neurological and neuro-surgical treatment such as: skull fractures, concussions and damage to the brain and meninges.
(ii) Injuries requiring surgery: broken bones, including fracture of the spine, facial and cranial bones, bruising of internal organs such as kidneys, deep tissue wounds, severe burns exceeding 30 per cent of the skin surface, etc.
(iii) Injuries requiring ophthalmological treatment: severe damage to the eyeball, internal eyeball haematoma, orbital fracture, burns, conjunctivitis, etc.
(iv) Injuries requiring treatment by other specialists such as: dermatologists (for burns); laryngologists (for contusions of the larynx, ears, and nose); physicians (for shock, pulmonary endema and circulatory insufficiency).

The most common cause of injuries were beatings inflicted by the ordinary police, the riot police and the security police.

The Basic Freedoms and the Courtroom

Another frequent cause of injury were tear-gas canisters and petards which were fired into crowds at close range and on a flat trajectory, causing burns and lacerations. Tear-gas petards were also fired into churches, blocks of flats and other public buildings. On days when public demonstrations were being held civilian hospitals in Nowa Huta were forbidden to admit those who were injured during the protests.

Many of those stopped by the police were beaten as they were being detained, beaten again as they were being pushed into police vans, beaten during the journey to the police station, beaten on leaving the van and beaten yet again at the police station. People who had been detained in connection with street demonstrations were beaten at the police stations as a matter of course. A number of people died as a result of injuries suffered at the hands of the riot police.

The case of Jan Witkowski

Jan Witkowski of Gryfino near Szczecin, a former supporter of the Workers' Defence Committee 'KOR', was detained in a police round-up on 30 August 1983 as he was leaving a church after a Mass commemorating the anniversary of the Gdańsk Agreement. As a result of a beating administered at the police station his hearing was impaired. He was held under temporary arrest and subsequently charged under Art. 237 of the Penal Code for 'publicly insulting the ZOMO riot police by marching and shouting 'ZOMO—Gestapo' along with other participants of an illegal demonstration'. Witkowski denied the charge. During the trial he said that he had found himself on Plac Zwycięstwa (Victory Square) where the demonstration was taking place quite by chance; the prosecution claimed that he could have gone straight to a bus stop and caught the bus home. The fact that he had resisted while the police tried to detain him was held against him as an incriminating circumstance. As a 'KOR' supporter and Solidarity activist interned during martial law, he had been on the secret police blacklist for a long time.

The act of indictment was not, however, supported by any evidence. It was based on the testimonies of two policemen — R. Grabowski and B. Poklep. During the trial before a regional court the latter changed the testimony he had given in the course of the investigation: during the court hearing he testified that the defendant had chanted 'Solidarity', whereas earlier in the investigation he had testified that he had heard him chanting 'ZOMO–Gestapo'. The other policeman, Ryszard Grabowski, testified in the courtroom that although he had seen the defendant at the head of the crowd, he was unable to hear exactly what he was chanting:

The Court: What did the people shout when Witkowski was dragged into a police van?
R. Grabowski: They shouted something against us, but I cannot remember exactly what it was since I was agitated.
Jerzy Chmura (defence lawyer): Could Jan Witkowski be recognized by his voice; in other words, was it possible to identify individuals among the crowd chanting 'ZOMO–Gestapo'?
R. Grabowski: I have no answer.

No other evidence was presented apart from the testimonies of the police officers. The court, however, found the defendant guilty and declared that he must have come to Szczecin for the specific purpose of taking part in the demonstration since he could have prayed in Gryfino just as well. The court further ruled that Witkowski had accepted the actions of the demonstrators. 'If a person moves his lips in a crowd' then, according to the court, 'it must be to repeat what the others are saying'.[91]

The rule of political expediency

Jan Witkowski, sentenced to one year's imprisonment, was, in fact, penalized for the probability of what he might have done, and not for what he actually did. His case demonstrates that the police have a free hand in formulating charges and deciding who will hear the case. Witkowski was well known to the security police in Szczecin and it was not considered sufficient to forward a mere request for punishment against him to the local petty offences tribunal.

This is not to say that a detainee with a record of anti-regime political activity will invariably be tried by a regional court for participating in a street demonstration. Concern for political expediency might dictate another approach: sentencing by a petty offences tribunal is less conspicuous, and enables those sentenced to be portrayed as hooligans. Władysław Frasyniuk and Józef Pinior were tried and imprisoned on the basis of a verdict passed by a local petty offences tribunal for participating in an

The Basic Freedoms and the Courtroom

independent pro-Solidarity march on 31 August 1984; Andrzej Gwiazda for taking part in a similar march on 16 December 1984 and again in February 1985 for 'refusing to show his identity papers'. In this way the authorities achieved their objective of removing well-known Solidarity activists from public at a time when they were introducing unpopular price rises or when Solidarity was celebrating national anniversaries.

It is worth remembering that 'the rule of thumb' is that the authorities are free to decide who will be charged and with what offence or petty offence. It is not surprising, therefore, that people detained in similar or identical circumstances have been treated quite differently.

Cases against well-known Solidarity activists are usually based on police testimony which is sometimes very unconvincing. In the case of Jacek Kuroń and Seweryn Jaworski, who were charged with organizing and leading an independent May Day march in Warsaw in 1985, Major Ryszard Macoch quoted as evidence against Kuroń a Radio Free Europe news item which said that Kuroń and Jaworski had marched at the head of a column of people, in spite of the fact that RFE's programmes are constantly labelled by PPR propaganda as slanderous, hostile or exaggerated. Both Kuroń and Jaworski were sentenced to three months' imprisonment. The former's sentence was later overturned by a regional court.

In some cases participants of independently staged assemblies were detained even before they had had a chance to commit the petty offence with which they were subsequently charged. Józef Pinior, for instance, was charged with 'attempting to place a wreath in a prohibited area' in Wrocław on 31 August 1985, and sentenced to three months' imprisonment.

Lubin — another cover-up

In Lubin, a small copper-mining town in south-west Poland, Solidarity members planned to heed the TKK's call to commemorate the second anniversary of the August 1980 agreements. A local underground publication dated 31 August 1982, appealed to its readers: 'Remember! The Legnica region of Solidarity calls on you to mark August 31 this year at 3.30 pm. We will gather for a peaceful demonstration at the designated places in the cities of our region, carrying banners reading 'Lift martial law', 'Solidarity fights on', 'Free Lech', 'Freedom for the imprisoned'. We appeal to you to behave calmly. Do not let yourselves be provoked.'[92] After 3 p.m. about 3,000 people gathered in the main square in Lubin and proceeded to arrange flowers in cross shapes and V signs. The arrest of an ambulance crew who, according to some reports, joined in the demonstration, provoked whistles and angry shouts from the crowd. The police began dispersing the crowd with tear gas. People threw gas canisters and stones back at the police who retaliated by firing warning shots from automatic guns over the heads of the demonstrators. A police patrol near the post office, however, started actually to shoot at people. An eye-witness reported: 'As I was going past the post-office, a police patrol went by me quite peacefully, unattacked by anyone. When the sound of shots rang out, I was convinced that they had fired blanks — even when I heard a shout and saw someone fall, I still thought he had just tripped. But then, with terror, I noticed the blood-stain spreading on his shirt. I also saw one of the patrolmen changing his magazine — had it been him? It was pre-meditated murder, coldly calculated...' [93] Three people were shot dead and several were wounded.

The Garrison Military Prosecutor's Office in Wrocław, in co-operation with the Silesian District Military Prosecutor's Office, conducted investigations into the street disturbances. On the basis of these investigations they compiled a document entitled 'Information concerning street disturbances on 31 August 1982 in Lubin'. The document presented by the Garrison Military Prosecutor's Office found on the basis of the evidence collected that: 'The use of firearms and the firing of live ammunition was unjustified. There was no evidence to suggest any direct risk of life and limb to the policemen involved in the action.' The three prosecutors proposed that the officers responsible be charged. This was not done, however, as the District Military Prosecutor's Office of the Silesian Military District in Wrocław discontinued the investigation and justified the police actions in Lubin.

In November 1983 the Court of the Silesian Military District in Wrocław passed sentences of up to five and a half years' imprisonment on a group of miners described as 'the bombers of Lubin'. The defendants, some of whom had been mistreated during investigation, had planted explosives not to kill but to frighten the local police and party officials. Although portrayed officially as terrorists, and excluded from the July 1984 amnesty, it is clear that their actions had their roots in what had happened in Lubin on 31 August 1982. They were people acting in desperation who could not find justice and therefore sought retribution.

The law on assemblies amended

The law on assemblies of 29 March 1962 distinguished between illegal assemblies (i.e. those that were organized by organizations denied legal recognition by the authorities, such as Solidarity) and legal assemblies. The latter were subdivided into those that required permission, those that required notification only, and those that required neither permission nor notification. Marches, rallies and demonstrations organized by the authorities and officially approved political parties or trade unions fell within the last category. Assemblies that required permission or notification could be dissolved by the police if they threatened security or public order as well as 'when their actual course contradicted their stated objective or violated penal provisions'. Wedding parties, funerals or religious processions could be dissolved under this pretext. Permission to organize an assembly is most commonly refused by the administrative authorities on two grounds: the proposed assemblies are declared to be contrary either to security and public order or to social interest. Needless to say, these very general reasons are arbitrarily interpreted.

The trend during martial law was to limit the number of assemblies that did not require permission under the law of 29 March 1962. The Act of 21 July 1983 gave the voivod the right to subject the following assemblies which had previously been excluded to the provisions of the law on assemblies:

(i) assemblies organized by the management of state enterprises as part of their statutory tasks (e.g. a general meeting of the staff);
(ii) meetings of local communities (e.g. groups of residents, etc.) even though such a meeting may only concern local issues;
(iii) meetings of the boards or members of recognized social organizations;
(iv) meetings of school pupils or their parents even though these have been approved by the school's director;
(v) student rallies.

The new law left it to the voivod to decide which of these assemblies were to be subject to the law of 29 March 1962, to what extent, for how long, and when 'the social interest' so demands.

The right to peaceful assembly was curtailed still further as a result of a legislative package adopted by the Sejm on 10 May 1985. The most ominous of the amendments to the Petty Offences Code concerned Art. 52.1, i.e. 'illegal assemblies'. Before this new amendment, 'organizing' or 'leading' unauthorized assemblies or 'making premises available for such an assembly' were punished by either a fine or a reprimand. Now perpetrators of these petty offences can also be punished with imprisonment.

Participation in 'illegal assemblies', which was hitherto not penalized at all, can at present also be prosecuted, and not simply with a fine but also with imprisonment. This means that the previous, at least theoretical, difference between 'illegal assemblies' and 'gatherings' has disappeared. A new Article 37a stipulated additional fines of up to 30,000 zloty 'if, in connection with a petty offence against public peace and order, units of riot police were used to quell the disturbance'. Yet another amendment to the Petty Offences Code introduced penalties of imprisonment or a fine for 'violating the laws on the state emblem, colours or the national anthem of the PPR' (Art. 49.2). This meant in practice that people could be punished for singing the national anthem in an independent rally, using national flags or printing a red Solidarity logo on a white background. Finally, Art. 57.1 of the amended Petty Offences Code made it an offence for anyone other than the defendant's family to provide the funds to pay a fine imposed by a tribunal. Previously only organizing or collecting funds on behalf of those fined by the petty offences tribunals was punishable.

A new role for the petty offences tribunals

Following the release of the majority of political prisoners in September 1986 the authorities passed amendments to the Code of Petty Offences under the law of 24 October 1986 and modified their penal policy. This manoeuvre was officially described as 'depenalization'. It enabled the petty offences tribunals to try some political offences previously under the sole jurisdiction of the courts. Most of the criminal acts downgraded from offences to petty offences came from Chapter XXXVI of the Penal Code and included: participation in a clandestine association or one which had either been dissolved or refused registration (Art. 278.1), public incitement to an offence or acclaim for such an offence (Art. 280.1), public incitement to civil disobedience (Art. 282), activities undertaken with the aim of causing public unrest and disturbances (Art. 282a.1), the publication, transportation and distribution of uncensored literature and recordings (Art. 45 of the Press Law). All these articles have been included in the Code of Petty Offences as Art. 52a.

This created an unclear situation in which one and the same act could in one case be treated as a petty offence and in another as an offence. Whether the case was to be heard by a court or a petty offences tribunal was determined by the gravity of the circumstances or consequences of the act. In other words, the amendment increased the discretionary powers of the police still further. The range of penalties available to the authorities to punish individuals for voicing their opinions in public, engaging in uncensored publishing, undertaking activities on behalf of Solidarity, or participating in independent demonstrations was extended.

Another amendment gave the police and certain other officials the right to conduct house or body searches in cases involving Art. 52a of the Code of Petty Offences. A conviction by a petty offences tribunal did not rule out further court proceedings under the Penal Code. Attempting, instigating and abetting in connection with the new petty offences were also made punishable.

Guidelines given to petty offences tribunals stressed fines in preference to the penalty of imprisonment. In addition, any property used or intended for use in connection with a petty offence could be confiscated. This includes cars used to transport unauthorized publications, and even apartments, should a copying machine or illegal publications be found there.

The shift from regional courts to petty offences tribunals involved certain disadvantages to the defendant. His case can now be heard quickly, often without the presence or with only the token participation of a defence lawyer. The political character of the repression can now be better hidden from the public eye and, instead of political prisoners, the authorities will have debtors.

* * *

After the pacification of active resistance to martial law in December 1981 and the realization that strikes were no longer an effective weapon, Solidarity sought a new formula for a struggle which would enable them to exert pressure on the authorities. Street demonstrations were an obvious and spontaneous form of protest and the underground Solidarity leadership, in response to grass-root pressure, supported and co-ordinated such actions. The Spring, Summer and Autumn of 1982 witnessed demonstrations in many towns. Some of them ended violently, usually as a result of police provocation. The authorities, however, remained unresponsive to this form of pressure and were determined to crush pro-Solidarity demonstrations with force.

This manifestation of anti-regime sentiments caught the authorities unprepared as they were planning gradually to relax some of the rigours of martial law and it was only in mid-1982 that they finally began to make changes in the law to make independent demonstrations too costly for Solidarity supporters.

Although independent demonstrations continued in the post-martial law period, they were less numerous and largely symbolic; their aim was to demonstrate that Solidarity lived on and that the policies pursued by the authorities were not accepted by the people at large. Demonstrations were a spectacular form of protest that showed to public opinion, both in Poland and in the West, that the cause for which Solidarity was fighting was far from defeated. At the same time, however, the demonstrations enabled the police to pick out the most active Solidarity supporters, in particular young people, and punish them in exemplary fashion at their place of work, school or university as well as imposing fines or putting them behind bars. Solidarity activists gradually realized that the authorities were too strong to be challenged and defeated on the streets and independent initiatives increasingly concentrated on the tactics of the 'long march', a less spectacular but more dogged and long-term struggle. In this way the failure of independent demonstrations as a method of struggle served as a catalyst for the formulation of a new strategy out of which new tactics were beginning to emerge.

5. The right to protest

The right to protest is an integral part of the general right to freedom of expression and is closely connected with the right to freedom of assembly. It is society's first means of self-defence against the arbitrary decisions of the authorities. The right to protest has been described as a minimum programme for the opposition. In the words of Jacek Szymanderski,

> The one thing we can do is protest loudly against the lawlessness, the way our country is being reduced to extreme poverty, the exploitation, etc. We have to protest, not because we believe our protests will lead us to a free Poland — indeed, they won't — but because no honest person can accept lawlessness. I regard this as the main political programme. If society proves to be strong and courageous, then our defence shall be successful and the days of the regime shall be numbered.[94]

The Martial Law Decree treated protest action on a par with strikes, imposing a strict ban on both and stipulating a penalty of up to five years' imprisonment for organizing or leading either of these (Art. 46.2). The same penalty could be imposed on whoever compelled another by force, unlawful threat or deceit, to refrain from taking up or performing work either in order to stage a protest action or while such was in progress (Art. 46.5). The penalty was increased to 10 years' imprisonment in case of a protest action involving damage to property or sabotage.

In practice, however, the term 'protest action' proved impossible to define. In a ruling of 10 May 1982 the Supreme Court failed to define the essence of a protest action in precise legal terms, contenting themselves with a specious verbal construction that only further obscured the issue: 'a protest action is any behaviour of its participants that aims, through various, externally manifested forms, to the achievement of a desired goal'.[95] The specific case which occasioned this general definition involved appeal proceedings on behalf of J. Mościcki who had been sentenced in the first instance to one year's imprisonment for passing round armbands in the national colours to his colleagues at a Ciechanów toy factory. The armbands had been taken off after 10 minutes, at the request of the management. The Supreme Court found that the aim of the action had been to put pressure on the prosecutor's office to release the imprisoned chairman of the local factory commission of Solidarity and upheld the sentence against Mościcki.[96] In other words, the simple act of passing round armbands was considered tantamount to organizing a protest action.

In another case the Supreme Court was asked whether a

three-minute stoppage at a workplace in order to commemorate the anniversary of the workers' riots that took place in the Baltic Coast region in December 1970 could be classified under Art. 46.2 of the Martial Law Decree as a protest action. The Supreme Court declined to answer, stating that this would have involved not an interpretation of the legal provisions but a critical appraisal of these events.

These two examples demonstrate that the Supreme Court was unable to present a satisfactory legal definition of what constituted a protest action. Would it not, therefore, have been better to have dropped this provision altogether, in keeping with the principle *nullum crimen sine lege?*

The notion of permissible 'protest action' subsequently appeared in both the Trade Union Act of 8 October 1982 and the Law on Agricultural Workers' Organizations of the same date. Neither of those stipulate, however, what form such an action might take while the conditions circumscribing it were so stringent as to make any organized protest action virtually impossible.

The universal right to stage protest actions was formally restored under the Act of 18 December 1982 provided that such actions 'were in accordance with the law'. At the same time the Act added a new provision to the Penal Code. As Art. 282a, this stipulated that 'whoever undertakes an action with the aim of causing public unrest or disturbances is liable for up to three years' imprisonment'. It did not, however, specify, what actually constituted 'an action aimed at causing public unrest or disturbances'. It was the legislators' deliberate intention not to define the forms of this offence putting the emphasis, instead, on the direct intent of the offender ('with the aim of causing'). In this way the legislators disregarded real life, in which 'public unrest or disturbances' are seldom caused for their own sake. What is more probable is that a peaceful meeting, rally or demonstration, organized in order to express dissatisfaction or put forward demands, escalates at some stage (for instance as a result of police intervention) into a public disturbance which was neither intended nor expected. The question then arises whether the organizers of a protest action should be held criminally responsible for an outcome which they might have foreseen, but which they would have wished to avoid?

In the case of Anna Walentynowicz, Kazimierz Świtoń and Ewa Tomaszewska, who were charged under Art. 282a.1 with organizing a protest march of about 300 people in December 1983 in order to embed a metal plaque in the wall surrounding the Wujek coalmine, the court's answer was yes. The prosecutor's office alleged that they had caused 'an organized disturbance of public order and the intervening police officers were physically assaulted and verbally abused'. In fact, this symbolic commemoration of the miners killed during the first week of martial law, would not have resulted in any disturbance of public order had the police not intervened. The prosecutor's office tried to substantiate the charge against Świtoń and Walentynowicz under Art. 282a.1 by saying that they had, by 'exploiting their personal popularity, attempted to gather as many people as possible around the cross'. According to the indictment 'their aim was not to honour the memory of the dead miners but to create public confusion and unrest and incite people to commit anti-state activities'. Were Walentynowicz and Świtoń not in fact being tried for 'their personal popularity'?

The amendments to the Penal Code of 28 July 1983 amplified Art. 282a by adding a second paragraph stipulating that the same penalty (i.e. up to three years' imprisonment) could be imposed on 'whoever organizes or leads a protest action carried out in violation of the existing legal provisions'. Art. 282a.2 breached the fundamental principle of law under which the individual is allowed to do anything that is not specifically forbidden by the law. Art. 282a.2 seems to allow the opposite interpretation, i.e. only that is allowed which is specifically permitted, while that for which there is no legal provision is forbidden. The onus of proving that he was within his rights is then placed on the suspect himself. This is an abuse of the principle *nullum crimen sine lege* which means that no one may be held to account before the law for a deed that is not specifically and precisely defined as an offence by the law. Art. 282a.2, which is, in fact, a new version of Art. 46.2 of the Martial Law Decree, does not specify the circumstances that would allow the court to determine what constitutes 'organization' or 'leadership' of a protest action. Thus, it can at any time be used to repress those who undertake such actions as collecting money to help the families of their victimised colleagues, circulating petitions or commemorating national anniversaries that the authorities prefer to ignore.

Art. 282a.1 was frequently used in conjunction with Art. 45 of the Press Law against those who engaged in independent publishing. The combination of these two articles, imputing a more serious offence, made it possible to impose heavier penalties.

The Basic Freedoms and the Courtroom

In PPR theory, the right to freedom of expression puts the printing presses at the disposal of the people; in practice, however, only a licence issued by the censorship office entitles the holder to publish. Anyone who applies for a licence to publish anything even remotely smacking of opposition not only has no chance of his request being granted but also runs the risk of drawing the attention of the security police to himself. Whoever tries to publish without a licence makes himself liable for prosecution under Art. 45 of the Press Law, and penalties of up to one year's imprisonment.

This 'catch 22' situation ensures that the vast majority of independent material is published underground. Anything to do with the underground — thus reason the prosecution authorities — must have links with foreign centres of political subversion, and, therefore, any publishing activity not bearing the censor's stamp of approval can only be undertaken with the aim of causing public unrest and disturbances. By the same token, anybody who prints, edits, stores, distributes, binds or even allows the basement of his house to be used for publishing uncensored material also acts 'with the aim of causing public unrest or disturbances'. Such a reasoning does more than falsely impute intentions to suspects; it implies that the intention is inherent in the deed. In the case of Marek Mickiewicz, who allowed his basement to be used in such a way, the court found that the defendant had no such intention but nevertheless sentenced him to two years' imprisonment for 'actively working to harm the state authorities'. Bogusław Porowski was sentenced to five months' imprisonment for his activity as a binder of independently published books. He pleaded not guilty to the charge, saying that he had not been aware that bookbinding could possibly have led to public unrest.

The Gdańsk trial of Frasyniuk, Lis and Michnik

The Gdańsk trial of the two well-known and popular Solidarity activists, former members of the underground Provisional Co-ordinating Commission (TKK), Władysław Frasyniuk and Bogdan Lis, and the equally popular Solidarity adviser Adam Michnik in June 1985 was one of the most blatantly manipulated trials of the entire post-martial law period. The three were accused of having 'performed leading functions and participated in the activities of an illegal association called the Provisional Co-ordinating Commission (TKK), which undertook actions with the aim of causing public unrest by organizing a 15-minute strike scheduled for 28 February 1985, in violation of the legal provisions'.

The indictment was based on Art. 278.1 and 3 of the Penal Code, in conjunction with Art. 282a.1 and 2, a combination of charges designed to aggravate the offence imputed to the three activists. The charges arose directly out of the fact that they had been present at a gathering on 13 February 1985 called at the request of Lech Wałęsa where the topics discussed included the latest round of price rises scheduled to go into effect on 28 February 1985. Four other Solidarity activists, Stanisław Handzlik, Jacek Merkel, Janusz Pałubicki and Mariusz Wilk had been present at the informal gathering which was broken up by the police before it had actually started. The police officials found Wałęsa's agenda for the day, as well as several copies of an unsigned typescript entitled 'On Prices', in an ashtray. All seven participants, excluding Wałęsa himself, were detained but only Frasyniuk, Lis and Michnik were placed under arrest. One copy of the typescript was actually found on Frasyniuk's person and this fact served as 'grounds' on which to accuse him of having 'performed on 13 February 1985 leading functions' in the TKK.

As far as Lis and Michnik were concerned, they had, at some time in January, attended a clandestine meeting as guests of the TKK. After this meeting, which was, of course, held without the knowledge of the police authorities, a communiqué dated 21 January 1985 was published. This dealt with several matters and included a call on trade unionists to oppose the authorities' decision on higher prices since 'they failed simultaneously to do anything to aid the economy or move towards a reform of the present inefficient economic system'. A separate document of the same date, co-signed by the TKK and Lech Wałęsa, announced a 15-minute strike for 28 February 1985. Incensed at being outwitted by Lis and Michnik, the authorities opened an investigation against them on 30 January 1985. The fact of their presence at the TKK meeting was subsequently used to substantiate the prosecutor's thesis that they had performed leading functions and participated in the activities of the TKK 'between January and 13 February 1985'.

A third event preceded the three arrests. Lis was approached by a security police official, Colonel Wacław Ulanowski, who had interrogated him on a previous occasion when he was being held under investigative arrest, and given him to understand that the authorities were interested in sounding out the possibilities of a resumption of dialogue with Solidarity. Lis agreed to an informal meeting which took place at the Heweliusz Hotel in Gdańsk on 25 January 1985, i.e. before the investigation against him had been formally opened. Their conversation was secretly recorded and the tape was later doctored to provide evidence against Lis. As the course of the trial subsequently showed, Ułanowski's offer to Lis had been set up to frame him right from the outset.[97]

By basing the charges against the three activists on Art. 278.1 and 3 of the Penal Code, in conjunction with Art. 282a.1 and 2, the prosecution attempted to by-pass Art. 47 of the trade union law which stipulates penalties only for the organization of an illegal strike. Unable to charge Frasyniuk, Lis and Michnik with preparing a strike or inciting others to participate in one (since neither of these is subject to penalization) the prosecutor made preparation for the strike synonymous with 'undertaking activity with the aim of causing public unrest or disturbances' (Art. 282a.1) and 'organizing a protest action carried out in violation of the provisions in force' (Art. 282a.2).

The evidence presented in this concocted case against the three scapegoats who were to be charged in lieu of the untouchable Wałęsa and the unattainable TKK included secretly monitored transcripts of Wałęsa's telephone conversations, a notebook confiscated during a search of Lis's flat, a document entitled 'Programme of Action for Lech Wałęsa' allegedly compiled by Michnik and confiscated during a search in his girlfriend's flat, copies of independent Solidarity publications, as well as transcripts of foreign radio programmes broadcast in Polish on the subject of prices and the Polish economy. All the evidence presented in the case was gathered by the secret police and the role of the prosecutor was limited to piecing it all together. Several abuses came to light even before the trial opened: Wałęsa's private telephone had been secretly monitored (this was not officially admitted until 23 November 1985); Lis's conversation with Ułanowski had been illegally taped, since it had not formally been undertaken as part of an investigation against him, and could not be classified as being of sufficient urgency to justify its recording before the investigation was opened; all three of the accused activists had been under constant secret police invigilation.

Still the prosecution had a thin case, and the authorities did not want to take any chances with the trial. The most important element of their scenario was, therefore, to ensure that the

The Basic Freedoms and the Courtroom

presiding judge understood what socialist legality was all about. Judge Krzysztof Zieniuk — the Chairman of the Voivodship Court in Gdańsk — was such a man. He understood his role at the trial not as that of an impartial arbitrator but one whose duty it was to convict three criminals. He was the real star of the proceedings; in Michnik's words, 'a sign of times to come ... times of the decomposition and degenaration of the dying totalitarian beast'. One of the defence lawyers said there was 'an atmosphere of horror in the courtroom'.

Zieniuk not only deprived the defendants of the opportunity to speak freely and conduct their own defence in the manner they thought most appropriate, but actually had them removed from the courtroom, on the pretext of contempt of court, imposed the penalty of the 'hard bed' on Frasyniuk, overruled not only the questions but also the procedural objections of the defence, ordered police to search all eight defence lawyers and relatives of the defendants, and refused to allow the relatives to hand over sandwiches they had brought for the defendants. All these things were unprecedented even by martial law standards and produced an atmosphere reminiscent of Stalinist trials.

The trial, to quote Barbara Szwedkowska, was 'a dramatic struggle of the defendants with the court to be allowed to speak freely. The court was afraid of becoming a political arena'. Afraid of becoming 'a political arena', the court turned the proceedings into a political farce. It did not even try to maintain the appearance of seeking to establish the material truth. When Michnik tried to explain his relations with the TKK within which he was accused of having performed 'leading functions', the judge said that this did not concern the case and when Michnik persisted, he continued to interrupt him, finally having him removed from the courtroom. His defence lawyer Jacek Taylor then requested the judge to specify in what way Michnik had infringed the rules, to which the court replied that it was not bound to do so. Following a break in the proceedings, Michnik made known his intention of submitting a formal request to have Zieniuk excluded from the proceedings on the grounds of his discriminatory and insulting behaviour with regard to the defendant, violation of procedural provisions, persistent blocking of the defendant's attempts to elucidate the truth. The judge announced a break and, when the hearing resumed, he overruled Michnik's request. Michnik protested saying that he had only expressed intent to submit such a request and that the court's decision had now made it impossible for him to do so.

The Basic Freedoms and the Courtroom

When defence lawyer Anna Skowrońska submitted a motion requesting the court not to admit the testimony of the two secret police officials who met with Lis at the Heweliusz Hotel, the presiding judge ordered the police to carry out a search of all those present in the courtroom (including the prosecutor) in order to distract attention from the motion. When the hearing resumed, Lis tried to give explanations before the security police witnesses but judge Zieniuk did not allow him to do so, and when Lis protested against this, he was removed from the courtroom.

During the questioning of the security police witness Ułanowski, the court dismissed some 40 questions from the defence lawyers. In some instances, the questions were dismissed even before the lawyers had been able to finish speaking. Those questions that were allowed by the judge were not always answered by the witness who said that they were irrelevant to the case. At one point defence lawyer Jan Olszewski asked the court to admonish the witness for deciding for the court which questions should be answered and which not. The judge replied that Olszewski was trying, in an inadmissible manner, to teach him his job and that since the court had not admonished the witness it meant that it approved what he had been saying.

Despite the court's efforts to admit the Heweliusz tape as a piece of bona fide evidence, it became clear as the proceedings progressed that the tape had, indeed, been tampered with. Defence lawyers drew the court's attention to the fact that the tape recording presented at the trial was only 55 minutes long, while the Gdavsk security official Andrzej Sieniuc who had recorded it stated that the conversation between Lis and Uqanowski had lasted some two hours and that the tape recorder had not been switched off at any point in the conversation. Admittedly, Seniuc later said that he could not recall exactly how long the actual 'questioning' had lasted. Judge Zeniuk then granted a defence motion to call the police experts who had authenticated the tape to testify before the court. These experts who identified the voices of three interlocutors, produced the specious theory that the tape recorder had been switched off in the course of the conversation while other interruptions in the recording had been caused by intermittent fading of the voices of the interlocutors. Lis insisted throughout the hearing that the tape contained faked material as well as edited fragments of a conversation that had been recorded in ill-faith without his knowledge. What had been proposed as an informal conversation was presented to the court as a formal warning to Lis.

The Basic Freedoms and the Courtroom

A hearing turned into such a 'political farce' could not but generate breaches of substantive law and rules of procedure. The Gdańsk trial provided many spectacular examples of blatant, undisguised abuse. For example, defence lawyer Olszewski realized, as he was reading the files in the case, that among the case documents passed on to the court by the prosecutor's office were five volumes of documents completely unknown to the defence. The defendants Michnik and Frasyniuk were not allowed to familiarize themselves with the evidence against them and were only read selected parts of it by the prosecutor who said that the rest was irrelevant to their case. The four other Solidarity activists who had been detained on 13 February 1985 in Gdańsk with the defendants were not called to testify. Written records of the court proceedings were falsified; in one instance the defendants were quoted as having admitted to the court that they had engaged in anti-state activities, something which they had never said. Defence motions to call other participants of the Gdańsk meeting as witnesses, and put the records of the proceedings in order, were simply ignored by the court.

In order to get away with such abuses, the court had to limit public access to the courtroom as well as intimidating the lawyers. The Gdańsk trial, albeit formally an open one with some 50 seats available to the public, was as good as closed since all of these were taken up by secret police officials. The defendants were denied private consultations with their lawyers and were only allowed to talk with them across a distance of some 30 feet and only in the presence of policemen. The defence lawyers, who refused passively to accept all these abuses during the Gdańsk trial, were threatened with disciplinary action for their 'tactless' behaviour by Zenon Jankowski, an official of the Ministry of Justice. Jankowski reproved them in particular for telling Western reporters that Zieniuk had shown 'exceptionally bad manners and a lack of knowledge of the elementary procedural rules of a trial'. Zieniuk himself, in his closing remarks, stated that the lawyers' first responsibility was to the state and not to their clients and charged that 'they had forgotten their duties as lawyers in a socialist state. They spared the court no invective. It was the court's duty to defend the socialist state and its legal order against the enemies of People's Poland.'

The judge handed down sentences on 14 June 1985. Lis was sentenced to two and a half years' imprisonment, Michnik to three and Frasyniuk, who was declared a recidivist, to three and a half.

The Basic Freedoms and the Courtroom

They were found guilty on all counts. The court dismissed Lech Wałęsa's testimony, as a witness, that the meeting on 13 February had not yet begun when the police intervened. The court believed the two police officers who had broken it up and said that it had already been in progress.

The Gdańsk trial can only be described as a 'secret policemen's ball'. The authorities, who were trying to re-assert themselves by showing their resolve to crack down hard on the opposition, in fact only undermined the credibility of their own legal system in which they would like Western governments and observers (if not the Poles themselves) to believe. None the less, the trial did serve the authorities' immediate as well as long-term objectives. First, three well-known opposition activists were neutralized at a time when unpopular price increases, always a sensitive issue, were being introduced. Secondly, the security police were compensated for the humiliation they had suffered at the Toruń trial of the murderers of Father Popiełuszko, where their methods had been publicly exposed and condemned, as well as getting their revenge on Frasyniuk, Lis and Michnik who had managed to outwit them and go underground for a meeting with the TKK. Thirdly, the trial was a prelude to possible court proceedings against Lech Wałęsa, whose special immunity the authorities wished gradually to dismantle and who was being investigated on the same charges. Finally, the trial was a kind of public opinion poll, with the authorities indicating that they were determined to deal decisively with all protests, to see how far public resistance to provocation and abuse had diminished.

The fundamental question arising from the Gdańsk trial is whether it signalled a new model of the political trial based on the Soviet norm. In other words, whether the PPR's criminal courts dealing with political cases were to be subjected to re-sovietization. Lech Wałęsa was aware of this danger when he described his three colleagues as the victims of 'political deviation'. He went so far as to call the deviation by name, calling the trial 'an act of state terrorism'.

The trial, which was intended to shock public opinion, did precisely that. The inconsistencies and abuses could not be put down to one individual — the judge, Krzysztof Zieniuk — who could promptly have been called to order or disciplined by the voivodship PUWP authorities or the Ministry of Justice.

The defendants themselves refused to make things easy for the court and play the parts ascribed to them by the secret police scenario. They demanded nothing less than acquittal and, unrepentent until the end, had no illusions as to the nature of the 'justice' they were being served. Michnik said: 'After what I have seen and heard here and, in order to be true to my conscience, there is only one thing I can say: I forgive those who lie about me and persecute me'. The judge said 'thank you' and turned to the next defendant.

All three defendants appealed against the sentences. In a sentence of 21 February 1986 the Supreme Court found no grounds for acquittal or re-trial; it did, however, discern mitigating circumstances in the cases of Lis and Michnik that the court of the first instance had not taken into account. Each of them had his sentence cut by six months. The court perceived no such mitigating circumstances in the case of Frasyniuk.

The Supreme Court also mentioned that the decision to cut the two sentences was connected with the general 'improvement in the situation as regards law, security and order in the country'. Indeed, the Gdańsk sentences had been passed only two weeks before the price increases took effect and their inordinate severity may well have been intended primarily as a warning to others not to undertake any strike or protest actions. Once the danger was past, the grounds for such severity ceased to exist. The three activists were all ultimately released on the strength of the Special Procedure Act of July 1986.

In fact, the authorities cheated Lech Wałęsa and the TKK into withdrawing their call for the threatened nationwide 15-minute strike on 28 February 1985 by pretending to back down on the price increases and then implementing them in a slightly different form: in three stages and at short notice. The TKK later called for a nationwide strike on the first working day after the new meat prices went into effect.

Although there was no widespread support for the nationwide strike, a few strikes nevertheless took place. The first to be tried for organizing such a strike was Henryk Grządzielski, a Solidarity activist employed at the agricultural equipment plant in Słupsk. Grządzielski was tried on the day after the strike had taken place and sentenced to one year's imprisonment on the same day, under Art. 282a.2 of the Penal Code, under accelerated procedure and according to the new Law on Special Criminal Liability of 10 May 1985 which had just taken effect on 1 July 1985. The court was unmoved by the plea of Grządzielski's defence lawyer, Anna Skowrońska, who said 'it would be unjust to pass a prison sentence on a man who wanted to prevent a deterioration in living standards for others'.

* * *

Both the trial of Frasyniuk, Lis and Michnik and that of Grządzielski clearly show that, for the purpose of adjudication, the distinction between a strike and a protest action has been obliterated, enabling the authorities to circumvent the Trade Union Act by calling a strike by another name and having it tried as a criminal offence, on a par with offences against public order. The use of Art. 282a.1 of the Penal Code in this way permits the courts to sentence dissenters, regardless of whether they actually took part in a strike or simply discussed such a possibility. Since the enactment of the Law on Special Criminal Liability of 10 May 1985, moreover, cases brought under Art. 282a can be tried under accelerated procedure. In this way, those who have been detained in connection with strike-related activities may be deprived of their right to a proper defence and a full trial and may be sentenced within hours and with immediate effect to long prison terms. The two severe precedents discussed above effectively prove that the right to strike or the right to protest in the PPR is written on paper only and that no attempts to make use of it will be tolerated by the authorities.

6. The right to work

State monopoly on employment

In the PPR the state owns the economy and the ruling elite collectively own the state. The virtual monopoly on employment is one of the means through which political control is exercised. This is reflected in the law. The PPR Constitution grants its citizens the right to paid employment, according to the amount and quality of their work (Art. 68). The PPR Labour Code of 1974 stipulates that the appropriate state authorities are obliged to assist citizens in finding work in accordance with their qualifications (Art. 10.3). Neither of these Acts, however, grants Polish citizens the right freely to choose their employer. They lack, moreover, any provisions that would prescribe discrimination of an employee on account of his or her political views.

The management of a state enterprise is responsible not only for production but also for political tasks. After the imposition of martial law it was the management staff who were charged with breaking the workforce into the contingencies of the new situation, and re-unionizing them. They were helped in this by members of the party committees and youth organizations, as well as secret police officers whose presence became more conspicuous than before.

The state's monopoly on employment serves to enforce conformity and obedience among the workforce. Repressive dismissals or the threat of them have not been applied solely against those who hold dissenting political views but also against anyone who tries to fight management inefficiency or corruption, against whom the director has a grudge or whom he may wish to blackmail into co-operation. The Polish Helsinki Committee has pointed out, in its Madrid Report, that 'the position of an employee versus the employer is such that practically any disagreement with the management carries a threat of dismissal, even if there is no political aspect to the conflict'.[98]

The vagueness of some of the Labour Code's provisions makes it easier for the management to practise repressive dismissal from work. Art. 52.1(1) of the Labour Code enables the management to terminate an employment contract without notice 'in the case of a serious breach of basic duties' on the part of the employee. This provision has been used as an anti-strike clause. Under Art. 53.1(2) of the Labour Code, the management may terminate an employee's contract without notice in case of a justified absence of more than one month for reasons other than illness. All those who were interned or imprisoned during martial law (this qualifies as a 'justified absence') risked losing their jobs under this provision and many did, indeed, find themselves out of a job. Finally, Art. 66.1 of the Labour Code provides for the automatic expiry, after three months' absence, of the contract of any employee who has been arrested and is awaiting trial. Although Art. 66.2 stipulates that the management is obliged to re-employ any employee who was either acquitted or against whom proceedings were discontinued, and who returned to his previous employer within seven days of the court's sentence becoming final, in practice, they are, in the vast majority of cases, refused re-employment. Art. 66.2 does not, moreover, cover those former prisoners who were released under amnesty or against

The Basic Freedoms and the Courtroom

whom the proceedings were conditionally discontinued.

Martial law verifications

In the course of the martial law period the provisions of the Labour Code were substantially altered by the Martial Law Decree, the militarization of key enterprises, the introduction of some forms of compulsory labour, the suspension of trade unions and special Supreme Court rulings.

During the early months of martial law the authorities considered strikes as the single most dangerous threat to normalization and were determined to deal with them swiftly and firmly. On the basis of a circular letter, dated 10 March 1982 and signed by the deputy prime minister responsible, the managements of individual enterprises and institutions were presented with the whole range of disciplinary possibilities and urged to make full use of them in order to stifle strikes and protest actions.

Under Art. 14.2 of the Martial Law Decree participation in a strike constituted 'a serious breach of the employee's basic duties' and, as such, could serve as grounds for immediate termination of employment under Art. 52.1 of the Labour Code. Participation in a strike was also penalized as a petty offence.

At the beginning of martial law not only strikers were threatened with dismissal but also those who refused to sign 'loyalty pledges' amounting to renunciation of their trade union membership and acceptance of martial law; those who, because of their prestige among their fellow workers, were potentially a focus for opposition to martial law policies; directors who had been elected to their posts by the workers' self-management; and anybody who had any reservations about the martial law regime and expressed them in public.

In some cases the suspension of Solidarity gave the management the opportunity to settle old scores with activists of this trade union. At the Municipal Transport Enterprise in Sandomierz where during the Solidarity period workers had successfully petitioned the authorities to remove the then director Mieczysław Sojda, and been able with the approval of the voivodship PUWP committee to elect a new director, many of those who had signed the petition were sacked by Sojda when he was reinstated as director after the imposition of martial law.[99]

The practice of forcing employees to sign loyalty pledges or declarations renouncing their membership in Solidarity was a

The Basic Freedoms and the Courtroom

particularly flagrant violation of the freedom of conscience, as well as being contrary to the labour law. Such a pledge had nothing to do with the duties as stipulated in the contract. Any ban on membership in a trade union should, moreover, only come into force when this union was disbanded and not while it was suspended. Finally, any renunciation of trade union membership should properly be addressed to the union authorities and not to the enterprise management.

There were several instances of concealed dismissal from work, as in the case of the Lenin Shipyard in Gdańsk which was closed down for a period. When it reopened new passes were issued to the employees and the old ones became invalid. Those who did not receive new passes simply found themselves out of a job.

Some occupations, in particular state employees, judges, public prosecutors, journalists and teachers, were singled out for a close scrutiny of personnel known as the 'verification procedure'. This usually took the form of an interrogation of individual employees by 'verification commissions' composed of representatives of the security police, the military, the relevant PUWP Committee, and the management. These commissions were illegal bodies whose prerogatives were not specified in any legal provisions.

State employees were verified on the basis of a circular letter dated 17 December 1981 and sent by the Director of the Office of the Council of Ministers, General Michał Janiszewski, to all central and local government offices and state agencies.[100] The letter said that membership in Solidarity was in times of martial law incompatible with one of the formal conditions of employment in the service of the state, i.e. the employee must be considered as 'warranting particular involvement, readiness to sacrifice and unequivocal loyalty in the service of the PPR'. In a letter to General Jaruzelski, Primate Józef Glemp expressed his concern that such directions constituted a denial of human rights as well as being contrary to both the PPR Constitution and the promises made by the General himself in his speech on the declaration of martial law. Cardinal Glemp's protest was disregarded and the verification procedure went ahead. General Janiszewski's directions were also used to weed out dissenting elements in the judiciary, resulting in the dismissal of some 25 to 40 judges.

The journalists' profession was the one that suffered the

greatest losses as a result of verification. According to the Polish Helsinki Committee, 10,000 journalists were subjected to this procedure.[101] Of this number some 1,200 were sacked and another 1,000 repressed in other ways. Widespread purges were carried out at the Radio and Television Committee where some 800 employees were sacked.

The academic profession, however, managed to resist such a large-scale purge and the verification procedure at institutions of higher education proved not altogether successful from the authorities' point of view. Special questionnaires were circulated among the staff and verification commissions were set up to assess the answers. These commissions then submitted recommendations on the termination of employment of certain employees to the rector's commissions but these managed largely to ignore them. Several independent-minded university rectors and departmental deans were, however, forced to resign their posts. Large-scale purges were avoided at the establishments of higher education in Warsaw, Kraków, Lublin and other centres. It was, however, a different situation in the Maritime Academy in Gdynia where the democratically elected rector, Mikołaj Kostecki, lost his post as rector on 15 December 1981 and was among the five members of the academic staff who were sacked in June 1982 by the new rector, Władysław Rymarz. On the whole, the purge of the academic world was not so swift and spectacular but rather protracted and conducted cautiously, if consistently, peaking in late 1985 following amendments to the Law on Higher Education.

A very thorough verification was, on the other hand, carried out in several stages among primary and secondary school teachers. During martial law those teachers who resisted indoctrination of the young people in their charge had to face disciplinary proceedings or were dismissed under the pretext of 'reorganization'. One such case involved Teresa Baranowska, a teacher from Katowice, who was sacked by the Teacher's disciplinary commission attached to the Voivod's Office for having an 'improper civic attitude' and 'anti-state extra-mural activities' (she was a member of KPN).

The Supreme Court played its role in making it easier for the authorities to 'verify' the workforce. In a resolution of 4 May 1982 it stated that Art. 39.1 of the Labour Code ensuring protection of contract for employees occupying elective trade union posts was invalid while martial law was in force. In another ruling of 19 July 1982 the Supreme Court stated that the voivod

The Basic Freedoms and the Courtroom

who was responsible for managing the assets of trade unions within his voivodship was empowered to hand notice of termination of employment to salaried employees of Solidarity's regional boards. The court's reasoning was that since Solidarity was suspended, the union's salaried employees had nothing to do, and paying their wages simply decreased Solidarity's assets.

It is difficult to establish the exact number of Solidarity activists who were sacked during martial law. Repressions in the sphere of employment took many forms: not only dismissal, but also transfer to another department, demotion to a lower-paid job, withdrawal of promotion prospects, forced early retirement, or — in the case of the judiciary — transfer to a court in another locality. A politically orientated dismissal or demotion was often disguised as 'structural reorganization' or 'contingencies of economic reform'. The number of those dismissed during martial law has variously been estimated from several tens of thousands,[102] to some 150,000 to 200,000.[103]

The case of the Institute of Nuclear Research (IBJ)

The Institute of Nuclear Research (IBJ) in Świerk was set up in 1955 and grew to be an internationally respected institution. After the Gdańsk Agreement of August 1980, a dynamic and sizeable Solidarity organization emerged there, publishing a fortnightly information bulletin and establishing co-operation with Solidarity commissions in other scientific institutes throughout the country. Democratic elections were carried out to the Scientific Council, a self-governing body with wide powers to award scientific degrees and titles. When the authorities at the IBJ decided to employ as of 1981 secret police officers as 'director's plenipotentiaries for security' the IBJ Solidarity organization demanded their removal from the Institute. The adverse publicity forced the secret police to withdraw from the Institute, though not for long. They returned after the imposition of martial law and proceeded to question the staff informally but had little success in their attempts to force employees of the Institute to sign loyalty pledges or to secure their co-operation.

Some 11 IBJ employees were on the authorities' internment lists; two, Zenon Nowak and Tadeusz Pacuszka, were tried and sentenced for leading a sit-in strike which took place on 13 December 1981 in one of the IBJ's branches at Żerań near Warsaw. 29 people participated in the strike as a protest against the internment of their colleagues. An active clandestine Solidarity commission was set up soon afterwards. It published its own journal *W okopach* ('In the Trenches') and set up a mutual aid fund providing material assistance to the families of prisoners. Almost each month of martial law was marked by some form of token protest. For instance, some 600 employees would queue for lunch or go for a smoke at the same time, thus creating a crowd, or they would all enter the Institute not through the main gate, but through one of the side entrances. All these actions occurred on specific dates which were days of protest throughout the country.

Following a token protest on 10 November 1982, the management handed notices of termination of employment to 32 employees of the Institute. The management did not, however, quote as grounds for termination the fact of participation in a protest action (i.e. entering the grounds of the Institute en masse through a side entrance), but reorganization of the IBJ. 16 of those dismissed were subsequently reinstated by the local appeals commissions (TKO), the management itself changed its decision about eight of the employees whose specialist training made them irreplacable and the remaining eight withdrew their claims. The first phase of sackings thus largely proved a failure.

A more drastic solution was implemented one month later. The Institute was formally split into three smaller institutes and the employees were told that they would not automatically be reassigned their posts at the new units. Indeed, some 40 employees found that there was no room for them within the new organizational structure.

The authorities did not hesitate to pay the huge costs of the whole operation which involved a growth in administration and rocketing of maintenance costs, as well as the general disorientation and uncertainty normally associated with any operation of such scale. Those who carried it out well knew that dismembering a well-established Institute served no scientific purpose at all, and that 'reorganization' had been carried out primarily as a repressive action against the personnel. The case illustrates the lengths to which the authorities were prepared to go in order to ensure the destruction of an independent-minded professional milieu and replace it with a collection of political conformists.

The Basic Freedoms and the Courtroom

Amnestied prisoners denied work

Solidarity activists released from internment or under one of the two amnesty acts of July 1983 and July 1984 or under the Special Procedure Act of July 1986 could not automatically claim' re-instatement in their former jobs. An employer is not bound, under Art. 66.3 of the Labour Code, to re-instate an employee whose contract of employment expired on account of his arrest and who was later amnestied. A number of secret circulars and guidelines ensured that this remained so. Former prisoners filed their claims for re-employment with the local appeals commissions or the labour courts and, in some cases, obtained a favourable verdict. This was not, however, necessarily honoured by the employer. To quote an example, the management of the Ursus Tractor Factory near Warsaw refused to reinstate three employees, Witold Kaszuba, Arkadiusz Czerwiński and Roman Bielański, in spite of the local appeals commission's ruling in their favour. The management appealed successively to the labour court and the Ministry of Machine Industries and Foundries. Both instances upheld the claims of the three workers. The management refused to be beaten and gave each of the workers notice of termination, together with three months' compensatory pay even before they had started work. The three workers again appealed to the local appeals commission, which upheld its earlier verdict that the three must be reinstated. The Ursus management then appealed to the labour court, which this time rescinded the reinstatement order.

In another case involving Andrzej Słowik, the Chairman of Solidarity's Łódź Regional Board, a bus driver by profession, who was amnestied in July 1984, it was the department of employment which refused to assign him to his former job with the Municipal Transport Enterprise (MPK). Słowik brought a successful lawsuit before the Supreme Administrative Court which ordered his reinstatement on the strength of the mandatory job placement priorities. Under these provisions (see Chapter I/5), the management of a state enterprise could not refuse to employ a person who was out of work and who had been referred to them by the department of employment. The Łódź city authorities, however, in the meantime, made use of their prerogative to change these provisions and exempted bus drivers from them. Słowik was rejected by the personnel department of the Łódź MPK. He brought another case before the labour court and this time he lost.

The Basic Freedoms and the Courtroom

Some former internees and amnestied political prisoners were only able to resume work with their former employer at the cost of being hired at lower level positions than previously. Others had to put up with increased surveillance at their place of employment. Others still were dismissed at the first opportunity. At the same time as the vetting of prospective employees generally became more pronounced, it became increasingly difficult for dismissed union activists to find any kind of job.

Those former prisoners who were not reinstated were bound by the law to register with departments of employment as job-seekers. Those who failed to register or refused to take up jobs to which they had been assigned were deprived not only of unemployment benefit but also of the ration cards entitling them to purchase basic foodstuffs, which were in short supply, and they risked being registered as persistent work dodgers (see Chapter I/5). These and other pressures forced ex-prisoners to take any job available, or to seek employment in the private sector, which was not easy either since private entrepreneurs could lose their concessions or be made to pay exorbitant taxes if the authorities wished to put pressure on them. Some chose emigration.

Former political prisoners were also discriminated against in various government guidelines. One such document, from the Ministry of Labour, Wages and Social Affairs and dated 30 July 1984, prohibited state enterprises from employing 'amnestied' prisoners, in particular those who had been sentenced for offences against 'the basic political and economic interests of the PPR'.[104] Similar instructions concerning the employment of former political prisoners were issued by party cells at various levels. In Warsaw, according to a confidential letter from the Warsaw City PUWP Committee, a former political prisoner could only be reinstated at his former job with the consent of the Warsaw City Mayor, after a request to this effect had been submitted by his enterprise director and approved by the local department of employment.[105]

Post-martial law restrictions

After the formal suspension of martial law the limitations on trade union freedoms and workers' rights were not eased. On the contrary, they were increased still further. Repressive dismissals gained in importance as an official means of ensuring peace on the streets, at the universities, in schools. The threat of dismissal was retained as a penalty for staging strikes or protest actions at one's place of work. Under Art. 5 of the Act of 18 December 1982, participation in a strike, a protest action or a gathering, as well as 'disturbing the peace and order at one's place of work' were all classified as 'a serious breach of the employee's basic duties'. In such circumstances, the management was empowered to terminate employment, without notice, under Art. 52.1 of the Labour Code. Any employee who had been dismissed in this way and who none the less managed to find himself a new employer could receive no more than the lowest pay for one year from the date of commencement. The most significant novelty of these provisions was that an employee could now be in 'breach of his basic duties as an employee' even outside his place of work and in a way that had nothing to do with these duties (for instance, by taking part in a street demonstration). The Act of 18 December 1982 also stipulated penalties for simple participation in a strike or protest action. In this respect it went even further than the Trade Union Act of 8 October 1982 under which only the organizers and the leaders of a strike or a protest action could be held criminally accountable.

State control over the workforce was maintained and reinforced still further after the lifting of martial law. The Act of 21 July 1983 made it difficult, if not impossible, for those who were employed in enterprises 'of special importance to the national economy' to terminate their contract. The list of enterprises 'of special importance' included those enterprises that had previously been militarized and extended the restrictions to other enterprises which had not been militarized during martial law. The management of such an enterprise was free to terminate the contract of any employee but the employee might be requested to give extended notice which could be as long as nine months, whereas previously it had been no longer than three months. Any employee deciding to leave before his extended notice was up was treated as though he had abandoned the job. This meant the loss of his right to various benefits and entitlements as well as putting him on the lowest pay scale in any new job. The Act of 21 July 1983 also introduced mandatory job placement and extended working hours.

The authorities were equipped with new repressive measures to discipline teachers without preliminary disciplinary proceedings. Art. 14 of the Act empowered the voivod to suspend a teacher in his duties, transfer him to another post or dismiss him if he 'undertook activity in flagrant breach of the law or the basic didactic and educational tasks of the school'. This provision was widely used in the aftermath of martial law to dismiss teachers for their extra-mural activities. Decisions issued by the voivod under Art. 14 of the Act of 21 July 1983 were not subject to appeal to the Supreme Administrative Court. The Act of 21 July 1983 expired on 31 December 1985 but many of its provisions were surreptitiously transferred to other laws and minister's orders before that date.

The authorities' experience during martial law and in its aftermath with regard to trade union issues and disciplining the workforce will doubtless be reflected in the forthcoming amendments to the Labour Code. The pre-martial law regulations empowered trade union bodies to voice their opinions with regard to the grounds for termination of employment by management as well as the procedure followed. Under the proposed regulations this would no longer be the case.[106] At a meeting of the Council of Ministers on 19 July 1985, the existing labour provisions were discussed and found wanting in that they were 'excessively elaborate with regard to the workers' rights and essentially incomplete with regard to discipline in the working process and the workers' duties'. In this way the Council of Ministers may have pointed the direction which future legislation on labour matters would be expected to take. It must be remembered that the pre-martial law labour legislation was obviated during martial law with various regulations and secret guidelines. Since the existing legislation is lagging behind reality, it must therefore be amended to catch up with the de facto state of affairs.

The Local Appeals Commissions and the Labour Courts

At the time of the introduction of martial law labour disputes were adjudicated by enterprise arbitration commissions (attached to some of the bigger enterprises), local appeals commissions (TKO, attached to local administrative authorities) and the labour courts which heard appeals against the verdicts of the TKOs. The role of the enterprise arbitration commissions in the period of martial law was a negligible one, with some of them being suspended by management, along with the trade unions and workers' self-management bodies. The role of the TKOs, on the other hand, greatly increased. This was due to the sheer increase in the number of cases brought before them. The growth in the number of cases (over 100,000 cases in 1982 compared with an average of 70,000 annually in previous years) was most pronounced in the heavily industralized voivodships of Warsaw, Katowice and Wrocław. One of the TKOs in Poznań noted a threefold increase in the number of cases, 80 per cent of which concerned employees' claims for reinstatement.[107] Some of the dismissals resulted from purely economic considerations arising out of the economic reform, such as the closure of certain slots, reorganization, dissolution of the 'unions of enterprises', etc. A great majority of dismissals resulted, however, from the repressive use of employment in order to discipline the workforce. Out of a total of 1,070 claims for reinstatement heard by the Labour Court in Warsaw in 1982 only 131 or 12.2 per cent concerned dismissals on economic grounds.[108] It can be assumed that the remainder involved political or personal grounds and that repressive dismissal on account of trade union activity was a widespread practice. Activists of Solidarity enterprise committees were its primary victims. Indeed, some employers understood the Supreme Court ruling of 4 May 1982 (see above) as meaning that the members of the enterprise Solidarity committees 'were not protected by any law whatsoever'.[109]

16.5 per cent of the cases heard by the TKOs and 25 per cent of those heard by labour courts were decided in favour of the employee.[110] Since the TKOs hear tens of thousands of cases annually, this proportion was seen as favouring the employees and the authorities stepped up the pressure to correct it.

On 28 July 1982 the Chief of the Office of the Council of Ministers, in a letter addressed to ministers and voivods, urged that they request the directors of state enterprises to lodge appeals against verdicts upholding employees' claims for reinstatement or, should the verdict be a final one, present requests for extraordinary reviews.

Judges hearing labour-related issues were given guidelines from the Supreme Court and risked disciplinary proceedings for ordering the reinstatement of employees who had led or participated in strikes or protest actions or who had been dismissed from service in a militarized enterprise. An outspoken judge of a Warsaw regional court, Mikołaj Kwiatkowski was brought up before a disciplinary court and found guilty in the first instance of having 'used inappropriate expressions which might be interpreted as incompatible with the dignity of the judge's office' in his verdict of 14 April 1982 in the case of Robert Palmowski, a member of the Solidarity factory committee in the Ponar-Plasomat factory in Warsaw. The expressions in question were: 'being unable to hand the employee notice of termination of his work contract in accordance with the obtaining labour provisions (i.e. protection of contract afforded under Art. 39.1 of the Labour Code which, contrary to the erroneous information spread by the Ministry of Labour, Wages and Social Affairs, remains in force), the employer (most probably submitting to pressure from political and police officials) accepted the notice of termination that the employee had been forced to give'. Judge Kwiatkowski concluded that 'the real reason for the employer's desire to get rid of such a valuable employee was that he was a member of the Solidarity factory committee'. On 5 November 1982 Judge Kwiatkowski was formally reprimanded by a disciplinary court. It was only over a year later, on 2 December 1983, that he was acquitted by a higher disciplinary court which was unable to find any specific provisions that Kwiatkowski's words might have violated.

Such pressure might well have had some bearing on the adjudication of cases but it is impossible to gauge its extent. Clearly, the authorities expected that still more cases would be decided against the workers. In some instances they were determined to ignore the verdicts that were not to their liking, as in the cases of the three Ursus employees or Andrzej Słowik described above.

The Ministry of Justice undertakes periodical reviews of the work of different courts. After one such review of the labour cases dealt with by the Warsaw District Labour and Social Insurance Court, the Deputy Director of the Courts Supervision Department, Władysław Tomyn, stated in a report of 2 December 1983 that judges had all too often let themselves be influenced by the emotional state of the workers and the public, as well as by the first instance verdicts handed down by the TKOs, 'verdicts for which no one in the country takes political responsibility'.[111]

After 1 July 1985 the TKOs, which evidently proved too independent, were wound up and all labour disputes were taken over by the 221 labour courts which were simultaneously integrated into the regional courts, and the 20 labour and social insurance courts which were integrated into the voivodship courts. Admittedly, the enterprise arbitration commissions were allowed to continue but their scope is fairly limited. Important issues, moreover, such as the establishment of new conditions of work and pay, application of productivity norms and disputes pertaining to the use of accommodation provided by the employer are not subject to the jurisdiction of labour courts. The law of 18 April 1985 made it incumbent upon the chairmen of the voivodship courts to call, at least once a year, a meeting of judges specializing in labour disputes and social insurance, with representatives of state enterprises and trade union organizations in attendance. At these meetings periodical analyses of the observance of labour discipline are to be presented, although it is not clear who is to prepare them. The judges will, doubtless, be served ready-made conclusions to be applied in their work. In this way, the indoctrination of judges adjudicating labour disputes has been written into the law.

* * *

The future of labour law in the PPR looks bleak. The general trend towards restricting employees' rights which originated during martial law will most likely peak with the amendments to the Labour Code which are currently in preparation. With Solidarity no longer able officially to fight for employees' rights and economic reform, the authorities, faced with a deepening crisis and resultant drop in the general standard of living, were emboldened to reach for administrative means of control over the workforce. Labour issues belong to those spheres of public life which have been most intensely modified by the authorities. The changes introduced from above are far reaching and include the extension of working hours, restriction of fluctuations in the workforce by making it more difficult for workers to leave their employer, mandatory job placement, curtailment of over-time work, and the elimination of free Saturdays. Increased control over the workforce is accompanied by decreased security of employment and still greater dependence of the workers on the monopolistic state employer. This was made clear in a report, compiled by experts commissioned by the TKK and sent in mid-May 1986 to the ILO Director General, Francis Blanchard, which draws attention to the increased prerogatives of management over employees; the restriction of employees' wage increases; the imposition of various fiscal penalties on employees; the extension of working hours; the subjection of managers and enterprise self-management bodies to stricter controls; and the concentration of decisions concerning wages in the hands of the central state bureaucracy.

The Basic Freedoms and the Courtroom

The more the authorities fear possible workers' unrest the more they legislate. The barrage of laws, ordinances and regulations in the form of administrative circulars resembles the bonds with which the Lilliputs attempted to incapacitate Gulliver. The right to work in the PPR in the post–martial law period became the primary means of enforcing conformity with the system: it was not only denied to those the regime deemed 'incorrigible non-conformists' but also served as a means of forestalling possible unrest.

7. Freedom of conscience and religion

The Church under martial law

Shortly before General Wojciech Jaruzelski was to appear on television to inform the nation about the imposition of martial law, personal envoys of the General were reportedly sent to the Primate's residence to inform the head of the Polish Catholic Church about the military coup. On 13 December 1981 Primate Józef Glemp delivered two sermons: in Częstochowa and in Warsaw. In both these sermons the Primate reaffirmed the Church's concern for human life, social peace, prevention of unnecessary bloodshed and the well-being of the nation. The Main Council of the Polish Episcopate condemned the introduction of martial law in its communiqué of 15 December 1981: 'This dramatic decision of the authorities to proclaim martial law is a blow to the hopes and expectations of society at a moment when there were hopes for the settlement of the issues still outstanding through national agreement.' In an appeal of 18 December 1981 addressed to General Wojciech Jaruzelski, Pope John Paul II stated: 'the universal desire for peace demands that martial law in Poland be discontinued'.

Although the imposition of martial law was an unexpected blow for the Polish Church, its hierarchy continued to believe in the possibility of 'national agreement' in the early months of martial law. On 5 April 1982 the Primate's Social Council prepared a document entitled 'Theses Concerning Social Accord'. The following month the same body published their 'Propositions Concerning Social and Economic Issues'. Despite their conciliatory wording both the Theses and the Propositions were ignored by the authorities.

The Basic Freedoms and the Courtroom

Briefly, the main objectives of the Church under martial law were as follows:

1. To prevent bloodshed and unnecessary suffering on the part of the people while keeping up the nation's spirit.
2. To articulate and defend social and national interests in accordance with the Church's teachings and historical experience.
3. To stand by the principles of 'social accord' and 'national dialogue', which involved playing the role of an intermediary between the authorities and the authentic representatives of society.
4. To provide charitable aid and pastoral service to the internees, prisoners and the needy.
5. To enable Pope John Paul II to make his second pastoral visit to Poland.

Three issues in particular dominated Church–state relations in 1982–3: the establishment of a Church–sponsored fund to aid private farmers, legislation to give the Church legal status which it had never enjoyed in Communist Poland and the regime's efforts to establish diplomatic ties with the Vatican. All these issues were inter–connected. The authorities seemed to be linking concessions on the first two points, which were important to the Church, with progress towards establishing diplomatic ties in which they themselves were interested in order to obtain an aura of legitimacy and break the international isolation in which they found themselves immediately after the imposition of martial law. The Church had a different perspective. 'How can you have diplomatic relations if there is no judicial basis on which they can be grounded', said a Church source quoted by a Western agency from Warsaw.[112] The bishops were, moreover, aware of the fact that direct links between the authorities and the Vatican could diminish their own role in Rome. The talks with the Church concerning legal status were suspended and the draft of an agreement reached with the Church negotiators was 'shelved indefinitely' in April 1984. Negotiations on the agricultural aid fund were finally abandoned in September 1986 because of the regime's insistence on maintaining control over the fund.

Following the imposition of martial law the role of the Church increased; it became the only repository of people's hopes that Solidarity, although defeated as an organization, would continue to endure as a spiritual idea uniting all Poles. The Church, in addition to its spiritual dimension, began to play a more obvious social role. It became the only place where people could openly meet, exchange opinions and establish contacts. The social, cultural and artistic activities that took place under the auspices of the Church gave a new dimension to its spiritual mission. The Church afforded a new hope for the people who were dejected and dispirited.

Despite their efforts, the authorities failed to achieve their objective of setting the Church against Solidarity which, although driven underground, still commanded widespread popular support. They knew that appeals for calm would be more readily listened to if they came from the Church. And calm was of essence if their self-proclaimed policy of normalization was to succeed. Despite the regime's efforts to win the Church's support or, failing this, its neutrality, it was not willing to pay too high a price for this and did not intend to alter its policy towards the Church in any fundamental way. Despite some concessions, such as the growth of the Catholic press and additional church building permits, the regime's fundamental animosity to the Church persisted.

These concessions, moreover, soon proved to have been tactical and they began to be curtailed at the end of 1984. By cutting back on the supply of paper the authorities forced several Catholic periodicals to either reduce their number of pages or the frequency of publication. In the case of *Przegląd Katolicki*, published by the Warsaw Curia, for instance, the paper allocation was cut back from 110 tons annually to barely 32. Among the other titles to suffer was *Powściągliwość i Praca* ('Temperance and Work') where many respected Polish journalists denied work in the official media had found employment. The programme of church construction in the country was sharply attacked in the Warsaw weekly *Polityka*.[113] The *Polityka* article was conceived as a response to a series of articles about the Church's pastoral work written at the beginning of 1985 by Bishop Ignacy Tokarczuk. The bishop had argued that changes in the character of contemporary society in the form of more widespread education, a greater diversity of professions, etc. required an expansion of the Church's pastoral activities as well as their adjustment to new circumstances. The reaction to Tokarczuk's articles came seven months later and the outrage expressed by *Polityka* was a sign of the authorities' hardening position on the crucial issue of the construction of new places of worship.

In the official interpretation, the 'constitutional principle' of the separation of Church and state meant that politics were the exclusive realm of the Communist party and that the Church should concern itself with spiritual matters alone, eventually becoming an anachronism. What constitutes 'politics' is constantly defined and redefined by the party, according to its current needs. One of the most serious charges levelled against Solidarity was that it engaged in politics. The charge of 'political clericalism' is perhaps the most serious that can be presented against the Church. In the PPR the separation of Church and state implies that the party is free to pursue its atheistic propaganda whereas the Church is solely to satisfy the internal spiritual needs of individual people. It is assumed that with the passage of time, as 'socialist morality' becomes stronger and more widespread, these needs will decrease. Another tenet of the 'constitutional principle of separation of Church and state' is that the Church must not 'abuse' its rights to the detriment of the state's interests. One of the practical consequences of this principle is that the authorities refuse to recognize in fact, if not in theory — the mission and the role of the Church in public life.

Although Arts. 67 and 81 of the PPR's Constitution forbid discrimination against people on the grounds of their religious beliefs and Art. 82 of the Constitution grants the people freedom of conscience and belief, in practice these legal provisions are subordinate to political considerations. The Communist state displays here its ideological nature, fulfilling the political objective of remodelling the traditional relationships among people. To quote Lenin, socialists are usually non-believers. The Catholics in Poland are discriminated against at places of work, especially with regard to promotion to positions of influence, and in public life. No religious association or parish is a person at law. Therefore, they cannot contest their rights at law, nor can they formally apply for redress.

The authorities emphasize on occasion their willingness to enter into dialogue with the Church for short-term pragmatic objectives but one may wonder why in Poland — a Communist-ruled country with a predominantly Catholic population — no such dialogue has really got off the ground. The reason is that the very concept of dialogue with the Church, as the Communists understand it, 'cannot obliterate the ideological contradictions'[114] between Christianity and Marxism. The Church, on the other hand, cannot acknowledge a doctrine derived from materialistic premises which aims at the atheization of society and, in the long run, aspires to make religion redundant.

Threatened by the Church's unequivocal stand on social issues, the regime issued warnings to those priests it considered politicized. To quote a few examples: Bishop Ignacy Tokarczuk was attacked in the media for his strong condemnation of the use of force against peaceful protests on 31 August 1982. During the 'war of the crosses' in Miętne in March 1984 the government spokesman Jerzy Urban emphasized that schools were state property. In September 1984 Urban told the Church to curb 'political demonstrations' by Solidarity supporters during religious pilgrimages and warned that, while the authorities were not planning to clamp down on pilgrimages, they would do so if necessary. In March 1985 Urban, himself a non-believer, declared in the name of the majority of Polish Catholics that 'they were against political clericalism'.

Art. 194 of the Penal Code

The 'constitutional principle of the separation of Church and state' is backed up by legal restrictions aimed at limiting the Church's freedom of action and expression in public matters. For this purpose the authorities are equipped with Art. 194 of the Penal Code which states that 'whoever, in the course of performing religious duties, abuses freedom of conscience and belief in order to harm the interests of the PPR' can be sentenced to between one and ten years' imprisonment. This article protects the ruling party establishment from critical remarks from the pulpit. It effectively restricts the freedom of expression of priests who may not speak openly about the public affairs which concern their parishioners. To quote the late Father Jerzy Popiełuszko, 'freedom of conscience can only be restricted, never abused'.

Art. 194 is used by the authorities to repress those priests whom they see as 'turbulent'. In the trial of Fr. Stefan Dzierżek, a 68-year-old Jesuit from Kalisz, the prosecutor alleged that the Nativity tableau which he had built in his church for Christmas was liable to incite public unrest and endanger social peace. The tableau referred symbolically to the events in the Wujek coalmine in December 1981 where several miners were shot dead in violent clashes with the ZOMO riot police. The Nativity tableau included Christ's weeping mother, the baby Jesus lying beside his crib which had been overturned by a tank and surrounded by barbed wire. Behind the crib, a large coloured picture showed several miners being killed by the ZOMO at the Wujek coalmine.

The prosecutor alleged that the symbolism of the tableau was of a political nature. Such a crib, according to the prosecutor, radically departed from tradition. Witnesses called in the course of the trial testified, however, that Nativity tableaux have often in the past contained contemporary messages. In his explanations before the court Father Stefan Dzierżek said that he had wanted 'to portray the Christ of our time' and that the essence of the trial was the issue of whether Christ was still alive. If he was, as Christianity taught, then it was normal to portray him in a contemporary setting. For seeking Christ's message in the tragedy of martial law in Poland, Fr. Dzierżek was sentenced to one year's imprisonment suspended for three.

In another case involving Reverend Henryk Jankowski, a close friend and adviser to Lech Wałęsa, the Gdańsk prosecutor presented him on 18 October 1983, with charges of inciting public unrest in sermons delivered between 18 February and 31 August 1983, disseminating 'false information' of a political nature and exhibiting emblems and inscriptions relating to the activities of Solidarity (Art. 194, 271 and 273 of the Penal Code). The substantiation for the prosecutor's decision to present charges against Rev. Jankowski proves that his parish Church of St Brygida was under the close observation of those for whom church-going was part of their official duties. The authorities did not go as far as trying Reverend Jankowski and the charges presented against him were covered by the amnesty of July 1984.

In the case of Fr. Jerzy Popiełuszko, the late curate of the Church of St Stanisław Kostka in Warsaw, presentation of the charges under Art. 194 and others on 12 December 1983 was preceded by a police provocation. A search in his flat revealed incriminating materials — 15,000 copies of underground leaflets, publications, tear gas canisters, fuses etc., were 'discovered'. In fact, they had been planted by the secret police in order to discredit him as someone with terrorist connections. One of the secret police officers subsequently sentenced for murdering Fr. Popiełuszko, Lt. Leszek Pękala, took part in the search. The government spokesman Jerzy Urban insinuated that Fr. Popiełuszko had concealed the fact that he owned a private flat from the Church hierarchy. The popular paper *Express Wieczorny* repeated this insinuation and added that Fr. Popiełuszko's flat was a bachelor's *pied à terre*, possibly used for romance.[115] Some of Fr. Popiełuszko's visitors and friends were harassed, coerced and blackmailed in an attempt to induce them to give evidence against him.[116]

These incidents were a continuation of a campaign of harassment against Father Popiełuszko that had started much earlier. As early as December 1982 someone had thrown a brick with an explosive substance through the window of the presbytery. The presbytery itself had been broken into twice but nothing had been taken. His car too had been vandalized. In August 1983 he was prevented from travelling to Gdańsk and detained for 8 hours. He was interrogated 14 times. In some cases summonses were delivered to him by as many as 10 plainclothes police officers, and he was told to appear for questioning the very same day that summonses were delivered. Normally, summonses are sent by post and some notice is given.

Fr. Popiełuszko refused to be silenced. The pulpit was for him a place from which people could hear the uncensored word. He condemned Communism on moral grounds. His vocation was not only religious but also patriotic, it was his moral duty to speak the truth. He described his task quoting the well-known verse from the Gospel in which Christ counselled his disciples to obey both temporal and spiritual authorities — 'Give unto Caesar what is Caesar's and unto God what is God's.' To this verse he added: 'No one can be silent when Caesar reaches out to take away the things that belong to God, that is, the hearts and minds of the people'. Fr. Popiełuszko did not think that his sermons were political. 'But, in fact, every matter that is raised in a church can be considered political, because it concerns men's hearts and minds.'[117]

And indeed men's hearts and minds sought refuge from the oppressive world of police violence and propaganda. The Church was the last such refuge still tolerated by the authorities. Popiełuszko symbolized the Church as people wanted to find it. His sermons represented hope, united people around a common goal, reaffirmed the values shared by all. The message of his sermons was that, although Solidarity had been disbanded as an organization, its ideals had survived: 'Solidarity remains a glorious word to which millions of Poles attach their hopes and desires', he said in his sermon of 27 May 1984, condemning the elections scheduled for 17 June 1984 as 'a mechanism of evil'.

On 12 July 1984 the Deputy Prosecutor Anna Jackowska,

the most promising protégée of the notorious prosecutor Wiesława Bardonowa (both participated in the legal cover-up of the manslaughter of Grzegorz Przemyk), filed an act of indictment with the voivodship court in Warsaw. The trial did not, however, take place and Father Popiełuszko was covered by the conditional amnesty of July 1984. It was not announced that he would be covered by it until 25 August 1984. Two days later Fr. Popiełuszko was once again urging the authorities to negotiate with the leaders of the outlawed union and saying 'Solidarity, born in August 1980, was not only a union ... it was the striving of the whole nation for truth, justice and freedom'. In September 1984, at a meeting in the Ministry of Internal Affairs called by Colonel Adam Pietruszka of the Fourth Department monitoring church affairs, the decision to murder him was taken. On 19 October 1984 Fr. Popiełuszko was abducted and subsequently murdered by three secret police officers from this department.

Priests sentenced on the basis of other Articles of the Penal Code

On 6 November 1982 the Voivodship Court in Gdańsk sentenced under summary procedure Fathers Tadeusz Kurach and Jan Borkowski of the Parish of the Sacred Heart of Jesus in Gdynia to three years' imprisonment. The organist from the same parish, Henryk Kardaś, was sentenced to three and a half years' imprisonment. All three had been arrested on 31 August 1982 outside the church by members of the ZOMO riot police, when the demonstrations staged in the area on the occasion of the second anniversary of the Gdańsk Agreement had already ended. They were subsequently charged under Art. 275.1 of the Penal Code with 'participating in an assault on officials of the forces of law and order, in particular leading a group of 300 demonstrators, erecting barricades of refuse bins, throwing stones at the ZOMO riot police, and shouting insults at them.'

The points of the indictment, which were based on the testimony of the ZOMO riot police, were challenged by a medical expert witness who proved that Fr. Kurach had lost the full use of his arm as a result of a major accident and was thus unable to throw stones. This was supported by X-rays. The court none the less upheld the 'evidence' supplied by the prosecution. The testimonies given by the ZOMOs during the investigation and in the course of the trial differed even with regard to certain basic facts, such as where the defendants were seen, what they were doing, where they were stopped or whether other people were present. The court refused defence motions to call a toxicologist and psychologist as expert witnesses to give evidence on whether the ZOMOs were capable of accurate observation of the course of the demonstration when the air was thick with tear-gas and they were, as they claimed, under constant threat from the demonstrators.

In its oral substantiation of the sentence passed, the court acquitted the defendants of the three charges: physical assault on policemen in the course of street riots, throwing stones and using insulting words, but found, none the less, that they were 'intermittently present' among those who had caused the street disturbance and that they had, therefore, participated in the riots. The court declared that being in a crowd was tantamount to approval of its actions and did not give credence to the defence witnesses who unanimously testified that there was no crowd on the street at about 6.40 p.m. when the priests were there, but chose to believe exclusively the testimonies of the ZOMOs.[118]

A special episcopal commission set up by Bishop Marian Przykucki of Chełmno at the Bishopric Court in Pelplin found, on the basis of independently collected material, that 'the priests and the organist were arrested without foundation, on the basis of maliciously and mendaciously stage-managed accusations, by members of the ZOMO riot police. The acts which were imputed to them certainly did not take place.' The two priests and the organist were released in April 1983 on the basis of the individual pardons procedure.

Another priest, Fr. Sylwester Zych from Grodzisk Mazowiecki near Warsaw, was sentenced in September 1982 to four years' imprisonment (increased by the Supreme Court to six) for 'active participation in an armed group and illegal possession of arms'. Father Zych had concealed a pistol stolen from a policeman by a group of adolescents. As described by his defence councel Władysław Siła-Nowicki, Fr. Zych was politically inexperienced and naive. He had wanted to help these adolescents but did not really know how. He had tried first of all to tame the violent actions of the adolescents who, following the imposition of martial law, had wanted to arm themselves to free the internees held in Białołęka prison. Such a project could, of course, never have been realised but it had resulted in the tragic death of police sergeant Zdzisław Karos whose pistol they had been trying to steal and who was accidentally shot dead in February 1982 during the scuffle in a Warsaw tram. Fr. Zych was released in mid-October 1986.

In June 1982 the Court of the Warsaw Military District in Rzeszów passed a suspended sentence of imprisonment against Father Władysław Drewniak, a curate from Jarosław, who was charged with storing and distributing anti-state leaflets and leading a group of seven youths from a local secondary school who were involved in this activity.[119]

On 4 March 1982 the Court of the Pomeranian Military District in Koszalin passed a sentence of three and a half years' imprisonment on Father Bolesław Eugeniusz Jewulski of the parish of St Joseph in Połczyn Zdrój. He was accused of publicly slandering and deriding the political system and the supreme authorities of the PPR, disseminating 'false information' about the political situation in the country and calling for resistance in his sermon of 20 December 1981. In that sermon he had said that there was increasing resistance against martial law in the country and that the workers would never give in.[120] In the prosecutor's view, expressing such an opinion was tantamount to inciting resistance.

Various forms of intimidation and harassment

Administrative chicanery

For the authorities the most convenient way of silencing outspoken priests is to induce the Church hierarchy to discipline them. This is one of the major tasks of the regional Departments of Religious Affairs, attached to the voivods's offices, which are usually headed by a security police official. These departments are subordinated to the Office for Religious Affairs and Denominations which is directly subordinate to the Chairman of the Council of Ministers. They co-operate with the police and informers. They gather information on priests, approve or oppose appointments made by the Church hierarchy on the parish level and try to persuade the local bishop to curtail the activities of recalcitrant priests.

One of many examples of their activity is the case of Father Leon Kantorski, parish priest at the church of St Christopher in Podkowa Leśna near Warsaw. In late November 1982, the Department of Religious Affairs of the Warsaw metropolitan area demanded, in a formal letter, that the Chancery of the Archdiocese of Warsaw remove Fr. Kantorski from his parish because of the outspoken character of his sermons and his support for the democratic opposition before August 1980.[121]

Father Jerzy Popiełuszko, whose case has been discussed above, was also the subject of such official representations. A letter dated 30 August 1982 and sent to the Warsaw Metropolitan Curia by the head of the Office of Religious Affairs Adam Łopatka alleged that he had 'inspired demonstrative behaviour on the part of the faithful ... not only with his sermons but also the background decor [of the church]'.

The Catholic Church hierarchy as a rule resisted such pressures, seeing them as inadmissible attempts to interfere in what was traditionally an internal administrative and pastoral province. In the case of Fr. Popiełuszko, although one of his murderers subsequently claimed his efforts had been successful and that Fr. Popiełuszko was soon to have been dispatched to Rome, there is no evidence to support such a claim.

Another outspoken priest, Reverend Henryk Jankowski, was harassed by customs officials who, at the instigation of the prosecutor's office, ordered him to pay duty on a Volkswagen van which had been sent to him as a gift from abroad to help him in his charitable work. At first the van was exempted from duty. A few months later, after the van had been damaged beyond repair in a road accident, the prosecutor's office found that it had been wrongly classified by the customs. Rev. Jankowski was then requested to pay duty on an item that no longer existed in breach of an earlier final decision. He appealed to the Supreme Administrative Court and won his case.

Another frequently applied form of administrative chicanery is threatening to deny or revoke a building permit for a new church, a chapel, a cross to be erected on church grounds, etc. Disregard for administrative rules, however unjustified they might be, exposes a priest to prosecution.

Defamation and Misinformation
The most important weapon in the sphere of defamation is the official, censored press which initiates propaganda campaigns at the behest of the authorities. Towards the end of 1983 it began to lambast certain priests with charges of 'political clericalism'. The attacks focused, in particular, on three priests: Bishop Ignacy Tokarczuk, Rev. Henryk Jankowski and Father Jerzy Popiełuszko. The government spokesman Jerzy Urban was notorious for his attacks on priests. His most shameful attack on

Fr. Jerzy Popiełuszko, describing him as 'the Savanarola of anti-communism', appeared in *Tu i Teraz* only four weeks before the priest was abducted and murdered.[122] Needless to say, rumours, insinuations, lies and even calumnies were written with official approval and the priests attacked were not given the right to refute charges.

What cannot be written in the official media can be printed in faked underground publications. One such pamphlet, entitled 'Samoobrona Wiary' (Self-defence of the Faith) and seen in the Małopolska region, attacked the late Fr. Franciszek Blachnicki and his 'Światło-Życie' Catholic youth movement in a scurrilous fashion.[123]

Attacks against the Church and its hierarchy also appeared in internal circulation party bulletins. One such bulletin issued by the Szczecin Voivodship PUWP Committee during Pope John Paul II's pilgrimage to Poland, criticized the 'programme of total Catholicization' of Poland which the Pope was alleged to have in mind. The bulletin focused its attacks on the allegedly political content of some of the speeches and homilies delivered by the Pope during his 1983 pilgrimage.

Another party cell, the PUWP's ideological commission in the city of Tczew, compiled a list of the local 'Oases' religious communities, a part of the 'Światło-Życie' movement, and sent it to school directors 'to be used in political and educational work with youth' with a view to prejudicing young people against the movement.[124]

In order to discredit the priests in the eyes of their local communities, rumours, graffiti, fly-sheets and even publications portraying the priests in an unfavourable light were circulated. In Warmia these reached such an intensity that Bishop Jan Obłąk described them as giving the impression of 'a planned campaign aimed at evoking hostile attitudes towards the clergy'.

In the parish of Zbrosza Duża, a centre of independent peasant activity, there appeared fly-sheets and posters insinuating that the local priest, Father Czesław Sadłowski stole charitable gifts and organized drinking bouts.[125]

Searches, Burglaries and Arsons
Searches were carried out to find 'incriminating materials' which could be used later as possible evidence against priests should the authorities decide to press charges. They usually took place in the early hours of the morning. On 1 March 1984 a thorough search

was carried out at the home of Father Stanisław Małkowski. As many as 56 Solidarity publications, various notes, post-cards, note-books, etc. were seized. During the search the house was surrounded. After the search had been completed Father Małkowski was taken to Warsaw Police HQ and held for two hours.[126] On 30 October 1983 Father Małkowski's flat was broken into. The burglars entered it through the basement and took away a file containing texts of homilies delivered by Father Małkowski between 1973 and 1979.[127] Similar methods used in the campaign of harassment against Fr. Jerzy Popiełuszko have already been described above.

In November 1982 several searches were carried out in the centres of the 'Światło-Życie' religious movement as well as in the homes of its supporters and sympathisers.[128]

In January 1983 two unidentified men tried to set fire to the parish house of Father Czesław Sadłowski from Zbrosza Duża, who was known for his sympathy for the democratic opposition movement even before August 1980.

Detentions
A number of priests were detained in connection with their sermons. A Dominican priest from Kraków, Father Kłosowski, was held by police because of his outspoken sermons and support for Solidarity, which was at that time still suspended.[129]

After the murder of Father Jerzy Popiełuszko two priests from the Sulejów parish near Piotrków Trybunalski, Fathers Jan Umiński and Roman Uchnicki, were detained and questioned after returning from the funeral mass for the murdered priest at the church of St Stanisław Kostka in Warsaw. Father Jan Umiński was questioned during the 10-hour-long interrogation about his alleged intent to distribute illegal publications. At the end of his interrogation he suffered a heart attack and was treated for six days at the municipal hospital in Piotrków Trybunalski.[130]

Secret police actions
The secret police monitored the activities and sermons of selected priests. Father Jerzy Popiełuszko's homilies were recorded on tape by plainclothes policemen. Information was gathered about his daily activities, background, material possessions, etc. Incriminating material was planted in a flat bequeathed to him which he seldom used. The inside of his church was photographed. He was harassed with frequent summonses for questioning. He

was not the only priest to be treated in this fashion.

A secret police operation codenamed 'Kruk' (Raven) mounted at the end of 1982 reportedly aimed at intimidating some of those on a list of 'extremist priests'. This task was entrusted to individual police stations. It was planned to arrest some of them, under various pretexts, in order to test the reaction of the Church hierarchy. If this proved to be weak or indecisive, a wider action might then be envisaged.[131]

Provocations, such as the forced entry of unidentified assailants 'who clearly had some form of military training' into the grounds of St Martin's Convent in Warsaw on 3 May 1983, were another method used by the secret police. Several voluntary workers of a Church charitable aid committee were beaten up and considerable material damage was caused. The Bishops' Conference protested to the authorities about the incident.

The police also tried to hinder non-pastoral activities organized by the Church. On a number of occasions, especially in Katowice voivodship at the beginning of 1984, the security police interfered in the work of students' chaplaincies. Persons invited to give lectures under the aegis of these chaplaincies were stopped on their way to Katowice and detained for several hours. Bishop Herbert Bednorz of Katowice listed three such cases in his letter of 24 February 1984 to General Jaruzelski.

Secret police actions included beatings, abductions and assassinations. On 6 April 1985 Father Tadeusz Zaleski from Kraków was attacked by a masked man in the basement of his Kraków home. He was rendered unconscious by a gas spray and subsequently burned with chemicals and cigarette butts. Two experts in forensic medicine from Kraków's Medical Academy, professors Kołodziej and Marek, presented the opinion that Fr. Zaleski had lost consciousness while walking down the stairs and had burned himself and set fire to his clothes with a candle he was carrying. On the basis of this opinion the regional prosecutor's office in Kraków refused to institute a criminal investigation into the assault on Fr. Zaleski, declaring that no offence had taken place. Neither Fr. Zaleski nor his lawyer Andrzej Rozmarynowicz were allowed to participate in any form in the limited proceedings that were undertaken. The six-member independent panel of doctors who examined Fr. Zaleski at the request of Cardinal Franciszek Macharski of Kraków stated that he had been deliberately attacked. Following the abduction and murder of Fr. Jerzy Popiełuszko, Fr. Zaleski lent his support to a newly formed citizens' committee in defence of human rights in Kraków and passed on to them documentation about Tadeusz Frąś, a teacher and a Solidarity activist from Zabierzów Bocheński, whose body had been found on 7 September 1983 in a Kraków suburb. The committee subsequently publicized this particular case of police murder. On the night of 3 December 1985 Fr. Zaleski was attacked yet again by two men and a woman. They claimed to be ambulancemen bringing news about a heart attack that the curate of Zaleski's parish was supposed to have suffered. Fr. Zaleski was gagged, his arms were twisted behind his back and tied with a wire cord. He was tied in such a way that any movement with his arms tightened the knots around his wrists and neck. He was beaten with closed fists and with a truncheon and was left unconscious. His flat was ransacked. As a result of this attack Fr. Zaleski was unable to go to Warsaw where he had arranged to meet a defence lawyer, Jan Olszewski, and a leading member of the Warsaw human rights committee, Jan Józef Lipski, in order to discuss the possibility of initiating proceedings against the prosecutor's office in Kraków for refusing to institute proceedings into the circumstances of the first attack against him on 6 April 1985. He also intended to sue the Polish Press Agency for defamation of character.[132]

Father Tadeusz Jancarz from the Nowa Huta parish church in Mistrzejowice was the victim on 24 February 1985 of an ambush reminiscent of the one staged against Fr. Popiełuszko. On that day Father Jancarz was travelling from Gdańsk to Warsaw to take part in Holy Mass at St Stanisław Kostka's Church in Warsaw, i.e. the parish of Father Popiełuszko. Between the towns of Olsztynek and Ostróda a rock was thrown from an oncoming car, smashing the windscreen of Father Jancarz's car. Fortunately no one was injured. It was only four months earlier on this very same stretch of road between Gdańsk and Warsaw that three secret police officers had made a similar, unsuccessful attempt on the life of Father Popiełuszko. Father Jancarz, who was known for his sermons supporting Solidarity, had for some time before this assault been receiving anonymous written and telephone threats. The experience of Father Zaleski and Jancarz forced some of the Kraków priests to hire full-time bodyguards.

Other actions against the Church
Special groups were organized to disrupt religious services or intimidate people on their way to Holy Mass. The sanctity of

The Basic Freedoms and the Courtroom

Church premises was violated on some occasions, for example on 24 February 1983 in Katowice when Kazimierz Świtoń was detained inside the Church as Mass was in progress. Churchgoers were attacked on their way home after Mass, beaten with truncheons, sprayed with water and pelted with tear-gas canisters. During street demonstrations people were prevented from seeking refuge within Church premises.

There was a much publicised campaign of removing crosses from schools, offices and factories. The Church which defended these symbols of faith was portrayed as a representative of obscurantism and backwardness. Two priests, Fathers Marek Łabuda and Andrzej Wilczyński, were tried and sentenced on 11 June 1985 for joining some 300 schoolchildren who had occupied their school in Włoszczowa for two weeks in December 1984 to protest against the removal of crosses they had put up in their classrooms. The priests were found guilty of resisting the law and refusing to leave the school despite repeated requests from the authorities. Fr. Wilczyński received a 10-month sentence of imprisonment, suspended for three years, and a fine of 60,000 zlotys, while Fr. Łabuda was sentenced to one year's imprisonment. The trial held before a regional court in Jędrzejów on 11 June 1985, was accompanied by official warnings about the perils of 'clericalism'. The sentences were only slightly modified by the voivodship court in Kielce during an appeal hearing on 12 August 1985. The convictions were upheld but the one-year prison sentence against Fr. Łabuda was repealed and he was placed on three years' probation. In addition Fr. Łabuda was fined 100,000 zlotys.

The authorities only grudgingly tolerated artistic events such as visual arts exhibitions, theatre productions, film shows and poetry readings, and the free legal aid offered by the Church. Their growing impatience with these kinds of activities was manifested, for instance, by the arrest of the Gdańsk writer Marian Terlecki in May 1985. Terlecki who had organized a video-film centre for the Pallotine Fathers in Gdańsk in 1984 and was the author of several documentary films produced by the centre, was arrested on his way to film a religious event in Ołtarzewo and charged, under Arts. 200 and 201 of the Penal Code, with having stolen television equipment belonging to Solidarity. Although the Church authorities presented proof of ownership of the equipment seized with Terlecki, the prosecutor kept on extending the temporary arrest order. Terlecki himself was told that the investigation in his case would take up to three years. He was 'amnestied' in September 1986.

Smaller scale chicanery includes vandalising church property, anonymous letters and phone calls, puncturing the tyres of cars belonging to visitors from other localities who have come to hear Mass, etc. A more sinister case involves a clothing factory in Warsaw which received an order from the Ministry of Internal Affairs for 200 cassocks.[133] Secret police agents dressed as priests could infiltrate the population and compromise the clergy. Since secret policemen give themselves away all too easily by their behaviour, however, it would probably not have been too difficult for the people to identify them, even if they had worn cassocks.

Divide et impera

From December 1981 until the party plenum in October 1983, the authorities were careful not to appear as though they were confronting the Church as an institution. After the second papal pilgrimage to Poland, the party made a move to strengthen ideological awareness within its ranks. The signal came from Leonid Zamiatin, the head of the Soviet Communist Party's International Information Department, who in August 1983 complained that following John Paul II's visits to Poland 'militant clerics were increasing their support for members of the Polish opposition'.[134] The head of the Office for Religious Affairs Adam Łopatka followed suit, stating in his interview with the PAP news agency during the CC plenum convened to chart a new ideological offensive, that 'there was a real danger of religious culture, especially the Roman Catholic one, going beyond its proper place in the national culture'.[135]

The task of Łopatka's ministry was to keep close watch over the clergy and to classify them according to their political attitudes. Łopatka estimated that, of the total number of 21,000 priests in Poland, some 2,000 were on the side of the authorities and co-operated with them. The silent majority was not concerned with politics, whereas about 800 were strongly anti–Communist, and of these about 100 travelled frequently outside their home parishes to preach against the authorities.[136]

In November 1983, Łopatka sent Cardinal Glemp a list of 69 priests whose activities were, in the opinion of the authorities, detrimental to the development of Church–state relations. The regime's intention was clear: either the Primate applied disciplinary measures against the recalcitrants or the authorities would have to do the unpleasant job themselves. Łopatka's letter was supported by documentation compiled by the secret police and consisting, as usual, of transcripts of sermons. Two bishops, Ignacy Tokarczuk of Przemyśl and Zbigniew Kraszewski of Warsaw, were said to be among those 69 priests mentioned.[137]

The regime subsequently denied the existence of such a letter. To admit that the list of 69 priests had been drawn up would have implied that the authorities were aiming at head-on confrontation with the Church. At that time they were thinking about raising food prices and perhaps they suddenly remembered Lenin's advice not to attack the Church directly when they were busy on other fronts.

The struggle was continued, however, on the local level by the voivodship Departments for Religious Affairs. Guidelines issued to these departments by Aleksander Wołowicz, a director in Łopatka's central office in Warsaw, stipulated that:[138]

- the departments should emphasize the contrast between the policy of Pope John Paul II and that of Primate Józef Glemp;
- priests who enjoy official favour should be set against whose whom the authorities dislike;
- the construction of new churches ought to be blocked or delayed, even when permission for a church building had been granted;
- the turnover and circulation of the Catholic press should be decreased and new publications not permitted. Gradually, some titles such as *Znak*, *Więź* and *Powściągliwość i Praca* ought to be eliminated.

Harassment of the clergy alternated with concessions. This dual tactic was part of a long-term strategy of eroding the influence of the Church by atheistic propaganda and ensuring that the clergy remained loyal to the regime. The party-state bureaucracy can create insurmountable obstacles for a priest who seeks planning permission, needs permission to buy building materials from the socialized sector of the economy or is applying for a passport to travel abroad. In such cases favours can cut through the red tape and the priest who accepts such a favour becomes subject to pressure from the authorities and dependent on their good will.

This policy, although seemingly inconsistent, gives the

authorities much scope for manoeuvre. They can, for instance, be accommodating on the local level with regard to the parish priest while adopting a rigid attitude in their dealings with the Episcopate. Or, on the contrary, be accommodating to the bishops and take a tough line with the local priests in order to test the resolve of the Episcopate. The latter reasoning lay behind the 'war of the crosses' when crucifixes were removed from school premises (as in Miętne and Włoszczowa as well as in other less publicized cases). The Episcopate defended these symbols of faith, which only fuelled propaganda attacks against the Church which was accused of engaging in politics. Had the Episcopate remained passive, the regime's aim of splitting the Church hierarchy from the faithful and the local priests would have been well served.

* * *

Freedom of conscience and religion in Poland is restricted on the one hand by preventing the Church as an institution from utilizing its full potential in influencing social life, forbidding the establishment of Catholic associations, hampering charitable work, discouraging cultural activities, ignoring the Episcopate's voice on public matters and rigorously guarding the state's monopoly in education and other fields; and, on the other, by preventing individual priests from addressing the most important current concerns of their believers, various forms of intimidation, the prospect of legal proceedings and the ultimate threat, as in the case of Fr. Jerzy Popiełuszko, of a martyr's death.

The struggle against the Church is one of the basic tenets of Communist doctrine. A sense of realism on the part of the authorities can result in a shorter or longer lull in the struggle or even in an armistice, but the propaganda machine is geared to expansion and without its imaginary enemies it would become redundant.

The martial law authorities knew they needed the co-operation of the Church to get on with their programme of 'normalization', i.e. to regain the initiative in social life lost to Solidarity and re-assert their monopoly of power. They needed the moderating influence of the Church in order to contain active social resistance. On the other hand, the people expected the Church to be uncompromisingly on their side. In consequence, the activity of the Church and public statements of its representatives acquired a political dimension. Primate Glemp's line was, to a large extent, a continuation of the policy of his predecessor, Cardinal Stefan Wyszyński: to be firm but flexible at the same time. His approach in dealings with the authorities was one of quiet diplomacy and *realpolitik*. There was, however, a dispute as to the very objective of his quiet diplomacy. Was he trading the real value — popular support — for vague promises from the authorities that could be revoked at a moment's notice? Or was he really guided by a clear-headed assessment of the situation, trying to protect what he could of the nation's striving for self-determination?

This dispute arose from a fundamental misconception as to the essence of the Church's mission among men. Many people, believers and non-believers alike, had expected the Church hierarchy to identify with the current political tactics of the opposition and failed to grasp the real meaning of the Episcopate's efforts which were dictated not by any short-term 'political defeatism' but by a long term perspective of man's spiritual destiny.

In Cardinal Glemp's first five years as Primate, the Church in Poland undoubtedly became stronger and more influential but, at the same time more vulnerable and exposed. The defeat of Solidarity as an organization meant that the Church in Poland was once again on the front line of the fight against Communism. It had to expand the scope of its activities in such 'secular' areas as charitable and legal aid or artistic events. Above all it had to satisfy a greatly increased popular demand for truth and self-organization in public life. It faced up to the task admirably. Still, the old warning contained in the Scriptures (I Peter 5:8-9) rings ominously true: 'Be calm but vigilant because your enemy, the devil, is prowling round like a roaring lion, looking for someone to eat. Stand up to him, strong in faith.'

Notes

1. *Palestra* no. 12, 1983.
2. Maria Budzanowska in *Życie Warszawy*, 26 October 1981.
3. *Palestra* no. 7-8, 1985.
4. *Kierunki*, 26 February 1984.
5. Polish Helsinki Committee's Report no. 1, 'Human and Civil Rights in Poland in the Period of Martial Law', (Poland, February 1983).
6. *Słowo* no. 22, 1 October 1983 and the Polish Helsinki Committee's

The Basic Freedoms and the Courtroom

     Special Report on Polish Defence Lawyers 'O adwokatach obrońcach ludzi i wartości. Czas próby'.
7. *Trybuna Ludu*, 10 June 1982.
8. *Newsweek*, 31 October 1983.
9. Ibid.
10. *Ład*, 6 June 1982.
11. *Tygodnik Mazowsze* no. 6, 13 March 1982.
12. Mentioned by the Polish barrister Jadwiga Grochowska at a meeting at the House of Commons organized by the East European Committee of the British Amnesty International Lawyers' Group in May 1983, *Amnesty*, August/September 1983.
13. *Praworządność* no. 6-7, 10 February 1985.
14. Kazimierz Buchała (a former Chairman of the Chief Barristers' Council) in *Państwo i Prawo*, October 1982.
15. Jerzy Nowomiejski, 'O środkach godnych celu', *Trybuna Ludu*, 1 March 1984.
16. *Wolna Trybuna* no. 26, 22 August 1984.
17. Karol Potrzebowski (ed), *Prawo o adwokaturze*, (Warsaw, Wydawnictwo Prawnicze, 1982).
18. Radio Warsaw, 22 March 1983.
19. *Solidarność Wiadomości Wojenne* no. 50, Łódź, 3 December 1983.
20. *Palestra* no. 7-8, 1984.
21. On 12 May 1981 the Minister of Justice approved the resolution of the Chief Barristers' Council of 21 February 1981 which had been adopted on the basis of the Poznań Convention and set the age limit at 75.
22. The Council of State also has this prerogative. It is, moreover, empowered to dissolve the entire district barristers' chamber and receives annual reports from the Chief Barristers' Council.
23. *Trybuna Ludu*, 3 October 1983.
24. *Prawo i Życie*, 15 October 1983.
25. *Trybuna Ludu*, 27 February 1984 and 12 April 1984.
26. *Argumenty*, 13 May 1984.
27. *Trybuna Ludu*, 16 May 1984.
28. *Tygodnik Mazowsze* no. 86, 3 May 1984.
29. *Palestra* no. 1, 1984.
30. *Odrodzenie*, 13 November 1984 and *Praworządność* no. 4, November 1984.
31. *Odrodzenie*, 13 November 1984.
32. *KOS* no. 63, 5 November 1984.
33. *Trybuna Ludu*, 24-26 December 1984.
34. *Trybuna Ludu*, 18 January 1985.
35. *Rzeczpospolita*, 31 January 1986.
36. Marian Rybicki in Tadeusz Fuks, Wiesław Skrzydło, Adam Łopatka and Marian Rybicki: *Ustrój polityczny PRL* (PWN, Warsaw, 1981).
37. 'Theses on Hope and Hopelessness', *Kultura*, June 1971.
38. Michał Kulczycki, Jerzy Zduńczyk: *Obywatel a prawo karne* (Instytut Wydawniczy Związków Zawodowych, Warsaw, 1981).
39. The sentences handed down by the Air Force Court in Poznań

were, in fact, relatively mild, ranging from six months' to one and a half year's imprisonment, and some of these sentences were suspended. Cf. *Observator Wielkopolski* no. 71, July 1983.

40. 'Patronat' was set up in 1909 and existed until the Warsaw uprising of August–September 1944. It was reactivated after the war in 1945 but was supressed by the Ministry of Public Security in 1948. It renewed its activities largely due to the efforts of KOR members, sympathizers and defence lawyers associated with KOR. It was registered on 21 July 1981, suspended with the declaration of martial law and finally disbanded on 18 December 1983.
41. The suspension of both the Writers' Union (ZLP) and the PEN Club was later extended for two months on the basis of the 1932 Law on Associations.
42. The Club was allowed to resume its activities one month later following a plenary meeting and new elections to the governing body. Cf. *Obraz* no. 3, 1984.
43. *Le Figaro*, 7 March 1983.
44. *Obraz* no. 3, 1984.
45. *Słowo* no. 4, 5 April 1984.
46. M. Rybicki in *Ustrój polityczny PRL*.
47. *Tygodnik Mazowsze* no. 108, 29 November 1984.
48. *Czas*, Poznań no. 1(2), 1985.
49. Ibid.
50. AP, Warsaw, 13 November 1984.
51. *Tygodnik Mazowsze* no. 161, 6 March 1986 and Radio Warsaw, 3 March 1986.
52. *Index on Censorship* no. 2, 1980.
53. Two volumes of confidential instructions and circulars from February 1974 to February 1977, published in two parts by Aneks, London, 1978.
54. Deputy Halina Ciszewska's speech in the Sejm on 28 July 1983.
55. Igor Andrejew, Witold Świda and Władysław Wolter, *Kodeks Karny z komentarzem* (The Penal Code with Commentary), (Warsaw, 1973), p.830.
56. *Nowe Prawo*, January 1983.
57. Ibid.
58. *Dziennik Bałtycki*, 12–14 February 1982.
59. WRONA — an acronym of the ruling Military Council of National Salvation (translates as crow) became a popular nickname for the regime.
60. *Solidarność Region Gdańsk* no. 23, 16 April 1983.
61. Appendices to the Polish Helsinki Committee's Report no. 1, unpublished.
62. Ibid.
63. *Żołnierz Wolności*, 16 February 1982.
64. *Tygodnik Mazowsze* nos. 6–8, 1982.
65. *Dziennik Łódzki*, 13 September 1982.
66. *Nowiny*, 18 May 1982 and *Trybuna Ludu*, 21 May 1982.
67. *Fakty* nos. 4–5, 1982.
68. *Kronika Małopolska* no. 10, 1 June 1982.

69. Appendices to the Polish Helsinki Committee's Report no. 1, unpublished.
70. *Informacja Solidarności regionu Mazowsze* no. 84, 1 October 1982.
71. Radio Warsaw, 29 October 1982, 1400 hours.
72. A ruling of 18 May 1982, commented in *Państwo i Prawo*, February 1984.
73. Jerzy Bafia, Danuta Egierska, Irena Śmietanka: *Kodeks Wykroczeń: Komentarz* ('Code of Petty Offences: A Commentary'), (Wydawnictwo Prawnicze, Warsaw, 1980), p. 140.
74. Out of the total number of 2,352 tribunals operating before they were reorganized under the Law of 20 December 1982, over 600 did not satisfy this requirement and over half of the remaining 1,700 did not receive proper legal advice. Cf. *Rzeczpospolita*, 26 November 1982.
75. *Rzeczpospolita*, 2 July 1984.
76. *Polityka*, 14 July 1984.
77. *Rada Narodowa, Gospodarka, Administracja*, 21 January 1983.
78. The authorities were not willing to allow a fully controlled 'selection' to be turned into an election whose outcome might have been unpredictable, given the generally freer atmosphere of the Solidarity period.
79. *Rzeczpospolita*, 2 July 1984.
80. *Rada Narodowa, Gospodarka, Administracja*, 11 July 1983 and *Polityka*, 14 July 1984.
81. *Życie Literackie*, 5 December 1982.
82. The law of 26 May 1982 quadrupled fines from 5,000 to 20,000 zloty. On the basis of the law of 10 May 1985 fines were raised still more: up to 50,000 zloty.
83. *Polityka*, 5 June 1982.
84. Z. Gostyński, *Państwo i Prawo*, April 1981.
85. Reuter, Gdańsk, 4 February 1982.
86. In violation of the standard practice the Voivodship Court in Gdańsk, which supervises regional courts in the voivodship, transferred all the appeals against prison sentences from the Regional Court in Gdańsk to the Regional Court in Stargard Szczeciński, making it difficult for families and friends of those sentenced to attend the court hearings in view of the restrictions on freedom of movement throughout the country. Cf. *Kontakt*, Paris, April 1982.
87. PAP in English, 7 September 1982 and *Trybuna Ludu*, 8 September 1982.
88. Reprinted in *Kultura*, November 1982.
89. The Minister of Justice Sylwester Zawadzki, the military commissar in the Ministry, Colonel Henryk Kostrzewa, and the Director of the Courts' Supervision Department in the Ministry, Romuald Soroko, all participated in the conference. This department was responsible for preparing special reports for the Central Committee, in particular on summary procedure, on the basis of information received from the chairmen of the voivodship courts. Cf. *Trybuna Ludu*, 7 October 1982 and the Polish Helsinki Committee's Report no. 1.

90. *Acta Medica Cracoviensia Tempore Status Belli* (Medical Report for Kraków during the period of martial law) translated and published in English by the Committee in Support of Solidarity, New York, 1983.
91. *Obraz*, July and October issues 1983.
92. 'What happened in Lubin'. An article by Wojciech Markiewicz set in type for the 11 September issue of *Polityka* but blocked by the censors. It was eventually printed in *Tygodnik Mazowsze* no. 27, 22 September 1982.
93. *Solidarność Zagłębia Miedziowego*, MKK Biuletyn Solidarność no. 39, 14 September 1982.
94. *Czas* no. 2(2), 1985.
95. Quoted by Zofia Radzikowska, *Palestra* no. 1, 1984.
96. Ibid. and *Prawo i Życie*, 9 June 1984.
97. Cf. Adam Michnik, 'The Lessons of Dialogue', a letter smuggled from the Kurkowa Street prison in Gdańsk.
98. Polish Helsinki Commission (sic), 'Human and Civil Rights in the PPR', (Warsaw, October 1980).
99. The testimony of Jerzy Las, unpublished.
100. The Polish Helsinki Committee's Report no. 1.
101. Ibid.
102. Ibid.
103. AFP, Warsaw, 15 September 1983, quoting Church sources.
104. The Polish Helsinki Committee's Report no. 4 'Human and Civil Rights in the PPR: September 1984 to February 1985'.
105. Ibid.
106. *Rzeczpospolita*, 20 November 1985.
107. *Głos Wielkopolski*, 14 April 1982.
108. *Życie Warszawy*, 27 October 1983.
109. *Polityka*, 16 October 1982.
110. Ibid.
111. *KOS* no. 49. 13 February 1984.
112. Reuter, Warsaw, 6 April 1984.
113. *Polityka*, 23 November 1984.
114. *Ideologia i Polityka*, April 1983.
115. *Express Wieczorny*, 27 December 1983.
116. AP, Warsaw, 20 December 1983.
117. UPI, Warsaw, 3 December 1983.
118. *Tygodnik Mazowsze* no. 38, 6 January 1983.
119. *Ojczyzna* no. 25 and UPI, Warsaw, 18 June 1982.
120. *Żołnierz Wolności*, 10 March 1982 and *Fakty* no. 2, 1982.
121. *Committee in Support of Solidarity Reports* no. 15, New York, 23 June 1983.
122. *Tu i Teraz*, 19 September 1984.
123. *Serwis Informacyjny RKW NSZZ Solidarność region Małopolska* no. 37, 9 December 1982.
124. *Tu teraz (pismo oświaty niezależnej)* no. 22, 15 December 1983.
125. *KOS* no. 33, 7 June 1983.
126. *Tygodnik Wojenny* no. 80, 17 March 1984.
127. *Tygodnik Wojenny* no. 72, 1 December 1983.

128. *Serwis Informacyjny RKW NSZZ Solidarność region Małopolska* no. 37.
129. Reuter, Warsaw, 5 March 1982.
130. AP, Warsaw, 5 December 1984.
131. *Informacja Solidarności*, 7-11 January 1983 and *Serwis Informacyjny RKW NSZZ Solidarność region Małopolska* no. 37.
132. *Hutnik* no. 114, 10 December 1985.
133. *Informacja Solidarności* no. 23, 9 February 1982.
134. AP, Warsaw, 17 November 1983.
135. Reuter, Warsaw, 15 October 1983.
136. Peter Godwin, *Sunday Times*, 18 November 1984.
137. AP, Warsaw, 17 November 1983, quoting Keston College and *Informacja Solidarności* nos. 172 and 173.
138. *Il Sabato*, 16 February 1985.

VII

THE POLICE AND THE PROSECUTION

A state within a state

The PPR's security services were formally set up on the basis of a decree issued on 7 October 1944 by the so-called Lublin Committee — stooges of Stalin who, having no legal title to form a government, simply usurped the right to rule with the aid of the Red Army and the NKVD. The security services which were organized and originally staffed by NKVD officers were from the very beginning an instrument of the sovietization of Poland. At the height of Stalinist terror they were used to crush real and potential opposition to Communist rule. In particular the security services crushed the underground Home Army, the pre-war intelligentsia and Mikołajczyk's Peasant Party (PSL) — the only opposition party originally allowed to operate, but which was, in fact, also destined for liquidation.

Their methods were also inherited from the Bolsheviks. Beating and torture were the norm during interrogation. Investigations never lasted less than one or one and a half years. The defendants were sentenced on trumped-up charges to long terms of imprisonment or death. Show trials usually featured elaborate charges of espionage. The security services offered an opportunity for rapid promotion to unscrupulous, ideological fanatics and opportunists. Loyalty to Stalin was the precondition for getting to the top. Stefan Kalinowski, who was Prosecutor General from 1950–6, had no formal education in law and owed his position to his loyalty to the First Secretary and President Bolesław Bierut. A metal worker and a Communist Party member before the war, he had fled to the USSR when Poland was overrun by the Nazis and the Soviets. He was first a political officer with the Kościuszko Division, then became a member of the National Home Council (KRN) which later founded the Communist government, and finally was transferred to the Military Prosecutor's Office. Such rapid careers were not by any means exceptional. Kalinowski survived de-Stalinization and, although he was dismissed from the PUWP Central Committee, he was never made to account for his actions. Many other security officers also survived de-Stalinization and continued to advance to higher positions. It is they, as well as their children and protégés, who still constitute the backbone of the security services in the PPR.

After the death of Bierut the discredited security apparatus was reorganized. While its excessive powers were curbed, its methods were not fundamentally changed. The post-Stalinist party leader Władysław Gomułka, according to Władysław Bieńkowski, a close associate of his at one time, needed its support to regain control over the party apparatus.[1] His half-hearted approach to reforming the security services, however, made their self-generation inevitable. According to Bieńkowski, the dynamics of the system are characterized by an inherent tendency for the party dictatorship to be transformed into a police dictatorship.[2] The security services have been called upon by successive Communist regimes to quell civic unrest. In the cyclical pattern of crisis in the PPR — the Poznań riots of 1956, the student unrest of 1968, the Baltic Coast riots of 1970, and the food price riots in Radom and Ursus of 1976 — the security services have played an important role not only using force to put down outbreaks of popular dissatisfaction but also providing the ruling elite with a propagandistic interpretation of the crisis and a follow-up in the form of repressions.

After the pacification of the workers of Ursus and Radom, who had taken to the streets in protest at food price rises in June 1976, the powers and the role of the police became one of the prime concerns of the emerging democratic opposition movement. The Workers' Defence Committee 'KOR' sent a motion to the Sejm calling for the appointment of a special commission to investigate police misconduct in Radom.

During the August 1980 wave of strikes in Poland the workers demanded that their social benefits be raised to the level of those enjoyed by the police. During the Solidarity period the people questioned the need to build additional police stations and demanded hospitals, schools and nurseries instead. Despite greater

The Police and the Prosecution

openness in public life, the police and the prosecution were used to provoke potentially inflammatory incidents and even to stage elaborate provocations such as the Bydgoszcz affair of 19 March 1981. This affair, which signalled a new offensive against Solidarity and led to a profound internal political crisis that threatened to erupt in a general strike, was criticized within police ranks where a grass-roots reform movement was already making itself felt. Reformist-minded policemen articulated various demands including the separation of the security branch from the uniformed police (the uniformed police were often used as a cover for the secret police), the removal of local police officials suspected of corruption and discredited by their illegal dealings with various party officials, and the recognition of a policemen's trade union. This last demand was absolutely ruled out by the authorities which were determined to crush the union, by force if necessary. Since the union claimed to have over 40,000 members, a widespread purge of police ranks was required.[3] This purge was carried out five months before the introduction of martial law. Reformist policemen were among those interned and forced to emigrate.

A similar fate met reformist prosecutors. As early as September 1981 those prosecutors who had joined Solidarity were told that their membership in the union could not be reconciled with their professional duties. The vetting of prosecutors and the general review of personnel in the prosecutor's offices intensified after the introduction of martial law.

The police: secret and uniformed

The Ministry of Internal Affairs (MIA) which is in charge of the secret and uniformed police is a highly centralized institution. Individual ministry departments and sections are not autonomous. The all-embracing Operational Division probes into all spheres of social life. In addition to regular intelligence work, protection of diplomatic posts, preservation of state secrets and economic counter-intelligence, it has special departments monitoring the major social groups. These departments not only concern themselves with those who have already expressed their opposition to the authorities but also seek to obtain foreknowledge of possible discontent or opposition, identify those who might emerge as leaders, and collect potentially incriminating evidence against

The Police and the Prosecution

them. The Operational Division monitors the working class, in particular in the larger industrial plants; private farmers; the intelligentsia; the Church; and the opposition. The MIA also has an Investigations Bureau which has an elaborate internal structure and conducts and supervises political cases as well as offering specialized services, and an Auxiliary Services Division offering technical support in the form of wire-tapping, forgery of documents, break-ins, mail censorship, as well as keeping personal files on individual citizens. They are rightly believed to be masters of dirty tricks. The Ministry of Internal Affairs should, in fact, more properly be described as the Ministry of Police.

As the front line of the regime's struggle against all forms of independent activity, the Security Police or SB systematically employ techniques of violence and intimidation in which their officers — as evidenced by the trial of Fr. Popiełuszko's assassins — have been trained. This trial also revealed the arrogance of the SB and their deep-rooted conviction that they were above the law. The atmosphere within the service is one of blind discipline, mutual fear and almost obsessive secrecy. The SB officials are the eyes, ears and muscle of the system. As a group they clearly have their own corporate interests and privileges. They constitute an exclusive caste, being not only better paid, but also able to jump long queues for scarce goods and services. They are as a rule well educated: in contrast to the early recruits for the SB, who were of peasant and working-class origin, those who joined the ranks of the SB in the 1960s and 1970s included a high percentage of university graduates. They tend to be loyal party members and hold an ingrained disdain for the Catholic Church. This is a symptom of the incessant indoctrination to which they are subjected. The SB regard themselves as the real vanguard of the party and guardian of the socialist system whose prime task is to hound political opponents.

Although they serve one master, the secret and the uniformed police are clearly distinct. The secret police identify much more closely with the system than the ordinary police (MO). Since it offers better career prospects the SB attracts more intelligent and better educated people. In an interview entitled 'I am a technician of socialism', an anonymous SB officer described his motives for joining the secret police:

> Contrary to the prevailing opinion people join the secret police for many different reasons, not just for the material

advantages. A number of failures who have lost out in other jobs or in their private lives end up in the SB. It is here that they try to find their necessary quota of admiration. Others think that such an institution is necessary, that the secret police have been active in all countries since time immemorial. Others still learned from their own experiences that the way to a career is open only to those who rule and those who ingratiate themselves with those who rule. I also think that in this profession the way into the 'firm' is through the family. Many join because Dad or Uncle or some other relative is in it, and he seems to live better than others do.[4]

Indeed, the family connection seems to be a widespread practice. Two of the murderers of Fr. Jerzy Popiełuszko had connections in the service. Grzegorz Piotrowski's father, General Władysław Piotrowski, was chief of the SB in Łódź. His mother used to be a women's prison director. His wife worked as a clerk in the MIA and his father-in-law was a General in the Ministry. Waldemar Chmielewski's father was a Colonel in the SB and his wife, also the daughter of an SB officer, worked at the MIA passport office. The SB's 'dynastic empire' extends through intermarriage also to the judiciary, the prosecution and the prison service.

In contrast to the Stalinist UB, the SB requires less ideological zeal of its employees but still demands discipline, obedience, lack of sensitivity, perennial distrust and suspicion of others. The SB officer who described himself as 'a technician of socialism' characterized the MIA as an institution which is ruled 'exactly according to the laws of the Mafia' in which 'fear is endemic: fear of failing to do the job or of being suspected of insufficient zeal'.[5] This fear is stronger than any possible scruples or qualms of conscience.

The ordinary and secret police are both part of the same state institution. They are recruited by the same personnel department. They wear the same uniforms. They often work side by side. None the less, each of the two services has its own institutional framework, with the SB taking precedence over the MO. Not only is the status of the SB employee higher than that of the ordinary policeman; the various departments of the SB also enjoy more prerogatives. Each service has, for example, its own investigative bodies, called the Investigations Bureau of the MIA and the

The Police and the Prosecution

Bureau of Inquiry and Investigations of the Police HQ, respectively. While the Investigations Bureau and its subdivisions on voivodship level specialize in political cases, the Bureau of Inquiry and Investigations and its local offices deal mostly with criminal cases. This is not, however, to suggest two distinct spheres of interest or a rigid separation of prerogatives. On the contrary, the dividing line is a fluid one. Some criminal cases can be taken over by the security service, particularly those which involve corruption of high-ranking state or party officials, embezzlement of public funds, large-scale economic crime. The distinction between what is criminal and what is political is never a clear-cut one. Offences committed by officials are as a rule investigated only when the appropriate party cell requests that this be done. By persecuting, harassing and imprisoning those who think and act independently and by shielding party apparatchiks from criminal liability, the political police is used to safeguard the PUWP's monopoly of power.

The extent to which the PPR's Ministry of Internal Affairs is controlled and supervised by the KGB is understandably hard to establish. Zdzisław Rurarz, the PPR's former ambassador to Japan, claims that 'the SB is penetrated and guided by the KGB. The SB is strictly forbidden to wage operations without KGB approval, whereas the KGB has a free hand to do whatever it deems necessary to maintain order in Poland. In fact, I know of some cases where the SB carried out KGB-organized operations without the knowledge of higher Polish authorities.'[6] Acccording to unconfirmed reports, after the visit to Warsaw in November 1983 of KGB chief General Chebrikov, General Jaruzelski was supposed to have agreed to readmit KGB officials to the SB.[7] Soviet advisers had already worked in the past in the Stalinist Ministry of Public Security and the Ministry of Defence. After 1956 their presence became less conspicuous. Following the imposition of martial law the GDR reportedly proceeded, in co-operation with the KGB, to build its own espionage network in Poland.[8]

During the Solidarity period the authorities built up the security forces in preparation for martial law. Since the police were ordered to purge uncertain elements and found it difficult to attract new recruits, it was decided that the police would to some extent be serviced by the military. Those who were called up to serve their mandatory two-year military duty were encouraged to serve with the ZOMO riot police instead. ZOMO could mean a move up the social ladder for recruits from poor backgrounds. ZOMO men could earn several times more money than ordinary conscripts, they had access to special shops selling goods in short supply, and they could complete secondary education for working adults, which gave them a better start in their subsequent civilian careers.

The ZOMO are trained for large-scale operations. They are screened for political liability (those who have relatives abroad are not admitted). While the ordinary police are organized on a voivodship basis with a commander in each region, the ZOMO units are controlled centrally.

The history of the ZOMO riot police is instructive. It reflects the history of post-war political unrest in Poland. The first ZOMO units were formed in 1956 after bloody clashes with workers in Poznań. Thereafter they were deployed to pacify the recurrent protest actions. After the police provocation in Bydgoszcz on 19 March 1981 the ZOMO entered a period of accelerated growth and modernization, apparently at the personal recommendation of General Jaruzelski. The revamped ZOMO made their first large-scale public appearance in Warsaw in early December 1981 when they carried out a lightning raid and broke up a sit-in strike by cadets at the para-military firemen's academy. This operation later came to be seen as a small scale dress rehearsal for martial law. In 1984 some 35 per cent of military recruits who had chosen to serve their mandatory military duty in ZOMO decided to remain in police ranks for good. Those who opted out after two years' service became ZOMO reservists — called the ROMO. Although they were considered to have served their military duty, they remained at the disposal of the MIA and not of the military.

Individual security officers enjoy immunity from criminal proceedings should they infringe the law in the course of their duties. Criminal liability is virtually non-existent. Internal discipline and unquestioned loyalty are of far greater importance within the MIA than respect for the law, and this is so at all levels of the police hierarchy.

The Police and the Military

The balance of forces between the police and the military deserves a brief mention. The imposition of martial law revealed the fundamental role of the military in a Communist state as the system's last reserve. When he said that 'our soldier has clean hands' Jaruzelski implied that the military were not responsible for the political and economic crisis but that they would put things in order. Martial law was presented as a crackdown not only on Solidarity but also on the corrupt and inefficient state and economic administration. Army officers took over key posts in the party, major enterprises and the state and local administration. This overhauling of the system's basic institutions had its obvious limits. The party's military cadres could not substitute for the rest of the *nomenklatura* indefinitely. The anti-corruption and pro-efficiency drive was, therefore, carried out less than wholeheartedly.

Since the advent of Solidarity and, even more so, the introduction of martial law greatly undermined the cohesion of the party and state apparatus, the rivalry for power and privilege between the police and the military inevitably increased. The army claimed to represent the national interest, while the police were openly relegated to being an apparatus of repression. The military were rewarded for their martial law operations with promotions. The police resented being forced to take a back seat. The bungled assassination of Fr. Popiełuszko undoubtedly placed the Ministry of Internal Affairs politically at a disadvantage. Even the partial exposure of the role of the secret police in planning and executing the assassination enabled Jaruzelski to clip the wings of the security services. Still the secret police were far from defeated. The secret police enhanced their role in determining employment policy by vetting prospective candidates; greatly expanded their network of agents and paid informers; inspired political trials and scored several propaganda victories over the underground Solidarity activists. Their position was greatly consolidated by the passage of the law of 14 July 1983 on the MIA (see below).

The tasks of the secret police

Although it has traditionally been the task of the secret police to act as an early warning system protecting the institutions of the state, their role in the Soviet-style state goes far beyond that. The PPR's Security Service (SB) operates in a state in which there no rule of law, no separation of powers, and which is not sovereign. Not only are the secret police not accountable to society but they are, at times, not even accountable to the country's political masters.

In the course of Poland's post-war history, the political police managed to emancipate themselves from the control of the party apparatus on several occasions. This was the case in the period of Stalinist terror when the UB kept files on high-ranking members of the party establishment; it happened again in 1968 when police chief Mieczysław Moczar challenged the PUWP's first secretary Władysław Gomułka for power; and most recently in the post-martial law period when the secret police attempted to rival the military in imposing the terms of the 'normalization' process. In the Communist system characterized by dogmatic phraseology, bureaucracy, inefficiency, chronic shortages of basic necessities and mismanagement, the police — especially its secret service — are the only institution which functions according to the principles of efficiency.

In addition to the police's preventative functions aimed at forestalling the emergence of organized opposition to one-party rule, they also serve to control people for control's sake by destroying social bonds, atomizing society, waging psychological warfare and intimidating individuals, social groups or society as a whole. Their operational activities include: surveillance, house searches, detentions, interrogations, interception of mail, wire-tapping, installing of bugging devices, infiltration, provocation, beating, abducting and killing, terrorism and propaganda campaigns.

Some of the SB methods

Surveillance.
Secret police interest is usually focused either on a particular person or on a particular locality. Quite apart from the material advantages of secretly tailing people, observing their movements, intercepting their mail and eavesdropping on their conversations, the police can also make their interest obvious in order to put pressure on individuals, create an atmosphere of fear and uncertainty and sow general mistrust. The secret police do not, as a rule, wait for the prosecutor's decision that is formally

required to violate the citizen's privacy in this way. They do not, moreover, institute surveillance on the grounds of reasonable suspicion that an offence has been or is about to be committed but in anticipation that the information collected might possibly be used against people at some later date.

Speeches made publicly by leading Solidarity activists long before martial law were secretly recorded. A secret recording of a speech made by Marian Jurczyk, the Chairman of Solidarity's Western Pomeranian Region during a meeting at a local furniture factory was passed on in October 1981 by the police to the prosecutor's office so that formal criminal proceedings could be instituted. In another case involving Patrycjusz Kosmowski, the Chairman of Solidarity's Podbeskidzie Region, the secret recordings of speeches delivered at various meetings before martial law were actually presented to the court during his trial in March 1982. The court, however, did not allow them as a valid evidence, arguing that trade union activity prior to the imposition of martial law had been covered by the Act of Abolition of 12 December 1981. After the introduction of martial law the SB increased their recording activities, concentrating in particular, on Church sermons. Secret recordings were also presented as valid evidence during the important political trials of Frasyniuk, Lis and Michnik in May 1985 and the Confederation of Independent Poland (KPN) in April 1986.

Detentions and house searches
These are two particularly widespread forms of police harassment of democratic opposition activists. Under the existing provisions the police can detain not only those who have actually committed an offence or a petty offence but also those whom they suspect of being about to commit an offence or a petty offence. In this way, anyone can be detained for up to 48 hours without the presentation of charges. Detention is regularly used as a preventative measure or as a sanction for behaviour which, although not illegal, is not approved by the authorities. In the first instance, detention is used to prevent certain individuals from participating in unofficial celebrations of patriotic anniversaries, protest actions, independent Church-sponsored activities. In the second, it serves to punish those who meet with prominent opposition personalities, wear Solidarity badges or other emblems, or participate in certain religious ceremonies. That such detentions are often used as pure harassment is well illustrated by the case

The Police and the Prosecution

of Jerzy Gnieciak, a Rural Solidarity leader from Opole who was detained for 48 hours six times in the course of one year. Each time, his poultry farm was left unattended. None of the five cases instituted against him and investigated by the prosecutor's office was ever brought to court.

Detention is usually accompanied by a house search. All kinds of publications — independent literature, Western publications and periodicals, books published before the war, as well as personal notes, diaries, address books, visiting cards, sellotape, cuttings from official newspapers — and reams of unused paper are confiscated with a view to procuring potential evidence. Although the law stipulates that the police must have a court or prosecutor's order in order to conduct a search, in practice it is the head of the local police station who orders the search. The police and the prosecutor's office co-operate closely with the censor's office, which has an important say in determining which publications confiscated in the search are to be held as 'incriminating evidence' and which can be returned to the owner. Short-term detention and house searches are standard methods of police operation. A person who is unjustly detained or whose house is searched cannot, moreover, seek redress from the police or have recourse to a court of justice.

'Unknown perpetrators'

This is a specialized form of intimidation which involves violence in the form of beating, abduction and even murder by secret squads of policemen. The victims of 'unknown perpetrators' are most commonly independent labour, rural or student activists, independent publishers and priests. Many of the victims were dragged into a car, gagged, blindfolded and taken to a secluded spot, usually in the woods. Here they were beaten, tortured or made forcibly drunk, threatened with loss of life and interrogated about their alleged contacts with the Solidarity underground. Some were blackmailed, others asked to become *agents provocateurs* and infiltrate the Solidarity underground.

'Unknown perpetrators' are at least as old as Bolshevism, but after de-Stalinization their activities remained largely sporadic until martial law when such incidents took on a more systematic character. A spate of abductions in the Toruń area between February and August 1984 was followed by the abduction and assassination of Fr. Jerzy Popiełuszko (19 October 1984) also in the Toruń area and the beating of Fr. Tadeusz Zaleski (6 April

1985 and 3 December 1985). One of those abducted, Gerard Zakrzewski, in a statement to the prosecutor's office, said that his assailants had claimed to belong to a group 'that was not bound by any law'. More clues to the identity of the assailants were provided by a leaflet found in the bag of another victim, Antoni Mężydło, when he was dumped on a waste disposal site in Brodnica. The leaflet, entitled 'Communiqué no. 1', announced the formation of the Anti-Solidarity Organization (OAS). The group pledged to strike at Solidarity which was described as 'a cancer' which the 'incompetent and bureaucratized security service under Jaruzelski had not managed to overcome'.[9]

Antoni Mężydło, who was abducted on 2 March 1984, recognized one of his oppressors in a secret police officer Marek Kuczkowski. Mężydło's testimony was corroborated by the testimony of Stanisław Śmigiel who had witnessed the abduction. The victims reported their cases to the regional prosecutor's office in Toruń which formally instituted an investigation but discontinued it, however, after Mężydło, Śmigiel and other victims of the abductions requested a confrontation with the SB officer Marek Kuczkowski. The prosecutor's office stated that 'no evidence could be found to confirm the hyphothesis that the abductions were the work of officers of the security service, whereas several circumstances established in the course of the investigation actually contradicted this hypothesis'. At the same time the prosecutor Antoni Białowicz said that 'it could not be ruled out that the abductions were the work of illegal Solidarity structures wishing to test the loyalty of former Solidarity members to their organization'. The victims appealed to the district prosecutor's office. Shortly afterwards, the chief witness Śmigiel was arrested on the trumped-up charge of possessing illegal broadcasting equipment. The investigation was finally discontinued on 5 October 1984. In the case of Father Zaleski, the prosecutor's office found that his injuries had been self-inflicted.

Official unwillingness to investigate cases of police-sponsored violence is even more evident in cases where the victim died. A formal investigation is promptly discontinued under the pretext of 'inability to identify those responsible' or 'no offence having been committed'. A victim of 'unknown perpetrators' is typically presented as a drunkard and his death as a result of drunken brawl, as in the case of Tadeusz Frąś, found dead in Kraków on 7 September 1983.

The Police and the Prosecution

The investigation is conducted in such a way as to rule out murder and suppress any evidence of secret police involvement. The investigation into the case of Piotr Bartoszcze, a Rural Solidarity activist, found dead on 8 February 1984 in the drainage pit on a farm near his home, was dropped on 13 May 1984 since 'no criminal evidence' had been found. The official media claimed that Bartoszcze had fallen out of his car drunk while driving over a bridge, crossed a muddy field in shock, fallen into the pit and choked himself with mud.[10] The official version of death by misadventure was challenged by the victim's father Michał, who wrote to General Jaruzelski stating 'with determination and deepest conviction' that his son had been murdered. Bartoszcze senior stated that his son had been chased by unidentified individuals across a field, beaten to death and then dumped in the drainage pit. He also recalled that his son had been repeatedly harassed and blackmailed by the police to end his involvement in Rural Solidarity. Bartoszcze senior's version was supported by evidence and confirmed by an independent investigative commission formed by an anonymous group of pro-Solidarity policemen who concluded that the death of Piotr Bartoszcze was most probably a murder, which was either premeditated or the unintended result of excessive beating.[11]

Provocation
This specific form of intimidation ranges from small-scale incidents, such as planting incriminating material to frame and discredit an individual, to large-scale operations such as the 3 May 1983 raid on the offices of the Primate's Aid Committee for Prisoners and Their Families. In the latter case, a group of about a dozen young males broke into the offices of the charitable committee situated in the Franciscan Convent attached to St Martin's church in Warsaw. The attackers demolished the pharmaceutical supplies collected by the Committee and then proceeded to beat up those who worked there. Four of those beaten were subsequently dragged outside, thrown over a fence that surrounds the convent grounds and forced into a waiting car. They were then driven out of town and dumped at the roadside, one by one. The entire action was well co-ordinated. At the time of the attack on the convent, the entire section of the Old Town in Warsaw was sealed off by police. The assailants were equipped with walkie-talkies and conducted conversations over them. The regional prosecutor's office who conducted the investigation into

the raid on the Primate's Aid Committee admitted that policemen had entered the grounds of the convent but claimed that they had done so in hot pursuit of young people who had been disseminating fly-sheets and insulting them. The victims of the attack were not, however, aware of any group of people who might have wanted to seek protection in the grounds of the convent. All they knew was that they had been attacked by a group of thugs for no reason at all. In the course of the investigation the group of thugs turned out to be plainclothes policemen. The reconstruction of events as presented by the prosecutor's office was made in such a way as to provide the policemen with the ridiculous, albeit formal, alibi of hot pursuit.

The Polish Bishops' Conference protested to the government over the incident. At that time, the bishops interpreted the provocation as an attempt by certain anti-clerical police or party elements to make it impossible for Pope John Paul II to visit Poland as planned in June 1983.

Such provocations present the state and party authorities with certain *faits accomplis*. By staging provocations the secret police can enforce their claim to influence political developments and determine the line pursued by the authorities with regard to society. The well-known Bydgoszcz provocation in March 1981, when police beat up three Solidarity activists who had been taking part in an official people's council meeting, created a gulf between the party establishment and Solidarity. The incident almost resulted in a general strike, which was only averted at the last moment. A general strike must have led to a police crackdown on Solidarity.

Whether the murder of Fr. Popiełuszko was, in fact, originally conceived as police provocation is not certain. It seems, with hindsight, to have been far more a coldly calculated assassination arising from the conviction of their omnipotence and impunity prevalent among the secret police. Jaruzelski's group decided, however, to treat the murder as a provocation. By revealing some details about secret police operations, Jaruzelski came out the stronger and succeeded in enforcing 'normalization' on his terms. By replacing some of the MIA's top officials he also clipped the wings of the police.

Infiltration
This method was used extensively to destroy the Solidarity underground. The first task was to catch a 'thread' — any useful

information on clandestine activities, usually obtained through an informer. The next step, known as the 'mangle', involves intensified surveillance using observation points and 'look-outs' near suspected buildings. The aim is eventually to plant an agent or 'wire' in the clandestine network. Such an agent can contribute such valuable items as paper or printing ink, offer contacts, help in distribution or act as a courier. He thereby not only wins the confidence of the others but also gains valuable information about the location of the printing, distribution and meeting points, as well as the identity of several activists. The 'wire' functions until the operational department of the secret police orders 'a clean-up'. This happens when the police feel confident that the underground network in question is sufficiently penetrated. Ideally, the 'clean-up' is conducted in such a way as to leave some people or places still active so that they might become the 'thread' to new operations.

A police-installed agent not only studies the organization he is sent to infiltrate, but also passes on misinformation and stages provocations.

Recruiting collaborators
A pre-condition of infiltration is the recruitment of police agents. These can be divided into three groups: residents (salaried, full-time SB employees), secret collaborators (used for special missions — usually infiltration — and rewarded with various benefits), and informers, who are often involved in the criminal underground, such as prostitutes or illegal money-changers. A criminal recruited to be a secret police agent is used to carry out particularly degrading tasks. Instances of the SB requisitioning criminals from the ordinary police for special tasks are not uncommon. Other methods of recruiting secret police collaborators include blackmail and beating.

Warning talks and informal interrogation
Solidarity activists detained in connection with an independent assembly, speech or private meeting may be 'let off' with a warning if the authorities do not wish or are not yet ready to institute formal proceedings against them. On 29 November 1984 a member of the Regional Board of Solidarity in Słupsk, Zygmunt Goliński, was detained in Wrocław as he was going to see Władysław Frasyniuk. Upon his release he was told that if he ever came to Wrocław again he would suffer the same fate as Fr.

Popiełuszko. Although meeting Frasyniuk is not in itself a punishable offence, the police wished to make clear that such meetings would not be tolerated. Such a warning could subsequently serve as an incriminating circumstance in a court case. Warnings can also be used, at the instigation of police, by the prosecutor's office. Warnings can be supplemented by threats of fresh prosecution. This happened in late December 1986 to Jacek Kuroń, Henryk Wujec and Janusz Onyszkiewicz, who were all summoned by the police and told that they would face further questioning. The threat of prosecution, together with regular interrogation sessions, was often used as a means of inducing Solidarity activists to scale down their activities.

Informal interrogation began to be widely used by the secret police in the aftermath of martial law as a form of establishing contact with the opposition. Under the PPR's Code of Criminal Procedure, an individual can only be summoned to the prosecutor's office in the capacity of suspect, accused, witness, expert witness or interpreter. He is obliged to answer summonses only if these contain the reference number of the specific case in question and indicate the capacity in which he is to be questioned. To by-pass these requirements secret policemen have tried to arrange meetings in cafés, private flats or public parks. They have tried to visit people at their places of work and informally interrogate them during their working hours. The aim of police interrogation is not only to extract information but also to bribe, blackmail or force individuals into becoming police informers. The biggest nationwide action of informal police interrogation took place in mid-September 1986, when 3,000 people suspected of having links with underground groups were visited at their homes or work places or summoned to police HQs. The move coincided with the announcement that 225 major political prisoners would be released under the Special Procedure Act of 17 July 1986.

Misinformation
The MIA has a special 'dirty tricks' department code-named the 'Studies Bureau' which is responsible for discrediting opposition activists, the Solidarity underground and any other independent initiative. They do this by various criminal means such as forgery, doctoring of tape recordings, falsification of documents and planting of evidence.[12] They have in the past produced counterfeit Solidarity publications and bulletins and broadcast

faked Radio Solidarity programmes. All of this was done in order to confuse the Solidarity underground and to score a few propaganda victories. They do not even balk at character assassination and defamation.

Psychological warfare
To create a climate of intimidation the secret police consistently attempt to link the Solidarity underground to Western intelligence centres or imply that their principal motives are terrorist ones. This psycho terror reached a crescendo a few days before the Tenth PUWP Congress when Deputy Interior Minister General Władysław Pożoga alleged that guerrillas were being trained near Munich and in New Jersey 'to attack Polish targets abroad and carry out sabotage raids inside the country'.[13] In mid-June 1986 several Solidarity activists and advisers were repeatedly questioned under the pretext of involvement in an espionage affair. Oddly enough, the alleged US spy, Stephen Mull, was not asked to leave Poland, as is normally the case. This does not prevent the authorities from trying to instil in the social consciousness the contradictory thesis that the Solidarity underground are a tiny and insignificant group posing no danger to the authorities, and enjoying no real support among the people.

Psychological pressure is also used to intimidate particular groups or professions. When the authorities wished to suppress the independent aspirations of scholars or writers, each of these groups in turn became the object of secret police interest and a few of their more prominent members were singled out for particular harassment.

The police often resort to arrests and interrogations at a time of potential unrest in order to create an atmosphere of intimidation and bring home to the people that the SB are omnipotent and omnipresent, and stand above the law. Preventive detentions always increased on the eve of an important national or Solidarity anniversary.

* * *

This presentation of some of the methods used by the secret police in the PPR illustrates that the fundamental role of the police is to counteract any independent social initiative or movement. To this end the police — and this is true of any Soviet-style state — must serve as an instrument of social disintegration. They must paralyze not only those independent-minded people whose organizational skills might prove troublesome for the authorities but also those who are capable of thinking independently. They must atomize society by breaking spontaneous social bonds. They must spread fear and psychological terror. Such a police force is always geared to expansion and always in need of enemies, not only to prove that it is indispensable to the party but also to influence political developments in the state.

The Prosecutor's Office

In the Soviet-style Communist system the office of public prosecutor is integrated into the single, all-embracing power structure. The prosecutor's office in the PPR is modelled on the Leninist prototype. Its task is not, as in Western democratic practise, simply to institute criminal proceedings on behalf of the state and represent the state in an independent court of law, but to exercise broad-ranging preventative and control functions designed to ensure the continuity and stability of the political order. The prosecutor's offices are not a part of the Ministry of Justice but constitute a separate state agency with a strict internal hierarchy headed by the Prosecutor General.

The Prosecutor General himself occupies a highly privileged position in the state. He is not accountable to the Sejm and is formally supervised by the Council of State. The PPR Constitution fails, however, to stipulate the disciplinary powers at the State Council's disposal. Apparently, such a possibility was not reckoned with and, indeed, the reports submitted by the Prosecutor General to the Council of State have, as a rule, been accepted without reservations. In fact, the Prosecutor General's formal subordination to the Council of State serves as a façade since he really works in close collaboration with the Ministry of Internal Affairs, the PUWP CC's Commission on Law and Order and the Council of Ministers' Committee on the Observance of Law, Order and Social Discipline.

The main task of the prosecutors' offices is to protect and to strengthen the political, social and economic system of the PPR, protect social property and ensure respect for citizens' rights (Art. 2.1 of the Law on the Prosecutor's Office of 20 June 1985). This law lists 12 areas in which the Prosecutor General and his subordinates are to carry out their tasks. Apart from the traditional areas of interest, such as conducting and supervising pre-trial investigations and acting as public prosecutor before the court, the PPR's prosecutors are responsible for ensuring the uniform and correct application of the law by the courts, state offices and state institutions. Their responsibilities also entail cooperation with people's councils in order to ensure that 'people's legality', 'social property' and citizens' rights are protected. Finally, the PPR's prosecutors have wide-ranging prerogatives to 'carry out other actions stipulated by the law and necessary for the strengthening of people's legality and the prevention of criminality' (Art. 4.12 of the law). To sum up, the Prosecutor General and his subordinates are responsible for ensuring that the state administration (excluding the supreme authorities), the managements of state enterprises and co-operatives and other state institutions act in accordance with the demands of the political order and the interests of the current political leadership.

The law of 20 June 1985 formalized the status of prosecutors as state employees, subject to appointment. The law increased the prerogatives of the Prosecutor General who is now empowered formally to request that the Council of State issue a binding interpretation of legal provisions or that the Council of Ministers submit a bill to the Sejm. He can also request the Constitutional Tribunal to determine whether a specific law or other provisions are compatible with the PPR Constitution.

The Prosecutor's Office during martial law

The prosecution played a subsidiary role during martial law and in the subsequent years. Individual prosecutors were expected to carry out orders and guidelines received from those higher up. The military prosecutors played a more important role than their civilian counterparts since they were responsible for the more sensitive political cases, and thereby charted the course of penal policy. The prosecution's preventative functions were greatly expanded. This was evidenced for instance by the numerous 'warning talks' carried out by the prosecutors. In the period under discussion the prosecution was identified with two notorious practices: imprisonment without trial through unjustified extension of pre-trial detention and the hushing-up of crimes and other abuses of law committed by the police and prison authorities. The Prosecutor's supervision of investigations which were conducted by security officials was no more than perfunctory. Their basic task was to compile the act of indictment and defend it in the courtroom. In a statement issued on 26 September 1981 a group of pro-Solidarity reformist prosecutors had stated that 'in the activities of the Prosecutor General's Office it is political considerations that take precedence over the law and its observance'.[14] The accuracy of this opinion was confirmed in the period of martial law and its aftermath.

Abuse of temporary arrest

In the PPR it is not the court but the prosecutor's office which determines whether a citizen should be placed in pre-trial detention or temporary arrest, as it is known in PPR law. Although PPR citizens may be detained or arrested only in cases permitted by the law and may be incarcerated only if charged with a specific crime (Art. 87 of the PPR Constitution), these provisions are often violated. Although Art. 209 of the Code of Criminal Procedure stipulates that temporary arrest is to be used only as a preventative measure to ensure the proper course of the investigation, in practice it is all too often used as a repressive measure. According to a Supreme Court ruling of 11 October 1980, temporary arrest can be used only when three conditions are simultaneously met. In the first place, the available evidence must be sufficient to substantiate the suspicion that the suspect had indeed committed an offence. Secondly, only those suspects who are likely to go into hiding or incite others to perjury, who have previous convictions, or if the degree of social danger of the criminal act imputed to them is high (Art. 217.1 of the Code of Criminal Procedure) may be held. Thirdly, temporary arrest is inadmissible if the criminal act imputed to the suspect is punishable by a penalty of imprisonment not higher than one year (Art. 217.2). The exceptional nature of temporary arrest is emphasized further in Art. 218 which stipulates that, subject to exceptional considerations, temporary arrest ought to be discontinued in particular when further incarceration might seriously endanger the suspect's health or life or result in hardship for his immediate family.

These regulations are self-contradictory and abused. Temporary arrest for criminal acts deemed to have a high degree of social danger or committed by recidivists need not necessarily 'ensure the proper course of criminal proceedings'. Yet, it is a widespread practice for the prosecutor's office to incarcerate suspects before they are tried on the grounds of the 'high degree of social danger' of the offence imputed to them. In political cases temporary arrest is the norm. The measure is applied not preventatively, but repressively; not on the strength of the evidence already available but to enable the police to soften up the suspect and get enough evidence to have him convicted.

The Code of Criminal Procedure does not specify the length of time a suspect can be held under temporary arrest. On prosecutor's orders he can be held in an investigative prison for up to six months. These orders are renewable by the court on a continuous basis, with no limits set upon the amount of time a prisoner may be held without trial or even without a formal indictment. In political cases the investigation very seldom lasts less than six months. Cases of suspects who spend over one year in investigative prison before they are brought before the court are not uncommon. Their plight is often worse than that of sentenced prisoners who are usually granted certain privileges including visits, parcels and pastoral care.

According to Art. 90 of the Code of Criminal Procedure, the prosecutor's arrest order ought to be substantiated. In practice, however, instead of a detailed substantiation of the charges with reference to specific facts, the prosecutor's office usually quotes a suitable provision of the Code of Criminal Procedure. A suspect held under temporary arrest may lodge a complaint with the court. Since most prosecutor's arrest orders fail adequately to substantiate the charges, especially in political cases, the court usually finds it difficult to determine whether the prosecutor's decision was justified or not. The court, therefore, tends to disregard the suspect's complaint. In exceptional cases a suspect may be released from temporary arrest when the case against him proves to be too weak or if an amnesty covering his offence is declared. A suspect released from temporary arrest can claim compensation only if his arrest was 'unequivocally unjustified'. The very fact that it was simply unjustified or illegal does not suffice. This practically precludes any possibility of winning compensation. The prosecutor's office bears no consequences for the misuse of temporary arrest, not even financial ones.

The Police and the Prosecution

The use of temporary arrest in the PPR is contrary to Art. 9 and 14 of the International Covenant on Civil and Political Rights. Art. 9.3 of the Covenant, which says: 'It shall not be the general rule that persons awaiting trial shall be detained in custody ...', and Art. 14.3(c), which stipulate that 'everyone shall be entitled to be tried without undue delay' to determine the substance of the criminal charges against him, are systematically violated, especially in political cases. The prosecutor's office has also frequently violated Art. 218 of the PPR's own Code of Criminal Procedure by continuing to incarcerate people who are seriously ill.

The consequences of the abuse of temporary arrest are manifold. In the first place, the secret police officer who conducts an investigation has the opportunity to prolong the investigation in the hope that, in this way, he can soften up the suspect and procure evidence later on. The facts that the courts have no real control over the issue of arrest orders by the prosecutor and that defence lawyers are as a rule barred from access to the suspect highlight the inquisitorial character of pre-trial proceedings in the PPR. They are a far cry from Poland's pre-1939 system of justice where pre-trial detention was the sole prerogative of the court and pre-trial proceedings were supervised by an investigative judge.

As far as the suspect is concerned he has to reckon with the loss of employment. His work contract expires automatically after three months of incarceration, whereas the investigation usually lasts much longer. While he is under temporary arrest the suspect or his family receive only half of his salary. The other half is paid out only in the event of an acquittal or discontinuation of the proceedings. Experience shows, moreover, that the fact of pre-trial detention influences the judge and affects the severity of the sentence. The pressure on the judge is to legitimate *ex post facto* a lengthy pre-trial detention by pronouncing a sentence of imprisonment not lesser than the time already spent in prison.

The widespread use and misuse of pre-trial detention in the PPR enables the secret police and the prosecution authorities to determine the character of penal policy. The use of imprisonment without trial and the removal of the penalty of imprisonment from the court's exclusive jurisdiction give the authorities scope to act swiftly and on a large scale to forestall the possible outbreak of social unrest or pacify dissenting workers or other social groups. Temporary arrest is a specific form of prosecutor's summary justice, in anticipation of a sentence of guilty. Although a major reform in this respect is long overdue, it is consistently blocked by considerations of political expediency.

Investigation

Although the investigation is theoretically instituted and supervised by the prosecutor's office, the prosecutor's influence over its course, duration and termination is, in fact, often purely formal. The political police are free to interpret the penal provisions and evaluate whether a citizen's activity is legal or criminal. During the investigation the suspect is at the mercy of the investigative authorities; they not only question him and present him with charges but they also can, and usually do, deprive him of contacts with the outside world, including contacts with his lawyer. The suspect is to be isolated and kept in uncertainty as to his own fate as well as to the intentions of the investigative authorities. The only thing he knows is what he is charged with, but this too can be changed at any time. It is only when the suspect becomes a defendant that he is allowed access to the files in his case and contact with a defence lawyer.

The PPR's criminal procedure does not provide for an investigative judge, i.e. a professional judge whose task is not to hear cases and pass sentences but to supervise the investigation by examining the suspects, deciding on their pre-trial detention and the termination of the investigation. The PPR Code of Criminal Procedure provides for the fusion of the investigative and prosecuting functions, which are performed jointly by the prosecutor's office.

For the police the best evidence in political cases is the suspect's own self-incriminating testimony. To achieve this the whole investigation is geared to making him willing to talk and engaging him in conversation. Once he has got the suspect to talk, the investigative officer proceeds to reconstruct, on the basis of the suspect's testimony as well as the testimony of his co-suspects, the course of events in such a way as to corroborate the often preconceived scenario of the case.

Although, in the great majority of cases, the suspects talk not because they are forced to but, ultimately, of their own free will, some of them must be broken down first. Various forms of psychological pressure are applied on the suspect in order to persuade him that his activity was futile, that it was not worth feeling any loyalty towards the other suspects in the case, that it was in his own interest to talk in exchange for a light sentence or conditional discontinuation of the proceedings. The precise nature of these pressures depends on the investigative officer involved, the case as such, and the weak points of the suspect himself. The investigative authorities can make the conditions of temporary arrest bearable or more severe. A suspect can be deprived of his much-needed medicines, books and letters, he can be put into a noisy, cold or badly-lit cell. He may be forced to share his cell with criminals or homosexuals. A suspect unwilling to talk might be threatened with being discredited within his profession, eviction from his flat or sacking from his job. He might be told that his family would suffer if he refused to co-operate. During the investigation the investigative officer might create an atmosphere of manifest lawlessness. He might, for instance, say that the secret police would make sure he got a long sentence if he refused to testify. He might also suggest that the police knew all about his activities anyway. Finally, the well-tried 'argument' of the clenched fist is always at the ready. One of the most disturbing instances of brutality in the course of post-martial law police investigation was the case of 17 miners from Lubin-Polkowice who were charged with and sentenced for storing explosives and preparing and carrying out bomb assaults. At least five of the suspects were beaten on the soles and had plastic bags put over their heads until they almost suffocated.[15] As a result of a severe beating one of the suspects, Stanisław Zabielski, suffered spinal damage. He was sentenced on 21 November 1983 for participation in the activities of a terrorist group to five and a half years' imprisonment.

Suspects held under temporary arrest are under constant surveillance. They are watched and surrounded by eavesdroppers. They are spied on by experienced fellow-prisoners who, free from moral scruples, inform on them to the prison authorities in exchange for various benefits. A prison informer will try to elicit a suspect's trust, provoke conversations, offer to smuggle a letter out of prison. One notorious prison informer was a certain Zenon Celegrat, a convicted offender who was still kept in an investigative prison where he enjoyed various privileges five years after his conviction. For some time he shared a cell with Adam Michnik at the Rakowiecka investigative prison in Warsaw. At the same prison three women, Elżbieta Stobbe (the MRKS case), Marta Walter (the case of *Tygodnik Mazowsze)* and Anna Owczarska (Radio Solidarity) were persuaded by a cellmate, Barbara Pieczka, to write letters which she offered to smuggle out of prison. All the letters landed on the desk of the investigative officer.[16]

In Kraków another prisoner would try to pass on to others oral or written suggestions allegedly coming from three well-known defence lawyers engaged in political cases. The lawyers, Rozmarynowicz, Kosiński and Ostrowski, were supposed to have requested detailed information on the suspect's contacts, ostensibly in order to warn them. Even seemingly unimportant details from a suspect's private life may play a role in breaking him when passed on to the investigative authorities by an informer. They can for instance be presented as 'evidence' that the police had for a long time kept tabs on him and knew all about him.

The third stage of the investigation involves the compiling of investigative records in the case. It is a common practice not to include in the written record the questions of the investigating officers and reproduce the answers of the suspect in the form of a continuous story about the events in question, as if they amounted to a confession.

The suspects can be grouped and re-grouped, according to the changing notion of the investigation and the trial. This may involve new or additional charges. In the case of Jacek Osuch, who was arrested in December 1982 when a considerable number of copies of the underground publication *Wiadomości Bieżące* were found in his apartment, at first the investigative officers tried to portray him as a member of the publication's editorial team. Later it was decided to include him in the case against distributors of the underground publication. In May 1983 Osuch was sentenced to one year's imprisonment, suspended for three.[17]

The courts all too often validate *ex post facto* the inadmissible methods used by the investigative officers to elicit testimony from the suspect. Statements elicited by such methods are often the only evidence against the defendant and are the deciding factor in pronouncing him guilty. Even if the defendant draws the court's attention to the fact that his testimony had been obtained under duress, more often than not the court will uphold it as valid evidence, especially if it is corroborated by other witnesses or material evidence. As a rule, however, one single incriminating evidence against the accused suffices to convict him. During the trial before the Voivodship Court in Gdańsk, in May 1982, of five participants and organizers of the strike at the Lenin Shipyard one of the defendants, Regina Jung, refused to testify, stating that the investigative officers had extracted testimony from her by preventing her from taking medicines for her ulcers until the pain became unbearable. The court none the less upheld her testimony on the grounds that since she had testified only a few hours after her arrest her testimony must have been a spontaneous expression of the truth before she had had time to think up a different version. She was sentenced to three years' imprisonment and her testimony was also used to incriminate a co-defendant, Alojzy Szablewski.

The investigation is a trial of nerves and character. Many passed it admirably, refusing to testify, maintaining their silence during the interrogation sessions. They did not panic and waited with their explanations until the main trial. This proved to be the only worthwhile attitude to take. The fact that the police had evidence against the suspect did not necessarily imply that they were prepared to reveal its origin in the courtroom or that they could prove it. In some cases the police actually preferred to discontinue the proceedings despite convincing evidence rather than unmask a valuable secret informer, if he were the only witness.

Investigation into the death of Grzegorz Przemyk: A case study

The death on 14 May 1983 of a 19-year-old Warsaw schoolboy, Grzegorz Przemyk, as a result of injuries sustained during a beating at a police station shocked public opinion in Poland. Przemyk's funeral was the largest post-martial law demonstration, with some 50,000 people, mainly young people, participating.

On 12 May, Grzegorz Przemyk and four friends had gone to celebrate after successfully passing the first stage of the matriculation examination. They drank no more than one or two glasses of wine in a Warsaw wine bar. On their way home they were stopped, apparently without cause, by a police patrol which requested to see their identity papers. Grzegorz said that he did not have them on him and he was taken together with two of his friends Cezary Filozof and Jakub Kotański to the police station on Jezuicka Street. There, Grzegorz became involved in an argument over whether he was still obliged to carry his papers on him since martial law had been suspended. When one of the policemen raised his truncheon as if to hit him, Grzegorz grabbed at it. He was then overpowered by six policemen who held him while others beat him on the stomach. The scene was witnessed by Grzegorz's friend. The police called an ambulance and Grzegorz was carried into it. At the first aid centre on Hoża Street, Grzegorz was met by his mother who had been told of what had happened by Cezary Filozof. The doctor on duty stated that Grzegorz had 'symptoms of a psychological disorder' and recommended treatment in a psychiatric hospital but, on the insistence of his mother, he was allowed to return home. He was unconscious most of the time but told his mother what had happened. The next day Grzegorz's mother Barbara Sadowska called an emergency doctor, who declared that it was no more than a 'bellyache'. She then called another doctor who recommended that Grzegorz be taken immediately to a hospital, where he was operated on. The team of doctors found burst intestines, a ruptured peritoneum and other internal injuries. The patient never regained consciousness. According to the post-mortem, death was due to beating.[18]

The authorities' first reaction was to ignore the whole incident. The first official communiqué described the victim as having been drunk and aggressive. It made no mention of the visit to the police station and tried to suggest that force had had to be used by the ambulance orderlies to pacify Przemyk. The investigation was finally instituted on 19 May by the regional prosecutor's office. In July the case was transferred to the voivodship prosecutor's office. In September the authorities announced that the investigation had led to preliminary proceedings against two police officers, two ambulance orderlies and two doctors.

On 23 December 1983 the first act of indictment was compiled. It charged two police officers, Ireneusz Kościuk and Arkadiusz Denkiewicz, and two ambulancemen, Michał Wysocki and Jacek Szyzdek, with manslaughter and deliberate beating of the deceased (Art. 158.3 of the Penal Code). Two doctors, Paweł Willman and Bronisław Jasicki, were charged with failing to assist a person whose life was in danger (Art. 163.1 of the Penal Code).

The Police and the Prosecution

The trial scheduled to begin in early February was postponed 'in view of new evidence.' As was officially announced, one of the ambulance orderlies had admitted that he had injured Przemyk 'in a way that might have been fatal'. The two ambulance orderlies had been arrested on 20 December but not in connection with the Przemyk case (carrying a maximum penalty of 15 years' imprisonment) but in another of lesser gravity, involving the alleged beating of an ill patient whom they were transporting on 4 May 1983 (carrying a maximum penalty of three years' imprisonment).[19] It was clear that the investigating authorities did not want to arrest the two ambulance orderlies under charges of manslaughter since they would have had to arrest the two policemen alongside them. Still, it was important to arrest Wysocki and Szyzdek in order to frame them as the major perpetrators of the crime, to play one off against the other, and induce them to accuse one another in order to protect the policemen and put the investigation on a different course.

After Wysocki's much publicized admission that he might have inflicted the fatal injury on Grzegorz Przemyk the indictment was scrapped and the investigation was re-started. The prosecutor who had signed the indictment resigned in protest. To shift the blame onto the two orderlies it was found necessary to silence the legal representative of Mrs Sadowska, Maciej Bednarkiewicz. He was suddenly arrested on 11 January 1984 following a search in his apartment. Some of the papers relating to Grzegorz Przemyk's death were removed. Bednarkiewicz was officially arrested on charges of aiding a ZOMO deserter, bribing him and asking him to find witnesses who would testify that the police were entirely responsible for the beating inflicted on Przemyk. The alleged ZOMO deserter was supposed to have given himself up to the police, and confessed everything. He was pardoned under the July amnesty of 1983.

As implied by Władysław Siła-Nowicki in his open letter to General Jaruzelski, the ZOMO deserter was a police provocateur who had simply tried to frame Bednarkiewicz. Bednarkiewicz had, in fact, been suspicious of him from the start and had taken no interest in him whatsoever. Some five months before his arrest Bednarkiewicz was summoned to the MIA where he was played a tape with the alleged deserter's testimony. It was a warning to him not to probe the case too far or even to withdraw from it. Bednarkiewicz was never actually tried under the offences with which he was charged and he was released on 17 July 1984, one day after the official verdict in the Przemyk murder case was handed down.

Grzegorz Przemyk's mother would have no part in the trial. In a statement delivered at the opening session she stated that: 'A straightforward case, in which there exists clear evidence, has been transformed, through a skilful shift in proportions, the exaggeration of certain aspects and the hushing up of others, in other words, through manipulations, into a monstrous case in which there is no chance of a just sentence.'

The trial was based on a new indictment in which the charges against the two policemen were reduced to inflicting bodily injuries without linking these to Przemyk's death. The two ambulance orderlies were charged, as before, with beating resulting in death. Finally the two doctors were charged with unintentional negligence.

The trial itself was very much in the shadow of the two women prosecutors, Wiesława Bardonowa and Anna Jackowska. They cast doubts on the credibility of uncomfortable witnesses, amplified circumstantial evidence irrelevant to the case, shielded the policemen from detailed examination. The entire hearing was given an anti-opposition flavour. Still the trial showed up the methods of investigation for what they were when Wysocki retracted his previous confession that he had 'dealt Przemyk a blow which might have been fatal' and said that it had been obtained by coercion by a colonel in the MIA. During the trial it was also revealed that Wysocki had accused his colleague Szyzdek of beating Przemyk in revenge for the charges he had been told Szyzdek had made against him.

Still Wysocki and Szyzdek were sentenced to two and a half and two years' imprisonment, respectively, not for beating resulting in death as charged but for criminal negligence of a person under their care. Since the two policemen were acquitted and the doctors convicted of unintentional negligence were amnestied, the trial left unanswered the fundamental question of who was responsible for the beating that resulted in Przemyk's death.

The Police and the Prosecution

Investigation into the murder of Fr. Popiełuszko: A case study

Jerzy Popiełuszko, a vicar at St Stanisław's church in Warsaw, paid the supreme price for his faith in his spiritual mission to defend the truth. He identified himself with the disadvantaged and persecuted, spoke the language of the ordinary working people, resisted evil wherever he saw it. He challenged the legitimacy of Communist rule on moral grounds. He died the death of a martyr on 19 October 1984, murdered by three secret police officers, and his body was dumped in a reservoir.

The investigation was entrusted simultaneously to the MIA's Investigations Bureau and to an internal task force whose real purpose was to cover up the crime. In the event, it proved impossible to blame the murder on scapegoats, as in the Przemyk murder case, to save the image of the police by skilful manipulation. The abduction and murder of Fr. Popiełuszko left too many traces of secret police involvement and no suitable scapegoat. Fr. Popiełuszko was a nationally known figure and his murder resulted in a major crisis for the authorities, forcing them to reveal at least some of the abuses of law practised within the MIA.

While much has already been written about the abduction and murder of Fr. Popiełuszko and the subsequent trial of his murderers, the course of the investigation itself is relatively unknown.

Shortly after Fr. Popiełuszko was abducted at about 10.05 p.m., a receptionist at a workers' hostel in Przysiek telephoned the Toruń police. According to the duty officer, she said only that she had with her a man who claimed to have been abducted and escaped his captors. The man in question was Waldemar Chrostowski, Popiełuszko's driver, who had managed to escape his captors by jumping out of a fast-moving car. The ambulance arrived before the police, and Chrostowski asked to be taken to the nearest church. He was taken to the Toruń parish priest, Fr. Nowakowski, who, on hearing about the abduction of Fr. Popiełuszko, also telephoned the local police. Chrostowski was taken to the local casualty department. There a duty secret police officer must have alerted his superiors since within minutes of Chrostowski's arrival 18 other SB officers and a representative of the regional prosecutor's office appeared. They wanted to take

The Police and the Prosecution

Chrostowski away with them but the doctors objected. Chrostowski was interviewed for two hours and an investigation was officially instituted. He was then taken to the police HQ for questioning. At about 2 a.m. he was transferred to the MIA hospital next door to the police HQ and detained there 'for his own safety' until 23 October. Chrostowski was questioned in hospital by the prosecutor Stronikowski. The case was soon taken over by another prosecutor, Białowicz, the same man who only a few weeks earlier had discontinued the investigation into several mysterious abductions in the Toruń area. Although Chrostowski was not formally detained, his son, as well as Fr. Popiełuszko's lawyer, Edward Wende, and a doctor appointed to deal with the case by the Church hierarchy, Zofia Kuratowska, could not gain access to him.

Despite official claims that the investigating authorities were following up all possible leads, Fr. Jerzy Osiński from the Holy Martyrs' parish church in Bydgoszcz in which Fr. Popiełuszko had delivered his last sermon before setting out on his return journey to Warsaw, was not questioned until 21 October and only after he had indicated to the police his wish to give testimony in the case.

Several circumstances mentioned by independent sources point to the fact that the abduction of Fr. Popiełuszko may have been co-ordinated with the Toruń police. On the day preceding the abduction and murder Col. Marcinkowski, a former chief of the voivodship police in Toruń, unexpectedly spent a few hours in Przysiek where the abduction was staged. Why was an SB officer on duty at the casualty department in Toruń? Had the abductors telephoned the Toruń police to warn them about Chrostowski's escape? Why were the SB officers who went to speak to Fr. Nowakowski interested above all in whom he had told about the abduction and escape?[21]

The authorities reacted nervously. On 20 October, at 7 a.m. the Toruń voivodship police chief informed General Zenon Płatek, head of the fourth department of the MIA responsible for monitoring the Church, of the abduction. Płatek gave instructions to hold Chrostowski for further questioning and to seal off the area where Popiełuszko's car had been found, examine it for evidence and comb the surrounding woods. He did not seem seriously to consider the possibility that Popiełuszko had been murdered and worked on the assumption that he was hiding somewhere. This futile mobilization of manpower and resources looks, with hindsight, like an attempt to simulate action in order to gain time. It is indicative of the way the MIA functions that it was Płatek's department and not the Investigations Bureau, which formally prepares the prosecutor's brief in politically sensitive cases, that took charge of elucidating matters. Płatek later involved the Ministry's Investigations Bureau, but it was not at first concerned with the internal implications of the crime and one whole month was to elapse before Płatek himself was questioned.

On the morning of 20 October, the day after the murder, one of its perpetrators, SB Captain Grzegorz Piotrowski, returned the 'W' pass, which gave senior SB officials freedom of movement throughout the country and immunity from police road-checks, to the deputy director of the MIA's fourth department, Col. Adam Pietruszka. During the subsequent meeting called by General Płatek, Piotrowski said he knew nothing about the previous night's incident and that nobody from his department had been in Bydgoszcz the day before. Płatek distributed tasks and Piotrowski was entrusted with elucidating several aspects of the case such as checking up on Popiełuszko's alleged contacts with the US Embassy and discovering whether the whole affair was a provocation by the underground opposition to discredit the authorities.

After the meeting at Płatek's office, Pietruszka summoned Piotrowski and asked, according to Piotrowski, whether Popiełuszko could be 'retrieved'. Piotrowski said that this was no longer up to him. Pietruszka asked whether they had been seen by anyone or left any traces and he replied in the negative. Another perpetrator of the crime, Leszek Pękala, came to work and submitted a use of petrol report for the previous day, stating that he had been to Kraków.

In the afternoon, a special task force headed by Płatek was set up within the MIA to 'supervise and co-ordinate the operational and reconnaissance activities' of the different ministry departments involved in the case. Płatek co-opted his deputy Pietruszka to the task force. Płatek subsequently claimed that he had devoted most of his attention to the search for Popiełuszko while Pietruszka had looked after the internal affairs of the fourth department. The fact is that Pietruszka not only had access to the information but was also in a position to obstruct the investigation by withholding or misdirecting vital evidence. In a conversation with his two subordinates, Pękala and Chmielewski who had been involved with him in the murder, Piotrowski described Płatek's task force as consisting of 'reliable people'. He assured them that 'everyone who should have known [about the abduction and murder] had known beforehand about the operation and that 'they would be protected'.

At this stage the authorities decided to inform the public of the abduction. Płatek and his immediate superior, Deputy Minister, General Władysław Ciastoń, then drafted a communiqué for the press and television. In the evening they received the news from Bydgoszcz that a car with the number KZC 0243 had been seen on 19 October in the vicinity of the Holy Martyrs' Church in which Popiełuszko had delivered his last sermon. The delay in passing on this information was later blamed on the fact that the duty policeman had had the day off and it had been impossible to contact him earlier. What has still not been satisfactorily explained, however, is why the number WAB 6031, which had been noted down by the same traffic policeman, was not passed on to Warsaw at the same time but several hours later.

Some hours earlier Płatek had despatched two colonels from his department, Stanisław Luliński and Wacław Głowacki, to Bydgoszcz and Toruń respectively to get first-hand information. They noted the traffic policeman's report that on 19 October a light-coloured Fiat 125P with the registration number WAB 6031, had been seen in the vicinity of the Holy Martyrs' Church with three young men inside. This same car had been seen later with the registration number KZC 0243. That same evening Luliński and Głowacki telephoned Płatek at his home and reported what they had learned, including the information that the suspected car KZC 0243 had also been seen with the numbers WAB 6031. Luliński realized at the same time that this was the number of one of the fourth department's official cars, albeit he did not mention this detail in his report. Płatek subsequently claimed that he did not remember being told the actual number at that time, only the fact that a car with a Warsaw registration had been seen, and that at the same time he was talking over another duty phone and was under the influence of sleeping tablets which he had taken earlier. It was not until 8 December 1984, when the investigation was nearing its completion, that Płatek admitted that he may have been told the actual numbers.

The next morning Płatek saw a car with the number WAB 6031 standing in the ministry car park, and he asked the duty officer whether it belonged to his department. Like certain other ministry cars, however, this one had two sets of licence plates: the official ministry number WAE 938B and a civilian number WAB 6031, and it was listed under the former. Płatek instructed Pietruszka 'to do something about the car'. Pietruszka, for his part, told Piotrowski to change the licence plates, which he did, together with Chmielewski, in some woods near Warsaw. They changed the false civilian number WAB 6031 to the official MIA number WAE 938B. The car was then sent to the ministry's servicing department for repair.

In an attempt to cover up the crime a written report submitted by Głowacki and Luliński to General Płatek on their visit to Bydgoszcz and Toruń on 20 October was forged by Colonel Pietruszka. Instead of the registration number WAB 6031 a new number appeared: WAE 8031. Pietruszka then passed an order to Toruń police to seek out the car with this forged registration number. Luliński and Głowacki noted the forgery on their second visit to Toruń and Bydgoszcz but did not seem perturbed.

A campaign of misinformation was conducted by the perpetrators of crime aimed principally at misleading the Church, the public and the investigators as to Popiełuszko's whereabouts. An anonymous letter with a ransom demand was written and sent to one of the Warsaw auxiliary bishops. The Toruń police were given false clues about the wanted car.

On 22 October the Director of the Criminal and Inquiries Bureau of the Warsaw Police HQ Jabłoński informed General Płatek that the police in Bydgoszcz had established that the number plates WAB 6031 and KZC 0243 had been used on one and the same car and that the former number was one of those reserved for the ministry. Płatek, who knew that the registration number WAB 6031 was used by his department, requested Pietruszka's subordinates to write personal statements on their whereabouts on 19 October and went to see one of the Deputy Ministers of Internal Affairs, Władysław Ciastoń.

Piotrowski wrote that he had felt tired that day and decided to go mushroom-picking. He had taken the departmental car without permission. In the vicinity of Toruń he had learned from two hitchhikers that Popiełuszko was expected in Bydgoszcz and had driven there to see for himself. Pietruszka persuaded Piotrowski to make changes in his statement and then, together with Płatek, took it to Ciastoń. Although they must by now have been suspicious of Piotrowski, they let him go home.

Another important piece of evidence was a travel permit

which, according to MIA rules, was to be left at the ministry's transport department on completion of each official assignment. Piotrowski did not return his document until 22 October. He handed it to one of the ministry's drivers, Kaczorowski. The latter became suspicious when he noticed the date, 19 October, on the permit, went to Piotrowski's secretary, Barbara Story, to check Pietruszka's signature against some other document in the office. She excused herself by saying that she had no documents with Pietruszka's signature. Kaczorowski did not go to Pietruszka since he was afraid of him and consulted another MIA employee Colonel Maj, whom he trusted.

On 29 October Maj went to Płatek, who seemed surprised and decided to pass the permit to the Ministry's Investigations Bureau. It was this document that ultimately sealed the fate of Pietruszka, who was arrested on 2 November and of Płatek who was suspended.

Earlier on the morning of 23 October Piotrowski was summoned to the Minister of Internal Affairs, General Czesław Kiszczak, who asked him outright whether he had abducted Popiełuszko. When Piotrowski denied having done so, Kiszczak ordered that he be taken to the director of the Investigations Bureau, Colonel Pudysz. He was then officially detained. All the members of Piotrowski's department were then asked to account in writing for their actions on 19 October, including any contact they may have had with Piotrowski. The secretary Barbara Story and Zbigniew Stromecki, who had stood in for her a few minutes that day, both of whom had mentioned in their statements that on leaving the office Piotrowski had said that Pietruszka knew where he was, were told by Pietruszka, through Major Dróżdż who had collected the statements and brought them to him, to be more concise and cut out the passages mentioning his (Pietruszka's) name, which he had marked. Pękala and Chmielewski were singled out for further explanations and later detained. Story broke down and came to Płatek asking what she should do and he sent her to the Investigations Bureau for questioning.

It was on this day that the key witness Chrostowski was released from the MIA hospital in Toruń.

Pękala and Chmielewski were first to confess their parts in the crime. They revealed where Popiełuszko's body had been dumped and police divers retrieved it on 30 October. The body was taken to the Forensic Science Institute in Białystok. It was examined by Professor Maria Byrdy and Dr Tadeusz Jóźwik with Prof. Edmund Chruścielewski in attendance on behalf of the Episcopate. Byrdy and Jóźwik issued a preliminary post-mortem on 30 October in which they pronounced that death had occurred as a result of asphyxiation. A second post-mortem, described as 'the final expertise', was issued on 31 November. This stressed that 'the injuries sustained [by beating], the gagging with the aid of gauze and plaster, and the noose whose ends had been tied to the bent and bound feet constituted a combination of factors which led to death within a period of time that cannot be exactly defined'. A third, supplementary expertise was issued by Byrdy and Jóźwik on 15 February 1985, that is, when the trial was already under way. This stressed that asphyxiation had occurred above all as a result of the aspiration of foreign matter (blood and vomit) into the respiratory tract, as well as the gagging and general concussion. The intention of this third expertise was to put the blame squarely on the shoulders of Piotrowski, who had earlier expressed his relief that he had not caused the death of the priest on hearing the initial opinion that death was caused by asphyxiation, assuming that this had had nothing to do with the beating which he had administered.

A strange incident, apparently unconnected with the political implications of the case, occurred on 30 November when two officials from the MIA Investigations Bureau and their driver were killed in a head-on collision with a snow plough (sic!) on their way back to Warsaw.

Neither the investigation nor the trial revealed any traces of a high-level conspiracy to kill Fr. Popiełuszko in the MIA. What little was revealed was hushed up or ignored. In the course of the investigation, for instance, a police officer from the Warsaw Police HQ Józef Bączyński who, together with his superior Lt. Col. Leszek Wolski, had attended policy meetings at General Płatek's office on 25 September and 9 October stated that during the second of those meetings Piotrowski had said that there was pressure 'from a very high level' to take action against Popiełuszko. During the trial Bączyński said that he had misunderstood Piotrowski's words. In the course of the trial General Płatek referred to three kinds of pressures to which his department was subjected: from above, from below and from the side. The presiding judge did not allow the defence lawyer to question Płatek in detail on this score. Neither the investigation nor the trial were concerned with the prolonged harassment to

The Police and the Prosecution

which Fr. Popiełuszko had been subject prior to his abduction. The disturbing series of abductions in the Toruń area were also ignored.

The Toruń Voivodship Court which heard the case of Popiełuszko's murderers did not probe into the decision-making process at the MIA nor into its channels of command. It was never established which of the five deputy ministers had approved the actions of General Płatek. It is one of the unwritten rules within the ministry that all officers assigned to operational tasks assure themselves of higher-level protection in order not to become a scapegoat in case things go wrong.

The course of the investigation indicates that its purpose was to prevent the truth from coming to the surface. This was the purpose of the special task force headed by General Płatek.

The murderers themselves felt sure that they would not be held accountable. This explains why they behaved illogically, at times. They did not, for instance, feel perturbed when they saw the Bydgoszcz traffic policeman taking down their car registration number. They did not make any attempt to catch Chrostowski after his escape.

The investigation and the trial concentrated on the 'technical' aspects of the crime itself, disregarding its conceptual aspects. During the investigation Pękala quoted Piotrowski as saying that the decision to take action against Popiełuszko was of a political character. It was to be put into effect on three levels: by the Warsaw Police HQ (Wolski's department), the MIA's fourth department — officially — by Piotrowski's deputy Major Dróżdż and the same department — unofficially — by Piotrowski himself. This last action was to be a secret one. Wolski did not need to know about the unofficial mission; it would be a kind of 'conspiracy within a conspiracy'. Pękala had been under the impression that the operation against Fr. Popiełuszko was inspired by important state considerations. In the courtroom he withdrew this testimony. Chmielewski also testified under investigation that Piotrowski had told him that the action against Popiełuszko had been 'agreed', meaning that his superiors knew about it and approved it. He did not ask about any of the details because he had trusted his superior. In the course of the trial Piotrowski struck the pose of a 'perfectionist' who, frustrated at official inaction, had taken the law into his own hands. The court recognized Piotrowski's 'professional frustration' as one of the motives leading him to inspire and carry out the crime.

The Police and the Prosecution

The Provisional Co-ordinating Commission in a statement of 19 November 1984 stated that: 'Those who are in charge of the investigation and publishing its findings are those who bear the moral responsibility for this crime, for it is they who have created the situation of pervasive lawlessness that made possible the commission of such a crime. The purpose of the investigation is to limit the culpability for the murder to the immediate perpetrators of the deed, cover up any traces of higher level complicity and mislead the public through a campaign of misinformation.'

The assassination of Fr. Jerzy Popiełuszko was a manifestation of the terrorist nature of the Communist system. Piotrowski did no more than act on Lenin's dictum: 'We have never rejected terror on principle, nor can we do so. Terror is a form of military operation that may be usefully applied ... under certain conditions.' Fr. Popiełuszko was a victim of a system that will tolerate no questioning of its legitimacy.

* * *

These two cases of criminal investigation and trials of police murderers are unique. The public prosecutor, as a rule, ignores offences committed by both uniformed and secret policemen when these are brought to their attention by the public. The case of Fr. Tadeusz Zaleski described in Chapter VI/7 proves that it is dangerous to bring these cases to the attention of the prosecuting authorities or to conduct an 'independent investigation'. Defence lawyers are discouraged from taking up cases involving official violence. In the case of Bogdan Włosik, who was shot dead by the plainclothes police officer Andrzej Augustyn in Nowa Huta on 13 October 1982, the military district prosecutor's office recommended to the Chief Barristers' Council that 'explanatory proceedings be instituted' against Andrzej Rozmarynowicz, the legal representative of the family of the deceased. The prosecutor's office alleged that he had abused the freedom of speech in documents prepared on his client's behalf. The investigation against Augustyn was discontinued.

The formulae most frequently quoted as grounds for the discontinuation of proceedings against police officers who have perpetrated crimes of violence are 'inability to identify the offenders', 'lack of evidence', 'lack of legal characteristics of an offence', or 'low degree of social danger of the act imputed to the suspect'. Police officers are not only seldom investigated and tried, they are usually not even suspended from their duties. Even when a policeman is sentenced it is by no means certain that he will serve his sentence in full.

All too often it is the victims of police violence who are portrayed as its perpetrators. The courts are involved in covering up offences committed by 'officers of law and order' in as much as they refuse to overrule 'evidence' extracted under duress or sentence the victim instead of his oppressor. PPR citizens are deprived of real legal protection against police abuse and violence. Although, for the sake of appearances, a decision may be taken to investigate or even try individual cases of police brutality, the authorities are keen to preserve the image of the police as flawless. It would be a commonplace to say that they need the police to maintain their grip on society. They need the police as they are, i.e. above the law, since the authorities themselves are above the law, and the police are modelled on their own image.

Freedom under the law and the Law on the Minister of Internal Affairs

The Law on the Minister of Internal Affairs and his Subordinate Agencies of 14 July 1983 was prepared secretly and presented to the Sejm only one day before it was to be voted, without even a formal appearance of consultation and discussion. It can be described as the constitution of a police state. Passed only one week before the formal lifting of martial law, it gave the Minister of Internal Affairs sweeping prerogatives with regard to all aspects of citizens' lives, making him the most powerful man in the country next to the Chairman of the National Defence Committee, State Council Chairman and First PUWP Secretary, Wojciech Jaruzelski himself. As 'the supreme agency of the state administration with regard to the defence of state security and public order', his first duty is to 'stand guard over the people's rule of law'. This role takes precedence over the defence of civil rights and freedoms.

The Law of 14 July 1983 established a new administrative structure of the police force, which no longer corresponds to the territorial division of the country, and involves an intermediary level between the voivodship and town or district police station called the Regional Office of Internal Affairs. The whole organization of the police apparatus has been made more uniform and renamed.

Another important innovation of the law is that, in a departure from previous practices, it mentions the SB specifically, and extends its powers at the same time. The difference between the criminal and the political police has, thus, been blurred. In the course of their official duties both plainclothes and uniformed policemen have been granted wide prerogatives to interfere under the flimsiest pretext in the activities of individual citizens. They can for instance stop not only those who are actually disrupting public order and security but also those who threaten to disrupt it. They can search any person or vehicle on the grounds of mere 'suspicion' that a crime or even 'other action' directed against the security of the state or public order has been committed.

Art. 9 stipulates that, should the means of 'direct coercion' prove insufficient, firearms might be used. The Law lists no less than 11 cases in which the use of firearms is permitted. Among them is 'prevention or repulsion' of an attack on state buildings, other important public buildings or public property of considerable value. The law fails specifically to state that firearms are to be used only as a last resort.

The provisions of the law are couched in euphemistic language full of conditional clauses and generalizations. From the point of view of civil rights and freedoms it is unacceptable since it does not strike a balance between the interests of the state and individuals' rights. It is heavily biased in favour of 'state security' and 'public order', which are not even defined in it. Too much emphasis is placed not on 'preventive' but rather 'anticipatory' action by the police. The police apparatus not only fails to protect individuals' rights and freedoms but looms ominously large over the state administration, economic institutions and social life.

The Law on the MIA is typical of the post-martial law tendency to enshrine in law the extraordinary prerogatives granted to the 'forces of law and order' in the martial law regulations. The authorities were very careful to create formal appearances of legality and thus give an aura of respectability to the much discredited police force. These appearances fail to hide the fact that the act is the very antithesis of freedom under the law.

The Police and the Prosecution

Notes

1. Władysław Bieńkowski:*Socjologia Klęski*(Instytut Literacki,Paris, 1971).
2. Ibid.
3. On 17 June 1981, for instance, the Minister of Internal Affairs Kiszczak dismissed 580 policemen under Art. 65.2(7) on the Law of the Police of 31 January 1959 on the grounds that this was 'in the superior interest of the service'. In some cases whole units were disbanded, purged and re-grouped.
4. *Most* no. 2, 1985.
5. Ibid.
6. *Wall Street Journal*, 2 November 1984. Rurarz, who defected to the West shortly after martial law was declared, has over 36 years' experience as a government and party official. For 25 years he worked in association with military intelligence.
7. *Le Matin*, 9 December 1983.
8. *Die Welt*, 11 July 1983.
9. *Toruński Informator Solidarności* no. 87, 14 March 1984.
10. *Trybuna Ludu*, 14 May 1984.
11. *CDN* no. 70, 24 April 1984.
12. *Die Welt*'s conversation with a former SB officer Eligiusz Naszkowski, *Die Welt*, 25 May 1985.
13. *Rzeczpospolita*, 24 June 1986.
14. *Goniec Małopolski* no. 49, 15 October 1981.
15. Reuter, 30 November 1983 and *Tygodnik Mazowsze* no. 71, 8 December 1983.
16. *Tygodnik Mazowsze* no. 47, 14 April 1983.
17. *Serwis Informacyjny*, Wrocław, no. 62, 1 June 1983.
18. Facts as established by the Polish Primate's Aid Committee for Prisoners and Their Families which based its findings on the testimony of Przemyk's mother, his friends and the doctors who operated him.
19. The beating of this patient was an additional charge for which they were tried during the main trial concerning the death of Grzegorz Przemyk. Two other trials concerning medical personnel and ambulance orderlies were held at about the same time in an obvious attempt to transfer public odium from the police on to ambulance personnel.
20. *Tygodnik Mazowsze* no. 91, 7 June 1984.
21. *CDN — Głos Wolnego Robotnika* no. 100, 24 January 1985.

VIII

THE PRISON SYSTEM

Treatment and conditions

The prisons of People's Poland, like prisons throughout the world, formally serve as places of confinement and resocialization for convicted criminals. In practice, however, the PPR's prison system not only fails to facilitate the reform of the offender and his reintegration into society but all too often breaks the character of its inmates or demoralizes them, destroying their human dignity as well as their physical health, their spirits as well as their bodies. Prisoners are not only deprived of their liberty but often also denied proper medical care, subjected to degrading treatment, cut off from contact with their families and the outside world, and denied adequate opportunity for recreation, study and religious ministrations. Reform of the existing prison system has been repeatedly demanded and is long since overdue.

The PPR's prisons have always been shrouded in official secrecy. The first to raise the problem of prison conditions in the post-Stalinist period was Emil Morgiewicz, a one-time member of the independence-orientated Ruch movement and later of KOR. In a 1975 memorandum on prison conditions addressed to the Sejm he drew attention to the various forms of mistreatment of prisoners. It was not until the advent of Solidarity, with its demand for greater openness in public life, that the plight of prison inmates was brought into the open. Many of those who spent time in prison after the imposition of martial law subsequently related their experiences. Zofia Romaszewska described the atmosphere in block 3 of the Rakowiecka investigative prison as one of 'terror and encirclement'. A group of political prisoners from

The Prison System

Hrubieszów reported that this atmosphere 'successfully creates in the prisoner a feeling of complete helplessness with regard to everything he comes across in prison'.[1] To quote Andrzej Mielczanowski, a prisoner of Potulice and later of Braniewo, 'the features and characteristics of the prison system are aimed at transforming people into objects, taking away their identity, personality and dignity, and making them into automatons ready to follow all orders of the prison guards, no matter how nonsensical, or contrary to prison regulations. In practice, the prisoner is deprived of his most basic and inalienable rights'.[2] This denial of rights is not restricted to a specific group of prisoners — political or criminal — but is a universal feature of the prison system, an additional form of punishment on top of the loss of liberty.

The number of prisoners in the PPR is very high in relation to the population — approximately 250 per 100,000 inhabitants. It was as high as 372 per 100,000 just before the amnesty of 1974. This was the highest since de–Stalinization — when the number of prisoners fell to the all–time low of 35,876 — some 124,685. No official statistics were published between 1973 and 1980 when the number of prisoners was officially acknowledged to be 105, 509.[3] The exact number of prisoners in Poland is difficult to assess since official data exclude those held under temporary arrest, usually 20 to 30 per cent of the overall number of prisoners.

Although the PPR's prison can accommodate a maximum of 80,000–84,000 prisoners, the number of prisoners remained in excess of 100,000. The amnesties of 1983 and 1984 and the Special Procedure Act of 1986 did not reverse this trend. Following the passage of the Law on Special Criminal Liability and the amendments to the Penal Code on 10 May 1985 the number of prisoners rose again to some 89,112 (excluding those under temporary arrest) at the end of June 1986 just before the Special Procedure Act of July 1986. At the end of November 1986 the prison population stood at 76,460 (excluding those under temporary arrest).[4]

In the PPR the prison is a specific place of work. The 'Provisional Regulations on Imprisonment' of 25 January 1974 emphasize the educational aspect of prisoners' work. For convicted criminals work, which may be paid or unpaid, is mandatory. Unjustified absence from work or refusal to work result in disciplinary penalties. An inmate who persistently refuses to undertake work as directed can be isolated from others in a punishment cell and served reduced food rations every second day, for up to 14 days. Although there are in theory no political prisoners in the PPR, in practice, those who have been sentenced on political charges are exempted from compulsory work in accordance with Order no. 8 of 30 June 1978 issued by the Minister of Justice on the basis of ILO Convention no. 105, which was ratified by the PPR in 1958.

Living conditions in PPR prisons have been described as very poor. In her open letter to the Sejm on the situation in Warsaw's Mokotów investigative prison, Zofia Romaszewska wrote about the lack of basic privacy due to overcrowding and the disregard for basic hygiene. She drew attention to the lack of fresh air and exercise, as well as to the disgusting, inedible food.

Reports from other prisons spoke of poor lighting inside the cells (windows have blinds made of metal sheets); lack of running water, dirt, dampness and cold; exposure of healthy prisoners to contact with sick inmates (through the use of a common bath and washing of linen at the same time); under-cooked meals to which bromine was added; insufficient time for walks and exercise in the exercise yard; difficulties in obtaining the books of one's choice; and lack of communal forms of recreation apart from the occasional opportunity to watch specific, carefully selected television programmes.

All reports speak of the inadequacy of the medical service, described in one of them as: 'impersonal, careless, incompetent and, at times, even cruel.'[5] It is difficult to gain access to the prison doctor. Even when a prisoner manages to gain admittance, he is all too often not examined at all or receives only a cursory check-up. The treatment — if at all recommended — is often improper. This is caused by lack of experience and proper qualifications on the part of prison doctors, indifference to prisoners' fate, shortage of medicines or simply ill-will.[6] Only exceptionally are prisoners sent to hospitals. If they are sent to a prison hospital or one administered by the Ministry of Internal Affairs, as opposed to a civilian one, their length of stay may not depend on their progress but on the orders of the secret police.

Medical staff are dependent on the prison administration and are often subjected to pressures from the governor and his staff. Prison doctors are more employees of the prison administration than practitioners of Hippocrates' profession. Deliberately false or misleading diagnoses have been put forward in political trials. The case of Tadeusz Jandziszak illustrates this fact. He was one of the four KPN members charged with sedition in October 1980. When their case came to court in July 1981, his case was excluded for separate proceedings on account of his diabetes and he remained at liberty. In December 1981, when the KPN case was reopened before a military court, Jandziszak was arrested to be tried alongside his three colleagues. In June 1982 the military court requested a medical report on Jandziszak. A few days later a report containing false details of his blood pressure, weight, etc., was submitted to the court. When it was revealed that Jandziszak had not, in fact, been examined and the details of the report were fictitious, the military court called a commission of army doctors to examine Jandziszak. They recommended his immediate release. He was saved by the fact that, unlike the doctors from the Mokotów investigative prison who signed the fictitious report, the army doctors did not co-operate with the secret police.

The prison administration usually consult with the doctors after force has been used against a prisoner. The doctors are also expected to pronounce on whether an inmate can be punished with 'the hard bed' or 'the straps', whether he should be force-fed, whether he is to be allowed a special diet, or permitted to lie on his bed during the daytime (a privilege normally denied to ordinary prisoners).

The independent Social Health Service Commission, in a report released in the Spring of 1984, stated that 'deterioration in [prisoners'] health persists, to a greater or lesser degree, for a long time after their release from prison and, in some cases, illnesses and ailments contracted in prison may be permanent'.[7] In a sample of 348 political prisoners arrested and sentenced during martial law, released under the July 1983 amnesty and subsequently examined by independent doctors, the most common was skin mycosis (caused by fungi), primarily evident on the feet, a direct result of the poor sanitary and hygienic conditions within the prison. The majority of those examined were victims of at least one, if not several, types of food poisoning. About 80 per cent of all the prisoners examined had advanced periodontosis. 20 per cent of the former inmates developed purulent skin infections. Over 60 per cent complained of disorders of the alimentary tract. Duodenal ulcers were diagnosed in 60 cases and gastric somewhat less frequently. This was often accompanied by pronounced gastritis. Ulceration present before arrest worsened considerably during imprisonment. The same applied to coronary disease. Other problems diagnosed included: liver pathology (nine cases), persistent pains in bones and joints (in over 75 per cent of cases), various kidney diseases (in approximately 10 per cent of the prisoners examined), and frequent deterioration of eyesight as a result of prolonged incarceration in poorly-lit cells.

Political prisoners have frequently complained about the lack of privacy as an additional and unjustified form of punishment. The prison system in the PPR is organized in such a way as to expose the prisoner to the all-pervading presence of those who are in control. This takes many forms: the prisoner is never alone, not even when he is examined by a doctor; his letters are not only censored but their contents are used to degrade him (as when the prison officer responsible for reading prisoners' letters divulges their contents to the guards who torment the prisoner with details from his own letter), or to supplement a case against him (as when a letter containing remarks on the situation in the country or prison conditions is included in the files of the case). In certain prisons an inmate is allowed to write to no more than four members of his immediate family, and visits are held under supervision (a guard interferes in the conversation and can terminate it if he does not approve of its content). For fear of bugging the prisoner communicates with his lawyer by writing on tiny scraps of paper which are subsequently destroyed.

Prisoners are often subjected to body searches, for example before they are administered certain disciplinary punishments, when some form of unrest is suspected among the prisoners or simply for no reason at all. The list of personal items an inmate is allowed to have in his cell is very limited and he needs the prison governor's permission to wear his own underwear or to put on an additional sweater. Prisoners are invigilated not only by the guards but also by other inmates. This is true especially of investigative prisons. Hardened criminals often agree to spy on their fellows in exchange for the promise of an early release, or because they have been blackmailed or incited to do so with money or privileges. They try to get the other prisoners into conversation, offer them their contacts to smuggle out letters, etc. Prisoners are not free to talk to those held in other cells or establish contacts with them in any other way (through letters, gestures, knocking on the wall, etc.). During walks in the exercise yard inmates walk in a line or in pairs and a distance of approximately two metres must be maintained between each prisoner or each pair. In practice they can talk only in the common room where they are allowed to watch television once or twice a week.

The Prison System

The prisoner's dignity is abused in many ways. He is exposed to the uncouth language and aggressive behaviour of his guards; forced to wear prison-issue clothing; he is powerless to change cells if he cannot stand his cell mates; he has to submit to the everyday ritual of making beds, attending roll-calls, etc. His access to information is limited. His contacts with the outside world (family, papers, television) can be cut off at a moment's notice. He knows that he is dependent on the prison administration in the trivial matters of everyday life and this dependence is consistently brought home to him in order to humiliate him.

A system of rewards and punishment is designed to create a model prisoner. He is to be obedient, carry out all instructions regardless of whether they are reasonable or not, not concern himself with the fate of his fellow prisoners and not engage in any additional pursuits that might seem in the opinion of the prison authorities to make imprisonment less severe. The authorities will tolerate only those initiatives that are undertaken with their knowledge or co-operation, such as reporting on cell mates. The model prisoner is one who does not show solidarity with those of his fellows who are mistreated or punished. Political prisoners who demand a separate status are considered a particularly recalcitrant and rebellious element.[8]

The powers of individual prison governors are very broad. Indeed, more often than not it is the governor's discretion and not Ministry of Justice regulations that determines the true scope of prisoners' rights and duties. It is he who decides whether a prisoner can pursue his studies, how often he may be permitted to meet his family, whether he may be assigned different work. He decides if a prisoner's request is to be granted or whether his complaint is justified. Above all, the prison governor metes out punishments. The Provisional Regulations on Imprisonment of 1974 list no less than 13 different kinds of disciplinary punishments. They include deprivation of the right to purchase foodstuffs in the prison shop; deprivation of the right to send and receive private letters and food parcels; solitary confinement; up to 14 days of the 'hard bed' (a punishment cell in which the prisoner sleeps on bare boards with one or two blankets depending on the season, may not smoke, lacks basic sanitation and is served a reduced food ration for non-working inmates); the 'thermos' (a cell built within another cell, making it not only sound-proof but also lacking sufficient air for breathing); the 'tiger cell' (or a cell with extra bars inside); and 'the straps' (a table with straps used to immobilize prisoners who are considered dangerous).[9]

Prisoners are punished for trying to establish contact with people in other cells; singing; conversing during walks in the exercise yard; putting inscriptions, religious or other symbols on the cell walls or prison clothing; writing things that are deemed inadmissible by the prison authorities in personal correspondence; neglecting the daily routine as set out in prison regulations; and refusing to carry out the orders of the prison guards, to note only a few typical transgressions.

The grounds for punishment are set out in a written report presented to the prison governor by the officer responsible for the section of the prison to which the culprit belongs. The governor does not as a rule institute any proceedings to establish whether the punishment is justified and although the requirement that the culprit must have a chance to explain himself is formally observed, it does not, as a rule, affect the decision of the governor who tends automatically to endorse the prison officer's request for punishment. This practice allows for arbitrary punishment of prisoners without any grounds. In some cases the inadmissible principle of collective responsibility is applied. All the inmates in a given cell may be disciplinarily punished for a transgression which could well have been committed by only one of them. Sometimes a prisoner may be punished for no reason but simply in order to test his resolve and wear down his psychological resistance. In this way the system of punishments which was theoretically conceived as an 'educational' aid to the prisoner's resocialization is, in fact, used as an instrument of repression to break a prisoner and humiliate him. The aim is to make him beg for mercy, denounce his fellow prisoners and acknowledge his own abjection.

The system of rewards presents the other side of the coin. A prisoner is rewarded when he breaks the common front (by refusing to sign a joint petition or by discontinuing a hunger strike), or shows a lack of moral scruples (by reporting on his fellow prisoners). Rewards may also be granted in order to discredit one prisoner in the eyes of his fellows, to sow distrust and suspicion (the reasoning is: 'since he accepted a reward denied to others he must be on their side'). Political prisoners have on the whole presented a common front in boycotting rewards and manifesting their disapproval for punishment of their colleagues.

An elaborate system of punishments was used by the Barczewo prison authorities against nine Solidarity and KPN activists who were incarcerated there at the end of 1983. To stop their protests against bad prison conditions, mistreatment and denial of political prisoner status, they were for several months deprived of visits, letters from their families, participation in Holy Mass, daily walks, purchase of food, studying, group activities and warm clothes. As if all that were not enough, they were handcuffed with their hands behind their backs, sprayed with tear gas from a distance of barely a few centimetres, threatened with the use of force, isolated from each other, deprived of proper medical care, kept in the 'thermos' or 'tiger' punishment cells, forced into straight-jackets and gagged with adhesive tape. They were also bound with the special constraints used on those who are about to be hanged. They were incarcerated in block 1 which was reserved for dangerous criminals and those who were being treated for jaundice. They protested against having to use the same bath. It was only as a result of the adverse publicity that this particular practice was stopped.[10]

The inmates of PPR prisons, especially the political prisoners who are, as a rule, more determined to fight for their rights than the average criminal, have often been threatened with the use of force. This threat cannot be taken lightly since, as every prisoner knows, there is a special 'intervention squad' in all penal establishments. This squad, which is known as the 'atanda', can be either permanent or set up in an ad hoc fashion from among the prison guards in case of an emergency. The squad, which is equipped with long truncheons, shields and helmets, is sometimes used to intimidate the inmates. On 23 July 1982 such an 'intervention squad' was used to beat prisoners in the Gdańsk investigative prison in Kurkowa Street under the pretext of preventing a hunger strike. Two separate complaints were submitted by individual victims and each was dealt with by a different prosecutor. Marian Kulwikowski of the Gdańsk Regional Prosecutor's Office refused to institute preliminary proceedings, finding that the use of force against the prisoners had been justified,[11] while Paweł Ejsmont of the Naval Prosecutor's Office in Gdynia discontinued the investigation on the grounds that, although the use of the truncheon had not been fully justified, 'the degree of social danger [of the beating] was minimal'. The provisions of the Code of Criminal Procedure are such that there is, in fact, no appeal against the prosecutor's decision in such a case.

Organized use of force appears to be more frequent in

investigative prisons and police jails than in ordinary prisons, albeit beating as such is a widespread and established custom in all prisons, an abuse added on to the penalty of imprisonment, resulting in severe stress and a general brutalization of prison life. Isolated incidents of beating quite often go unreported since the prisoners do not want to risk further reprisals and do not, in any case, believe in the course of justice. One can distinguish three levels of prison violence: against one particular inmate, against all the inmates of a particular cell or against an entire wing. The most serious instances of organized violence against prisoners occurred during martial law in the internment prisons of Kwidzyń, Wierzchowo Pomorskie and Iława as well as in the Gdańsk investigative prison in Kurkowa Street and at the Kleczkowska Street prison in Wrocław. Since martial law was lifted there have been fewer reports of large-scale beating in prisons, but the potential for violence is none the less still there. Inmates who wish to protest against the prison conditions must take into account the possibility that force may be used to pacify them.[12]

Among those political prisoners singled out for particularly harsh treatment was Władysław Frasyniuk. In order to break him the prison authorities applied an elaborate system of punishment. His testicles were squeezed, he was beaten and his jailers poured cold water over him in December 1985. 'There is no punishment I did not have', he said.[13] In another disturbing case, Seweryn Jaworski was allegedly kept naked in a soundproof cement cell for 24 hours.[14]

The PPR prison authorities rarely resort to the Soviet practice of prolonging a prisoner's stay in prison by sentencing him on trumped up charges of improper behaviour. In at least four cases, however, political prisoners were accused of insulting a prison guard and brought to trial, but they did not actually serve the additional time since they left prisons as a result of the amnesties of July 1983 and 1984.[15]

Political prisoner status

The authorities refused to recognize Solidarity activists sentenced for their role in the strikes of December 1981 or pursuing independent trade union activity as constituting a separate category of prisoners. Apart from the fact that they did not have to work, political prisoners were subjected to the same restrictions as criminal prisoners. In some prisons both categories of prisoners were kept in mixed cells although, on the whole, the authorities were careful to separate them. This did not stop them from occasionally playing one group off against the other. In Hrubieszów prison the criminal prisoners were told that they got no amnesty in 1982 because of the political prisoners. Criminal prisoners were often used as informers, especially in the investigative prisons. Since political prisoners were not recognized as a separate category, they were not exempted from the re-socialization programme pursued by the prison authorities. This programme is theoretically aimed at making the criminal aware that what he did was morally blameworthy and instilling in him a desire to change his ways. In the case of those imprisoned on political grounds, their motives cannot be said to have been morally reprehensible or anti-social; on the contrary, what they did or propagated was dictated by their convictions. Society did not on the whole disapprove of their actions. It was the authorities who had made independent trade union activity a punishable offence. The actions (or political views) of those sentenced for defending Solidarity's right to exist were incompatible with the interests of the ruling elite but not with those of society as a whole. Therefore, re-education of this group of prisoners could not be anything other than ideological indoctrination and all attempts at such brainwashing were resisted by the political prisoners as an additional form of repression.

This re-socialization of the political prisoner took several different forms, the basic one being warning talks. These were conducted by the education officers, block governors or other employees of the prison service. The arguments put forward tried to discredit Solidarity and its leaders. Occasionally, an argument smacking of 'political realism' would be offered, e.g. 'one had to adjust to the realities since there was no place for Solidarity in Poland'.[16] Some political prisoners were offered freedom and even a chance to leave the country in exchange for co-operation with the police or counter espionage[17] (providing a valuable insight into the links between the prison service and the secret police). In some prisons special programmes slandering Solidarity were broadcast over the internal radio network. In Kielce prison the inmates were compelled to watch the daily television news bulletin which was also recorded and re-broadcast over the internal radio network.

The Prison System

The political prisoners of martial law were predominantly workers with a small group of intellectuals who acted as advisers to Solidarity, as well as students. The experience of prison was unknown to most of them and they found the prison ritual imposed upon them to be irritating, humiliating and pointless. They strove to change it to preserve their personal dignity. In particular, they demanded that they be kept apart from the criminal prisoners, and exempted from re-socialization, as well as from some of the routine duties stipulated under the Provisional Regulations on Imprisonment (such as making beds in the strictly prescribed manner, standing to attention when speaking to a guard, attending roll-calls, not lying on beds at times other than the prescribed 1.5 hours a day). They also demanded new rights, such as the right to unlimited correspondence, not restricted to family members alone; visits at least twice a month instead of once a month from people other than relatives and without surveillance; the right to receive books and papers from outside the prison; parcels at least twice a month instead of once a month; longer exercise periods with the opportunity to talk freely; unrestricted access to religious practices; open cells; adequate medical supervision; the right to use private clothing; more contact with the plenipotentiary judge; and the right to participate in group self-education and cultural activities.[18]

As part of their campaign to win better treatment the political prisoners challenged the prison authorities' resolve in enforcing the Provisional Regulations and refused to comply with some of their provisions. They would undertake protest action in support of a punished colleague. When Father Sylwester Zych was punished with the 'hard bed' and moved to an isolation cell his cell mates at the Braniewo prison refused to sleep on their mattresses and placed them outside their cell.[19] When force was used against Władysław Frasyniuk in Łęczyca prison in August 1983 in order to make him leave his cell, his cell mates rallied to his defence and were also beaten. Frasyniuk was punished with 14 days' 'hard bed'. His cell mates began a hunger strike in solidarity with Frasyniuk, and as a result his punishment was suspended by the prison governor. The political prisoners also initiated a campaign of letter-writing to the authorities, public opinion at home, international organizations and the Polish Episcopate. They continued to demonstrate their unbroken spirit by singing together or by making symbolic ornaments with whatever materials were to hand. If all else failed, they would stage hunger strikes.

The Prison System

The prisoners at Hrubieszów, Potulice and Łęczyca, who were evidently more persistent than those in other penal establishments, won considerable improvements. In Hrubieszów, for instance, the political prisoners were, as of August 1982, allowed to possess their own books, listen to radio news twice daily and to the Sunday Mass broadcasts; they were allowed an additional family visit once a month, to write and receive letters without restrictions, pursue studies, watch television after 8 p.m., take to their cells any food parcels they had been given during a family visit, and lie on their beds in the afternoon. The prison authorities promised, moreover, to improve the standard of medical care. In Łęczyca the political prisoners won the right to longer exercise periods and an additional weekly bath. All these and other concessions were, however, only of a transitory nature, and were not formalized in a special political prisoner status that would have stipulated the rights of such prisoners under the provisions of law. These concessions were forced only on individual prison authorities and did not apply universally. To quote the Solidarity Chairman from Łódź, Andrzej Słowik, who was incarcerated in Barczewo, 'The prisoner's worst enemy is his fear of standing up for his rights'.[20] Regulations are interpreted very loosely and it is up to the individual prison governor to decide whether to apply the regulations to the letter in order to break the prisoners' spirit or whether to bend the rules in order to keep his prisoners quiet.

After the amnesty of July 1983 the number of political prisoners in Poland decreased. Those who were not amnestied found that conditions became generally worse. This led to hunger strikes in several prisons. The five political prisoners in Barczewo refused food for 18 days (13 September–1 October 1983). The concessions that had been won there before the amnesty were retracted. The new prison governor insisted on stricter discipline. The remaining prisoners tried to defend their hard-won concessions by undertaking a rotational hunger strike with each prisoner fasting every fourth day, but even this failed to move the new governor. Political prisoners transferred from Potulice and other prisons where they had won concessions found, on their arrival at Braniewo, that they were again subject to normal prison regulations only stricter, with more body and cell searches, punitive roll-calls and disciplinary punishments such as withdrawal of family visits, correspondence and canteen privileges. After a hunger strike lasting from 6–14 October 1983, the prison governor withdrew punishments that had been the direct cause of the protest and gave assurances that he would not punish the political prisoners for failing to observe prison regulations.

The hunger strike is the most dramatic form of struggle for political prisoner status. It involves possible damage to the prisoner's health and serious mental stress, made even worse by force-feeding of the prisoner through a tube forced down his throat. One of the hunger strikers Wieńczysław Nowacki, an activist of Rural Solidarity, described the dilemma of the hunger striker: 'I felt the authorities were trying to break me. I felt completely alone and walking a tightrope, with the authorities risking my death and I myself risking a breakdown.'[21] Still, for many this form of protest made profound sense. It was not only a means of fighting for political prisoner status but also the only form of self-defence against mistreatment as well as the only way of reasserting their own dignity.

The public were undoubtedly sympathetic to the cause of political prisoners, and were ready to offer charitable aid and demand their release. There was initially some confusion, however, as to the issue of political prisoner status. Some of the lawyers close to the opposition argued that martial law was an abnormal situation and the only way out of it was to abrogate all the provisions introduced on 13 December 1981. All attempts to persuade the authorities to create political prisoner status — they argued — would have the effect of consolidating the existing abnormality. Other legal experts argued, on the other hand, that there was no discrepancy between the struggle for political prisoner status and refusal to accept the provisions of martial law, and that a formal status for political prisoners would significantly improve their conditions of imprisonment.[22]

This dispute faded into insignificance with the gradual institutionalization of martial law and growing public concern about the conditions prevailing in PPR prisons. The underground press spearheaded the campaign for recognition of political prisoner status, while lawyers (judges, scholars, barristers) and the prisoners themselves joined in by writing letters, petitions and appeals to the authorities. In one such appeal addressed to the Sejm and the Minister of Justice 111 signatories, including 40 fellows and professors of law, said that treating criminal and political prisoners alike offended the dignity of political prisoners and violated Art. 7 of the International Covenant on Civil and Political Rights. They demanded that the Minister of Justice issue separate provisions concerning this category of prisoners, exempting them from re-socialization programmes and stipulating that they should be kept in separate cells.[23]

The proposals put forward by the Scientific Council of Warsaw University's Institute of Criminal Law during a session held on 25 October 1982 in Warsaw went even further. The Council proposed that political offences (stipulated in Chapters XIX and XXXVI of the Penal Code) should not be tried under summary procedure or before a military court; that a special procedure be set up to establish whether a prisoner merited political prisoner status; that no political trial might be held without the obligatory participation of a defence lawyer; that the conditions attendant on political prisoner status be defined and that they should include separate cells, exemption from re-socialization programmes, the right to pursue studies and maintain wider contacts with the outside world; and that the Penitentiary Association set up during the Solidarity period to provide aid for prisoners and their families and subsequently suspended and disbanded, be allowed to resume its activities.[24]

The authorities' response was predictably negative. Apart from exempting political prisoners from work and separating them from the criminal prisoners, they offered concessions only in those rare instances in which the prisoners succeeded in winning them themselves. Concessions were to be an exception and not the prisoners' right. New prisoners would have to start the struggle afresh. The reasons for this intransigent policy were three-fold: ideological, legal and practical. By recognizing political prisoner status the Communists would have had to recognize that the opposition had certain rights (if not to pursue open activity then, at least, to be treated in a privileged manner while in prison). Since, however, the Communists lack moral and legal legitimacy, they are keen to maintain a fiction of mass popular support and, far from being granted certain rights, the opposition must, according to the Leninist dogma, be eliminated. Secondly, the legal institution of political prisoner status would have shown up the political context of the law and criminal proceedings, something the authorities, maintaining a democratic façade, have always been anxious to avoid. Finally, the authorities' reluctance to grant a separate status to political prisoners can also be explained by the practical consideration that they would have had to reckon with unrest among the criminal prisoners who would have demanded improvement of their conditions as well. As a result, the authorities' approach was to turn a deaf ear to public demands and to present the whole issue as insignificant. This also explains the difficulty in ascertaining the real number of political prisoners. It is a mark of the cynicism of the regime that its press spokesman Jerzy Urban regularly reported (however underestimated his figures may have been) how many prisoners were being held for 'politically motivated offences'.

Zbigniew Romaszewski rightly observed that it is impossible to separate the struggle for the rights of political prisoners from the more general issue of humanization of the prisons in general and the re-socialization programme in particular.[25] The primary fault lies, of course, not in the fact that the regime denies a separate status to its imprisoned opponents, but in the fact that it imprisons them in the first place. It is the existing laws that must bear the major responsibility for the existence of political prisoners, since they do not tolerate independent civic activity and enable the authorities to prosecute people for their convictions.

The amnesties of 1983 and 1984

The problem of political prisoners was a direct result of Jaruzelski's repressive policies. The steady growth in their number contradicted the authorities' claims that the situation was returning to normal and that the people had on the whole accepted the rigours imposed by martial law. Political prisoners were a constant reminder of the illegal and repressive nature of martial law. As time passed they became the embarrassing legacy of martial law. Equally embarrassing was the persistence of the underground Solidarity structures and other independent initiatives. The authorities, therefore, sought a formula that would both neutralize public opinion at home and abroad by satisfying demands for the release of political prisoners and put an end to underground activity by offering magnanimously to let off with a warning those who gave themselves up.

The two amnesties of July 1983 and July 1984 were practical expressions of this formula. They had much in common, in particular their conditional character, i.e. the prisoner's slate was not wiped clean and he was only released on the condition that he did not commit a similar offence within the next two and a half years. Whoever did so would not only risk new proceedings

The Prison System

but would also have to serve the remainder of his original sentence. This made the amnesty seem more like parole. The intention was to buy abstention from independent political and trade union activity in exchange for release from prison. Neither of the two amnesties was full. Both were limited in two important aspects. First, neither offered a full pardon for offenders (except those convicted of petty offences). Secondly, neither included all the political prisoners. The 1983 amnesty excluded those sentenced for or charged with sedition and the 1984 amnesty excluded those charged with treason. In both cases by manipulating charges, the authorities retained considerable scope for manoeuvre and could exclude certain prisoners from the terms of the amnesty as, indeed, happened in the case of the underground Solidarity activist Bogdan Lis. He was arrested in August 1984 and charged with treason. In this way he could not benefit from the amnesty of July 1984. As a result of public pressure at home and abroad the charges against Lis were modified. He was no longer charged with treason but with sedition, thus qualifying for release under the terms of the 1984 amnesty.

Both amnesties were compulsory, i.e. a suspect or a prisoner was obliged to accept it as such and forego the possibility of other proceedings that might have helped him to prove his innocence (cf. the Kwidzyń case, the KOR trial). The amnesties were also applied to suspects held under temporary arrest (in some cases extending over a period of several months) who had not been proven guilty but only presumed to be guilty (by virtue of the amnesty) of the charges with which they had been presented. This clearly contradicted Art. 14.2 of the International Covenant on Civil and Political Rights stipulating that 'Everyone charged with a criminal offence shall have the right to be presumed innocent until proved guilty according to law'. In this respect both the amnesties offered the authorities an opportunity to cover up the widespread use of temporary arrest as a de facto form of imprisonment without trial.

The two amnesties also included provisions for underground activists. They covered political offences that had 'not yet been revealed or tried', i.e. supposedly committed by those Solidarity activists who chose to remain in hiding seeing little or no opportunity for themselves to act openly, those who feared repressions, those who were active in the underground but had not gone into hiding, and those who had decided to remain abroad following the introduction of martial law. No proceedings would be taken against such people provided that they reported voluntarily to the authorities and signed a statement renouncing their activity and revealing its nature.[26] The amnesty of July 1984 was more restrictive in that those deemed to have engaged in anti-state conspiracy and related offences were required to reveal all relevant circumstances pertaining to their activity, as well as handing over all the equipment and other materials used in connection with it. This also applied to the underground Solidarity leadership. In the event only two prominent underground activists, Janas and Szumiejko, came out of hiding, although they revealed nothing. The rest of the Provisional Co-ordinating Commission and the regional leaders chose to stay underground, demonstrating that they stood by their values, continued to reject martial law and its consequences and that the struggle for free trade unions would go on despite the inevitable setbacks.

In fact, the amnesties of 1983 and 1984 offered the underground little choice. They were more an ultimatum than a gesture of good will and conciliation. The Provisional Co-ordinating Commission in a statement dated 3 July 1983 rejected the post-martial law status quo: 'The lifting of martial law, without repealing all the legislation that renders impossible any independent initiative or social activity, would be simply an empty gesture devoid of political significance'.

A cynical side-effect of the 1983 amnesty was the release under its provisions of police officials sentenced for having abused their powers in pacifying strikes and other protest actions. It also had a grotesque postscript in February 1985, when the infamous Maciej Szczepański, who was serving a sentence for embezzlement and corruption, was released on the strength of its provisions.

Table 2 gives a compact overview of the official numbers of those who were released from detention as a result of individual pardons and the two amnesties.[27]

Table 2

	Number of releases		
	Serving sentences of imprisonment	Held under 'temporary arrest'	Voluntarily admitted unrevealed or untried political offences
Individual pardons	894	—	—
Amnesty of 21 July 1983	730 released 130 had their sentences reduced by half	1,764	1,132
Amnesty of 21 July 1984	635	1,152	405
Total	2,259	2,826	1,537

These figures show that over 5,000 people were arrested, and/or tried and sentenced for political offences during the first two stages of normalization (from 13 December 1981 to 21 July 1984), and that the major repressive measure was in fact, not the political trial but imprisonment without trial. This practice violated the provisions of the International Covenant on Civil and Political Rights which in its Art. 9.4 stipulates: 'Anyone who is deprived of his liberty by arrest or detention shall be entitled to take proceedings before a court, in order that that court may decide without delay on the lawfulness of his detention and order his release if the detention is not lawful.' Since the authorities had no intention of changing their policies or acknowledging the will of the people, the two amnesties could not and did not solve the problem of political prisoners. They were forced on the authorities by social pressure, the attitude of the Church hierarchy and international opinion. The authorities would undoubtedly have preferred to have done away with the issue of political prisoners through the application of the procedure of individual pardons instituted in December 1982 with the suspension of martial law, since this required a sentenced political prisoner to repent and ask for pardon himself and was, moreover, less conspicuous since the prisoners were released in a small trickle and not en masse. The amnesties remitted guilt which, in the overwhelming majority of cases, had not been proved. To quote Karol Modzelewski, one of the group of 'eleven hostages', released in July 1984: 'The amnesty, behind its façade of humanism, conceals the lawlessness of keeping people imprisoned for two years under false charges'.[28]

The Special Procedure Act of 17 July 1986

The Special Procedure Act of July 1986 was not, strictly speaking, an amnesty. It was, according to its full name, 'special procedure with regard to the perpetrators of certain offences'. The main characteristic of the Act was that its provisions could but did not have to be applied and that it gave the authorities very wide discretionary powers to decide whom to release and on what conditions. Major political offences stipulated under Chapter XIX of the Penal Code, as well as Arts. 276 (participation in a criminal association) and 278 (participation in a secret or delegalized association) of the Penal Code were excluded. With regard to Solidarity activists in hiding the decision not to institute or to discontinue proceedings was made conditional on their 'disclosure of all essential circumstances of their activities and handing over the equipment with which they had committed their offence ...'

The PPR authorities decided none the less to take advantage of one of the provisions of the Act which empowered the Supreme Court, acting on the request of the Prosecutor General, to release political prisoners accused of or sentenced for other offences, including serious political offences. They released 225 political prisoners, and discontinued proceedings against 278 opposition activists. Some 575 underground activists were said to have turned themselves in to the police.

The 1986 Special Procedure Act also had a twist to it: three of the four secret police officers convicted in the Popiełuszko murder trial had their prison terms decreased.

* * *

The Prison System

A New Penal Policy

Although amnesties became an established part of the post-martial law cycle, the release of the majority of political prisoners on the strength of the Special Procedure Act of July 1986 proved to be more than just another exercise in the annual filling and emptying of prisons. It marked the end of the post-martial law chapter and the beginning of a new phase in societal relations: one of uneasy coexistence between the Communist authorities and the opposition, with the former forced unofficially to tolerate a degree of de facto pluralism and the latter forced to regroup and rethink their tactics as their room for maneouvre was increasingly circumscribed.

A new penal policy, reflected in the law of 24 October 1986, stressed fiscal penalties in preference to imprisonment, suggesting that — for the time being, at least — the authorities would attempt to contain the opposition with recourse to petty offences tribunals, administrative controls and invisible means of repression. This new penal policy, which the authorities somewhat incorrectly call a 'depenalisation', has been officially presented as evidence of progressive internal stability and liberalisation. The chairman of a newly established Solidarity Commission monitoring the legal system and its abuse, Zbigniew Romaszewski, has, on the contrary, spoken of the 'complete degradation of the legal system'[29].

In practice, the policy means that personal property is being confiscated as a reprisal against independent activity. The petty offences tribunals, sitting under accelerated procedure, confiscate cars and other personal effects without any legal grounds, without a fair hearing, on the basis of a policeman's whim and with no appeal. The new penal policy is clearly aimed at sapping the opposition's financial resources and reducing the number of people willing to support unofficial initiatives.

Since the law of 24 October 1986 did not annul the previously existing penal provisions but only gave the prosecuting authorities greater flexibility in dealing with independent activities, it is not the law itself that has changed but only the current official policy. As long as there is a lack of legal and political solutions that would preclude the political discrimination of those who hold views differing from the official ones and who wish to express them and act on them, the existence of a large contingent of political prisoners remains a potential threat in the PPR.

The Prison System

Notes

1. This report of some 150 pages was prepared by a group of 28 prisoners in mid-1983. It is henceforth referred to as the Hrubieszów Report.
2. *Obraz* no. 6, Szczecin, October 1983.
3. Andrzej W. Małachowski, *Przegląd Tygodniowy*, 11 January 1987.
4. Ibid. and the Polish Helsinki Committee's Report no.4: 'Human and Civil Rights in the PPR', September 1984 — February 1985.
5. *Zeszyty Niezależnej Myśli Lekarskiej*, no. 2, December 1984. An issue commemorating Father Jerzy Popiełuszko, published by the independent Health Service Commission.
6. Ibid.
7. *Praworządność* no. 2, July 1984.
8. Cf. the Hrubieszów Report.
9. It has been known for prisoners to have been beaten as they were being strapped in and the straps to have been fastened so tightly over arms, legs and chest that the blood circulation was restricted. Several hours of such immobilization makes the prisoner unable to walk unaided for at least two hours after he is untied. Prolonged restriction of the blood circulation can cause permanent damage to arms and legs. There is no record of this form of punishment having been used specifically against political prisoners.
10. Details were leaked in messages smuggled out of the prison by two KPN members Tadeusz Stański and Romuald Szeremietiew and published in *Zeszyty Niezależnej Myśli Lekarskiej* no. 2 and *Niepodległość* (pismo KAB) published by the KPN group in Kraków, no. 3, 15 March 1984, respectively, as well as in a letter of 16 April 1984 signed by six of the prisoners addressed to General Jaruzelski (UPI, Warsaw, 27 April 1984).
11. Unpublished. Kulwikowski was dealing with a request from one of the victims, Antoni Grabarczyk, that those responsible for the beating be prosecuted.
12. At the Bydgoszcz investigative prison, for instance, force was used by the officers of the special anti-riot squad ('atanda') against prisoners who had damaged window blinds (10–12 July 1984). The protest was sparked off by the installation of special window reinforcements which blocked the circulation of air. These reinforcements had been installed to make it impossible for inmates to communicate through the windows. Cf. *Tygodnik Mazowsze* no. 89, 20 September 1984.
13. *Chicago Tribune*, 30 September 1986.
14. UPI, Warsaw, 11 September 1986.
15. They were A. Michalak (Łowicz internment prison), Zygmunt Berdychowski (Hrubieszów prison), Władysław Frasyniuk (Barczewo), Andrzej Słowik (Barczewo). Using offensive language towards prison officers was the most frequent charge.
16. The Hrubieszów Report.
17. Ibid.

The Prison System

18. Andrzej Mielczanowski in *Obraz* no. 6, October 1983.
19. *Tygodnik Mazowsze* no. 71, 8 December 1983.
20. *Tygodnik Mazowsze* no. 67, 31 October 1983.
21. *Washington Post*, 7 March 1984.
22. 'The Second Five Months of Martial Law in the Małopolska Region', Kraków, November 1982.
23. *Tygodnik Mazowsze* no. 33, 10 November 1982.
24. *Państwo i Prawo*, February 1983.
25. *Praworządność* no. 4, November 1984.
26. Such conditions were unacceptable to most underground Solidarity activists who neither considered their activity illegal nor were prepared to inform the police about it. Those wishing to come out of hiding as a rule simply returned home and waited for the police to come to them instead of reporting directly to the police. They were usually taken for questioning to the police station where they refused to sign any statements, although, for propaganda purposes, they were still declared to have 'benefited from the amnesty'.
27. These data are based on Radio Warsaw of 13 July 1983 and 24 August 1984, as well as *Rzeczpospolita* of 25 January 1984 and 28 February 1985.
28. *Praworządność* no. 3, August 1984.
29. *Washington Post*, 5 February 1987.

IX

FREEDOM UNDER THE PPR LAW

Martial law was a re-conquest of civil society by the totalitarian, one-party state. Political trials were an important element of the politically motivated penal repression that formed the backbone of martial law and survived as its legacy. The role of these trials was to protect an insovereign state from its citizens who wished to live in freedom and dignity in accordance with their national traditions. In the Soviet model of Communism imposed upon the Soviet Union's East European dependencies, the state is deprived of its sovereignty and the citizens of their rights. The Communist party, although wielding a monopoly of power and controlling all forms of participation in public life, is insovereign *vis-à-vis* society, since its right to rule has never been acknowledged by democratic means. It is also insovereign with regard to the Kremlin by virtue of the limits imposed upon it by the 'Brezhnev doctrine'.

The system imposed on the Poles was imported from the Soviet Union and its basic role was to guarantee Soviet domination in 'the Polish corridor'. It had no roots in Polish history and the crises that have repeatedly shaken it show it to be fundamentally flawed. Its prime flaw is its unrepresentativeness: society is deprived of any influence over decision-making and the party is not accountable to society. The party aspires to control all aspects of political, economic and social life. The party elite is a collective owner of the state, the economy and the law. Its 'leading role', an euphemism for domination, extends to the army, the factories and the courts.

In Communist doctrine the state is an instrument of coercion ensuring the domination of one social class over the others. In the practice of Soviet-style Communism one of the ways in which this coercion is exercised is through the courts. In such a system the judge can be neither impartial nor apolitical. He is appointed to protect the interests of the 'working class' which are identified with the interests of its avant garde, i.e. the party or, more precisely, the ruling elite which, in the case of the PPR, had been installed to serve Soviet interests. These doctrinal and political considerations have resulted in the sovietization of the PPR law.

Law in the PPR is not, as in the West, a contract binding on both the rulers and the ruled; it is one of the many channels through which the ruling elite communicate their decisions to the people. 'The owner of the law' is not bound by its provisions. The ruling elite in a Communist state use the law as their tool in order to mould society to their own liking.

Immediately after the Communists took power in Poland they passed laws, usually in the form of decrees, to re-structure society, destroy economically 'the exploiting classes' and silence the political opponents of the regime. Although some of the pre-war legislation was preserved, the bulk of it was revised to reflect the new conditions. In particular, the concept of 'social danger' was introduced as a criterion determining the substantive content of an offence; the protection of the 'people's state' from real and putative enemies became a priority; the severity of punishments increased, especially for those offenders whose acts were considered to involve 'a high degree of social danger' at a time when the new political order was being constructed; and the scope of penalization was broadened, leaving little room for independent social activity. These Stalinist laws provided a model for all subsequent Communist regimes. Although the degree of repressiveness differed, the basic function of the law remained unchanged. It was to entrench the monopoly of power enjoyed by the Communists, enforce conformity with the system, eliminate market forces and replace them with a command economy, and politically disarm the people by preventing them from coming together and evolving alternative programmes independent of the state. The law has consistently remained an instrument of domination by the ruling elite over the people as a whole.

The legislative process in the PPR is controlled by the ruling elite at all its stages, beginning with the drafting of a bill and ending with its enactment into law by the Sejm deputies. The contents of bills are often not even revealed to the public. Acts of law and their official interpretations are prepared by anonymous 'experts' whose names, positions and qualifications are not made public.[1] Law in a Communist state is not based on a consensus since diverse interests cannot be freely articulated. The provisions concerning censorship, the issuing of passports or the functioning of the prison system are deliberately vague, leaving room for secret regulations on their implementation that are unknown to the general public and ad hoc instructions that change in accordance with the political line pursued by the ruling elite.

The Communists may offer tactical concessions as far as secondary issues are concerned, and they may retain a façade of democratic legality, but they are not willing to change their fundamental approach to the law as a means of domination and control. The idea of law as a compromise and a contract is alien to their mentality. They treat law as no more than an administrative act. The authorities have repeatedly demonstrated their total disregard for professional opinion and the interests of those directly concerned by the laws. The amendments to the Law on Higher Education of 26 May 1982, the Trade Union Act of 8 October 1982 or the Law on Special Criminal Liability were passed despite widespread opposition.

In the Western democratic tradition the judicial system does not serve any objectives other than the impartial adjudication of cases; in particular, it does not serve any political objectives. The Communist approach reflects a fundamentally different notion of law and of its function. In the PPR the courts are used to protect the socio-political system and are integrated into the state's monolithic power structure. In times of crisis when the people demand the right of self-determination the political pressure on the judiciary intensifies.

The following official statements on judicial policy during martial law well illustrate this tendency:

> We require sentences to be passed quickly, in accordance with the law, the kind of sentences required in martial law conditions, that is — severe ones. The front line of battle runs through the courts.[2]

> The moment demands utmost efficiency on the part of the courts which in turn requires a fundamental review of the way in which penal policy in cases of a political nature has so far been interpreted.[3]

> A fierce political battle is being waged, a battle in defence

of the socialist system, a battle for law and order which are necessary conditions of the process of normalization. In such conditions *correct* [my italics — AS] adjudication by the courts takes on a particular importance.[4]

In a system based on the rule of law and division of powers, the law is a final guarantee of the individual's rights and freedoms. Any individual can seek protection and the respect of his fundamental rights through the independent courts. He can have recourse to the courts should he feel that his rights are restricted or abused by the state administration. The law, being universally binding and equal to all — the government and all its officials as well as the humblest individual — can act as a restraining force to check administrative arbitrariness.

In the PPR the law lacks these attributes. The rulers do not feel bound by the law, even though it is of their own making, its content is heavily politicized and the principle of equality of all citizens is not reflected in it. In particular, Art. 3 of the PPR Constitution stipulates that 'the leading political force of society in the construction of socialism is the PUWP'. This Article is clearly contrary to other provisions of the Constitution which formally grant all citizens equal rights and freedoms. The leading role is performed by the party apparatus (i.e. full-time paid officials of the party) and the *nomenklatura* which is both the extension of the party and the method through which it wields its power. The *nomenklatura* is a body of people who, after a complicated selection procedure, having satisfied the required criteria, in particular that of political loyalty, have been allowed to participate in the exercise of power and enjoy the privileges it offers. The *nomenklatura* includes central and local state and government appointments, management posts in the economy, important posts in education, the arts and culture, as well as leadership positions in social and professional associations. It applies also to judges, since the Communists abolished the pre-war ban on political activity for judges. Candidates are assigned to posts by the personnel departments of the relevant central or local PUWP committees. The *nomenklatura* is not identical with the party but it is primarily from the ranks of the party that candidates for the *nomenklatura* are recruited. The interests of the *nomenklatura* are safeguarded by the law.

One of the most important battles in which Solidarity was engaged during its legal existence involved *nomenklatura* appointments in the economy. Solidarity rightly considered that without a limitation of the *nomenklatura* managers' privileges and a delineation of their duties, the economic reform had little chance of success. Solidarity demanded that the criterion for selection of candidates to managing posts in the economy should not be political loyalty but professional qualifications, relevant experience and readiness to co-operate with trade union and self-management bodies. Under the protective shield of the military, the *nomenklatura*, with its inbuilt tendency to 'negative selection', has recovered its former position.[5]

Those who demand the right to participate in public affairs outside official structures are liable to various forms of repression even if the cause for which they wish to campaign is officially supported. This is well illustrated by the fate of the temperance protesters who picketed liquor stores in Gdańsk and Warsaw on the fifth anniversary of the signing of the Gdańsk Agreement in August 1985. The demonstrators, who were members of the 'Temperance Brotherhood' were detained and later heavily fined by the local petty offences tribunals. The authorities who are themselves committed to a campaign against alcoholism reject any form of public support for the campaign that is not initiated or organized by the establishment. The reason for this is that they do not want the people to acquire the habit of organizing themselves outside the official bodies or to entertain the notion that they could play an independent role in politics. It was in order to root out such notions which arose after August 1980 that the repressive machinery of martial law was devised and set in motion.

The people have felt the post-martial law restrictions on the right freely to associate, in order to participate in the affairs of the local community or the nation as a whole, the more keenly for having made full, albeit shortlived, use of this right during the legal life of Solidarity. Indeed, one of the fundamental dimensions of the Polish crisis is the clash between the people's demands for self-determination and the political establishment's intransigent defence of its usurped powers to control and direct the people who are reduced to being mere numbers or pawns of the party's and government's decisions. The formal participation by the people in government — under the control and direction of the party — is central to the ruling elite's legitimation of their monopoly of power. It is only by refusing independent, active and open participation by the people in the decision-making process that they can preserve their self-appointed absolute right to make decisions on behalf of society. This holds true for all Poland's post-Stalinist regimes: the authoritarian Communism of Gomułka, the Communist consumerism of Gierek and the bureaucratic-military Communism of Jaruzelski.

These totalitarian practices are reflected in the PPR Constitution, which fails to guarantee the citizens equal rights irrespective of their political beliefs. It glaringly omits to mention that — alongside racial origin, sex, creed and nationality — political beliefs cannot be held as reasons for discriminating against an individual and barring him from holding administrative and other public posts.

The PPR Constitution is somewhat reticent in its enumeration of human and civil rights. Although the PPR guarantees citizens 'freedom of conscience and religion' (Art. 82), 'freedom of speech, publication, assembly, rallies, marches and demonstrations' (Art. 83), 'the right to associate freely with others' (Art. 84), and 'inviolability of body, privacy of home and correspondence'(Art. 87), it does not present these rights as natural and inalienable human rights, but as a consequence of the state's magnanimity. The use of the words 'the PPR guarantees its citizens' instead of 'every human being has a right to ...' is characteristic in this respect. Human and civil rights in the PPR are neither inalienable nor protected by the state. Those who take seriously the civil rights stipulated in the Constitution sooner or later find themselves in conflict with the law since constitutional norms concerning human and civil rights are not expressed in the statutory legal provisions and often clash with them. For instance, exercising one's constitutional right to freedom of speech can be classified under a variety of criminal offences such as 'the dissemination of false information liable to cause serious harm to the interests of the PPR', or 'public slander of the PPR, its socio-political system, the Polish nation or the supreme authorities of the PPR'. Criticism of the government — the very essence of democracy in the West — can be classified as 'inciting unrest' or 'calling upon people to break the law', etc. Naturally, most governments do not look favourably upon the activities of the opposition but it is the very essence of democracy that opposition groups are able to organize, propagate their programmes and seek to implement them. Where there is rule of law the administration cannot ban such opposition activity, as long as it remains within the limits of the law. Any doubts in this respect can be settled by a court which is independent of both the government and the administration. Not so under a Soviet-style system, where the lack of an independent judiciary makes constitutional guarantees of civil rights a dead letter. Criminal law in the PPR is characterized by extreme severity, excessive penalization of independent political activity, precedence of the state and its officials over the ordinary people and their rights, and extreme rigidity of the judicial system, restricting the independence of judges in passing sentences. These features date back to the Stalinist period and have survived since then.

The degree of severity of the PPR's Penal Code has undoubtedly affected the size of the prison population which has been rising steadily. After the upheaval of August 1980 reformist lawyers presented several demands to the authorities, the principal among them being that criminal law be made less severe and that it afford better protection of civil rights. The Ministry of Justice set up a special commission of experts who were to prepare a reform of the criminal law. The commission presented their proposals for general discussion. These were very conservative in comparison with the independent draft and they did not meet social expectations. Even so, they were never implemented.

Martial law not only reaffirmed but also enhanced the much criticized negative features of the PPR's criminal law. The general trend towards even greater repressiveness and rigidity continued in spite of the fact that, as far as the authorities were concerned, the situation was becoming progressively stabilized. This trend was reflected in two interim acts of law marking first the suspension and then the lifting of martial law, as well as in the Law on Special Criminal Liability of 10 May 1985. The punitive hand of the Ministry of Internal Affairs, the official voice of 'socialist legality', was clearly visible behind this trend.

In the PPR it is the police and the prosecution that are responsible for violating most of the human and civil rights. The PPR citizens have virtually no recourse to law to protect themselves from the repressive and arbitrary actions directed against them. It is only exceptionally that the prosecutor's office agrees to prosecute policemen suspected of having abused the law and bring charges against them. The limited prerogatives of both the Supreme Administrative Court and the Constitutional Tribunal to reverse unjust decisions taken by police officials and the Tribunal's impotence with regard to the unconstitutional character of the laws and regulations on the basis of which the police operate, only serve to confirm the supremacy of the police in the state. Thus it is that human and civil rights are known to PPR citizens only from the Constitution and not from real life. There is a self-evident contradiction between the crucial constitutional provision for 'the leading role of the PUWP' and the constitutional guarantees of human and civil rights.

The 'leading role' pertains also to the judiciary, thus depriving the Poles of recourse to independent courts in order to safeguard their rights. This is undoubtedly the principal factor circumscribing freedom under the law in the PPR. In order to be able to function as a guarantor of civil rights the courts have themselves to be independent and in the PPR this is not the case. The judge in Poland is more like a state administrative employee. This is apparent in a statement made by the Minister of Justice, Lech Domeracki:

> When dealing with a specific case the judge comes face to face with the legal provisions and his own conscience. But this conscience can and should be formed by the verification of the judge's political attitude lest he err in interpreting legal norms and in order that he may be capable of applying the provisions in accordance with the intentions of the lawmakers and the interests of the state.[6]

Although Art. 62 of the PPR Constitution states that 'judges are independent and subject only to the provisions of the law', they are, in point of fact, subject not only to the provisions of law but also to the Council of State's interpretation of their content and the way they should be applied. The judges are, moreover, subject to the 'guidelines on the administration of justice' which are issued by the Supreme Court at the request of the Minister of Justice, the Prosecutor General or the Supreme Court Chairman. These 'guidelines' are binding on the judiciary, as are also various secondary regulations, ordinances, and supporting legislative acts, which are often contrary to the spirit of the laws they purport to implement. Since the PPR Constitution does not prescribe a systematic hierarchy of legal acts the judges are obliged to apply not only the letter of the law but also the ordinances instituted by various administrative bodies.[7]

Penal policy is decided outside the courts by the PUWP Central Committee's Commission on Law and Order chaired by the Politburo member responsible for the army, the regular and secret police and Church-state relations; the Council of Ministers'

Committee on the Observance of Law, Order and Social Discipline headed by the Minister of Internal Affairs; the General Prosecutor's Office; and the Ministry of Justice. The recommendations on penal policy stipulate the penalties appropriate to the different categories of offences. The recommendations vary according to the needs of the moment and judges are required to attend special briefings in this connection. They are also obliged to participate in the periodic ideological campaigns against 'the enemy within' — variously identified as the speculator, the hooligan, the bribe-taker, the larcener of public property or violator of public order — by meting out suitably severe sentences to those exemplary scapegoats brought up before the court. It is on their application of the guidelines and the recommendations, as well as on the number of cases completed each month, that individual judges are assessed. According to current norms, a criminal judge is expected to complete 20 cases a month while a civil court judge is expected to complete twice that number. Since the number of cases heard by the judiciary — both criminal and civil — has been steadily rising, at a rate of some 200,000 a year (without a corresponding increase in the number of judges), the discrepancy between high standards of adjudication and keeping up with work norms has been growing.[8] A judge who is too slow or who has been saddled with complex cases is more likely to be passed over for promotion or financial reward.

The PPR's penal policy is realized not only by establishing guidelines and imposing work norms but also by taming the judiciary, shaping their consciousness, instilling in them respect for the ruling apparatus' *raison d'état*. To this end judges are summoned to regular meetings with representatives of the prosecutor's office, the police, the local PUWP committee (usually at voivodship level) and the Ministry of Justice. It is during such meetings that they are made to feel joint responsibility for the state of law and order in the country, for 'social property', the prevention of delinquency, etc., and are encouraged to play their part in the overall division of tasks between the police, the prosecution and the judiciary. It is here that they are presented with the current official interpretations of legal provisions.

The authorities also have at their disposal wide-ranging material means to influence the judges' sense of 'responsibility for the state and its socialist contents'.[9] A judge whose sentences do not find approval with the court chairman or are repealed by a higher court can find it difficult to get promotion, can be encumbered with complex cases requiring additional time and effort, banned from adjudicating certain cases, transferred to another department within one court or to another court altogether or, finally, recalled by the Council of State as 'not warranting the proper fulfilment of his judiciary tasks'. The lack of the indispensible conditions of judges' independence — their irremovability and non-transferability — makes them susceptible to administrative pressures and control. The various elements of the 'carrot and stick' approach enable the judge promptly to realize what is expected of him. To be on the safe side, the typical judge will ask his colleagues, consult with his superiors and finally agree his sentence before he pronounces it. A one-time judge in the CSSR Otto Ulc had described the dilemma of the judge in a Communist state:

> In about 90 per cent of the court agenda there was not the slightest sign of interference in our decision making. This observation, however, does not warrant the conclusion that some sort of '90 per cent judicial independence and integrity' existed. Both the sorry experience with the remaining 10 per cent and the awareness that someone might at any time inflict his 'suggestion' upon us, conditioned *all* our adjudication. One had to distinguish between 'hints' and 'orders'. One had to weigh the importance of the interfering apparatchik against the issue involved...[10]

The position of the judge is, therefore, a very delicate one. He must try to find a middle road between the objective demands of justice and righteousness, application of the actually existing legal provisions such as they are, and response to pressures from the ruling apparatus of power. A number of judges try to reconcile their consciences with the demands of the system by offering what they think is the best deal for the defendant under the circumstances, not by referring to the facts and merits of the case but by seeking procedural loopholes. They might, for example, conduct the proceedings in such a manner as to intimate to the defence the weaknesses of the prosecutor's case or provide the defence with grounds for a subsequent appeal to a higher court.

It would, certainly, be a gross oversimplification to suggest that the majority of judges in the PPR were either acquiescent or unscrupulous lackeys of the regime. Judicial reality in today's

Poland is far more complex and differentiated. Nor is it possible to draw a line between good and bad judges. Most of them are realists who know their limitations, 'ordinary people who are concerned for their own well-being. They will be impartial in their sentences only if they can be certain that such impartiality will not adversely affect their positions.'[11]

Judges adjudicating in cases of a political nature are carefully vetted. The task of assigning a specific judge to a specific case is entrusted to the head of department in a court or the chairman of the court himself. When none of his subordinates can be trusted to do the job as required, the court chairman assigns the case to himself. This rule applied in the most important political trials discussed in this book (the Kwidzyń case, the Toruń trial of the murderers of Father Popiełuszko, the Gdańsk trial of Frasyniuk, Lis and Michnik, etc.). More commonly, however, the court chairman's role is limited to behind-the-scenes instruction: how to conduct the case, what evidence is to be admitted, what sentence is to be passed, etc. A judge who is also a party member is additionally bound by party discipline and can receive instructions directly through party channels.[12] A judge who resists such pressure might in certain specific cases be allowed to continue in office, although his career prospects would undoubtedly be diminished.

In contrast with the 1960s and 1970s, when the judiciary were steered indirectly and fairly discreetly, in a manner noticeable only to professionals, the pressure upon them markedly intensified with the declaration of martial law. Since then the judiciary has been subjected to more regular and more thorough instruction. Those judges who had joined Solidarity or the autonomous trade union movement were pressed by the court chairmen to dissociate themselves from the union.

The number of judges recalled by the Council of State at the request of the Minister of Justice following the imposition of martial law has been variously quoted as being between 25 and 44. Many more left voluntarily, moving to other legal occupations or choosing early retirement. Judges continue to leave the bench by the dozen. At least 10 per cent of the total number of 3,460 judges and 553 trainee judges left between 1982 and 1984. The most frequently quoted reasons for the decision to leave the profession were the deterioration in the conditions of work caused by a dramatic increase in the number of cases brought before the court, low pay, nervous stress and last but not least, opposition to official penal policy. The judiciary has become increasingly dominated by women and inexperienced university graduates as the prestige of the profession has suffered.[13] The influence of the secret police over the course of political trials has greatly increased.

The roots of the malaise were not new and had been fully understood in the Solidarity period. At the bottom of the problem is a recruitment policy which puts greater value on political loyalty and personal connections than on qualifications and experience in accepting candidates for judge traineeship. Secondly, there are no clear-cut criteria for assigning specific cases to individual judges. Thirdly, judges are financially dependent on the court chairman who is able to administer the flexible system of pay and distribute rewards and bonuses largely at his own discretion. Most importantly, judges lack job security. They are appointed by the state administration and any judge can be recalled once he loses the confidence of those in power. The worst situation is that of Supreme Court judges who do not hold a life tenure but are appointed for a period of five years only: and can even be recalled during their term of office. Finally, judges are not barred from engaging in party or party-sponsored political activity; they are, on the contrary, encouraged to do so.

During the Solidarity period a few judges fought to regain their independence and change the conditions of their work. Their struggle for independence in adjudicating was, in fact, a struggle for freedom under the law for all. Although they were too cautious to demand depoliticization of the profession, they hoped to influence policy through the judges' self-government which was only beginning to take shape. They hoped that the long overdue Law on the Courts would equip them with the means with which to resist external pressures.

Martial law put a stop to all these projects. The extraordinary legislation did not find acceptance with all the judges who were expected, without notice and without being asked for their views, to continue their work within a new legal system different from the one they knew when they had chosen their profession. The authorities' response to the reformist tendencies among the judiciary was the Law on the Courts of 20 June 1985 which subjected the judiciary to still greater control by the Ministry of Justice and virtually transformed the court chairman into an arm of the Ministry. Similarly to previous regulations dating back to 1950, the Law on the Courts of 1985 makes such demands of the judge as to ensure a 'correct political attitude' on his part. In their oath they pledge to stand on guard of the socio-political and economic system of the PPR and the rights of the citizens — in that order. It has been emphasized by the Deputy Minister of Justice Jan Brol that independence of the judges does not mean that they are 'independent of the state, its objectives and tasks'.[14] The judges are in this way reduced to the role of being guardians of an undemocratic system of government who, as such, do not need any independence. Since the rulers do not feel bound by the provisions of the laws which they themselves have passed, an independent judiciary must seem to be an anachronism.

Indeed, throughout the entire period of the PPR's existence the judicial apparatus have obediently served party and government, and the courts have been staffed with many products of the *nomenklatura's* 'negative selection' policy. Aniela Steinsbergowa has drawn attention to the fact that the judges who were responsible for the draconian sentences of the Stalinist period were never held to account, although the sentences they passed were subsequently repealed, and that this has led to the widespread conviction that justice can be travestied with impunity.[15] Those judges who had abused the law were never publicly condemned, either in 1956 or in 1980-1. Before 1956 judges who could be counted on to do whatever was required of them were recruited from the ranks of the security apparatus after completing special eight- or ten-month crash courses. Supervised at first by their Russian comrades, they survived in the midst of the judiciary in subsequent years and trained a new breed of judges who could likewise be relied on to defend the system. The 'registration crisis' of October-November 1980 failed to alert Solidarity activists to this fact.[16]

Reducing the very concept of judicial independence to an anachronism was a condition and a consequence of the authorities' instrumental use of law. A second important factor circumscribing freedom under the law in the PPR is the existing 'inquisitorial' model of preparatory proceedings which is very different from the Anglo-Saxon 'adversary' model. The investigation, although formally dominated by the prosecutor, is, in fact, conducted by security police officers. There is no such institution as the investigative judge which would have restricted the often arbitrary practices of the prosecutor's office and allowed the judiciary a supervisory role in the preparatory pre-trial proceedings. Bail is unknown. The practice of temporary arrest is abused, and exploited as a cover for imprisonment without trial. There is no set maximum time limit for detention under temporary arrest in court proceedings.[17] In cases of a political nature the prosecutor performs the role of a figure-head, while the fate of the suspect is in actual fact in the hands of the political police.

The prosecution is a hierarchical and highly disciplined organization with wide-ranging prerogatives. Although it is formally independent of the government and answerable to the Council of State, in fact it works closely with the Ministry of Internal Affairs and the police and there is no way of bringing it publicly to account. Some of the most important posts in the prosecutor's office are occupied by employees of the secret service or its collaborators.

The main burden of criminal proceedings in the PPR has shifted from the main trial itself on to the pre-trial investigation. The proceedings before the court are increasingly being reduced to reading out the files in the case as compiled by the prosecutor conducting the investigation, instead of being an impartial hearing by the court of the defendant's and witnesses' testimonies. The courts tend to favour testimony given by the suspect in the course of the investigation to the detriment of his statements to the court during the trial. The criminal trial is thus reduced to confirming or, at best, verifying the findings reached by the prosecution in the course of the preparatory, pre-trial proceedings.

Indeed, one might be forgiven for thinking that the roles have been reversed. On the one hand, before the trial begins the prosecutor enjoys certain prerogatives which should normally be within the province of the court, such as conditional discontinuation of the proceedings. On the other hand, once the trial has actually begun, it is the judge who must ex officio rectify the deficiencies in the evidence presented by the prosecution, while the prosecutor keeps a low profile. The judge cannot acquit the defendant simply because 'there is nothing in the circumstances of the case that would point to the existence of any evidence that might be presented against the defendant',[18] i.e. because the prosecutor had failed to prove his guilt. The failure of the judge to exhaust all the possibilities in searching for evidence of the defendant's guilt has frequently in the past resulted in the prosecutor's appeal against acquittal on the grounds that a certain piece of evidence had been overlooked or misinterpreted even though he had not presented such evidence in the course of the trial or even requested its admission. The role of the judge in the PPR is not simply to pronounce on the guilt or innocence of the defendant on the basis of the evidence and testimony presented to the court by the two sides but, rather, actively to seek evidence by questioning the suspect and witnesses, referring to the materials of the investigation and interpreting them. All too often the court chooses itself to cover up the inadequacies of the investigation rather than discontinuing the proceedings or, at least, returning the case to the prosecutor's office for completion. The courts, moreover, consistently accept incomplete files in cases forwarded by the prosecutor's office for trial and proceed to trial on the basis of such incomplete evidence.[19]

The precedence of the prosecutor's office over the courts is evidenced by the fact that it is very rare for a court to overrule a prosecutor's order and grant a suspect's request to be released from temporary arrest. This is especially true in cases of a political nature.

It is only with the utmost reluctance that the prosecutor's office institutes an investigation against police officials or party apparatchiks and then only after they have been expelled from the party. In such exceptional cases only the most trusted prosecutors are involved lest they conduct the case too eagerly. A formal pretext is usually found to discontinue the investigation and prevent the case from being brought to court.

The degree of political involvement of a prosecutor matters more than his experience and professional qualifications as far as career prospects are involved. His professional career often depends on his degree of involvement in extra-curricular, party-sponsored activities. In the opinion of a former prosecutor from Kalisz, Bogusław Śliwa, the existing legal provisions which give a prosecutor wide prerogatives are not consistent with his actual status. The office of prosecutor is all too often used as a cover for the activities of the secret police. It is the prosecutor who is summoned to meetings at the security policeman's office and not the other way round. The decision to close the investigation in politically sensitive cases, or to give it a specific direction, rests not with the prosecutor's office, but with the secret police or the party voivodship committee. In cases of serious economic crimes, or those where priests or party officials are involved, it is the police — secret or uniformed — who have the exclusive prerogative of initiating the proceedings. The prosecutor does not act until he gets the go-ahead and then only in so far as the formal side of the proceedings is concerned. Although the majority of prosecutors can no longer be said to be ideologically motivated (and certainly not to the extent of their Stalinist colleagues active in the late 1940s and early 1950s), they are still, on the whole, interested in preserving the system. Some of them resent being used in cases of a political nature but a majority have been tamed and corrupted by years of indoctrination, intimate, comradely involvement with the real power-holders in the country, and access to scarce goods and privileges denied to ordinary citizens.

In short, the PPR is a country in which freedom under the law is circumscribed in four ways:

1. The rights formally granted to the people by the Constitution are fictitious and serve as a façade to cover undemocratic provisions concerning the functioning of the state (there is no division of powers; the government is not accountable to its citizens; real power is wielded by the party which has its own structure parallel to that of the government; access to posts of influence in public life is limited by the nomenklatura system).
2. Any attempt to exercise their political rights makes PPR citizens liable for criminal proceedings. The Penal Code is in many instances contrary to the PPR Constitution.
3. The principle of judicial independence is treated as an anachronism.
4. The investigative authorities (the police and the prosecution) are not accountable to society and are dependent on and controlled by the ruling party elite.

In view of the above one might be prompted to conclude that the rule of law and one-party Communist rule are mutually exclusive. The supreme justification of the Communists' activity is their consolidation of power. The law which lacks the attributes of durability, predictability and integrity has been subordinated to political expediency. Since the system has not been devised to suit the needs of the people there is always a danger that their passive grumbles will some day assume the form of open resistance. The ruling elite's response to the chronic in-built deficiencies of a system officially referred to as socialist has been to inject still more 'socialism'. The former Politburo member Mirosław Milewski, speaking at the Eleventh Congress of the Association of Polish Lawyers (ZPP), remarked characteristically: 'In all those spheres of social life where there exists a deficit of socialism, its enemies gain a chance to pursue their activities.'[20]

And who are these enemies, one might ask? The answer — since the Communist party's right to rule has not been acknowledged by the people — is that potentially everyone is a suspect. In the words of Peter Archer: 'The ruler who does not offer his people a chance to pass judgement on his regime must deny them a right to raise their voice. He must treat every man as a potential enemy for he cannot be sure where the enemy lurks. Every critic is a traitor; every argument a counter-revolution.'[21]

The ruling elite in a Communist state are, none the less, keen to retain a democratic façade of legality and project the image of law-abiding rulers ready to listen to the public. They do this in the belief that terror is, in the long run, counter-productive. The people can be made to work, but to work effectively they must not only be neutralized with material incentives but also have a sense of security under the law and a conviction that the fruits of their labour are not wasted. It is only in times of crisis for the regime that the terrorist nature of the system comes to the surface. When the ruling elite feel themselves firmly at the helm they resort to less conspicuous methods of social control such as 'the carrot and stick' approach, mild repression or the marginalization of dissidents. Law is then used as a means of restraining social change, controlling the people, and affording a sense of security — not so much for the people, as for the ruling elite themselves.

These appearances of democratic legality — a body of laws generously granting the people all sorts of rights — are maintained in order to demonstrate that not only the Communist ideology, but also the Communist legal system are superior to Western democracy. According to the apologists of the ruling doctrine, socialism (i.e. Communism) not only offers traditional human and civil rights which exist in the West, but also provides for and extends the list of social and economic rights. These are said to be underestimated in the West and, moreover, to be more important to the individual than civil rights. At the same time the people are told that they can only avail themselves of the rights granted to them on condition that they fulfil their civil duties. The power elite in a Communist state would like the people to find the system just, and, at the same time, themselves to feel secure in their power.

This is an impossible task if one realizes that the starting point of many independent initiatives has been the desire to rectify injustices inherent in the system. The Workers' Defence Committee (KOR) defended the workers of Radom and Ursus who had been victimized for their part in the protest against the authorities' decision to raise food prices. The Movement for the Defence of Human and Civil Right (ROPCiO) was formed to defend the human and civil rights formally granted to the PPR citizens, but never respected by the authorities in practice. It was a characteristic of the democratic opposition movement which emerged in the mid 1970s that they did not question the merits of the law as such but concentrated on the fact that it was not observed by the authorities. As they re-claimed their due rights, the activists of the democratic opposition movement helped to re-awaken political thinking and awareness.

Solidarity went a step further. They not only demanded that the law be observed by the authorities but also that it be just, i.e. equal to all citizens, regardless of their social standing, ideological outlook and political affiliation, and that it should afford a sense of security to all people by protecting them from arbitrary official decisions and state violence. The law was not only to guarantee basic civil rights but also to enable the people to make use of their rights. The Gdańsk Agreement was a political act which was to result not only in improved conditions but, more significantly, in changes in the law. The new Trade Union Act, which was to reflect the provisions of ILO Convention no. 87 stipulating that trade unions were independent of political parties and employers, was considered particularly important. Although the Gdańsk Inter-Factory Strike Committee did not specify a reform of criminal law among their 21 demands, it was clear that they were in favour of such a reform. It was as a result of the Gdańsk Agreement that the need to introduce changes in criminal law became widely felt.

The demand for a reform of criminal law came out into the open in the 'Theses' adopted by Solidarity's National Congress in October 1981. Thesis no. 23 stated explicitly: 'the system of government must guarantee the basic civil freedoms, respect the equality of all citizens and all public institutions before the law', while thesis no. 24 read: 'the judiciary must be independent and the prosecution subject to social control'. Finally, thesis no. 25 read: 'In a law-abiding Poland no one may be persecuted for his views and no one may be forced to act against his own conscience.' Solidarity did much to alert the public to the need to reform the law and inculcate legal and democratic patterns of behaviour. The union stripped 'socialist legality' of its false pretences by demonstrating that the 'rule of law' and the 'law of the rulers' were not one and the same thing.

Freedom Under the PPR Law

KOR and ROPCiO, as well as Solidarity, were movements for the liberation of society; neither had political ambitions. They worked on the assumption that the ruling elite could be made to abide by the provisions of the laws which they had themselves established (the Constitution) or which they had ratified but failed to translate into domestic law (the International Covenant on Civil and Political Rights, the ILO Conventions).

Martial law was a serious setback to the long-term opposition strategy to force the authorities by peaceful means to abide by the provisions of laws they had themselves passed. But the authorities suffered their setbacks too. They realized that the use of politically motivated penal repression could never be fully successful since those interned for independent trade union activity, sentenced to prison terms or dismissed from their jobs, far from being socially stigmatized, only earned greater public respect. Repressions increased the cost of normalization and demonstrated that the people were not responding positively to the policies pursued by the martial law regime. The authorities, moreover, could not hope to win respectability in the West as long as they continued to apply repressive measures. The coup of 13 December 1981 was not the unequivocal success the authorities would have liked. To quote Adam Michnik, 'The Poles have travelled a great distance on their journey from totalitarianism to democracy.' Noting that even after the official dissolution of the independent institutions that were active in the Solidarity period, independent 'civil society' still lived on, Michnik continued: 'Poland had now become a battleground for the conscious struggle to set limits on the power of the Communist *nomenklatura* and to create a de facto pluralism in conditions imposed by the Brezhnev doctrine'.[22]

Since this 'de facto pluralism' is not recognized by the authorities but barely tolerated, the question is whether the law can still be used for the articulation of dissent to the system of rule. Since the authorities have shown time and time again that they would not in the long run tolerate any independent organization, be it a trade union, a political party, a citizens' campaign, or self-government, is it still advisable for the opposition to seek a common ground with the authorities? In other words, should independent initiatives reject the actual Communist-dominated power structure as the terms of reference of their activities?

Several different approaches to the authorities can be

distinguished among the post-martial law opposition. Lech Wałęsa and his advisers appeal to the authorities to 'return to the spirit of August 1980' and argue that since none of Poland's basic problems can be solved without some form of public support, the authorities cannot go on ruling in a void and must sooner or later seek some kind of accommodation with the people. The underground Solidarity Provisional Co-ordinating Commission (TKK) opted in 1983 for the 'independent society' programme which envisaged society as continuing to exist side by side with the authorities but organizing itself independently of the authorities around specific initiatives such as clandestine trade unions, free publishing, independent education and aid to people persecuted on account of their political convictions or trade union activity. Finally, the third trend among the opposition is evolving in the direction of a greater politicization of independent initiatives. The representatives of this trend say that what the Polish opposition needs is to think more politically and devise political programmes so that they may not be caught unprepared by the next Polish crisis. Their position is, broadly, that since the party has usurped the right to rule in the name of the people, any dialogue with them seems to be legitimizing their rule and should therefore be avoided. This third tendency assumes that fighting for freedom under the law is not enough and that the entire system of law in a Communist state ought to be rejected as unsuitable for reform. However some of the representatives of this third tendency would not rule out an intermediate stage involving a strategic compromise with the party.

The failure of Solidarity's bid to increase the degree of freedom under the law proves indeed that any movement which aims at reforming the law in the PPR faces a formidable task. It is not so much the legal provisions themselves as the balance of forces between the authorities and society that determines their content and application. A weak society is likely to invite invisible violence, whereas an independently organized 'civil society' will make the application of violence a costly exercise for the authorities. The ruling elite are more likely to push forward with unpopular measures when resistance is low. Where would Poland be now had it not been for those thousands who resisted the imposition of Stalinism at the cost of so many lives? Would the authorities have desisted in 1984 from staging the trial of the Solidarity Seven, or would they have declared three amnesties for political prisoners, had it not been for the social pressures and public condemnation of their repressive policies?

Those who participate in sham elections and are not prepared to fight for their rights cannot complain that they are governed unjustly since they do not know any alternative to the Communist idea of justice. If such a concept of alternative justice exists in the social consciousness, however, it is difficult, if not impossible, to sovietize the people. In fact, destruction of the ideal of justice is a precondition of sovietization. It is only when the people believe that 'might is right' that the Communists, or for that matter, any other totalitarian regime, will gain a measure of acceptance. They will have succeeded in creating 'a new man' who will be free to dissent only because there will be no one left who would wish to do so.

Fighting for the concept of alternative law gives the opposition a language through which they can express their aspirations. Władysław Frasyniuk has said: 'The greatest misfortune is that in a totalitarian system the people have no opportunity to learn their due rights'.[23] These rights must first be learned before they can be fought for.

The opposition may be powerless to stop the authorities from pursuing repressive policies but they can raise the cost of such policies to the authorities. This can be done (and, in fact, has been done) by giving adverse publicity to the abuse of law as practised by the judiciary, the police, the prosecution and the prison system. Such pressure has proven successful in individual cases. The names of those who flagrantly abuse the law should be made public.

The state of the judiciary ought to become a matter of universal concern for it is in the courts that unjust sentences reveal the absence of civil, political and trade union rights. Political prisoners are not criminals but victims of a dogma. Instead of defending the authority of the state, the judiciary bears witness to the fact that the state has no recognized authority.

Martial law, with its destruction of Solidarity as an organization, and the subsequent period of normalization, with its attempt to subject the people to a military discipline, were new experiences for the opposition in their struggle for freedom under the law. Władysław Frasyniuk spoke for many when he denounced the illegitimacy of Communist rule:' 'The fundamental paradox of martial law is that the authorities which do not enjoy the confidence of the people and are therefore illegal, have suspended [and later disbanded — AS] a legal trade union inasfar as [its authorities] were chosen in genuine elections.'[24]

Freedom Under the PPR Law

The realization that the Communists had no moral or indeed legal right to rule in the name of society as a whole led many opposition activists to deny them the appearance of legality they would very much like to enjoy. Today, the opposition challenges the Communists' right to rule because of their specific practices such as denial of free elections, disregard for public opinion, lack of constitutional guarantees of civil rights resulting from the subordination of the judiciary to the requirements of political expediency, the use of terror against political opponents of the regime, denial of human, civil and trade union rights, the sovietization of culture, and economic incompetence.

The struggle for freedom under the law has created a new political awareness in Poland. Today the struggle is still primarily for a trade union movement free from government and party control. The trade union formula is attractive since it demonstrates that the Communists' claim to have established an 'ideal worker state' is false. It reveals not only the ideological bankruptcy of the regime, but also its lawlessness, economic exploitation and political unrepresentativeness. This kind of struggle helps the opposition to internationalize the cause of Polish workers. It holds greater appeal than the struggle for openly political objectives. At the same time it offers an opportunity to gain political experience in independent social activity.

The deeper significance of martial law lies not in the destruction of Solidarity as an organization but in its consolidation as an idea marking the failure of the Communist totalitarian utopia. The emergence of Solidarity proves that this utopia has definitely failed to stamp itself permanently on the fabric of social life. The ruling elite can no longer claim to represent the whole of society but must fall back on their real legitimacy—force. The experience of Solidarity proves that the struggle for independent trade unions and other social organizations, rational economic policies, scientific, cultural and creative freedoms, genuine elections and justice are inter-dependent and inextricably linked with the issue of national sovereignty. Indeed, the Western powers, having at Yalta relegated Poland to the Soviet orbit, have only increased Moscow's appetite for further conquests and will continue to bear the consequences of their trust in the Soviet Union's war-time pledges. With Poland in the Soviet orbit, the political, military, economic and psychological dividing line between East and West runs through the heart of a Europe which can therefore be neither united nor peaceful. None the less, as long as the Polish people desire freedom and justice—despite the odds—in their individual and national life, and are ready to sacrifice themselves for these ideals, there is hope that Poland will some day regain its sovereignty and its place among those nations which enjoy freedom under the law.

Notes

1. These 'experts' hide behind the Council of State which is empowered under the PPR Constitution to issue rules concerning the application of specific legal acts as well as formal interpretations. Both the rules and the interpretations are binding on all courts, including the Supreme Court. The Council of State, often referred to as the 'collective presidency', is, in fact, an organ of government.
2. Colonel Henryk Kostrzewa, martial law commissar at the Ministry of Justice, 18 December 1981, *Kontakt* no. 1, April 1982.
3. The Deputy Minister of Justice Tadeusz Skóra in a telex of 1 September 1982 sent to the chairmen of voivodship courts. *Kultura*, November 1982.
4. The Minister of Justice Sylwester Zawadzki speaking during a meeting with judges in Warsaw on 6 October 1982, *Trybuna Ludu*, 7 October 1982.
5. As Stefan Bratkowski observed, it was the *nomenklatura* that proved to be the main beneficiary of the economic reform introduced by Jaruzelski at the outset of martial law. It was to be implemented by the very same people whose power it was supposed to restrict, hence it was doomed to failure. Cf. *Kultura*, January/February 1983.
6. *Kierunki*, 26 February 1984.
7. Cf. Ludwik Dembiński, 'Prawo i władza', *Aneks* no. 20, 1979.
8. In 1981 the PPR courts heard one million cases, and 1.3 mln one year later. In 1983 the figure was 1.5 mln and in 1984 over 1.6 mln cases. The courts were given new tasks such as the registration of trade unions or, since the local appeals commissions (TKO) were abolished, hearing labour disputes in the first instance.
9. An expression used by the Minister of Justice Sylwester Zawadzki in June 1982 in Wrocław, *Gazeta Robotnicza*, 23 June 1982.
10. *The Judge in a Communist State. A View from Within* (Ohio University Press, 1972).
11. *Tygodnik Solidarność* no. 4, 24 April 1981.
12. Between 50 and 60 per cent of the judiciary belong to the PUWP.
13. Out of a total of 3,460 judges and 553 trainee judges in 1984, 55.6 per cent were women. The proportion of women judges was greater in the regional courts (61,3 per cent) and smaller in the voivodship courts (34,2 per cent). 40 per cent of all the judiciary were under 30. Cf. *Rzeczpospolita*, 19 December 1985.

14. *Państwo i Prawo*, November/December 1985.
15. *Kultura*, July/August 1983.
16. On 24 October 1980 Judge Kościelniak of the Warsaw Voivodship Court manifestly abused his rights when he formally registered Solidarity after having written a new clause into the union statutes without the knowledge or approval of the union. This clause, repeated the Gdańsk formula that the union recognized 'the leading role of the PUWP' and the PPR's 'international alliances'. Solidarity insisted that the clause was not necessary in the statutes as such since the text of the Gdańsk Agreement was enclosed as an appendix and Kościelniak's addendum was eventually deleted although he himself survived in his post, unabashed. He is said to have been very much surprised about Solidarity's outrage.
17. District prosecutors may detain a suspect for a period of up to three months and voivodship prosecutors for up to six months. Further extensions of the detention period (temporary arrest) during pre–trial proceedings must be decided by a voivodship court which, in political cases, usually grants the request of the prosecutor.
18. Cf. Stanisław Zimoch, *Nowe Prawo*, April 1981.
19. In this respect the court has little room for manoeuvre since the prosecutor whose files in the case have been returned to him by the court is entitled to lodge a complaint with the Supreme Court, which in turn all too often takes the view that the deficiencies of the investigation can be rectified in the course of the main trial. Cf. the interview of Judge Julian Karsznia of the Wrocław Voivodship Court for *Gazeta Prawnicza* of 1 October 1985.
20. *Prawo i Życie*, 12 November 1983.
21. Peter Archer, *Communism and the Law* (Bodley Head, London, 1963).
22. 'Letter from Gdańsk prison', *The New York Review of Books*, 18 July 1985.
23. A speech made before the Wrocław Voivodship Court during his trial in November 1982.
24. 'An open letter to members of Solidarity on a programme of action', Wrocław, 25 September 1982.

GLOSSARY OF TERMS USED IN THIS BOOK

absentia (in)	zaocznie
accelerated procedure	tryb przyśpieszony
acclaim for an offence	pochwała przestępstwa
adjourn	odroczyć
adjudication	orzecznictwo
adversary model	zasada kontradyktoryjności
amendment	nowela, nowelizacja
appeal (against)	wnieść rewizję, odwołać się (od)
appeal proceedings	postępowanie odwoławcze, rewizja
arrest warrant	nakaz aresztowania
assault (physical or verbal)	napaść (czynna lub słowna)
assembly	zgromadzenie
association of greater public benefit	stowarzyszenie wyższej użyteczności publicznej
the Bar	adwokatura
barrister	adwokat
barrister's chamber	izba adwokacka
body search	rewizja osobista, przeszukanie osoby
breach of law	obraza przepisu
breach of the employee's basic duties	naruszenie podstawowych obowiązków pracowniczych
chairman of the court, tribunal	prezes sądu, przewodniczący składu orzekającego
circumstances as established	stan faktyczny
circumstantial evidence	poszlaka
classify (as an offence)	zakwalifikować
closed doors (hearing behind)	rozprawa niejawna
command procedure	tryb nakazowy
commissar (military)	komisarz wojskowy
complaint	skarga, zażalenie
concurrence	zbieg przepisów

Glossary

conditional release	warunkowe zwolnienie
conjunction with (in)	w zbiegu z
consider a request	rozpatrzeć wniosek
conspiracy	spisek
contempt of court	obraza sądu
continuous offence	przestępstwo ciągłe
court proceedings	przewód sądowy
court record	protokół rozprawy
criminal agreement	porozumienie przestępcze
criminal association	związek przestępczy
criteria of criminal liability	przesłanki odpowiedzialności karnej
decision (court's or prosecutor's)	postanowienie (sądu lub prokuratora)
defence lawyer	obrońca
defence plea	wniosek obrony
defendant	oskarżony, podsądny
deliberate	rozpatrywać
detention	zatrzymanie (na 48 godzin)
discontinue an investigation or proceedings	umorzyć śledztwo lub postępowanie
dissemination	rozpowszechnianie
distribution	kolportaż, rozprowadzanie
district military court	sąd okręgu wojskowego
elements of an offence	znamiona czynu przestępczego
evidence	materiał dowodowy
exclude for separate proceedings	wyłączyć do odrębnego postępowania
expert witness	biegły
explanations (by the defendant)	wyjaśnienia (oskarżonego)
extraordinary review	rewizja nadzwyczajna
false information	fałszywe wiadomości
files in the case	akta śledztwa/sprawy
final sentence	wyrok prawomocny
find	rozstrzygnąć
findings	ustalenia sądu
fine	grzywna
garrison military prosecutor's office	wojskowa prokuratura garnizonowa
gathering (public)	zbiegowisko
group legal practice	zespół adwokacki
guidelines	wytyczne
hearing	posiedzenie sądu, rozprawa

Glossary

house search	przeszukanie pomieszczenia
imputed criminal act	zarzucany czyn
incite	podżegać, nawoływać
incite unrest	wzniecać/wywoływać niepokój
incriminating circumstances	okoliczności obciążające
indict	postawić w stan oskarżenia
indictment (act of)	akt oskarżenia
individual pardons procedure	procedura ułaskawień
inquiry	dochodzenie milicyjne
inquisitorial procedure	postępowanie inkwizycyjne
instigate	inspirować
institute proceedings	wszcząć postępowanie
intent (direct or indirect)	zamiar (bezpośredni lub pośredni)
interpretation	wykładnia prawa
investigation	śledztwo
Investigations Bureau	Biuro Śledcze MSW
investigative arrest/prison	areszt śledczy
investigative judge	sędzia śledczy
inviolability of the person	nietykalność osobista
job placement (mandatory)	pośrednictwo pracy (obowiązkowe)
judicial supervision	nadzór sądowy
judiciary	sądownictwo
jurisdiction	jurysdykcja, właściwość sądu
jurors' panel	skład orzekający kolegium
labour exchange (compulsory)	pośrednictwo pracy (obowiązkowe)
lay adjudicator	ławnik
legal adviser	radca prawny
legal characteristic (of an offence)	znamiona (czynu przestępczego)
legal definition	kwalifikacja prawna
legal representative	pełnomocnik
legal status	osobowość prawna
liability (criminal)	odpowiedzialność (karna)
limitation of personal freedom	kara ograniczenia wolności
local appeals commission	terenowa komisja odwoławcza
loss of public rights	pozbawienie praw publicznych
main trial	rozprawa główna
martial law decree	dekret o stanie wojennym
militarized enterprise	zakład zmilitaryzowany
military prosecutor	prokurator wojskowy
misdemeanour	występek
mitigating circumstances	okoliczności łagodzące

Glossary

objection	sprzeciw
offence	przestępstwo
offender	sprawca przestępstwa
order (government or minister's)	rozporządzenie Rady Ministrów, zarządzenie ministra
ordinance	przepisy/rozporządzenie wykonawcze
overrule a request	oddalić wniosek
overrule a verdict	uchylić orzeczenie kolegium
penalization (scope of)	zakres karalności
petty offence	wykroczenie
petty offences tribunal	kolegium d/s wykroczeń
perpetrator	sprawca
point of law	kwestia prawna
police record of the investigation	protokół śledztwa
police report	notatka milicyjna
police surveillance	inwigilacja policyjna
premeditated	z rozmysłem
present charges	przedstawić zarzuty
pre-trial proceedings	postępowanie przygotowawcze
prison governor	naczelnik więzienia
procedural law	prawo procesowe
promulgate a law	ogłosić ustawę
prosecutor	prokurator, oskarżyciel
Prosecutor General	Prokurator Generalny
prosecutor's office	prokuratura/urząd prokuratorski
protest action	akcja protestacyjna
public unrest	niepokój publiczny
questioning	przesłuchanie
regional court	sąd rejonowy
request	wniosek
resolution (Council of Ministers')	uchwała (Rady Ministrów)
return for re-trial	przekazać do ponownego rozpatrzenia
return the case for completion	przekazać sprawę celem uzupełnienia śledztwa
review	rewizja
revocation of arrest	uchylić postanowienie o tymczasowym aresztowaniu
revoke a sentence	uchylić wyrok
rule of law	praworządność
ruling	orzeczenie

Glossary

secret association	tajny związek
sedition	przestępstwo przeciwko podstawowym interesom politycznym państwa
self-management, -governing body	samorząd
sentence	wyrok sądu
simplified procedure	tryb uproszczony
slander	lżyć, znieważyć, szkalować
social danger (of an act)	społeczne niebezpieczeństwo czynu
special procedure	szczególny tryb postępowania
special regulations	szczególna regulacja prawna
statutory law	prawo stanowione
submit (evidence)	przedstawić (dowód)
substantive law	prawo materialne
substantial evidence	dowód istotny
substantiation	uzasadnienie
substitute imprisonment	zastępcza kara pozbawienia wolności
summary procedure	tryb doraźny
suspended sentence	wyrok z zawieszeniem
Supreme Court	Sąd Najwyższy
suspect	obwiniony, podejrzany
task force (military)	wojskowa grupa operacyjna
temporary arrest	areszt tymczasowy
testimony	zeznania
trainee barrister	aplikant adwokacki
treason	zdrada ojczyzny
universal military service	powszechny obowiązek obrony
universal obligation to work	powszechny obowiązek pracy
unknown perpetrators	nieznani sprawcy
uphold a sentence	utrzymać wyrok w mocy
verdict	orzeczenie kolegium
voivodship court	sąd wojewódzki
withdraw testimony	wycofać zeznania
work dodger	osoba uchylająca się od pracy

INDEX

Abolition Decree of 12 December 1981 (Act of Abolition) 16, 128, 207, 219, 332
Accelerated procedure 57–59, 61, 260–261, 283
Adamowicz Zofia 170, 197, 201
Affenda Stanisław 183, 196, 200–201
Air Force Court 175, 318
Albrecht Erwin Ginter 80, 82
Amnesty of 21 July 1983: 137, 175, 207, 291, 365, 378–381
Amnesty of 21 July 1984: 13, 191, 268, 291, 365, 378–382
Anderson Ken 10
Andrzejewski Piotr 26, 119, 123, 195–198, 202–203, 208
Anti-Solidarity Organization (OAS) 334
Antończyk Julian 112–113
Archer Peter 401
Association of Barristers and Trainee Barristers 193, 208, 221
Association of Polish Lawyers (ZPP) 193, 401
Augustyn Andrzej 360

Balina Tadeusz 114
Bałuka Edmund 150–153, 230
Baranowska Teresa 288
Barańczak Stanisław 235
Bardonowa Wiesława 145, 232, 305, 351
Bartold M. 83

Bartoszcze Michał 125, 334
Bartoszcze Piotr 335
Bądzyński Józef 358
Bednarkiewicz Maciej 197, 199, 200, 207–208, 350
Bednarz Piotr 163, 165, 186
Bednorz Bishop Herbert 311
Bełczewski Józef 115
Berdychowski Zygmunt 385
Berger Aleksander 175
Będkowski Ryszard 93
Białowicz Antoni 334, 353
Bielański Roman 291
Bielecki Czesław 38, 164–165, 170, 179–180
Bieliński Konrad 180
Bieńkowski Władysław 324
Bierut Bolesław 323–324
Blachnicki Fr. Franciszek 309
Black Book of Polish Censorship 235–236
Blanchard Francis 297
Blek Andrzej 188
Błasikiewicz Lt. Col. Stanisław 152, 232
Błaszczyk Hubert 187–188
Błaszczyk Marianna 248
Bober Andrzej 118, 122
Bonek Jacek 248
Borkowski Fr. Jan 305–306
Borowski Adam 169–170, 176–177, 198
Borusewicz Bogdan 38, 164, 168, 179, 180
Bratkowski Stefan 220, 408
Brezhnev Leonid 88–89, 250
Brezhnev doctrine 386, 404

Index

Brol Jan 397
Brzeziński Zbigniew 134
Buchała Kazimierz 207, 212
Budzanowska Maria 207–208, 210–212
Bujak Zbigniew 38, 158, 161, 163–165, 179–180
Bukowski Roman 246
Bydgoszcz affair 4, 125, 325, 329, 336
Byrdy Maria 358
Bzdyl Krzysztof 144, 148

Celegrat Zenon 133, 346
Chebrikov Gen. Viktor 328
Chief Barristers' Council 13, 193, 205–212, 239, 360
Chłopecka-Pszczółkowska 202
Chmielewski Lech 98
Chmielewski Stanisław 100
Chmielewski Lt. Waldemar 327, 354, 356, 359
Chmura Jerzy 201, 266
Choina Bogusław 247
Chojecki Mirosław 127, 132, 169, 235
Chrostowski Waldemar 352–353, 357, 359
Chruścielewski Edmund 358
Chrzanowski Antoni 42
Chrzanowski Maciej 243
Ciastoń Gen. Władysław 355–356
Cieślicki Jacek 88–89
Citizens' Care Movement (ORO) 226–227
Clandestine Factory Commissions (TKZ) 160–161
Clubs for a Self-Governing Republic — 'Freedom Justice Independence' (WSN) 131, 136
Clubs in the Service of Independence (KSN) 219
Code of Criminal Procedure, amendments to
  of 18 December 1982: 251
  of 28 July 1983: 38
Commission on Internal Affairs and the Judicial System (attached to Sejm) 209
Commission on Law and Order (PUWP CC's) 195, 207, 211, 340, 393
Committee for the Defence of People Imprisoned for Their Convictions 145
Committee on the Observance of Law, Order and Social Discipline (attached to Council of Ministers) referred to also as Kiszczak's Committee 8, 10, 14, 393
Committee of the National Self-Determination Compact (KPSN) 219
command procedure 60
compulsory labour 46, 48, 50–51
Confederation of Independent Poland see under KPN
Constitution of the PPR (of 1952) 18, 20, 22–23, 46, 113, 149, 213, 228, 232, 284, 287, 301, 340, 342, 389, 391–393, 401, 403
Constitutional Tribunal 392
Co-ordination Bureau of Solidarity, Brussels 167, 178, 179
Court of the Pomeranian Military District 151, 172, 217, 248, 307
Court of the Warsaw Military District 37, 113, 115, 139, 147, 168, 176, 219, 307
Court of the Silesian Military District 43, 93–95, 97, 100, 174, 186, 189, 268
Craxi Bettino 133
Criminal and Inquiries Bureau of the Warsaw Police HQ 356, 359
Czachór Marek 90–91
Czarnecki Piotr 204
Czerwiński Arkadiusz 291

Danielewicz Stanisław 243
Dejewski Zdzisław 82, 84, 86

Index

Demczuk Mirosław 100
Denkiewicz Arkadiusz 349–351
Department of Press, Radio and Television (attached to the PUWP CC) 221, 234
Dębiński Marek 248
Dłużniewski Jerzy 99, 172, 194, 249
Domeracki Lech 194, 210, 393
Downarowicz Zbigniew 56
Drewniak Fr. Władysław 307
Dróżdż Mjr. Janusz 357, 359
Duszak Mirosław 118, 121
Dużyński Czesław 212
Dyląg Stanisław 43
Dyrcz Władysław 249
Dzierżek Fr. Stefan 302–303

Ejsmont Paweł 371

Fighting Solidarity (SW) 162
Filozof Cezary 349
Force Ouvrière 150
Frasyniuk Władysław 13, 133, 152, 163, 172, 181–185, 196, 200–201, 231, 232, 262–263, 266, 276–284, 332, 337–338, 372, 374, 396, 406
Free Democrats Movement 145
Free Poland 144
Free Trade Unions (WZZ) 95, 103, 237

Garnys Kazimierz 235
Garton Ash Timothy 15
Gauza Władysław 155
Gdańsk Agreement 3–4, 67, 103, 144, 145, 183, 223, 224, 236, 289, 390, 403
Gdańsk Portworkers' Strike 78–88
Geneva Convention of 12 August 1949: 30
Giedroyć Jerzy 165
Gierek Edward 103, 390
Glemp Cardinal Józef (Primate of Poland) 287, 298, 314, 317
Głogowski Karol 194, 196, 207
Głowacki Edward 100, 110

Głowacki Col. Wacław 355–356
Gnieciak Jerzy 333
Gniza Bronisław 70, 80–81, 86
Goliński Zygmunt 337
Goławski Andrzej 118, 123
Goławski Krzysztof 112
Goławski Zygmunt 118, 121, 144, 148
Gomułka Władysław 324, 331, 390
Gonciarz Lt. Tadeusz 146, 219
Grabarczyk Antoni 86, 384
Grabiński Andrzej 196, 201, 207
Grabowski Lech 194
Grabowski Władysław 196
Grembowski Józef 93
Grochowska Jadwiga 318
Gruba Col. Jerzy 144
Grządzielski Henryk 283–284
Grzywa Karol 95
Gwiazda Andrzej 127, 130–131, 267

Handzlik Stanisław 99, 171–172, 277
Hardek Władysław 170
Helsinki Committee in Poland 60, 154, 194, 287
Helsinki Commission in Poland 154, 285
Helsinki Final Act 22, 154
Hinz Mariusz 245
Home Army (AK) 34, 323
Human Rights Charter 232

Instytut Literacki (*Kultura*) 136, 154, 165
International Covenant on Civil and Political Rights 24–26, 52, 62, 72, 75, 149, 214, 252, 344, 376, 379, 381, 403
International Labour Organization (ILO) 30, 297, 404
Convention no. 29: 46, 50
Convention no. 87: 223–225, 403
Convention no. 98: 223, 225

Index

Convention no. 105: 46, 50, 366
Inter-Factory Strike Committee (MKS) Gdańsk 225, 403, Wrocław 144
Inter-Factory Strike Committee of Western Pomerania 99
Inter-Factory Worker's Solidarity Committee (MRKS) 162-165, 167, 169-170, 176-177, 198, 202, 347
internment 25, 203, 292
Investigations Bureau of Ministry of Internal Affairs 10, 118, 166, 235, 326, 328, 352, 354, 357-358

Jabłoński Col. 356
Jabłoński Leszek 70
Jackiewicz Zbigniew 84, 86
Jackowska Anna 304, 351
Jagodziński Ryszard 242

Jałowiecki Stanisław 174
Jancarz Fr. Tadeusz 312
Jandziszak Tadeusz 144-145, 366-377
Janiszewski Gen. Michał 287
Jankowski Krzysztof 91
Jankowski Rev. Henryk 107, 303, 308
Jankowski Zenon 281
Jarosz Stanisław 78-80, 82-83, 86-88, 102
Jaruzelski Gen. Wojciech 6-10, 12, 14, 20-23, 49, 64, 68, 127, 157, 211, 237, 298, 328-330, 336, 390
Jasernik Kazimierz 249
Jasicki Bronisław 349-351
Jatczak Cpt. Jacek 218
Jaworski Seweryn 127, 131, 267, 372
Jedynak Tadeusz 38, 164, 166, 178, 179, 180
Jewulski Fr. Eugeniusz Bolesław 307
Jędryczka Grzegorz 248

Johann Wiesław 198
John Paul II Pope 298-299, 309, 314, 336
Jóźwik Tadeusz 358
Jung Regina 348
Jurczyk Marian 127, 332

Kaczorowski (MIA employee) 357
Kalinowski Stefan 323-324
Kałudziński Władysław 118, 122
Kamiński Zygmunt 100
Kantorski Fr. Leon 307
Kapica Krzysztof 248
Kapuściński Marek and Elżbieta 249
Kardaś Henryk 305
Karnicki Marek 98
Karos Sgt. Zdzisław 306
Karpiński Andrzej 233
Kaszuba Witold 291
Katowice Steelworks strike 68-70, 88-90
Kazior Wojciech 245
Kelus Jan 27
Kern Andrzej 194, 196
Kędzierski Zygmunt 227
KGB 328
Kiciński Wacław 243-244
Kieszkowski Zbigniew 56
Kiszczak Gen. Czesław 8, 49, 118, 165-166, 357, 363
Kiszyna Aranka 207 113
Klich Bogusław 112, 113
Kłosowski Fr. 310
Kochanowski Janusz 73
KOK see under National Defence Committee
Kołakowski Leszek 1, 7, 214
Kołodziej Professor, forensic medicine 311
Konik Krystian 114
KOR (Workers' Defence Committee) 154, 164, 218, 265, 319, 324, 364, 402-403; See also KSS KOR
KOR's Intervention Bureau 133, 135

Index

Kosmahl Ireneusz 40–41
Kosmowski Patrycjusz 323
Kostecki Jan 230–231
Kostecki Mikołaj 91
Kostrzewa Col. Henryk 320
Kostrzewa Ryszard 194
Kościelniak Zdzisław 409
Kościuk Ireneusz 349–351
Kościuszko First Infantry Division 34, 324
Kotański Jakub 349
Kotowski Stanisław 233
Kowalczyk Jerzy 37, 90–93
Kowalewski Stanisław 107–108
Kowalski Ryszard 68–69
Koza Jacek 217
Kozaczyński Adam 118, 122, 125
Kozłowski Feliks 124
KPN (Confederation of Independent Poland) 142–144, 154–155;
    First trial of 144–150, 151, 153, 367;
    Second trial of 231–233, 332;
    Members mistreated in prison 370, 371
Kramarczyk Adam 248
Kraszewski Bishop Zbigniew 315
Kropiwnicki Jerzy 74, 75
Król Krzysztof 231
Krzysztofiak Krzysztof 113
KSS KOR (Social Self-Defence Committee 'KOR'), trial of 12, 126–142, 153, 173, 202–203, 206, 379. See also KOR
Kubala Col. Włodzimierz 134, 219
Kubasiewicz Ewa 37, 60, 90–93
Kubisowski Edward 248
Kucharski Janusz 98
Kucharski Maciej 70
Kuczer Bronisław 115
Kuczkowski Marek 334
Kukliński Col. Ryszard 6
Kulik Ewa 38, 179, 180
Kulwikowski Marian 371
Kupisiewicz Zbigniew 88

Kurach Fr. Tadeusz 305–306
Kuratowska Zofia 201
Kurcyusz Jerzy 201
Kurcyusz-Hoffmanowa Teresa 201
Kuroń Grażyna 30
Kuroń Jacek 2, 127, 133, 135, 140, 161, 231, 267, 338
Kuzian Jerzy 97
Kwiatkowska Wiesława 90
Kwiatkowska Zofia 42, 43
Kwiatkowski Mikołaj 295–296

Labour Code of 1974: 39–41, 44, 46, 284–286, 291, 293–294, 296–297
Labour Courts 294–297
Las Jerzy 31, 115
Law of 24 October 1986: 386
Law on Assemblies of 29 March 1962: 269
    amended on 21 July 1983: 269
Law on Associations of 1932: 214–215, 227, 231, 319
Law on the Bar of 1950: 192
Law on the Bar of 19 December 1963: 192, 199
Law on the Bar of 26 May 1982: 198, 203–206, 209–213
Law on Censorship of 31 July 1981: 18, 237–238
    amended on 28 July 1983: 12, 238
Law on the Courts of 20 June 1985: 13, 397
Law on Fighting Hooliganism of 22 May 1958: 57–58
Law on Higher Education of 26 May 1982: 388
    amended 25 July 1985: 288
Law on the Journal of Laws of 30 December 1950: 72, 74
Law on Jurisdiction in Labour Disputes of 18 April 1985: 296–297
Law on Legal Advisers of 6 July 1982: 205

Index

Law on the Minister of
   Internal Affairs and his
   Subordinate Agencies of 14
   July 1983: 12, 330, 361–362
Law on the Prosecutor's
   Office of 20 July 1985: 13,
   340–341
Law on Special Criminal
   Liability of 10 May 1985:
   13, 60–61, 283–4, 320, 365, 388,
   392
Law on State and Service
   Secrets of 14 December
   1982: 12
Law on the State of
   Emergency of 5 December
   1983: 8, 12, 21, 33, 60
Law on Universal Military
   Service of 21 November
   1967: 20, 23, 36, 37, 38–39
   amended on 21 November
   1983: 7, 12, 21
Law on Workers' Self-
   Management of 25
   September 1981: 222
Law on Work Shirkers of 26
   October 1982: 47–50
Lenin Vladimir I. 39, 301,
   360, 377
Leszczyński Juliusz 192
Lewandowski Henryk 43
Liberal-Democratic Party,
   Independence 233
Lipiński Edward 138
Lipiński Jerzy 100
Lipski Jan Józef 127, 132,
   141, 154, 228, 313
Lis Bogdan 13, 152, 164, 166,
   168, 178–180, 191, 231–232,
   276–284, 332, 379, 396
Lis-Olszewski Witold 195
Lisowski Władysław 66
Lityński Jan 127,132
Local Appeals
   Commissions;(TKO) 41, 47,
   290–291, 294–296
Lovas Istvan 10
Lubin 185, 267–269
Lublin Committee 323
Luliński Col. Stanisław 355–356

Łabętowicz Mariusz 125
Łabuda Fr.Marek 313
Łaski Stanisław 249–250
Łęgowski Krzysztof 248
Łodyga Jan 25, 119, 202
Łojewski Kazimierz 212
Łopatka Adam 203, 314–315
Łyczywek Roman 201

Macharski Cardinal
   Franciszek 311
Mackaniec Romuald 187
Macoch Mjr. Ryszard 267
Main Office for Control of the
   Press, Publications and
   Performances (GUKPPiW)
   234, 235, 239
Malcher George 3, 9
Małcużyński Karol 51
Małkowski Fr. Stanisław 310
Maj Col. 357
mandatory job placement
   (Order of 8 August 1983
   issued by the Council of
   Ministers) 45, 293
Manifest Lipcowy coalmine
   94–97
Marcinkowski Col. Zenon 353
Marek Zdzisław 311
Markiewicz Marek 204
Markiewicz Wojciech 321
Masiak Kazimierz 70, 244–245
Matuszewski Wiesław 27
Mazowiecki Tadeusz 222
Merkel Jacek 277
Mężydło Antoni 334
Miastowski Sławomir 169
Michalak A. 114,385
Michałowski Andrzej 79,
   82–83, 85–86, 168, 180
Michnik Adam 3, 13, 127,
   133, 139, 140, 152, 157,
   231, 232, 276–284, 332,
   346, 396, 404
Mickiewicz Marek 252, 276
Mielczanowski Andrzej 365
Mierzewski Piotr 166
Miętne 302, 316
Mikołajczyk's Peasant Party
   (PSL) 323

Index

Milewski Gen. Mirosław 195, 207, 211, 401
militarized enterprises 36–45
Military Council of National Salvation (WRON) 6–7, 20–22, 23, 113, 127, 194, 217, 244, 319
military courts 33–38, 179
Military Courts Decree on 16, 36, 38
Ministry of Public Security 319
Mirecki Roman 104
Mizio Marian 185
Młotkowski Lt. Edmund 122
Mnich Jerzy 94–96
Moczar Mieczysław 331
Moczulska Maria 145
Moczulski Leszek 142–149, 152, 231–233
Moćko Robert 95
Modzelewski Karol 127, 133, 382
Molczyk Col. Zenon 79
Morgiewicz Emil 364
Mościcki J. 77, 273
Movement for the Defence of Human and Civil Rights (ROPCiO) 143, 145, 218, 402, 403
MRKS see under Inter-Factory Workers' Solidarity Committee
Mrożek Sławomir 5
Mull Stephen 339

Naszkowski Eligiusz 363
National Alliance of Russian Solidarists (NTS) 144
National Commission (of ISTU Solidarity) 64, 78, 85
National Consultative Commission (KKP) of ISTU Solidarity 145
National Congress (Solidarity's) 403
National Council of Legal Advisers 193
National Defence Committee (KOK) 7, 8, 14, 20–22, 38, 361

National Farmers' Resistance Committee (OKOR) 162
National Home Council (KRN) 324
National Resistance Committee (OKO) 160
National Strike Committee 78, 80, 81, 83, 86
Naval Court in Gdynia 37, 42–43, 80–88, 90–93, 98, 101, 197, 202, 242, 244, 248
NKVD 34, 323
Noël Roger 169
Nogajewski Ryszard 187–188
nomenklatura 3, 389, 398, 408
Nowacki Wieńczysław 376
Nowak Czesław 80–81, 83–87
Nowak Zenon 54, 98, 202, 289
Nowakowski Fr. 352
Nowakowski Marek 133

'Oases' (Światło-Życie movement) 309, 310
Obłąk Bishop Jan 117, 309
Okraj Jerzy 42
Oleksyn Jacek 76
Olivarez Emilio de 139
Olszewski Jan 195, 200, 202–203, 208, 280–281, 312
Onyszkiewicz Janusz 338
Order no. 165 of 13 December 1981 issued by the Minister of Justice 27
Order of 30 December 1981 issued by the Council of Ministers (universal obligation to work, self-management) 18, 46
Order no. 189 of 31 December 1981 issued by the Council of Ministers (internment) 27–28
Order of 8 August 1983 issued by the Council of Ministers (mandatory job placement) 45
Order no. 51 of 13 December 1981 issued by the Prime Minister (proscribing trade union activity) 17, 41

Index

Orłoś Kazimierz 133
Osiński Fr. Jerzy 353
Ostrowska-Kasprzyk Krystyna 204
Ostrowski Kazimierz 347
Osuch Jacek 347
Owczarska Anna 169, 347
Ozimek Stanisław 225

Pacuszka Tadeusz 54, 98, 202, 289
Paczko Zdzisław 247
Paczyński Włodzimierz 57
Palka Grzegorz 127
Palus Janusz 94
Pałubicki Janusz 164, 166, 168, 174–175, 190–191, 277
Patronat 221
Penal Code amendments of 18 December 1982: 12
of 28 July 1983: 12, 275
of 10 May 1985: 365
Penitentiary Association 377
Perestaj Stefan 210
Perez de Cuellar Javier 138
Petty Offences Code 254–257
amendments of 28 July 1983: 256
amendments of 10 May 1985: 254, 270
amendments of 24 October 1986: 180, 270–271, 383
Petty Offences Tribunals 180, 242, 257–261, 320, 383, 390
Pękala Lt. Leszek 303, 354, 357, 359
Piast coalmine 70–71, 94
Piątkowski Jan 195
Pieczka Barbara 347
Piekarski Jerzy 113
Pieńkowski Janusz 100, 110
Pietruszka Col. Adam 305, 354, 356, 357
Pinior Józef 163, 165, 166, 170, 171, 175, 266, 267
Piotrowski Edward 169
Piotrowski Cpt. Grzegorz 327, 354, 356–359
Piotrowski Leszek 201
Piotrowski Gen. Władysław 327

Płatek Gen. Zenon 353–357, 359
Płoski Mieczysław 78, 101
Pobłocki Cpt. Juliusz 119, 121
Podgórski Marian 80, 82
Polish Government-in-Exile 136, 154
Polish Socialist Labour Party (PSPP) 150
Popiełuszko Fr. Jerzy 178, 228, 235, 302–305, 308–310, 312, 316, 326–327, 330, 336, 338, 352–360, 396
Porowski Bogusław 276
Pożoga Gen. Władysław 339
Press Law of 26 January 1984: 12, 239, 252, 271, 275, 276
Primate's Aid Committee for Prisoners and Their Families 29, 117, 335–336, 363
Primate's Social Council 298
Provisional Board of the Wielkopolska (Poznań) Region (TZR) 164, 175
Provisional Co-ordinating Commission (TKK) 31, 160–162, 164–167, 170, 172, 175, 181, 183, 184, 262, 263, 276–279, 283, 297, 360, 380, 405
Provisional Regulations on Imprisonment of 25 January 1974: 365, 369, 374
Przeciechowski Tomasz 200, 201
Przemyk Grzegorz 197, 199, 305, 348–351, 363
Przybylski Mariusz 195
Przybyłka Włodzimierz 118
Przykucki Bishop Marian 306
Pstrąg-Bieleński Maciej 44, 145, 155
Pudysz Col. Zbigniew 357
Pyzio Wiesław 98

Radio Free Europe 104, 106, 136, 152, 201, 267
Radio Moderata 201
Radio Solidarity 27, 132, 152, 161, 164, 168–169, 172–173,

Index

251, 339, 347
Radio and Television Committee 18, 236
Rajmont–Proch Maria 188
Regional Co-ordinating Commission of the Gdańsk Region (RKK) 87, 164, 168, 180
Regional Executive Commission of the Małopolska (Kraków) Region 170, 171
Regional Executive Commission of the Mazowsze (Warsaw) Region 164, 173, 180
Regional Executive Commission of the Śląsko-Dąbrowski (Katowice) Region 164
Regional Social Citizen's Committee for the Defence of the Rule of Law (Szczecin) 230–231
Regional Strike Committee of the Lower Silesia (Wrocław) Region (RKS) 164, 172, 181–185
Regulations for the Period of Overcoming the Socio-Economic Crisis (Act of 21 July 1983) 45, 50, 222, 223, 269, 293–294
Regulations for the Period of Suspended Martial Law (Act of 18 December 1982) 37, 45, 55, 221, 250–251, 263, 274, 293
Resolution (Council of Ministers')
  no. 533 of 1961: 205
  no. 185 of 28 April 1981, unpublished 18
  no. 262 of 12 December 1981: 19
  no. 189 of 30 August 1982: 263
Resolution of 12 December 1981 (issued by Council of State) on martial law 38
Resolution of 12 December 1981 no. 9 (issued by National Defence Committee KOK) on militarization of some enterprises 38
Robotnik 237
Romanowski Col. Wincenty 118
Romaszewska Zofia 168, 364, 366
Romaszewski Zbigniew 132, 135, 164, 168, 173, 378, 383
ROPCiO see under Movement for the Defence of Human and Civil Rights
Rossa Henryk 200
Rozmarynowicz Andrzej 198, 311, 360
Rozpłochowski Andrzej 127, 198
RUCH movement 364
Rulewski Jan 125, 127
Rurarz Zdzisław 328, 363
Rusek Franciszek 55
Rymarz Władysław 92
Rzeszótko Tadeusz 187–189

Sadkowski Stefan 247
Sadłowski Fr. Czesław 309, 310
Sadowska Barbara 197, 199, 349–350, 363
Sadowski Sławomir 91
Sarnicki Radosław 118, 121–123
security police (SB) 326–328, 330–340
security police (UB) Stalinist 327, 331
self-management 18, 220–223, 286
Sieniuc Andrzej 280
Sienkiewicz Jarosław 94
Siła-Nowicki Władysław 97, 107, 176, 177, 195, 196, 199–201, 206–208, 222, 306, 350
simplified procedure 59–60
Skalecka Krystyna 196

Index

Składanowski Aleksander 42, 43
Skłodkowski Wojciech 249
Skowronek Jarosław 91
Skowrońska Anna 106–108, 207, 279, 283
Skóra Tadeusz 262
Skrzypczak Edward 64
Skuza Marian 145, 155
Słowik Andrzej 74–75, 291, 296, 375, 385
Small Penal Code of 1946: 240
Sobczak Lech 98
Social Association for the Defence of Human Rights in Toruń 228–230
Social Committee for Science (SKN) 162
Social Council for National Economy 131
Social Health Service Commission 367
Sojda Mieczysław 286
Solak Zbigniew 113
Solidarity Seven, trial of the 19, 126–132, 134, 137–139, 153, 206
Sopuszyńska Alicja 80, 82, 86
Soroko Romuald 320
Special Criminal Liability (see the Law on)
Special Procedure Act (Law on Special Procedure for Perpetrators of Certain Offences) of 17 July 1986: 14, 180, 283, 338, 365, 382–383
Special Procedure, Decree on 16, 51–60
Stalin Josef 323
Stalinism 35
Stalinist period 11, 35
Stalinist show trials 11, 131
Stalinization 10, 35, 218, 324, 365
Staniszkis Jadwiga 7
Stański Tadeusz 144–145, 147–148, 384
Stasiak Czesław 187–189
Stecki Zbigniew 76

Steinsbergowa Aniela 35, 136, 398
Stępień Jerzy 112
Stobbe Elżbieta 169, 347
Stojak Longin 42
Story Barbara 357
Stromecki Zbigniew 357
Stronikowski (prosecutor) 353
Strzyżewski Tomasz 155
'Studies Bureau' (Ministry of Internal Affairs') 338–339
summary procedure 37, 53–57, 60–61, 104–105, 108, 246, 320
Supreme Administrative Court 237–238, 253, 291, 308, 392
Supreme Court resolution of 4 May 1982: 288–289
Supreme Court rulings
  of 11 October 1980: 342
  of 12 January 1982: 65
  of 22 January 1982: 53–54
  of 18 February 1982: 76
  of 27 February 1982: 39
  of 1 March 1982: 74
  of 10 March 1982: 241–242
  of 25 March 1982: 76
  of 26 April 1982: 77
  of 4 May 1982: 288, 295
  of 10 May 1982: 77
  of 18 May 1982: 250–251
  of 11 June 1982: 40
  of 15 July 1982: 40
  of 11 August 1983: 205
Supreme Court, Law on 13
Swatko Commander 79
Sychowski Wojciech 98
Sychut Jerzy 144, 148
Szablewski Alojzy 107, 348
Szachowicz Zenon 122
Szadurski Karol 101
Szczepański Jan Józef 221
Szczepański Maciej 380
Szczęsny Ryszard 196
Szeremietiew Romuald 144–145, 147–148, 384
Szerer Mieczysław 35
Szomański Andrzej 231
Szulc Andrzej 43
Szwed Ewa and Wiesław 246

Index

Szwedowska Barbara 279
Szymala Eugeniusz 197
Szymanderski Jacek 228–230, 273
Szymecki Eugeniusz 79, 81, 85–87
Szyzdek Jacek 349–350
Śmigiel Stanisław 334
Świdziński Tadeusz 248
Świtek Leszek 79, 81, 83, 86–88, 102
Świtoń Kazimierz 274–275, 313

Tarniewski Marek 141
Tatarowski Konrad 116, 125
Taylor Jacek 108, 121, 279
Temperance Brotherhood 390
Terlecki Marian 313
Thibaud Paul 2–3
TKK (see under Provisional Co-Ordinating Commission)
TKO (see under Petty Offences Tribunals)
Tokarczuk Bishop Ignacy 300, 302, 308, 315
Tomaszewska Ewa 274
Tomyn Władysław 296
Trade Union Act of 8 October 1982: 175, 222, 224–225, 274, 284, 293, 388, 403
Trotsky Leo 6, 38
Trzciński Władysław 90–93, 101, 197
Turowiecki Ryszard 106

Uchnicki Roman 310
Ulc Otto 395
Ułanowski Col. Wacław 277–278
Umiński Fr. Jan 310
UN Charter 22
Underground Solidarity of the Świebodzin Region 186–187
Universal Declaration of Human Rights 32
universal obligation to work 46–47
Urban Jerzy 137, 138, 200, 302, 303, 308–309, 378
Ustasiak Marian 99

Virion Tadeusz de 54, 73, 75–76, 100, 146, 196, 198, 202, 232
Voivodship Defence Committees (WKOK) 8,14, 21

Walania Eugeniusz 120
Walentynowicz Anna 97, 102–109, 274–275
Walter Marta 196, 347
Wałęsa Lech 12, 13, 102, 109, 120, 127, 133, 140, 144, 154, 160, 166, 201, 263, 277, 278, 282, 283, 303, 404
Wende Edward 200, 232, 353
Wesołowska Alicja 139
Węgliński Zdzisław 146
Wierzbicki Alfons 120, 196
Wierzbicki Piotr 133
Wika-Czarnowski Teofil 78–79, 82, 97
Wilczyński Fr. Andrzej 313
Willman Paweł 349–351
Wilk Henryk 101
Wilk Mariusz 277
Witkowski Jan 265–266
Witoń Krzysztof 30–31
Włosik Bogdan 198, 360
Włoszczowa 313, 316
Wojewodzic Edmund 100
Wolski Lt. Col. Leszek 358–359
Wołowicz Aleksander 315
Workers' Defence Committee see under KOR and KSS KOR
Woroszylski Wiktor 133
Woźniak Jerzy 120, 140, 196
Wójcik Dariusz 231
WRON see under Military Council of National Salvation
Wujec Henryk 127, 338
Wujek coalmine 71, 84–87, 93, 97, 303
Wysocki Michał 349–351
Wyszyński Józef 227

425

Index

Yalta accords 150, 151, 218, 233, 407

Zabarnik-Nowakowska Jolanta 201
Zabielski Stanisław 346
Zadrąg Krzysztof 122
Zając Rudolf 78-81, 85-87
Zakrzewski Gerard 334
Zaleski Fr. Tadeusz 311-312, 333-334, 360
Zalisz Paweł 187-188
Zamiatin Leonid 314
Zaniewski Krzysztof 93
Zawadzki Sylwester 24, 72, 137, 204, 320
Zbroński Klemens 249
Zieja Fr. Jan 133
Zieliński Zbigniew 217
Ziembiński Wojciech 155, 218-219
Zieniuk Krzysztof 278-282
Zierhoffer Marek 166
Zych Fr. Sylwester 306-307, 374

Żabiński Andrzej 94
Żygliński Stanisław 118
Żyta Józef 118, 125

For Product Safety Concerns and Information please contact our EU representative GPSR@taylorandfrancis.com
Taylor & Francis Verlag GmbH, Kaufingerstraße 24, 80331 München, Germany

www.ingramcontent.com/pod-product-compliance
Lightning Source LLC
Chambersburg PA
CBHW052138300426

44115CB00011B/1426